The Science of Religion

A Framework for Peace

The Science of Religion

A Framework for Peace

Howard Barry Schatz

TONE CIRCLE PUBLISHING • NEW YORK

Published by Tone Circle Publishing, LLC

www.tonecircle.com
info@tonecircle.com
TheScienceOfReligion.com

ISBN-13: 978-0-9787264-1-6

Printed in the United States of America

Cover art by Anita Weiss

"They wanted to find the kernel of truth that lay at the heart of all the various historical religions, which, since the dawn of history, had been trying to define the reality of the same God."[1]

- Karen Armstrong

1 Karen Armstrong, *A History of God* (New York: Random House, 1993), 170-173; A description of the *Faylasufs*, a sect of 9th century Muslims, in their search for religious truth.

Table of Contents

Part II: The History and Science of Monotheism (continued)

Acknowledgements

The most logical title for this text would probably be "The History and Science of Religion." However, the current title reflects the profound notion that modern science is capable of anchoring the diversity of religious dogma within a comprehensive scientific framework. But to even suggest that a science of religion exists as an objective common ground is to swim against a very strong worldwide current of religious tradition and academic scholarship.

As a college student I had the good fortune to study with friend and mentor Dr. Ernest McClain, who taught me that the ancient mathematical discipline of music was the only way to unlock the deepest meaning of history's great religious and philosophical texts. McClain's writings survey crucial mathematical passages in texts of world literature — the Bible, the Rig Veda, the Egyptian Book of the Dead, Plato — points that often challenged or eluded experts in the concerned disciplines.

McClain credits colleagues Ernst Levy and Siegmund Levarie for introducing him to Pythagoreanism via the insights of 19th century scholar Albert von Thimus. Von Thimus was a pioneer in suggesting that a Pythagorean approach to the mathematics of music might help explain the many confusing mathematical passages in Plato's dialogues. McClain applied this Pythagorean approach to Plato, and to many other important texts of world literature, revealing music as the key to deciphering the deepest meaning of many ancient texts. My own writings are an attempt to expand on this thesis by considering the scientific, historical, theological, and sociological implications of McClain's work, in order to synthesize a comprehensive history and science of gnosticism, as a plausible framework for interfaith discussion.

First, I would like to thank Dr. McClain for giving my life meaning with all that he taught me. Few texts are written without extensive help from others, and I am grateful to Linda Prudhomme for continually encouraging me to keep the text as simple and clear as possible. I would also like to thank my mother, Anita Weiss, for her painting of "The Garden of Eden" featured on the book's cover. I'd like to thank Charles Bentz for his drawing of "The New Jerusalem"; Jonathan Clark for his poem "Autumn Rhapsody"; Duane Christensen, Ivan Matetic, Gregory Rosen, and Arthur Lindberg for their insight and edits; and finally, to Charles Weiss, Lisa Moose, Ted Weg, Donna Kasmer, Terrence Bazylewicz, Pete Dello, Faisal Malik, Asad Gilani, Peter Duff, and Jonathan Clark for their comments, criticisms, suggestions, and encouragement.

Preface

TThe only writings attributed to the great patriarch Abraham by the Orthodox Jewish community is a tiny sacred text called the Sefer Yetzirah (Book of Creation). Most Orthodox rabbis believe that this text somehow reveals the great mysteries of Scripture. I am convinced that the oldest monotheistic text on the Jewish mystical tradition of Kabbalah has not been properly understood for more than 2500 years. That may explain why so few people are even aware of the book's existence. Rabbis and scholars have filled libraries with their Kabbalistic speculations about the inner meaning of Scripture. These views are based on the fact that Hebrew letters also function as numbers. After years of my close association with the Orthodox Jewish community, I have found that rabbis and Jewish scholars have never understood how Hebrew letter/numbers actually extend into mathematics and science. When read through the eyes of Abraham I would suggest that there is a great deal more depth to the Bible than people realize.

The reader might wonder what could possibly distinguish my effort from the efforts of the great rabbis and scholars of the past, who have tried but failed to penetrate the great mysteries of the Sefer Yetzirah and the Bible. I would never have guessed that a degree in music composition and theory was exactly the right educational background necessary to explore the origins and history of a very real science of religion. For more than 40 years, I have been fascinated, and even obsessed, with Pythagorean music theory. Two great Jewish scholars, Gershom Scholem and Leo Baeck, both tell us that the ancient Greek Pythagorean tradition might be the only way to decipher the meaning of the Sefer Yetzirah. Although neither of these learned men understood the mathematical/musical details of this tradition, my work suggests that both men were correct in their assumption. The Pythagorean tradition, which academics often call "The Harmony of the Spheres," is based upon the mathematical structure of sound that integrates the exact sciences of antiquity into a complete cosmology and cosmogony. The key to Abraham's writings, and to many of the great religious and philosophical writings of the ages (including Plato's dialogues and the Bible), must include a basic understanding of ancient music theory.

During the early 1970's, I wrote a college paper on Pythagorean music theory for my first course in music history. The paper completely baffled my professor. I was called into the chairman of the music department's office, and was asked to explain it to my professor, to the chairman, and to the deputy chairman. After hearing my explanation, they decided to give the paper to Professor Ernest McClain, who had spent much of his life studying this obscure subject. On Dr. McClain's recommendation, school administrators established an honors graduate seminar that would enable him to teach me independently. Only years later did I find out that, during his long teaching career, I was his only student in Pythagorean studies.

What McClain taught me over the next few years would transform my life. He taught me that music theory unlocked the meaning of the oldest Hindu text, the *Rig Veda*. He also taught me how to understand Plato's mysterious mathematical allegories in terms of Pythagorean music theory. During this period, to help defray my living expenses while attending college, I taught 4th grade in a private Chasidic school in Williamsburg, Brooklyn. It was a Belzer Yeshiva, named for a town in the Ukraine called Belz. The 2nd grade teacher in the next room brought me to Crown Heights, also in Brooklyn, suggesting that I study with the Lubavitch (another Chasidic sect, named after a town in Russia called Lyubavichi). For a brief time I studied the Torah and Talmud at Hadar Hatorah, a rabbinical seminary in Crown Heights. I had been putting most of my effort into learning the "Bible of Chasidus," called the Tanya, when I discovered the community's library of English translations. After spending many months in this library, I realized that the mathematics and music theory that McClain had taught me during our study of Plato was also showing up in sacred Jewish texts. Before graduating and parting ways with McClain I brought him a copy of both the Tanya and the Sefer Yetzirah and mentioned to him that these were the texts we would need to fully understand if we ever hoped to decipher the secrets of the Bible. After graduating with a degree in music composition, I lost contact with McClain for more than 30 years, but I never gave up on my research.

It took me all of those 30 years to solve the Sefer Yetzirah's mathematical riddles, which became the focus of my first book, The Lost Word of God (Tone Circle Pub., 2007). Just before publication, however, I searched for and found my old professor, Dr. McClain. He was now close to 90 years old, but still as sharp as ever. My wife and I visited him at his home in Washington, DC. Both McClain and I were thrilled to reestablish contact, and he was gracious enough to write the foreword to my first book. Once it was published, he asked me to send a copy to his mentor, Dr. Siegmund Levarie, who was 93 at the time. After Levarie read my book he told McClain that he wanted to meet me.

I arrived at Levarie's beautiful brownstone in Park Slope, Brooklyn. He sat me down in his living room, but he wasn't one for small talk. The first thing he said to me was: "You know son,... you are the only living person to have figured out the Sefer Yetzirah." I was a bit rattled by his words, because I thought that I was the only person to have figured out the Sefer Yetzirah since ancient times. After seeing my incredulous reaction, he waved for me to follow him upstairs to his *sanctum sanctorum* — his library — where he reached up to remove a large and dusty leather bound book. As he set it down on his desk, he told me it took him 35 years just to locate this book. It was by a 19th century German judge and music theorist named Albert von Thimus. Back in the 1970's, McClain taught me about the mathematical table that von Thimus had uncovered in Plato's Timaeus. It was the key to unlocking Plato's mathematical allegories in terms of Pythagorean music theory.

Thumbing through the pages of this wonderful German text was a real adventure for me. Since Levarie was Austrian the language was no issue for him. As we proceeded, it was a bit eerie to find several of what appeared to be my own painstakingly calculated diagrams. But, what shocked me was the realization that Von Thimus was describing the Sefer Yetzirah and not Plato's Timaeus! Levarie was right. I wasn't the first person to "crack the code." The Pythagorean interpretations within the Von Thimus work remained in obscurity until brought to light by Hans Kayser and Ernst Levy in Switzerland during the 1920's. Levy then taught them to Siegmund Levarie after Levy emigrated to the United States in 1941.

After relating this story to Dr. McClain, he was a bit upset that Levarie never mentioned Von Thimus's extensive work on the Sefer Yetzirah to him. Perhaps Levarie didn't want to distract McClain from his work on Plato. Nevertheless, I had to find my own way to the texts of the Orthodox Jewish community, and I was left to my own devices with respect to the Sefer Yetzirah. Although I was not the first to decipher Abraham's writings, my afternoon with Levarie and Von Thimus was an absolute validation of my work. To philologists who incorrectly date the Sefer Yetzirah's content to a period no earlier than the 2nd century AD, I have responded to them by directly linking Yetzirah's mathematics to the mathematics of several Old Babylonian period cuneiform tablets (written during the time of Abraham: circa 1800 BC). To further establish that the mathematical content of Abraham's writings predate the Torah, *The Science of Religion* attempts to demonstrate exactly how the embedded Von Thimus table functions as the Bible's Rosetta Stone — providing the mathematical/musical framework that would later shape all Biblical allegory — and, almost 1500 years later, become the foundation of Plato's writings. Confident in my knowledge of how Abraham's writings structured the Bible, I realized that the Quadrivium also shaped the mythology and religious symbols of the most ancient cultures. So, like detectives "following the money," I ask the reader to join me in my search for the origins and common scientific foundation of religion.

In writing this book I have attempted to follow the advice that Plato attributes to Socrates: "We must follow the argument wherever it leads." Since religion was born in the cradle of science — the exact sciences of antiquity: arithmetic, music, geometry, (trigonometry) and astronomy — this text begins its narrative at the dawn of civilization, and lets the history of the science of religion unfold before us in logical sequence. I hope the reader enjoys the journey as much as I have.

Introduction

As we reflect on the history of civilization, we tend to view modern man as the culmination of a long evolutionary process. We view ourselves as the highly sophisticated product of all the Ages of man, each contributing to what we have become as a species. But, perhaps that is a self-centered view. What if the evolutionary curve actually reached its peak several thousand years ago, and mankind is now in decline? Is that possible? Don't the great advances of modern science prove that mankind has been taking great strides forward? We can certainly talk about the ascent of rational man. But, perhaps the evolution of man's rational mind occurs at the expense of his intuitive, holistic mind, and its ability to integrate accumulated knowledge in order to guide us forward. We will take a closer look at the arc of history in an attempt to determine what might actually constitute "progress" for the species.

This text will explore the history of the dynamic between science and religion; between the exoteric material world and the esoteric spiritual world; between the conscious waking world of logic and science, and the meditative world of dreams, myths, allegory, and prophecy. Civilization has lost access to its rich legacy of ancient knowledge and wisdom, because people are no longer in the habit of accessing their inner world. As a result, civilization seems to have lost its way. We have lost our inner compass. Some may call it our intuitive mind, but others might say that we must relearn how to listen to the "voice" of our soul — the ever present guardian angel that guides us through life.

The challenge of living in today's fast-paced world requires highly specialized knowledge, if we are to satisfy civilization's requirements for an effective division of labor. Specialization is simply a fact of modern life. Modern man seems narrow-minded in comparison to the great ideal of Renaissance humanism: the ability to acquire and integrate knowledge. Were Leonardo da Vinci and Thomas Jefferson considered Renaissance men because they were unique geniuses, or was it because they understood what it took to achieve the Renaissance ideal? Is it fair to call a subject matter expert narrow-minded? And, is the Renaissance ideal of integrating knowledge even relevant in today's world?

If we go back further in time, to the Middle Ages, we would find that today's liberal arts education is based on the 7 liberal arts, namely: the mathematical disciplines of the *Quadrivium* (Latin: four roads). The Quadrivium is comprised of: arithmetic, music, geometry, and astronomy; plus the language disciplines of the *Trivium*: grammar, logic, and rhetoric.[2] But, the Quadrivium has much more ancient roots. And, although there are those who would argue that the evolution of religion is largely a reflection of human psychological needs, economics, the politics of power, and other material circumstances, this text will attempt to establish that it is the mathematics and science of the Quadrivium that defines the origins of religion, while the aforementioned socio-economic factors have only served to distort religion's basic tenets throughout history — the exact sciences of antiquity as "eternal truth" filtered through a parlor game of telephone — with a calamitously divisive impact on civilization.

This text will attempt to establish that archetypal myths, as well as the complete warp and woof of Biblical allegory, have been structured by the exact sciences in antiquity. In ancient Greece, Pythagoras, Plato, and Aristotle believed that music was central to the Quadrivium because the science of sound provided a way to logically integrate these disciplines into a coherent framework of knowledge.[3] For Plato, the mathematics of music defined what Euclid would call "first principles." Here are Plato's own words, taken from his dialogue *Laws*:

> As I have stated several times, he who has not contemplated the mind of nature which is said to exist in the stars, and gone through the previous training, and seen the connection of music with these things, and harmonized them all with laws and institutions, is not able to give a reason of such things as have a reason.[4]

In Plato's *Timaeus,* mathematics and music were described as the language of the *Demiurge*[5] who fashioned and organized the universe. Since man was considered an important part of that universe, Pythagoras and Plato believed that man's soul, as well as the entire universe, could be expressed in terms of both number and sound.[6] Pythagoras and Plato were not alone in their efforts to describe "first principles" in musical terms. The Tantric tradition that straddles Hinduism, Buddhism, and Jainism, also teaches that: "The ultimate Reality is unfathomable creative vibration (*spanda*), the basis for all distinct vibrations composing the countless objects of the subtle and material realms,... omnipresent vibrancy."[7]

2 An important connection to our knowledge of the 7 Liberal Arts was Boethius (ca. 480-524), a scholar of the early Middles Ages, who is said to be the first to use the term Quadrivium.

3 We should be clear that when Plato spoke about music he was not referring to music composed for pleasure, like the songs or symphonies we typically hear on the radio or in the concert hall. Plato was referring to the mathematical discipline of music that exists within the Quadrivium as the science of sound, which has developed into a branch of modern physics called acoustics.

4 Plato, "Laws," *The Collected Dialogues of Plato*, ed. by Edith Hamilton and Huntington Cairns, trans. A.E. Taylor (Princeton, NJ: Princeton University Press, 1961) 967e.

5 This ancient Greek term refers more to an *artisan* as "organizer of the universe" than to monotheistic notions of a Creator.

6 Ernest G. McClain, *The Pythagorean Plato* (New York: Nicolas-Hays, 1978).

7 Georg Feuerstein, *Tantra: The Path of Ecstasy* (Boston: Shambhala Pub., 1998) 75; *Spanda* is a Sanskrit term that roughly translates to "vibrational essence."

In the educational systems of ancient Greece and the Middle Ages, students were taught how to integrate the Quadrivium's disciplines into a logical and coherent framework of knowledge based on the science of sound. The rigor of a holistic approach to the liberal arts was thought to provide a foundation for *sophia* (Greek: wisdom). But, great knowledge does not necessarily imply great wisdom. So, what then is wisdom? And, how would we describe Plato's understanding of *philo-sophia* (Greek: love of wisdom)? Both knowledge and wisdom are widely acknowledged as virtues that have somehow been embedded within the great religious and philosophical writings of antiquity, like the Bible and Plato's dialogues. Since we struggle to find meaning in these ancient texts, could it be that we have not been properly prepared to hear their message? Even if a proper liberal arts education empowers us to integrate our knowledge into the logically consistent framework of a comprehensive cosmology and cosmogony, we would still need to learn how the ancients transformed knowledge into wisdom.

Substantial evidence will be presented in an effort to establish meditation as the "wisdom practice" of religion since the dawn of civilization.[8] Deep meditation goes beyond the logic of the brain's frontal lobes, to access an older part of the brain called the limbic system. Modern research suggests that meditation enhances, and provides a level of control over the limbic system, which influences both the autonomic nervous system and endocrine system. The limbic system is a set of brain structures that include the amygdala, the hippocampus, the hypothalamus, the thalamus, and the pituitary gland ("master gland"). It is the "inner brain" that surrounds the brain stem, functioning as the "gatekeeper" between the neocortex (newly developed rational brain) and the brain stem and spine (oldest reptilian brain). Every second, our brain's sensory apparatus receives and filters millions of signals that are prioritized by the limbic system and passed on to the hippocampus for further processing by the cognitive regions of the cerebral cortex.[9]

More simply put, the brain creates theories through pattern recognition in an attempt to make sense of the millions of sensory inputs per second while the ego continuously and selectively sifts through these inputs looking for patterns that tend to support its world view. If it finds new or even ambiguous patterns that undermine or threaten our highly nuanced and memorized patterns, then the limbic system, or "emotional brain," triggers our threat response mechanism. It prioritizes the memorized pattern and release's the appropriate stress response hormones, like fear, anxiety, anger, sadness, lust, etc. During stress nothing gets into the frontal lobes for reasoning. Conversely, it is possible to create an optimum learning environment, one that even creates entirely new neural circuits, but only if we learn to switch off

---

8 Generally speaking, although meditation remains the core practice of the various Eastern religions, it has been pushed to the periphery of the three Abrahamic faiths: Judaism, Christianity, and Islam.
9 Daniel J. Schneck and Dorita S. Berger, The Music Effect: Music Physiology and Clinical Applications (London: Jessica Kingsley Pub., 2006) 82-89.

our stress mechanism. We must learn how to calm the mind and transcend our emotions through meditation. In order to access the limbic system we must learn to relax our brain's wave patterns until we are almost, but not quite, asleep.

As people drift between waking and sleeping, their brain waves vary in frequency as they enter what is called the hypnagogic state. A meditator can train to maintain this state for long periods of time during which they are essentially dreaming, while still remaining partially conscious. During this lucid dream state an adept may gain some level of control over his autonomic nervous system, enabling him to slow his heart rate and breathing, etc. With the help of the Dalai Lama, science is busy documenting studies regarding the effects of meditation on man's physiology. This semi-conscious state enables the meditator to harness the power of his unconscious mind in order to integrate intellectual knowledge into a matrix of expanded neurological circuits, as suggested by recent MRI research.[10] Here is how Carl Jung describes the power of dreams and the unconscious mind:

> The dream is a little hidden door in the innermost and most secret recesses of the soul, opening into that cosmic night which was psyche long before there was any ego-consciousness... For all ego consciousness is isolated: it separates and discriminates, knows only particulars, and sees only what can be related to the ego. Its essence is limitation ... All consciousness separates, but in dreams we put on the likeness of that more universal, truer, more eternal man dwelling in the darkness of the primordial night. There he is still the whole, and the whole is in him, indistinguishable from nature and bare of all egohood. It is from these all uniting depths that the dream arises ...[11]

The great Taoist teacher Chuang Tzu famously said: "Now I do not know whether I was then a man dreaming I was a butterfly, or whether I am now a butterfly, dreaming I am a man." It is from this perspective that the well-known scholar Joseph Campbell writes about the origins of myth:

> The notion of this universe, its heavens, hells, and everything within it, as a great dream dreamed by a single being in which all the dream characters are dreaming too, has in India enchanted and shaped the entire civilization.[12]

Campbell echoes Chuang Tzu as he describes the ultimate dreamer, Vishnu:

---

10 Dan Gilgoff, CNN Culture & Science Editor.
11 C.G. Jung, trans. by R.F.C. Hull, "The Meaning of Psychology for Modern Man ," *Civilization in Transition*, The Collected Works of C.G. Jung (Princeton: Princeton University Press) 304-306.
12 Joseph Campbell, The Mythic Image (New York: MJF Books, 1974) 7.

> ...floating on the cosmic Milky ocean, couched upon the coils of the abyssal serpent Ananta, the meaning of whose name is "Unending." In the foreground stand five Pandava brothers ... with Drupadi, their wife: allegorically, she is the mind and they are the five senses. They are those whom the dream is dreaming... Behind them a dream-door has opened, however, to an inward, backward dimension where a vision emerges against darkness. Are these youths, we might ask, a dream of that luminous god, or is the god a dream of these youths?[13]

Just as modern science describes cause and effect within the material "waking" world, we question the nature of that reality as we delve into the recesses of our own inner, "hidden" world of the unconscious mind. It is there that we integrate our personality, our knowledge, and the events of the day. Meditation gives us "waking" access to our hidden world of dreams, and to what Jung called the "collective unconscious," mankind's shared sea of dreams, archetypes, and myths.

A comprehensive history of *gnosis* (Greek: knowledge) will be presented as a function of the history of mathematics, music and meditation. It offers solutions to the great religious mysteries of all time — mysteries long hidden from the masses — that will unlock the ancient and sacred doors of knowledge and wisdom. This "gnostic hypothesis" will provide us with insight into the ancient methods of acquiring knowledge and wisdom, and put us in a better position to examine our own belief systems, with an unprecedented empirical understanding of God and the cosmos. For the first time, we will be empowered to modernize and revitalize our faith within the context of modern science, and conversely, the science of religion will bring atheists to the doorstep of spirituality.

The reconciliation of science and religion requires a profound common ground that describes verifiable, objective, and scientific truths to which all could subscribe. An informed discussion on this subject can reflect a dynamic between science and religion that is powerful enough to tear down the walls of dogma, bigotry, and exclusivity that separates cultures and religions from one another. History's divisive sectarian violence and chaos can finally be replaced by a comprehensive framework for interfaith discussion, reconciliation, and peace. Learning the science of religion will teach us the ancient approach to acquiring knowledge and wisdom, and provide us with an entirely new way to read ancient religious and philosophical texts. This will enable us to understand our own holy books, and give peace loving people everywhere the power to wrest control of their faith from the tyranny of fundamentalism that has commandeered its high ground with uninformed teachings. Within this scientific context, mankind's search for inner and outer peace might even be the tipping point for our survival as a species.

13 Ibid., 7.

PART I:
THE HISTORY & SCIENCE OF POLYTHEISM

Chapter 1: The Gods on the Mountain

In the Beginning ...

Biblical Scholars generally agree that God would have created Adam somewhere around 4000 BCE, but the Biblical timeline clearly conflicts with that of science. There has been genetic evidence accumulating for years suggesting that modern science's answer to Adam would have been born in Africa.[14] This "out of Africa" theory takes into account the fossilized remains of man's earliest *hominid* ancestors (family of great apes), discovered in Ethiopia as much as 5.9 million years ago. A trail of *hominid* fossil discoveries in East Africa confirms that the genus *homo* evolved through many different species, culminating in our own genus and species *homo-sapiens* (literally: "wise" or "knowing man").

The remains of the oldest anatomically modern humans were discovered near the Omo River in south-western Ethiopia about 200,000 years ago. DNA testing confirms that these Cro-Magnon hominids should be more appropriately called Early Modern Humans (EMH). Theoretically, we know that "Y" chromosomes in men can be traced back to the first anatomically modern man. Therefore, by studying Y chromosomes from around the world, professors of molecular biology and evolution have determined that patterns of DNA, well known in India among man's earliest populations, were found in the earliest form of that pattern in approximately 1000 breeding couples living in Ethiopia around 70,000 BCE. But, if mankind was traced back to a small Ethiopian population of 2000, then *homo-sapiens* appears to have been close to extinction.

In 1998, professor Stanley Ambrose proposed a theory that helps to explain this apparent catastrophe. In Sumatra, the super-eruption of Mount Toba caused the equivalent of a 6 year nuclear winter and may have started the last Ice Age.[15] Mount Toba's eruption initiated a 1000 year glacial period in an Ice Age that lasted from about 70,000 to 10,000 BCE. During this extended period there were alternating "glacial" and "interglacial" phases. Ice formed during cold periods and melted during warmer periods, dramatically affecting sea levels and climate around the world.

14 Robert Foley, *The Context of Human Genetic Evolution*; Genome Research vol.8 (Cold Spring Harbor Laboratory Press, 1998) 339-347.

15 Stanley Ambrose (1998). "Late Pleistocene human population bottlenecks, volcanic winter, and differentiation of modern humans," *Journal of Human Evolution* 34: 623–651.

Huge volumes of fresh water flowed into the ocean as a result of icebergs breaking off from glaciers during warmer interglacial periods, causing severe global climate fluctuations. These occurrences were named after the marine biologist Hartmut Heinrich.

> "Heinrich events, which occurred episodically throughout the last glacial cycle, led to abrupt changes in climate that may have rendered large parts of North, East, and West Africa unsuitable for hominid occupation, thus compelling early Homo sapiens to migrate out of Africa."[16]

During the last Ice Age, the climate of Northern Africa became colder, and the highest mountain peaks of equatorial Africa became glaciated, while the plains of northern Africa were transformed into the arid and uninhabitable Sahara desert. Sometime after 70,000 BCE, there was a migration from Ethiopia that crossed the Red Sea into Yemen at the Horn of Africa, heading through India toward Australia. This text, however, focuses on a second wave of migration, that made its way into the Middle East. It is this group that appears to have discovered science and religion and founded the sophisticated civilizations of Sumer, Egypt, and Harappa.

Important Middle Eastern archeological sites have been discovered yielding EMH skeletal remains and artifacts at Üçağızlı Cave (Turkey), Ksar 'Akil (Lebanon), and Zar, Yataghyeri, Damjili and Taghlar caves (Azerbaijan). Physical characteristics that distinguish the transition of EMH to modern man deserve our close attention. The EMH were generally bigger and stronger, and had a larger cranial capacity, averaging about 1600 cm^3 to 1750 cm^3, as compared to the cranial capacity of modern humans, who average about 1450 cm^3. A larger cranium might be considered appropriate for a larger, more robust *homo-sapiens* skeleton. When comparing different species, the ratio between brain weight and body weight clearly correlates with intelligence. But, when comparing the brain:body ratio within the same species, results appear to be inconclusive. For example, there has been no measurable change in cranial capacity over the last half of the 20th century, yet IQ points are believed to have risen by about 3 points per decade. It would be a mistake, however, to extrapolate on this data to presume that we must be smarter than our ancient EMH ancestors. In fact, there is evidence to suggest that the opposite might be true.

16 Shannon Carto, Andrew Weaver, Renée Hetherington, Yin Lam, and Edward Wiebe, "Out of Africa and into an ice age," *Journal of Human Evolution* (Royaume-UNI: Elsevier Journals, 2009 Feb;56(2))139-51.

Discovering the Wisdom Practice

It is well known that early man survived the Ice Age by finding shelter in the numerous Middle Eastern caves. It is also safe to assume that the logistics of cave life would have imposed a new set of biological constraints that may have had a significant impact on the natural selection process across tens of thousands of years. For example, by living in darkened caves EMH appear to have evolved with eye sockets that were 15% larger than those of modern humans.[17] That observation might help explain the discovery of ancient carved figures at different key archeological sites across the Middle East that exhibit greatly exaggerated eyes (see Figure 1b). It is also reasonable to speculate that life in a darkened cave implied staying isolated and quiet, especially when we consider that EMH tribes might be cohabiting in close proximity to their Neanderthal enemies. My hypothesis suggests that the natural constraints of day-to-day life in an Ice Age cave effectively imposed a meditative posture of isolation and quiet on the cave's inhabitants. Himalayan monks still meditate within the seclusion of caves.

Perhaps these constraints had the unexpected result of enriching man's "inner life." Just as any bored student might resort to daydreaming, early meditators might have come to appreciate the "visions" of lucid dreaming. Or, perhaps, the first meditators may have needed to stay vigilant during sleep and found the happy medium in a hypnagogic state. Somewhere along the way, EMH learned that quieting their mind was an effective way of detaching from the harsh realities of their perpetual winter while still remaining "in the moment." Meditation detaches the practitioner from stimuli that continually bombard the senses. Hindu yoga calls this *Pratyahara,* or sense-withdrawal. Thus, the limbic system's pattern-matching algorithm is put on hold, preventing the release of hormones that cause stress and emotion. This allows brain waves to slow down to the hypnagogic state somewhere between waking and sleeping. In his efforts to explain meditation in more scientific terms, Zen practitioner and medical doctor, Dr. James Austin describes speculation that "... regular meditation was a kind of practice in developing a certain skill. The skill lay in freezing the hypnagogic process at later and later stages (first in the predominantly alpha wave stage, later in the predominantly theta wave stages)."[18] This hypnagogic state can be characterized by a "loosening of ego boundaries ... openness,

---

17 Robert Connolly, Bea Connolly, *The Search for Ancient Wisdom* (a documentary TV series airing on Life Network, 1997; also a CD by Apple and Cambrix Publishing, 1995); Physical anthropologist in the University of Liverpool's School of Biomedical Sciences took photos and presented narrative about ancient civilizations.

18 James Austin, *Zen and the Brain: Toward an Understanding of Meditation and Consciousness* (Boston: MIT Press, 1999) 92.

sensitivity...[19] Modern-day studies of yogis and lamas who have entered this state have demonstrated that the hypnagogic state has given them a level of control over their autonomic nervous system and endocrine system.

The hypnagogic state has been the subject of much study, and is even discussed in the writings of Aristotle and the Neo-Platonist, Iamblichus.[20] Around the time of the First Ecumenical Council, the Church did its best to dispense with the works of Iamblichus. However, the writings of Proclus and Stobaeus helped preserve his work.[21] These writings, and other works of the Greek Stoics, shed an important light on our understanding of the ancient Greek meditation practice.

During the First Ecumenical Council, in 325 CE, the Church's Orthodox position refutes the beliefs of the deacon Arius as heresy, linking him to Greek pantheistic thinking. The Arian heresy suggests that any man could become deified like Christ through the ascetic practices of the ancient Stoics. Plato called that practice *theoria*[22] (contemplation). For the Greek Stoics, theoria brought *sophia* (wisdom). For the religious prophets of Scripture, it brought revelation. Arius maintained that Christ, like any man, could be "deified" by liberating his soul. Many modern Christians equate Christ with God, and Orthodox Christianity rejects any suggestion that Christ was just a man who became deified through meditation.

On-going MRI research into brain activity suggests that meditation creates additional electrical circuits within the nervous system. If new circuits channel additional electrical energy up the spine to "wake up" and expand brain capacity, then it logically follows that cranium size may have also increased over thousands of years. Archeological evidence exists to support this idea, including the discovery of enlarged skulls at sites closely associated with the origins of science and religion.

Physical anthropologists and archeologists have discovered a number of skulls that are considered well outside the range of a normal size Cro-Magnon skull. These have been categorized into types, including "conehead" skulls ranging from 2200 cm^3 to 2500 cm^3, and "J" type skulls with enormous capacities ranging from 2600 cm^3 to 3200 cm^3.[23] A study by Dudley Buxton and Talbot Rice of ancient Sumerian skulls (Figure 1d) from the earliest known historical civilization, has found "that of 26 Sumerian crania 17 were Australoid, five Austrics and four Armenoid. According to Penniman who studied skulls from Kish and other Sumerian sites, these three: the Australoid (Eurafrican), Austric and Armenoid were the "racial"

19 Andreas Mavromatis, *Hypnagogia: the Unique State of Consciousness Between Wakefulness and Sleep* (London: Routledge, 1991)3-4.
20 Ibid., 82.
21 And, expanded our knowledge of Pythagorean number-symbolism and ancient Greek philosophy.
22 Armstrong, Op.Cit., 114.
23 Connolly, Op.Cit..

types associated with the Sumerians."[24] A dolichocephalic, or enlarged skull, was found to be a common trait of all three. "Sir Arthur Keith says that the people who spoke Sumerian were dolichocephalic, with large brain capacity, like a section of the pre-dynastic Egyptians."[25] Dolichocephalic skulls have also been discovered in Egypt and South America (Figures 1f & g) and appear to reflect derivative cultures.

Figures 1a - Ubaid Period ca. 5400 BCE *Figures 1b & c - Jarmo c. 6750 BCE*

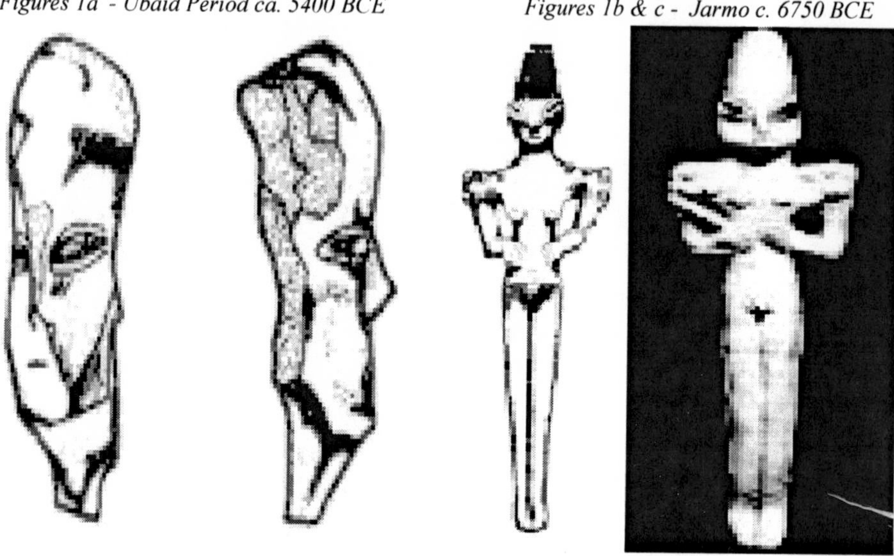

I am suggesting a history of gnosticism tied to the existence of an ancient shamanistic meditation practice that helped drive human evolution. This theory at least provides a plausible explanation for a dynamic growth in cranium size and IQ during the last Ice Age. Could meditation be the missing link between caveman and civilized man?

Figure 1d - The "Serpent-Headed People" of Eridu

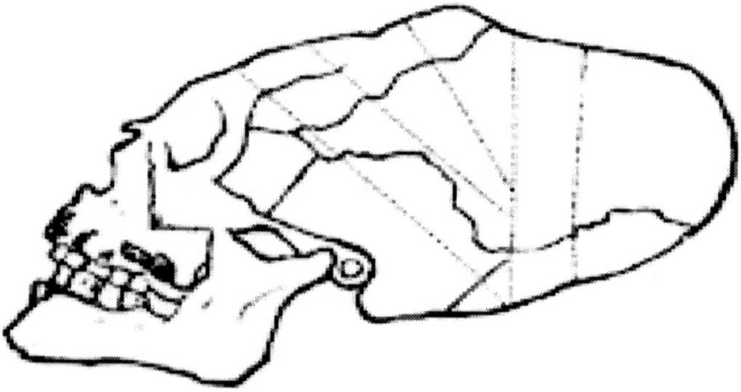

---

24 Dr. Ashok Malhotra, *Tracing the Origin of Ancient Sumerians* (syndicated article appearing in the Armenia Encyclopedia; Chayah Bayith Elowahh; EZine Articles)
25 John Marshall, *Mohenjro Dara and the Indus Civilization* (Asian Educational Studies, 1931) 109; Sir Arthur Keith in H.R. Hall and C.L. Woolley, "Ur Excavations Al'Ubaid," (Oxford University Press, 1927) vol.i, 216-240.

Figure 1e -Homage to Egyptian Nobility

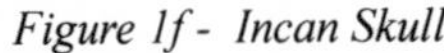

Figure 1f - Incan Skull

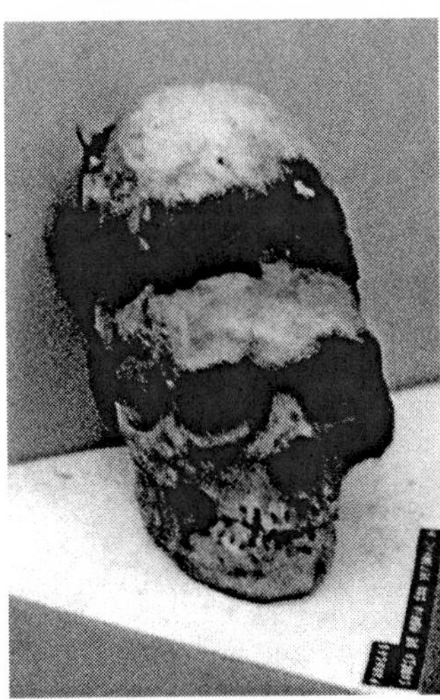

Figure 1g - Peruvian Skulls

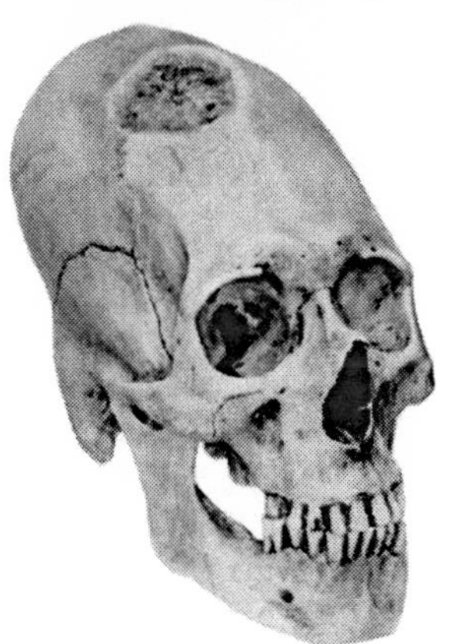

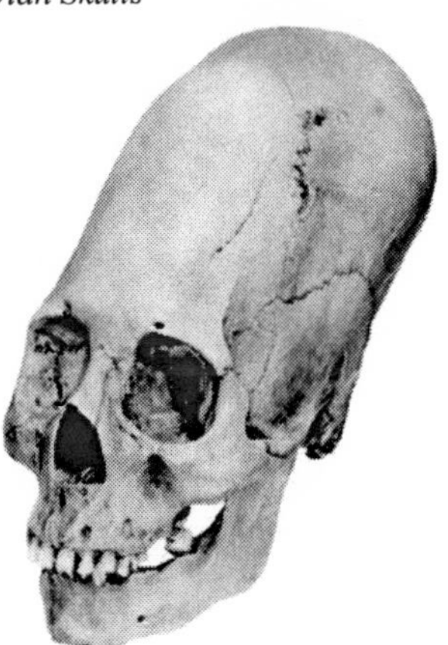

Modern research has already established that meditation has many physiological benefits, and it is generally acknowledged as mankind's most ancient and sacred vehicle for achieving spiritual Enlightenment. There is considerable evidence to suggest that Middle Eastern cave dwellers became the great catalyst in moving civilization forward. This implies that the revelations of early man played an important role in developing the axioms of the various mathematical disciplines. Perhaps meditation provides the means to integrate these disciplines into a holistic perspective that is greater than the sum of its parts. EMH "Enlightened" tribes thus became the stuff of legend. They were worshipped as gods by the many civilizations that followed. They have often been called *Aryans* (Sanskrit: Noblemen), and I believe them to be the *Nephilim* described within Hebrew Scripture. The word *Nephilim* can be most accurately translated from the Hebrew as "Men of Renown" or "Heros of Old." Later cultures paid homage to the Sumerian "gods" by binding the heads of their infants during early skull formation. This was practiced in the Armenian Highlands, in Nubia, and in Egypt, as well as in South America. Armenian mothers still practice it to this day, albeit in a modified, more acceptable way.[26] It appears unlikely, however, that the binding of infant skulls adequately accounts for the enormity of the largest dolichocephalic skull-types that have been discovered.

Ancient legend, traditions, and artifacts indicate — and the oldest examples of cuneiform writings, suggest — that a highly evolved people did exist. Perhaps due to their imposing physical appearance and special "gifts" they became both feared and worshipped as gods. Ancient sculpture and stelae depict elongated skulls as the trademark of divine blood (see Figure 1e).[27] Historically, the headdress of kings, priests, pharaohs, wizards and witches should also be considered a significant cultural remnant of these so-called gods (see Figures 2a - e). Those who came into contact with the "serpent-headed ones" depicted them as "giants" in artwork scattered across the Neolithic sites of the Ancient Near East, including Jericho, Jarmo, Susa, Eridu, etc. (Figures 1a, b & c). The number and diversity of relevant archeological discoveries reflect the syncretistic notion that this unique spiritual community became the "gods on the mountain" for many ancient cultures. The mythology of these legendary shepherd-gods made its way into the art, architecture, science and literature of the entire ancient world, including: Sumer, Babylon, Egypt, India, Mitanni, Israel, Assyria, Media, Elam, Greece, Rome, etc..

Our hypothesis suggests that a bigger, more utilized brain evolved as a result of thousands of years of meditation. This might account for the dramatic transition between caveman and the sophisticated sexagesimal mathematics of the first historical civilization. In more recent historical memory, one can appreciate the prophet Mohammed's Koranic revelations as a function of his well-known cave practice meditation. Similarly, Buddhism, Hinduism, Taoism, Jainism,... have all been founded on the bedrock of "Enlightenment" brought about by a life of meditation. What has been largely lost in the West is the awareness that the three main Abrahamic religions: Judaism, Christianity, and Islam, are also rooted in the same priestly meditation practice.[28] Within the Abrahamic religions, meditation has largely been relegated to the practices of fringe mystical groups, such as the Muslim Sufis, Christian Rosicrucians, and Jewish Kabbalists.

---

26 Gevork Nazaryan, *Armenia: the Cradle of Civilization, unpublished.*
27 Ibid.
28 Howard Schatz, *The Lost Word of God* (New York: Tone Circle Pub., 2007).

Figure 2a - Pharaoh's conical Headdress

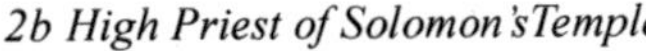

2b High Priest of Solomon's Temple

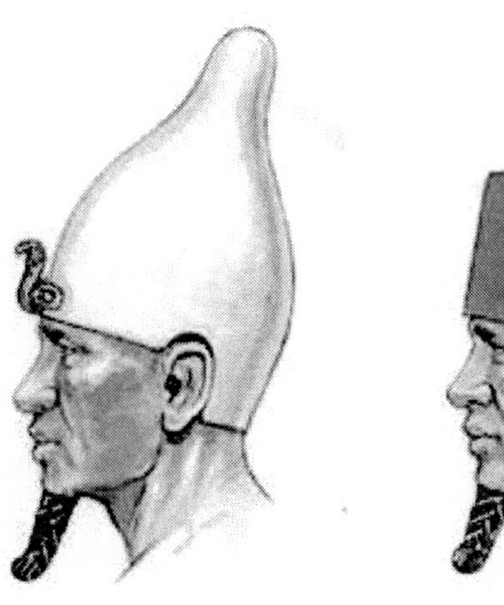

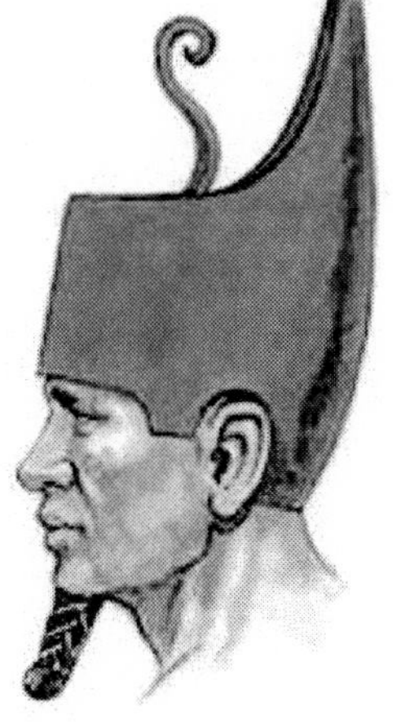

Figures 2c, d & e - Pope's Conical Hat; Dalai Lama's Conical Hat; Arab Turban

The Good Shepherds

With the end of the last Ice Age, circa 10,500 BCE, the EMH were no longer captives of cave life. They domesticated sheep and goats and wandered the perimeter of the Tigris-Euphrates and Indus River Valleys. It seems likely that their greater size and strength was the genetic result of tens of thousands of years of excursions into the perpetual winter as hunter-gatherers. When they finally left the safety of their caves, they also left behind the constraints of cave life — the original impetus for assuming a meditative posture as a way of life. Over the course of the next several thousand years, it is also logical to assume that meditation was no longer practiced by the entire community. At some point in time the benefits of a "sitting practice" would have been limited to, and preserved by, spiritual leaders, priests, shamans, and the like.

The end of cave life also accounts for the relatively quick disappearance of EMH distinguishing physical traits. My thesis suggests that man began to devolve from their evolutionary peak attained at the end of the Ice Age, and slowly lost their meditation-derived traits and skills. Today's more frontal lobe oriented humans have smaller brains and skulls, and a less robust physical stature. After the extinction of Neanderthal Man (ca. 29,000 BCE), and without the brutality of Ice Age weather, we can also speculate about a time when highly evolved EMH would have experienced a pastoral golden age, wandering the mountain foothills as wise and spiritual shepherds. These tribes became the protagonists of history's great religious allegories.

From this scenario, we might conclude that whatever it is that we now call civilization, did not really begin in the Tigris-Euphrates River Valley's Fertile Crescent, as most academics would have us believe. It appears to have begun in the unbroken mountainous perimeter of Iraq (Figure 3), where these Aryan "shepherd-gods" came to inhabit the Taurus and Nur Mountains of Turkey, the southern Caucasus in the Armenian Highlands, the Elburz, Kurdistan, and Zagros Mountains of Iran, as well as Pakistan's Central Makran Range, bordering the Indus Valley.

Melting glaciers overflowed the Black Sea and flooded the river valley between roughly 14,000 - 7,000 BCE. The Bible's timeline for the Great Flood (ca. 2348 BCE) does not match the geological record, although there is said to have been some local flooding around that time. The Genesis allegories, especially the Biblical flood myth, shares many common elements with the Sumerian *Epic of Gilgamesh* and the Babylonian *Epic of Atrahasis.* If we were to closely compare these stories with one another, we could observe what is essentially the same flood myth being told from different cultural perspectives. Bible stories, in fact, may be one of our best modern guides to prehistoric times. From this perspective, we might consider the Biblical allegory of Noah and his family emerging from the Ark on Mount Ararat as metaphor for the EMH emerging from their mountain caves around Lake Van and Mount Ararat, circa 10,500 BCE.

When EMH came out of their caves, they would have avoided the flooding by herding sheep and goats in the foothills of the mountains. They eventually settled the land, growing wheat and barley, to begin the Neolithic Revolution circa 9000 BCE. The earliest farming settlements included: Jericho, Jarmo, Susa, Çatal Höyük, and Mehrgarh. The earliest EMH settlement appears to have been the Mesolithic (Middle Stone Age) site of Tell es-Sultan (Sultan's Hill), a couple of kilometers from the current city of Jericho. It is a

40,000 square meter settlement surrounded by a stone wall, with a stone tower built into the wall. Jericho is considered the oldest continuously inhabited settlement, and its stone architecture was built by the *Natufian* civilization (circa 12,500 - 9500 BCE). EMH were probably accustomed to living within the protective shell of their caves, and their need to build a settlement surrounded by a stone wall at Tell es-Sultan was a practical solution to the problems of keeping out any flood waters or unwanted intruders. Over the next few thousand years, the EMH migrated across the seven mountain chains already mentioned, which framed the perimeter of the Fertile Crescent.

Figure 3 - The Mountain Ranges Framing Iraq

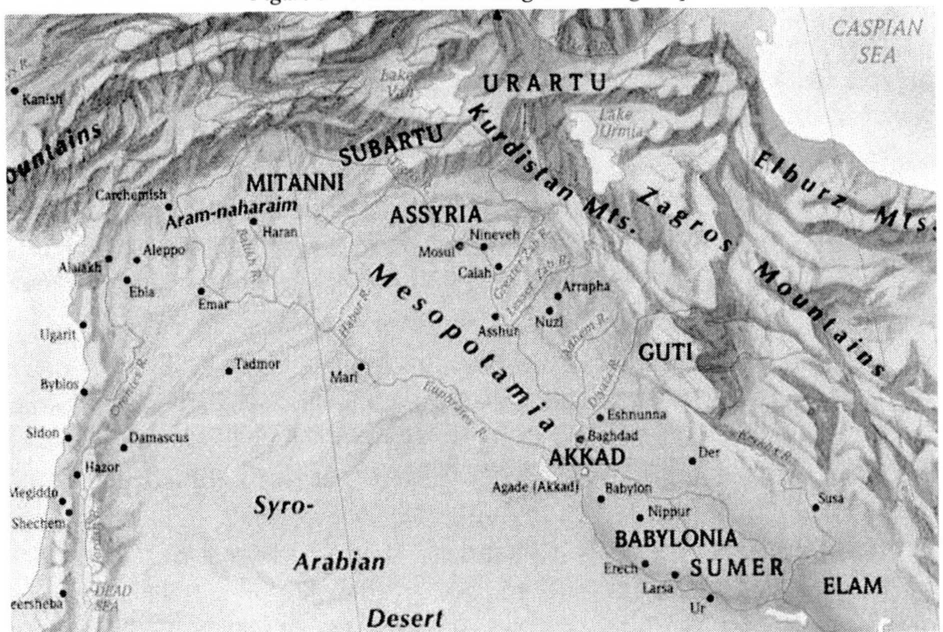

EMH survived the Ice Age in the shelter of Middle Eastern caves for anywhere from 20,000 to 50,000 years. Meditation probably began as a natural coping mechanism for tribes and families who survived during that period. Meditation significantly strengthened the practitioner's limbic system, and provided unprecedented access to the brain's untapped potential. My hypothesis suggests that this "cave practice" was a widely established and cherished practice that came to define the sacred priestly tradition. I believe it to be the missing evolutionary link between caveman and the sophistication of pre-Sumerians "who were culturally far more advanced than were the Sumerians..."[29] Samuel Noah Kramer, a renowned scholar on ancient Sumer, discovered a vastly superior pre-Sumerian culture that emerged from the Iranian mountains. This aligns well with my own theory about Aryan "shepherd-gods on the mountain."

29 Samuel Noah Kramer, History Begins at Sumer (Philadelphia: University of Penn Press, 1956) 237.

Chapter 2: The Founders of Civilization

The Founding of Sumer

The Aryans migrated to Eridu from Susa in the province of Elam at the dawn of Iranian history.[30] Susa was named for Noah's granddaughter Susan, while Elam was named for his grandson Elam. Both were children of Noah's son Shem. In this earliest period of Iranian history, this region was first known as Arana (Āryānā), meaning "land of the Aryans." The Sanskrit word Aryan (or Arya) means "noble" or "honorable," and can be literally translated as "one who strives upward." In the Persian language, this evolved to "Erān," and finally to "Irān," in modern Persian.

By 5400 BCE, any flood waters would have cleared. At this point, the Aryans/Iranians who founded the Zagros Mountain Neolithic settlement at Susa descended into the valley along the Karkheh River (which I believe is the Bible's Pishon River) and founded the city of Eridu, the first city of ancient Sumer. "Henri Frankfort argued that the Sumerians were the first settlers in southern Mesopotamia and came from the Iranian highlands in the beginning of the Ubaid period. Next, the Semites arrived in the Uruk period..."[31] Kramer echoes these thoughts: "Not long after the establishment of the first settlement by the Iranian immigrants [circa 5400 BCE], the Semites probably infiltrated into Southern Mesopotamia [circa 4000 BCE]."[32] Kramer describes the pre-Sumerians as "culturally far more advanced than were the Sumerians."[33] This pre-Sumerian civilization was actually responsible for the "material and spiritual heritage" of ancient Sumer, which positioned Sumer to play such a predominant role in the Ancient Near East.[34] Kramer also speaks of an important Irano-Semitic cross-fertilization in Southern Mesopotamia.

If we can accept the premise that a superior race existed, then we are in a position to consider the syncretistic perspective that these "shepherd gods" became legendary figures, known to each derivative culture by different names. The existence of a single "master-race"[35] would therefore describe the origin of the Greek

30 Ibid., 239.
31 Arkadiusz Soltysiak, "Physical Anthropology and the Sumerian Problem," *Studies in Historical Anthropology*, Vol.4: 2004[2006] 145-158.
32 Samuel Noah Kramer, Op.Cit.,239; "Iran" and "Aryan" are etymologically related. This area in the Zagros Mountains was called the "Land of the Aryans."
33 Ibid., 237.
34 Ibid., 237.
35 To rehabilitate the reputation of the Aryans, we might reconsider our negative reaction to the phrase "Aryan Master Race," and attempt to disassociate the actual Aryans with Hitler's maniacal justification for genocide.

pantheon of gods on Mount Olympus, the shepherd-gods of Sumer, Egypt, and Babylon, and the "Sons of God" in the Bible. As a further example, Noah had many syncretistic names, including: the Sumerian *Ziusudra*, his Akkadian counterpart *Atrahasis*, and the Babylonian Noah, *Utnapishtim.*

Soon after the first city was founded, according to Genesis 11:4, a Tower of Babel was said to have been built by Noah's great-grandson, Nimrod, in dedication to the glory of man, rather than to the glory of God. This "idolatry" caused God to confuse language, and each language would evolve its own distinct culture. Thus, the 70 nations were dispersed to the "four corners of the earth." The Tower of Babel allegory implies that there was originally a proto-language and a proto-culture, once again suggesting a single set of shepherd-gods on the mountain. The word *Aryan* has often been used to categorize the gentile Caucasian descendants of Noah's son Japheth, whereas the term *Semitic* generally refers to monotheism's patriarchal descendants of Noah's son Shem. This text uses "*Aryan*" interchangeably with the Biblical term "*Nephilim*" to describe the founders of civilization. The Book of Genesis, however, describes a father-son relationship between the "Sons of God" and their *Nephilim* offspring, which Jewish Biblical commentators mistakenly, I believe, characterize as the Good "sons of Seth" versus the Evil "sons of Cain."[36]

In further support of a syncretistic approach to this subject matter, we note that the ancient Jewish historian Flavius Josephus (circa 58 CE) writes about Adam's belief that the earth would be destroyed by flood and flame. Based on that belief, the "sons of Seth" would record the sacred mysteries for posterity on two pillars, one of stone and the other, brick, believing that if the flood destroyed the brick, the stone might still survive.[37] This early record of the ancient knowledge was therefore said to be written on the "Pillars of Seth." The rabbis are clear that it was someone in the "line of Seth" that carved those pillars. If we were to follow the Biblical timeline, it would have been the 7th generation from Seth, Enoch, the first holy man and scribe, who is believed to have carved the ancient secrets into stone and brick.[38] These writings would then constitute the actual "Book of Enoch," authored during the time that the Biblical Enoch would have lived, as opposed to the non-canonical "Book of Enoch," authored around 300 BCE, thousands of years after the Biblical timeline for Enoch.

Three hundred years before Josephus, the writings of Manetho state that he actually saw these pillars, but he understood them to be inscribed by the Egyptian Thoth, who the Egyptians believed was the inventor of writing and keeper of the secret knowledge. Within Egyptian culture, the two pillars were believed to symbolize

36 Adam's sons included Cain, Abel, and Seth.
37 Flavius Josephus, *The Antiquities of the Jews*, trans. By William Whiston (Virginia: IndyPublish.com) 8.
38 Schatz, *The Lost Word of God*, Op.Cit., 24; The "Secret of the Torah" (Hebrew: *Raza d'Oraita)* is also known as the "Secret of the Twenty-Two Letters" or the "Secret of Knowledge." The *Sefer Yetzirah* explains how the primal light of God's *Ten Sefirot of Nothingness* descends across 22 Foundation Letters (the 22 letters of the Hebrew alphabet), extending His light into the essence of man (the soul) and all living creatures, the essence of time, and the essence of the Universe.

Upper and Lower Egypt. In addition to the "Two Pillars of Seth" and "Two Pillars of Thoth," there was also the "Two Pillars of Hermes" within the Greek culture — also said to contain the secret knowledge. Like Enoch and Thoth, Hermes was said to be the first scribe, carving the science of religion's mysteries into stone. This accounts for the etymology of the word *hermeneutics*, the art of interpreting hidden meaning.

Correspondences between Greek and Roman gods are widely accepted in the academic world. The Greek Hermes became Mercury in the Roman culture; the Greek Dionysus equates to the Roman Bacchus, while the Greek Artemis equates to the Roman Diana, etc. Our recommended syncretistic approach suggests that the Hebrew Enoch equates to the Egyptian Thoth, the Greek Hermes, and the Roman Mercury. We have also mentioned the many names of Noah. These are just a few examples of how a narrow syncretistic view of the ancient gods and epic heros needs to expand in its scope to include a matrix for all the ancient cultures. I am suggesting that these shared myths are describing a single "golden age of the gods" viewed from different cultural and linguistic perspectives.

A broad syncretistic approach suggests that there was only one source allegory and one protagonist, whether or not the protagonist was a purely mythical character, an unknown person, or a known historical figure. But, even more significantly, the science of religion enables us to explain the underlying mathematical framework for these shared myths and gods. A syncretistic approach is made possible by a shared scientific legacy among the world's religions that began with the Aryans. In Part II, we will study the *hermeneutics* of Abrahamic monotheism, and see exactly how it evolved directly from the Aryan science of polytheism.

We might want to think of this first civilization as preliterate, but that would be inconsistent with Kramer's belief that a pre-Sumerian civilization was actually responsible for the "material and spiritual heritage" of ancient Sumer.[39] Joseph Campbell writes: "...the new spiritual aim of humanity that was formulated for all future time in the culture of that mysterious Sumerian race to which our whole world owes all its basic arts of literate civilized life.[40] Both scholars stress the significance and mystery surrounding the beginnings of civilization in ancient Sumer. There appears to be a consensus that the Ubaid period (5400 BCE) arrival of the Aryan fathers — the "gods on the mountain" — preceded the later arrival of Semitic tribes during the Uruk period (4000 BCE). Therefore, the Aryans appear to be the pre-Sumerian founders of civilization. Thousands of years of meditation provides a plausible explanation for the appearance of a genetically superior race whose significantly higher IQ, knowledge, skills, and wisdom, empowered them to become the founders of civilization.

During the Neolithic period of agricultural settlements, there was a significant migration of enlightened tribes from Eastern Turkey's *Göbekli Tepe* and

39 Ibid., 237.
40 Campbell, Op.Cit., 325.

Çatal Höyük, across the mountainous perimeter of Iraq and Iran. Knowledge of the science of religion that was enshrined within *Göbekli Tepe* and *Çatal Höyük* traveled along with them. The Aryan "gods on the mountain" would control their own urban destiny from about 5400 to 4000 BCE, at which point Semitic tribes began invading from the West. Without taking the Biblical timeline too literally, perhaps we can make use of its chronology as a guide. Enoch and Noah would have been Aryan masters, while Noah's son Shem would have been patriarch to the Semitic tribes. After the flood, the Bible's Diaspora to "the four corners of the Earth" was associated with Noah's triplet sons: Shem, Ham, and Japheth (Figure 4). Traditionally, monotheism proceeded to Abraham through the patriarchal lineage of Enoch, Noah, and Shem. The earliest Aryan polytheism, however, up to and including its oldest written text, the Rig Veda (circa 1700 - 1100 BCE), might best be described as a multi-faceted unity that is closely related to Abrahamic monotheism.

Figure 4 - The Great Diaspora in the Time of Noah

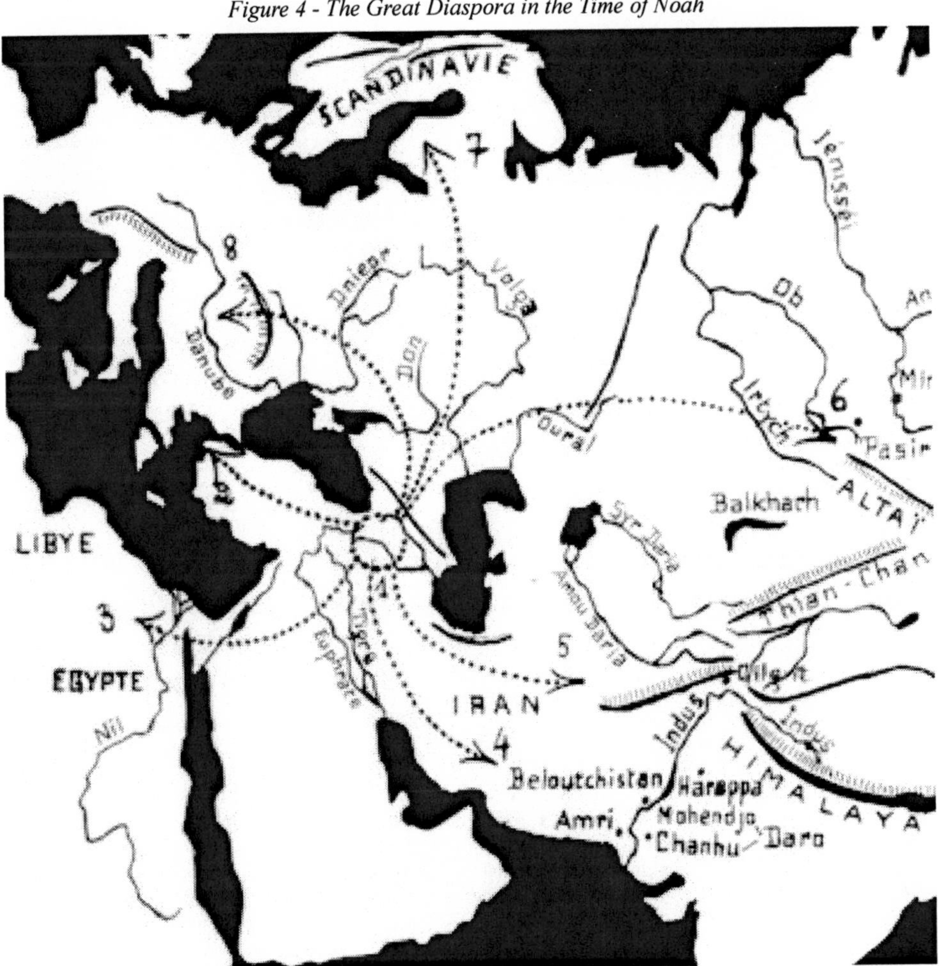

The Invention of Writing

Joseph Campbell writes that "Babylon was, according to a consistent tradition, the home of astronomy, and there the science of the stars formed the basis of intellectual culture."[41] This position is supported by Otto Neugebauer, an authority on ancient astronomy, who admits: "We know absolutely nothing about an earlier, presumably Sumerian, development."[42] Neugebauer's focus is on the sophistication of the Old Babylonian period (circa 1800 BCE).[43] In more recent challenges to Neugebauer's ideas, scholars like Jöran Friberg discuss earlier "evidence for a possible common origin of the mathematics of various civilizations."[44] Joseph Campbell also surveys earlier mythologies, specifically those of ancient Sumer, where he concludes that "the mythological systems of the great civilizations share a significant body of motifs, many of which have been derived from a single historic source: the mathematically structured astronomical systems of the Early Bronze Age Near East."[45] The Early Bronze Age begins with the Sumerian invention of cuneiform writing, ca. 3300 BCE. So, Campbell too stresses the significance of an earlier Sumerian mathematical contribution. However, if writing did not exist when the pre-Sumerians founded Eridu (ca. 5400 BCE), we might wonder how Kramer is able to justify crediting them with the "material and spiritual heritage" of ancient Sumer. How is it possible to gauge the level of Aryan pre-Sumerian contribution between 5400 BCE and 3300 BCE without any written historical records?

Perhaps, it would be a mistake for historians to assume that people were necessarily primitive before the invention of writing. We have hypothesized that an ancient meditation practice was the main impetus behind EMH evolution, and the reason for Aryan sophistication. We should not assume that the pre-Sumerian mind, which might have been far superior to our own, had no way to comprehend or communicate complex and highly sophisticated mathematical and scientific ideas before the invention of writing. Today's historians are aware of a rich oral tradition that existed in the ancient world for transmitting long and complex texts to posterity. It is not unlikely that this oral tradition began before writing developed.

In Chapter 5, we will be carefully examining an ancient document called the Sumerian King List, in order to understand its mathematical construction and profound significance for both religion and astronomy. The document is writ-

41 Campbell, Op.Cit., p 149.

42 Otto Neugebauer, *The Exact Sciences in Antiquity* (New York: Dover Pub., 1969) 29-30.

43 Otto E. Neugebauer, "The Alleged Babylonian Discovery of the Precession of the Equinoxes," Journal of the American Oriental Society, Vol. 70, No. 1. (Jan. - Mar., 1950)1-8.

44 *Reader's Guide to the History of Science* , edited by Arne Hessenbruch (London: Fitzroy Dearborn Publishers, 2000) 196; Jöran Friberg, ed. by J.W. Dauben, *Mesopotamian Mathematics* (American Mathematical Society, 2000)..

45 Campbell, Op.Cit., 278.

ten in the Sumerian language, and many scholars believe it was compiled long before Babylon became the "home of astronomy." It should also become clear, by the visual nature of these particular mathematical constructs, that a geometric template for this mathematics existed thousands of years before the invention of cuneiform phonetics and sexagesimal notation. Therefore, prior to the invention of writing, we must look to the existing archeological record for clues suggesting Aryan knowledge about the origins of the pre-Sumerian Quadrivium.

Kramer believes that the Sumerian King List was compiled sometime during the 3rd millennium BCE. It appears that Sumerian astronomer-priests wanted to understand the physical context for the soul's migration to its Heavenly destination once meditation liberates it from the body. In Chapter 5, we will decipher this famous document's encrypted mathematics, music, and astronomy; and, for the first time, we can explain how the science of polytheism is based on the "Clock of Heaven and Earth." This effort will demonstrate that the most famous of sexagesimal artifacts, the clock, is tightly coupled to a natural phenomenon in astronomy known as the Precession of the Equinox. The Sumerian King List appears to be nothing less than religion's foundation document. Understanding this document from the perspective of ancient science suggests that a knowledge of precession existed before the Babylonians — perhaps long before.

The technology of writing that accurately recorded this great legacy depended on the development of phonetic script. But, the earliest attempts to write on clay used pictographic and ideographic script, circa 4000 BCE.[46] Kramer writes: "The Sumerian language was denoted by an earlier pictographic script, attested in some archaic tablets found in the remnants of ancient cities Unak/Uruk, Ur, and Jamdet Nasr..."[47]

Eventually, this sophisticated Aryan-Semitic civilization would collapse, precipitated by a steady stream of less desirable invaders. Kramer writes:

> Turning now from the pre-Sumerian, or Irano-Semitic, period in the earlier history of Lower Mesopotamia, to the following Sumerian period, we find the latter to consist of three cultural stages: the preliterate, the proto-literate, and the early-literate. The first, or preliterate, stage of the Sumerian period began with an era of stagnation and regression following the collapse of the earlier and more advanced Irano-Semitic civilization, and the incursion of the Sumerian barbaric war bands into Lower Mesopotamia.

The centuries of barbaric Sumerian war lords created a struggle between them and more cosmopolitan Sumerians. The only cultural bright

46 Kramer, Op.Cit., xxi.
47 Soltysiak, Op.Cit., 145-158.

spot was the continued attempt to chisel their pre-dynastic legacy onto clay tablets. The extant Sumerian literature dates back to this period. Kramer calls it "the Heroic Age of ancient Sumer." And, from a syncretistic perspective, he comments on the theological similarities between the earliest heroic epics of Sumer and those of ancient India and Greece:

> These gods form organized communities in a chosen locality, though, in addition, each god has a special abode of his own... At death the soul travels to some distant locality that is regarded as a universal home and is not reserved for any particular community. Some of the heros are conceived as springing from the gods, but there is no trace of heroic worship or hero cults.[48]

A brief survey of the extant literature reveals only nine Sumerian tales. Two of these focus on the hero Enmerkar, two revolve around Lugalbanda, and five describe the star of ancient Sumer — Gilgamesh. It is important to note that all three heros were inscribed on the Sumerian King List.[49] The King List begins with the statement, "When kingship was lowered from heaven the kingship was in Eridu."[50]

The Aryan-Semitic Roots of Religion

Pre-Sumerian Aryans had been studying the sky ever since their ancestors left the confines of Ice Age caves. During that early period, they discovered a significant anomaly in the motion of the sun in relation to the background stars. In Chapter 4, we will take a close look at this anomaly: the annual drift of the stars across the celestial dome (Vedic astronomy's *ayanamsa*). It created a tiny gap each year that suggested an opening, or "gateway" leading onto the Sun's spiral path. The Aryans believed that their liberated soul traveled through this "gateway" and followed the Sun's voyage across the heavens, to the dwelling place of immortal souls. The Aryans had discovered what they believed to be Heaven. However, invading Semitic tribes regarded the ayanamsa as an imperfection in the cosmos, and concluded that they too, like the cosmos, must be imperfect. From either perspective, the ayanamsa became critically important to both the Aryan and Semitic traditions.

Within the Torah, and within Jewish Kabbalistic tradition, two holy men overcame this "imperfection" — Enoch and Noah — and thus, they are said to have "walked with God." Historically, they both would have been born into the Aryan tradition, a tradition that considered each soul that reached Heaven an immortal god.

48 Kramer, Op.Cit., 224.
49 Ibid., 227.
50 Jack Finegan, *The Archaeological History of the Ancient Middle East* (Boulder, Colorado: Westview Press: 1979) 23.

The 10 generations from Noah to Abraham roughly corresponds to the transition period of cross-fertilization described by Kramer. The Semitic tribes would have considered their inability to achieve *Moksha* (Sanskrit: Liberation) as one of "exile from Paradise." Teaching Semitic tribes the necessary skills to achieve *Moksha* would have to wait for the emergence of a Semitic High Priest. Genesis tells us that it was Melchizedek who initiated Abraham into the ancient tradition of High Priests. Orthodox rabbis believe Melchizedek to be the reincarnation of Shem.

The rapid development of writing, mathematics and science seems to coincide with a Semitic presence in the region, possibly suggesting that written communication, previously unnecessary for such a superior race, suddenly became critical in order to educate Semitic neophytes. The pre-Sumerian Aryans may have been meditating and liberating their soul for tens of thousands of years, whereupon late-coming Semitic tribes were likely to have had great difficulty in achieving the desired spiritual state. The Semitic conclusions about their own spiritual shortcomings is supported by the mathematics. We will see how the mathematics of sin takes on a dominant role in the history of Semitic monotheism. Mathematics and science evolved quickly from this point forward, driven by a great spiritual quest. With the advent of Semitic monotheism, the theological focus began to shift from the liberation process to the purification process, a necessary remedy for man's perceived imperfection and inherent sin. These mathematically articulated concepts became the scientific justification for the Bible's moral imperative.

Cultural differences between the Aryan and Semitic tribes were preserved in the two earliest extant treatises on the science of religion: the *Rig Veda* and the *Sefer Yetzirah*. Philologists date the *Sefer Yetzirah* to a period no earlier than 200 CE. However, it is fair to say that even the greatest philologists and religious scholars have little or no knowledge of the music theory that is so critical to the understanding of these two texts. Without knowledge of the *Sefer Yetzirah's* arithmetic, music, geometry, and astronomy, and how it all integrates to explicate Scripture, we gloss over the meaning of Scripture, with little concern for its deepest meaning, or the derivation of that meaning. And, by addressing only the extant text of the Sefer Yetzirah, philologists date the text based on form rather than content. Conclusions are drawn solely from linguistic principles with no consideration of the well-known oral tradition that transmitted ancient texts, nor of the hermeneutics of religious science. A mathematical analysis of the book's content dates back to the Old Babylonian period, to the approximate time of Abraham's birth as described by Genesis. Its mathematical content is considerably older than the oldest pages of Scripture.

Approaching the *Rig Veda* and the *Sefer Yetzirah* through ancient science reveals identical mathematical constructions, providing strong evidence that they were authored at about the same time, in about the same place — in the ancient city of Haran during the early to middle part of the 2nd millennium

BCE. Today, this is considered northern Iraq. The *Rig Veda* was begun soon after Aryan tribes migrated from the Southern Caucuses to defeat the Hurrians and rule a kingdom called Mitanni. The Torah tells us that Abram and his family (before he was called Abraham), were en route to Canaan, but settled in Haran, a city in the kingdom of Mitanni, on the Euphrates River. The patriarch finally migrated to Canaan with his family when he was 75 years old.

Both the *Rig Veda* and the *Sefer Yetzirah* are based on the mathematical construction of the *Navel of Order.* From this mathematical construction, Aryan thought became the foundation of Eastern religion, while the Semitic interpretation became the foundation of monotheism. The Semitic interpretation of the Aryan "Pathway to Heaven" became familiar to the Semitic mind as a closed "Gateway to Heaven"—a cosmic "flaw" that manifested deep within the Semitic psyche as inherent sinfulness or "original sin." Western religion's optimism about their ability to overcome that flaw was dealt a fatal blow by the loss of the ancient meditation practise of High Priests during the destruction of Solomon's Temple, whereas *Moksha* has always described the core and foundation of Eastern faiths.

Within the *Rig Veda*, Yama was the first mortal to "ascend" and pave the way to the celestial abode of Heaven for all who followed (Figure 5a). He was the King of the Dead. *Yama* thus belongs to the earliest stratum of Vedic mythology. Those following in Yama's footsteps become ascetics who drink of the Divine Elixir, *Soma*. A 2nd millennium Vedic hymn, *The Long-haired Ascetic* (quoted below), describes sacred figures "riding on the wind" (Figure 5b). These verses describe figures that have been set in shrines at the Neolithic site of *Çatal Höyük* (ca. 6500 BCE). The shared mathematics of the Navel of Order encrypted the metaphysics of a sacred practice that would empower the practitioner to reach Heaven in the footsteps of Yama. If Vishnu was dreaming the world illusion (Sanskrit: *Maya*), then learning to remain within the hypnagogic state was the only true existence, and the only way to discern what was real and what was unreal.

Figure 5a & b - Rig Vedic Hymns Describe Sacred Figures Discovered at Çatal Höyük

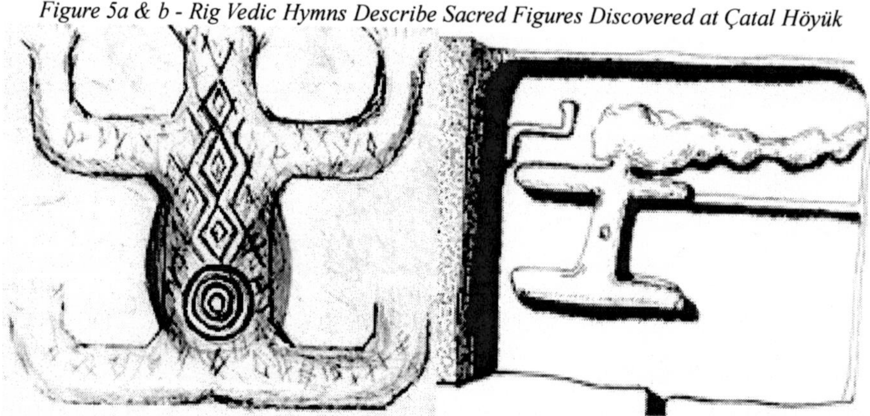

> *Long-hair holds fire, holds the drug, holds sky and earth. Long hair reveals everything, so that everyone can see the sun. Long-hair declares the light... These ascetics, swathed in wind, put dirty red rags on. When gods enter them, they ride with the rush of the wind...Crazy with asceticism, we have mounted the wind. Our bodies are all you mere mortals can see...He sails through the air, looking down on all shapes below. The ascetic is friend to this god and that god, devoted to what is well done...*[51]

As already mentioned, the "drug" being referenced within the caption of Figure 5b has been called Soma juice, Amrita, Bodhicitta drops, ambrosia, snow, anointing, a true Baptism of the Spirit, etc., depending on the cultural context. It is the Divine Elixir that is metaphorically drunk, but it is actually an inherent component of the meditation process. After years of "flaming and dripping," a practitioner's sacred practice progresses, and ultimately, the "Fire" ascends and the "Water" descends until the soul liberates "on the Winds." This should provide some insight into the Rig Veda's expression of "riding on the Wind." The soul's liberation on the subtle "Winds of spirit" create out-of-body experiences that result from either death, near-death, or *Moksha.* "Beyond death" experiences are as old as civilization itself.

The founders of civilization discovered the common mathematics of the universe that linked the microcosm to the macrocosm. In Chapter 5, we will see how the 12 divisions of Heaven's clock was understood to be marking time on a spiritual clock as a mirror reflection of the 12 divisions of Earth's material clock. The world of man and the world of immortal souls were "tied" together at the navel by man's umbilical cord. The clock, as a measure of astronomical cycles, is our oldest and most significant sexagesimal artifact. Archeologists and mathematical historians may eventually discover even earlier references to the Quadrivium and the clock within pictographic and ideographic script that preceded phonetic cuneiform.

After the pre-Sumerian Aryans founded Eridu (ca. 5400 BCE), Sumer lasted about 3000 years. We have stressed the significance of cross-fertilization that occurred between the Iranian (Aryan) founders and the first wave of invading Semitic tribes (4000 - 2300 BCE). By 2300 BCE, invading Semitic Akkadians soon replaced the powerful priests overseeing Sumerian city-states. These tribes were led by Sargon of Akkad, who founded the kingdom of Babylon circa 2300 BCE.[52] Akkadian rule would soon be followed by Gutian and Amorite kingdoms. But, before we discuss Babylon, it is important to discuss the fate of this superior Aryan race after the collapse of the Irano-Semitic civilization at Eridu. Some may have intermarried with the invading Semitic tribes, but, the evidence suggests that a good number of them migrated in river boats by 4000 BCE, to become the founding fathers of Egypt.

51 *Rig Veda, 10.136,* Op.Cit., *137-8.*
52 In the Book of Genesis, Nimrod was said to be the first "mighty King." He was Noah's great-grandson.

Rediscovering the Aryan Fathers

The first archeologist to journey eastward from the Nile Valley was the Russian scholar Vladimir Golenischeff in 1887. He traveled through the Wadi Hammamat. Before the Mediterranean rain belt moved south, circa 3500 BCE, this wadi was once a great river connecting the Nile to the Red Sea. Golenischeff was also the first to discover abundant hieroglyphic inscriptions at the siltstone quarries along the wadi.[53] In 1908, Englishman Arthur Weigall traveled along the nearby Wadi Barramiya to discover prehistoric images inscribed along the cliffs of the wadi. He was the first Egyptologist to publish large numbers of boat drawings discovered along these cliffs. In 1936-37, German scholar Hans Alexander Winkler searched through the Wadi Hammamat, studying its ancient rock art for clues about Egypt's earliest inhabitants. He noticed a resemblance between the high-prows and sterns of boats inscribed on the Eastern desert walls, with similar vessels depicted on Mesopotamian cylinder seals that were in his possession. Winkler theorized that Egypt was invaded from the East by a "master race" who brought civilization with them in river boats.[54] Winkler also found numerous swastikas inscribed on these cliffs. He knew the swastika to be the *Axis Mundi* symbol of the Aryan tribes in the Armenian Highlands (see Figure 24c).

Nazi Alfred Rosenberg, Hitler's aide-de-camp, convinced Hitler to adopt the swastika based on Winkler's theories regarding an Aryan master race. Rosenberg's racial ideas were reinforced by the work of another German scientist, a "craniologist" named Johann Blumenbach, the acknowledged father of racial classification.[55] Blumenbach categorized five different races by studying and measuring human skulls:

- The Caucasian or white race
- The Mongolian or yellow race
- The Malayan or brown race
- The Negroid or black race
- The American or red race.

Based on these distinctions, he also applied a now defunct pseudo-science called phrenology, in which personality traits were determined by "reading" the skull. He theorized, for example, that the high brows of Caucasians

53 Tony Wilkinson, *Genesis of the Pharaohs* (London: Thames & Hudson, 2003) 13.
54 Ibid., 147.
55 Nell Irvin Painter, *Why White People are Called Caucasian?* (New Haven, Connecticut: Yale University Press, 2003).

were physical expressions of a loftier mentality. He also found great similarities between a German skull in his collection and what he considered to be the most perfect and beautiful human skull, taken from the Caucasus Mountain region:

> I have taken the name of this variety from Mount Caucasus, both because its neighborhood, and especially its southern slope, produces the most beautiful race of men, I mean the Georgian.

Blumenbach's work was followed by decades of debate among early 20th century anthropologists that had less to do with science, and more to do with ideology. Among the ideas that surfaced was an observation that blond, blue-eyed, beautiful Caucasians appeared to be best exemplified by the Nordic people. This appealed to Rosenberg and Hitler, who then declared that a Nordic-Aryan master race was the ancient ancestor of the German people. In Hitler's twisted mind, a contrived German link to an idealized master race was transformed into Hitler's distorted version of "Aryan supremacy," which became his justification for genocide.

Historian Nell Painter remarks that Blumenbach used the word "beautiful" compulsively to describe the Georgian skull, suggesting that his conclusions were something less than scientific. In an article that questions the very identity of white people as Caucasians, Ms. Painter suggests that Blumenbach's theory depicting the Caucasian race as the "primeval race," "the oldest race of man," and the "first variety of humankind," was based on the very unscientific Biblical notion that Noah's Ark came to rest on Mount Ararat in the Caucasus Mountains, and further, that the great dispersion of people after Noah's Ark landed, began their migration from the Caucasus Mountains.[56]

From the perspective of Ms. Painter's "American black experience," the term "master race" brings to mind the trauma of slavery and oppression. Obviously, it has similar overtones within the Jewish psyche. It is easy to get caught up in exaggerated notions of Hell and mortal sin, just long enough to dole out Semitic justice to the likes of a Hitler. Indo-Aryan karmic justice does not seem severe enough to satisfy Western sensibilities, and as a result, there has been a strong desire to discredit the work of Winkler, Blumenbach, and the Aryan founders of civilization. They have been unjustly slandered, primarily because Hitler took an interest in them. Today, the very mention of an Aryan master race elicits a visceral reaction from descent people the world over.

Since the time of Hitler's distortions, major strides have made in biology resulting from the discovery of DNA, revealing that far too much

---

56 Ibid.

has been made of racial differences. It is now well established that skin color readily adapts to changing climate, since dark skin is a way to filter ultra-violet rays. EMH originated in Africa some 200,000 years ago, where people were very dark. During the earliest migrations out of Africa, those who traveled to the Middle East and Asia, circa 50,000 - 60,000 BCE, became moderately dark. By the time Cro-Magnon skeletons were discovered in French caves, they were believed to have the size and coloration of the robust Finnish people, with pale skin and red hair, circa 30,000 BCE.

Ms. Painter essentially dismisses the story of Noah and the Biblical Diaspora as non-factual, but she fails to recognize that the Caucasian Mountains has long been considered the gateway between Europe, the Middle East, Asia and Africa, functioning as a virtual turnstile of ethnicity and language. In the Biblical story of the Great Flood, Noah landed on Mount Ararat in the Armenian Highlands in order to repopulate the world like a second Adam. The story continues with Noah's great-grandson, Nimrod, building a Tower of Babel (Hebrew: Babylon) to reach Heaven.[57] God considered this idolatry, so He confused the "tongues" of all those on the Tower, dispersing various races and languages to the "four corners of the earth." Ms. Painter might consider the possibility that the Bible is a reasonably accurate chronology of pre-historic events. It turns out that the geographic region situated between the Black Sea and Caspian Seas has long been the most ethnically and linguistically diverse area in the world. Sanskrit developed right along side Hebrew, as well as numerous other Indo-European, Semitic, and non-Semitic languages and cultures.

A great flood has been documented across many ancient cultures as the Ice Age drew to a close. The last glaciers melted and flooded the plains from about 14,000 to 7,000 BCE. Noah, emerging from his Ark on Mount Ararat in the Caucasus Mountains, can be thought of as metaphor for the Aryan tribes emerging from the extensive network of Ice Age caves that border Iraq. When Early Modern Humans first emerged from the nearby Shanidar Cave in the Zagros Mountains of Kurdistan, some linguists suggest that the language they spoke might be called proto-nostratic, meaning that it would have been spoken at an earlier time than the language families descended from it.

The Bible refers to the Aryan fathers as "Sons of God" (Hebrew: *Bene Elohim*).[58] The Book of Enoch elaborates on this Biblical passage by describing 200 "Watchers" who descended from Heaven to Mount Hermon (Deuteronomy 4:48 calls it Mount Sion), located in the northern most section of today's Golan Heights in Israel on the Syrian and Lebanese border.

57 Nimrod is often associated with Sargon of Akkad, the founder of Babylon.
58 Genesis 6:1-4

Those who emerged from caves in this area would have also emerged from the Kebera Cave within nearby Mount Carmel. There is archeological evidence of an advanced Early Natufian culture (12,500 - 10,800 BCE) that was sedentary before the advent of agriculture. The very first agriculture in the world is said to be the small Natufian settlement of Abu Huyeyra, on the banks of the Euphrates in northern Syria (ca. 9000 BCE).[59] Some evidence of Natufian dolichocephalic remains have been discovered (enlarged skulls). And, in 2008, the remains of the oldest shaman's grave was discovered. Buried with this Natufian priestess was the wing tip of a golden eagle, the tail of a cow, and the pelvis of a leopard — significant symbols of the four fixed astronomical signs (to be discussed in Chapter 3). Another important early Natufian settlement was the Mesolithic site of Tell es-Sultan, a couple of kilometers from Jericho, the famed "walled city" mentioned in the Bible.

As the Neolithic period got underway, ca. 8000 BCE, early farming settlements included Jericho, Catal Höyük, Jarmo, and Susa. In addition to founding Eridu in the river valley below, the diaspora spread other Aryan tribes through the Zagros Mountains as far as Mehrgarh, Pakistan (ca. 8000 BCE). A 4th millennium Aryan migration from Mehrgarh descended in6to the Indus Valley to begin the advanced Harappan civilization (ca. 3000 BCE). The ancient name of India is *Aryavarta*, which literally means "abode of the Aryans."

My own research on Aryan migrations suggests that we must look deeper into Winkler's theory about Aryan tribes founding Egyptian civilization. Hitler's inhumanity cast an enormous shadow over Winkler's work, initiating a major effort to discredit him. His discovery of swastikas in the Egyptian wadis have since been dated more accurately, to about 1800 BCE, which would have been more than 2000 years after the beginning of Egyptian civilization. Winkler also suggests that the Aryans would have had to cross the Mediterranean Sea in river boats, circa 4000 BCE, and then portage across the Suez. Since these boats were considered too flimsy to cross the Mediterranean, his theory was ultimately rejected, and largely ignored for the next 50 years. Ironically, Winkler was drafted into the German Army and was shot and killed in WWII during active duty in Poland.

Modern Egyptologist, Toby Wilkinson, provides some background about his own first expeditions in the eastern Egyptian desert, as part of his own effort to revive Winkler's theory:

> After half a century of neglect, Winkler's "Eastern Invaders" hypothesis was brought back to life in the late 1990's by historian David Rohl. His book *Legend* tries to use diverse archeological data,

59 Andrew Moore, Gordon Hillman and Anthony Legge, *Village on the Euphrates: From Foraging to Farming at Abu Hureyra* (London: Oxford University Press, 2000).

> supported by alternative etymologies of important ancient names to demonstrate the historical accuracy of Old Testament stories... Rohl identified these ancestors ... as Mesopotamians, citing the boat petroglyphs of the Eastern Desert as important supporting evidence.[60]

Rohl never won over the academic community. He subsequently teamed up with Ancient World Tours to launch adventure safaris in the Eastern desert, in an effort to train participants to follow in Winkler's footsteps, in order to perpetuate his theories. Wilkinson's first exposure to the Eastern desert was as a member of one of these expeditions. Winkler was guilty by association — Hitler distorted his theory — and without new evidence, it has been difficult to reestablish the validity of Winkler's original theory.[61]

However, I believe that significant new evidence did appear within the last 20 years. Mesopotamian river boats did not need to travel the Mediterranean Sea, as Winkler's detractors presumed. Satellite photos taken in the 1990's have established that ancient rivers existed under the Saudi Arabian desert before the rain belt moved south, quite possibly capable of carrying Aryan river boats from Basrah to Mecca and on to the Nile. The existence of just such a navigable river is substantiated by the Bible as one of the Four Rivers of Eden known as the Gihon River.

Consider the possibility that tribes of Aryans migrated across Saudi Arabia to Egypt in riverboats between 4500 - 3500 BCE. We might recall Sir Arthur Keith's already mentioned observation that the Sumerians were "dolichocephalic, with large brain capacity, like a section of the pre-dynastic Egyptians."[62] Of course, Sumerians would have brought the science of religion along with them, including an astral theology of the four fixed signs (Chapter 3), the Clock of Heaven and Earth (Chapter 4), and the Sumerian notion of local city-gods:

> At Memphis, Ptah, the power of the earth was the creator. At Heliopolis and Hermopolis it was the power in the sun [the god Re], and at Elephantine it was said that Khnum [god of water] made all living beings on a potter's wheel...[63] Amon, the wind, was also, as breath, the mysterious source of life in man and in beast...[64] The dead lived in the great cosmic circuit of the sun and stars.[65]

60 Wilkinson, Op.Cit., 30.
61 Ibid., 30.
62 John Marshall, *Mohenjro Dara and the Indus Civilization* (Asian Educational Studies, 1931) 109; Sir Arthur Keith in H.R. Hall and C.L. Woolley, "Ur Excavations Al'Ubaid," (Oxford University Press, 1927) vol.i, 216-240.
63 Henri Frankfort, *Ancient Egyptian Religion* (New York: Columbia University Press, 1948) 20.
64 Ibid., 22.
65 Ibid., 109.

The Four Rivers of Eden

Many evangelical Christians believe Genesis literally. They believe that Adam and Eve were historical people, and that the Garden of Eden was a historical place. One reason for this is our knowledge that at least two of the Four Rivers of Eden actually exist. These rivers are described in Genesis 2:10-14 as the Tigris and Euphrates.[66] However, the other two rivers: the Pishon and Gihon, have never been decisively located. Eden is also called Heaven or Paradise, and although Eden is considered a spiritual realm, the musical mathematics in Part II describes exactly how Adam's exile from Heaven bridges the spiritual and material realms. Since the spiritual Eden has a material reflection, it is logical to assume that the other two rivers would also have a physical presence here on Earth. According to Genesis 2:10-14:

> A river issues forth from Eden to water the garden, and it then divides and becomes four branches. The name of the first is Pishon, the one that winds through the whole land of Havilah, where the gold is. The gold of that land is good; bdellium is there, and lapis lazulli. The name of the second river is Gihon, the one that winds through the whole land of Cush. The name of the third river is Tigris, the one that flows east of Asshur. And the fourth river is the Euphrates.

According to Samuel Kramer:

> "The very idea of a divine paradise, a garden of the gods, is of Sumerian origin. The Sumerian paradise was located, according to our poem ["Enki and Ninhursag"] in the land of Dilmun, a land that was probably situated in south-western Persia. There is good indication that the Biblical paradise, which is described as a garden planted eastward in Eden, from whose waters flow the four world rivers, including the Tigris and Euphrates, may have been originally identical with Dilmun, the Sumerian Paradise-land.[67]

The story of "Enki and Ninhursag" is just one example of a Bible story that closely resembles its Sumerian or Babylonian predecessor, as deciphered from cuneiform tablets. It begins in the paradise of Dilmun, where there was no sick-

---

66 Carol A. Hill, *The Garden of Eden a Modern Landscape*, Perspectives on Science and Christian Faith 52 (March 2000): 31-46..

67 Samuel Noah Kramer, Op.Cit., 143.

ness or death.[68] The two-faced Isimud plucked precious plants in the divine garden and gave them to Enki to eat. As a result, Enki's health quickly began to fail, until Ninhursag (Mother Earth) brings him back to life. This resembles the duplicity of the serpent offering Eve the "forbidden fruit" that resulted in Adam and Eve's "sickness" of exile on Earth, and implies that Eve acquired a temptress persona from the serpent. In another story, Noah's Sumerian counterpart, king Ziusudra, was sole survivor of the great flood and preserver of the seed of mankind. He was given "life like a god" and "breath eternal." Similarly, Noah "walked with God."

Scientific evidence suggests that the man who would be Adam, migrated out of Ethiopia in several waves, along different possible routes. The first wave is believed to have crossed into Yemen at the Horn of Africa, and continued on to India and Australia. The second wave of migration is believed to have entered the Middle East, and with this second wave, the Bible begins its narrative. Our gnostic hypothesis provides insight into the Biblical narrative that guides our speculation about prehistoric migrations. Adam's "Out of Africa" journey, or his tribes journey, would have begun at the Eden-like headwaters of the Blue Nile in Ethiopia. We can trace their route along the Gihon River (Figure 38) as the Blue Nile merges with the White Nile at Khartoum. The Gihon proceeds north along the Nile to the wadis in the Eastern Egyptian desert, and then follows the Wadi Hammamat to the Red Sea.

There is some geological evidence to suggest that the Gihon entered Saudi Arabia around Mecca. Following Biblical and geological clues, we can speculate that Adam's descendants traveled the length of the Gihon in Saudi Arabia to the spot where it "cross-cuts" the Pishon, the Tigris, and the Euphrates. This would corroborate the legend of the Kabah in Mecca as Adam and Eve's first home after they were exiled from Eden. The next 6 generations after Adam would have settled nearby, along the Gihon, leading up to what would be Basrah today. At some point, during glacial periods, and certainly during the Last Glacial Maximum (circa 28,000 BCE), the descendants of Adam would have had to escape to Zagros Mountain caves in order to survive. This area is referred to by Samuel Kramer as southwest Persia, "the land of the Aryans."

Today, the Zagros Mountains in Iran are known for its mining of natural resources, including: bauxite, coal, iron ore, lead, zinc, chromite, manganese, silver, tin, and tungsten, and various gems, such as: amber, agate, lapis lazuli, and turquoise. In the Sumerian story "Enmerkar and the Lord of Aratta" an emissary had been dispatched to this region to obtain gold and lapis lazuli to decorate a temple. A three month trek was made through the "seven passes" to procure the precious stones. Gold and lapis lazuli were mentioned in both the Sumerian cuneiform account of Dilmun and in the Biblical description of Eden. If we refer to the preceding quote from Genesis 2:10-14, the gold and lapis lazuli helps us to locate the Pishon

---

68 Hill, Op.Cit., 31-46.

River as one of the two major rivers that run through southwest Iran. They are the Karkheh and the Karun. "These two rivers provided a route of communication between the heart of Susa (or Susiana) and southernmost Mesopotamia. In the third millennium BCE, caravan routes along both rivers went through Susiana to Sumer and Akkad."[69] The ancient settlement of Susa was built on the east bank of the Karkheh River as it flowed down from the Zagros foothills, for about 150 miles, to join the other Biblical rivers in the delta. If we were to retrofit the Bible stories to the known facts, we might speculate that the first holy man, Enoch, the 7th generation after Adam, would have traveled toward the divine "Source" of Eden's four rivers, along the Pishon River, ascending the first holy mountain within the Zagros.

The Genesis narrative, considered against local geography, history, and the archeological record, suggests that Enoch's descendant, Noah, would have settled along the Pishon in nearby Susa (circa 10,000 BCE), which later became the capital of Elam. We know this because Susan and Elam were the eldest children of Shem and the grandchildren of Noah. The Aryan settlement of Susa (or Susiana) became a Neolithic farming settlement, high enough in the Zagros Mountains to escape the melting glaciers flooding the river valley. But, imagine the end of the Ice Age melting the last Zagros glaciers, and a great flood sweeping Noah's Ark from his Susa home in Elam. The Ark would have descended along the Pishon River until it reached the intersection of the four rivers, somewhere near Basrah. We know this to be the shortest path from Susa to the Tigris because "Alexander the Great was said to follow this path and reach the Tigris in four days."[70] The Ark would have followed the same path as the great migration of Aryans who descended from Susa during the early Ubaid period (circa 5400 BCE) to start the ancient Sumerian city of Eridu. To corroborate this, remarkable conehead figurines were discovered at both Susa and Eridu, dating back to the Ubaid period (Figures 1a). Once the Ark descended the Pishon and changed direction with the currents, it headed up the Tigris toward Mount Ararat in the Caucasus of Eastern Turkey.

Thus, the story of Noah's Ark provides Biblical readers with two well known "lands of the Aryans": the Zagros and Caucasus Mountains. The implications suggest that the Aryan tribes came out of Africa with Adam, settled in the Zagros with Enoch, and migrated to the Caucasus with Noah. Then, as part of the great Diaspora to repopulate the Earth, the descendants of Noah's triplet sons began at Mount Ararat and traveled down the Tigris River toward Akkad and Babylon. The descendants of Ham continued along the Gihon to Ethiopia, while Japheth's descendants traveled up the Euphrates and continued on toward Turkey, Greece and Europe. At 75 years of age, Abraham traveled to Haran, which sat on a bank of the Euphrates. His subsequent journey

---

69 Ibid.
70 G. Long, "On the Site of Susa," Journal of the Royal Geographical Society of London, Vol. 3, (1833) 257-267.

from Haran to Canaan breaks with these great river migrations and might be considered metaphor for the Hebrew invasion of Canaan. With Kramer's Iranian-Semitic cross fertilization firmly established in Sumer, some Aryan tribes may have refused to accept the decline of their civilization, and hopped into Gihon River boats that would cross Saudi Arabia, and bring the Aryan fathers to Egypt (ca. 4000 BCE). Hans Winkler's theory of "Eastern Invaders" would still be viable if the Aryans were able to sail their river boats inland, along the Gihon River, as long as they could reach Egypt's Eastern wadis.

In the passage below, geologist Carol Hill presents some relevant facts for consideration, however, my own findings suggest she has reversed the locations of the Pishon and Gihon (see Figure 38); and, has named the Karun rather than the Karkheh, which is said to have flowed into the Karun during Biblical times.

> The now-dry Wadi al Batin was probably the Pishon River, the Gihon was probably the Karun River, and the Hiddekel (Tigris) and Euphrates Rivers flowed in approximately the same courses as they occupy today. The confluence of these four rivers was located at the head of the Persian Gulf, but a Gulf that may have been inland from where it is today... There is evidence that such a river did flow there sometime in the past. Only four inches of rain a year now fall in Saudi Arabia, but during the periods from about 30,000 to 20,000 years B.P. (before present) and from about 10,000 to 6000 years B.P., the climate was much wetter than it is today. Even as late as 3500 B.C. (before Christ), ancient lakes are known to have existed in the "Empty Quarter" of Saudi Arabia, which is today the largest sand desert in the world. A somewhat drier but still moist phase existed from about 4000 to 2350 B.C., followed by a more arid phase from about 2350 to 2000 B.C. It was then, at about 2000 B.C., that the climate turned hyper-arid and the rivers of Arabia dried up.[71]

Ms. Hill also cites an article by James Sauer called "The River Runs Dry," which describes how satellite images have detected an underground riverbed along the Wadi al Batin (Figure 6). On its eastern end, the Wadi al Batin confluences with the Tigris and Euphrates. Recent satellite photos show "that the Wadi al Batin continues to the southwest, beneath the sand, and emerges as the Wadi Rimah (both wadis may have been part of the same river system in the past, before being covered by sand dunes). About eighty miles further in the upstream direction, the Wadi Rimah bifurcates into the Wadi Qahd on the northwest, and the Wadi al Jarir on the southwest." This geological evidence suggests the possibility that in the centuries before the rain belt moved south, there may have been a navigable river to the Red Sea.

71 Hill, Op.Cit., 31-46.

Figure 6 - The "Upper" Gihon across the Saudi Desert

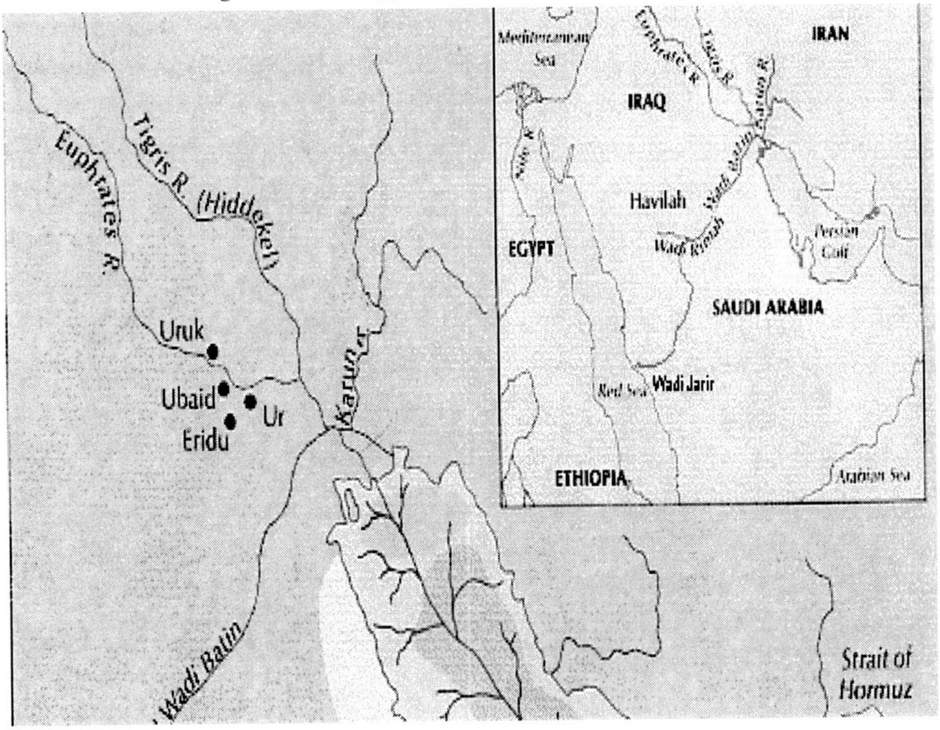

Figure 7 - The "Lower" Gihon across Egypt's Eastern Desert

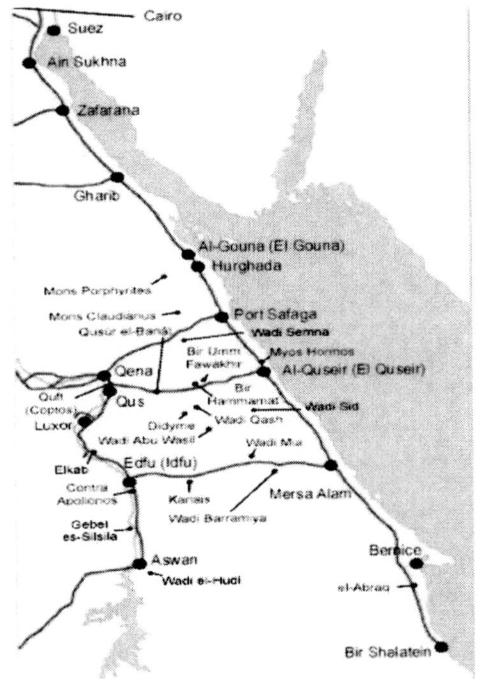

In order to be properly identified as the Gihon River, Genesis tells us it would have to "wind through the whole land of Cush" (Ethiopia: see Figure 38). Cush was the son of Ham, the grandson of Noah, and the father of Nimrod. It is believed that Ham's descendants settled in Africa, and soon afterwards, spread north, east, and west. Josephus states: "For of the four sons of Ham, time has not at all hurt the name of Cush; for the Ethiopians, over whom he reigned, are even at this day, both by themselves and by all men in Asia, called Cushites."[72] Adam's route "out of Africa," along the Bible's Gihon River, helps to guide our analysis of the EMH path into the Middle East. Invading Aryan river boats that made their way across Saudi Arabia to the Red Sea appear to have retraced mankind's path back to Egypt. The Aryans would have headed North after reaching the Red Sea near Mecca, and then headed West along the Wadis Barramiya and Hammamat until they reached the Nile (Figure 7). Drawings on the cliffs of these wadis document the event. Locating the Gihon River in this manner provides a plausible route for Hans Winkler's late 5th millennium Aryan invaders, perhaps making his theory viable once more. Winkler's erroneously dated swastikas would have been carved into the Egyptian wadi cliffs during a 2nd millennium Aryan migration, called the Hyksos migration.

Establishing the location of the Bible's Gihon River (Figure 38) is further supported by the Nile's southern path through Khartoum, in the Sudan, where a tributary called the Blue Nile proceeds to "wind through the whole land of Kush." The prophet Isaiah spoke of a land beyond the rivers of Nubia (Isaiah 18:1), while the prophet Zephaniah speaks about invoking the LORD by name from "beyond the rivers of Kush" (Zeph. 3:10). Before the 4th century, and throughout classical antiquity, Nubia was known as Kush. In ancient Egyptian inscriptions Ethiopia is called Kesh. The Greek speaking Jews who translated the Hebrew Scriptures into the Septuagint, consistently translated the word Cush as "Ethiopia."

During the Hyksos migration, Hebrew, Canaanite, and Aryan tribes were part of the same migration into the Levant out of the southern Caucasus Mountains (circa 2000-1700 BCE). This powerful wave had a great impact on Turkey, Iraq, Syria, Lebanon, Canaan, and Egypt. The Hebrews invaded Canaan (at 75 years of age, Abraham left Haran for Canaan), then Canaan invaded and came to power in Egypt (Abraham's great-grandson Joseph became magistrate over Egypt). Also, as part of the Hyksos migrations, the Aryans invaded the Hurrians with their powerful war chariots (Figure 8) to create the Mitanni Kingdom (circa 1800-1350 BCE), which included southeastern Turkey, northern Syria, and northern Iraq.

After the fall of Mitanni to Hittite forces (ca. 1360 BCE), the Aryans of Mitanni migrated toward the Indus Valley where they gave a much needed boost to the existing Aryan Harappan culture (founded ca. 3000 BCE) that was winding down. The recent arrivals brought a new influx of knowledge and wisdom that became the

72 Flavius Josephus, *Antiquities of the Jews,* 1.6.

foundation of Hinduism, as recorded in four "Vedic" *Samhitas* (Sanskrit: collection): the *Rig-Veda, Sama-Veda, Yajur-Veda,* and *Atharva-Veda.* The Vedas greatly influenced Hinduism, Buddhism, Jainism, and in Persia, Zoroastrianism.

Figure 8 - Aryan "Chariot of the Gods"

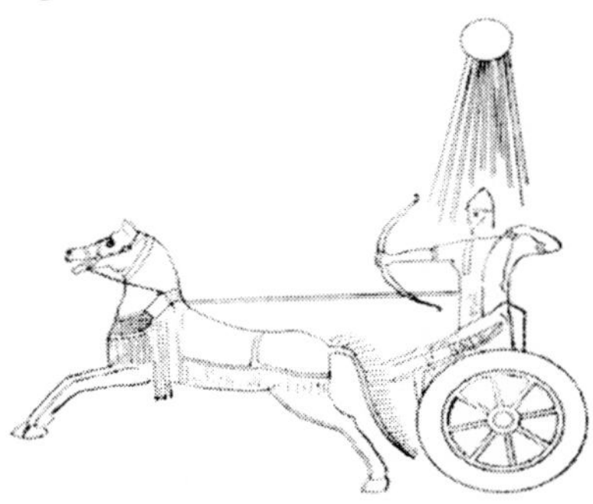

When considered alongside later Indo-Aryan texts, the Vedic writings are the closest in character to the oldest Aryan tradition, with frequent references to One Supreme God. Vedic monotheism can be traced back to the Sumerian goddess Inanna and her sexual "integration" with the other 6 Sumerian "gods who decree." The 7th god, Inanna, sexually "integrates" these energies into a Divine Unity. Inanna was later known as: Isis, Ishtar, Venus, Aphrodite, etc.. Inanna's gradual motion through the skies "unites" the astrological emanations of the Sun's universal energy. Vedic polytheistic deities began as mortals, but their liberated soul either dwelled in Heaven, or was somewhere in transit between Heaven and Earth. The Vedas are considered *Apauruseya* (Sanskrit: "unauthored" implying divine origin)," and are considered *mantras* that were revealed to man through 22 *śruti* ("what is heard"). Similarly, the only text attributed to Abraham, the *Sefer Yetzirah*, speaks about *22 Foundation Letters*. Both texts are referring to the 22 chromatic tones of the *Navel of Order* (see Figure 25): an ascending 11-tone scale (Heavenly Fires) and a descending 11-tone scale (Heavenly Waters) describing the ancient Aryan spiral "ladder" that spans Heaven and Earth (Figure 21b). Also, in both texts, the centerline of the circle (the path of Heavenly Winds) depicted in Figure 25 is the World Soul that arises from Vishnu's Navel as a 7 tone scale. Within the microcosm, we might think of the 22 vibrations of the surrounding circle (*mandala*) as the torso of the body, while the "*Axis Mundi*" of 7 vibrations depicts the soul (Figure 47a, b & c).

Demonizing the Aryans

Before the world discredited the man who first realized the possibility of an Aryan "master race," the effort to discredit him drew upon two ancient texts that, in the minds of many, cast the Aryans themselves in a negative light. Those two texts were the Bible and the Book of Enoch. The Book of Genesis states:

The sons of God saw that the daughters of men were beautiful; and they took for themselves, whomever they chose... It was then, and later too, that the Nephilim [Hebrew: men of renown] appeared on earth — when the sons of God came in to the daughters of men, and they bore children to them. Those were the mighty, who, from old, were men of renown. -- Genesis 6:1-4

This passage has confounded Church fathers, presumably because it speaks about multiple "sons of God" — a concept that appears to contradict the First Ecumenical Council's edict that Christ was the only son of God. This passage does, however, make perfect sense if we consider the theory that the "sons of God" were actually the Aryan "gods on the mountain."

In an attempt to explain the identity of the "sons of God," an important Jewish Kabbalistic text called the Zohar, alludes to the great mysteries of the science of religion. It begins with Adam in the Heavenly garden, where God gave him a book written by Raziel, the angel in charge of the holy mysteries. The Zohar states that Adam studied it diligently, learning its sacred mysteries. But, when Adam was banished from the Garden, the book flew out of his hand, and Adam beat his breast and wept. The Zohar (55b) tells us what happened next:

God thereupon made a sign to Raphael [the archangel] to return to him the book, which he then studied for the rest of his life. Adam left it to his son Seth, who transmitted it in turn to his posterity, and so on until it came to Abraham, who learned from it how to discern the glory of his Master, as has been said. Similarly, Enoch possessed a book through which he learned to discern the divine glory.

After Adam bequeathed this birthright to his son Seth, Zohar 37b identifies the "posterity of Seth" as "the sons of God":

It came into the hands of the 'sons of God,' the wise of their generation, and whoever was privileged to peruse it could learn from it supernal wisdom... Tradition further tells us that Enoch also had a book, which came from the same place as the book of generations of Adam. This is the source of the book known as 'the book of Enoch.' When God took him [Enoch], He showed him all supernal mysteries, and the Tree of Life in the midst of the Garden and its leaves and branches, all of which can be found in the book.

From a historical perspective, Seth and Enoch would both have been Aryan patriarchs. The *Zohar* speaks about the Book of Enoch with reverence, although it was never part of the Hebrew or Christian Canons.[73] Scholars generally consider it the most significant non-canonized Apocryphal text.[74] There are three known versions, usually dated around 300 BCE. It was also part of the Dead Sea Scrolls discovered around the Wadi Qumran in 1947. The Book of Enoch was written thousands of years after the Biblical Enoch would have lived, and it can be argued that any text written after Solomon's Temple was destroyed (586 BCE) must be considered less than authoritative. After that decisive event, prophecy was considered dead. The last High Priest of Solomon's Temple was considered the last person to understand the "Secret of Knowledge"[75] that gave rise to the Biblical prophets.

Early Church fathers, most notably Origen and Clement of Alexandria, held the Book of Enoch in the highest esteem.[76] The introduction to Richard Laurence's translation of the Book of Enoch states that this book is nothing less than "the Ethiopic key to the evolution of Christianity." Notes to this edition of Enoch also state that the first mention of "Fallen Angels" was taken by early Christian writers from the Book of Enoch. We should note that the Church did its best to hide this text from the public. Possibly because it speaks of 200 "sons of God" who descended to Mount Armon[77] as "Fallen Angels" in order to procreate with mortal women.

We have described the "sons of God" as Aryan's like Enoch and Noah, who understood how to purify the body and liberate the soul in order to "walk with God." In Abrahamic terms, they understood how to "pronounce" the Word of God, YHVH, in order to achieve liberation. The *Nephilim* offspring of the sons of God simply refers to a continuation of the spiritual Aryan lineage. The most reputable Jewish sources render the Genesis translation as either "men of renown" or "heros of old." The Book of Enoch and the Book of Jubilees appear to be attempts at providing the back story for Genesis 6:1-4. From that perspective, the Book of Enoch's story line decides to cast the *Nephilim* as evil "Giants," and their fathers as "Fallen Angels." So, in order to clarify, we have to dig a bit deeper. The Hebrew suffix "im" is the plural form of the word *Nephilim*, while the root of the word NPL (נְפָל) literally means "to fall." There are some who might translate the word as those who "cause others to fall." We might recall that when the Aryan coneheads first left their caves, legend suggests they were very large and robust, especially with their elongated skulls. It is not surprising, therefore, that people were awestruck when encountering these giants, which may help explain how they "caused others to fall."

We have already mentioned the translator, Richard Laurence's belief that the first Christian notion of "fallen angels" was taken from this text. But, it was not the offspring *Nephilim* who were considered "fallen angels," it was their fathers.

73 It is, however, part of the Ethiopic Canon
74 The word Apocrypha comes from the Greek verb crypto, which means to hide.
75 Tanya, Likutei Amarim 53.
76 Ibid, 192.
77 Mount Armon is also called Mount Hermon or Mount Sion. It is located in the northern most section of today's Israel

The Book of Enoch usurps the meaning of the root NPL (נָפַל) as "to fall" and erroneously applies it to the "sons of God." Twisting the translation in this manner was intended to cast aspersions on the moral character of the sons of God, who "took wives among the daughters of men." The Book of Enoch goes a step farther, and borrows a term from the Book of Daniel[78] to describe the "sons of God,"the Hebrew word *Irin* (Watchers), suggesting that the "sons of God" were more than watchers of mankind, they were also lecherous "watchers" of mortal women who gave into temptation and thus became "Fallen Angels," mating and giving birth to *Nephilim* "demon" offspring. The Book of Enoch misinterprets both Abrahamic meaning and Aryan history, asking us to believe that the Biblical "sons of God" were avatars, who could in no measure be considered mortal, despite their apparent mortal vulnerability to sin. Here is an example of Enochian exaggeration from 1 Enoch Chap.7:

- Then they took wives, each choosing for himself; whom they began to approach, and with whom they cohabited; teaching them sorcery, incantations, and the dividing of roots and trees.
- And the women conceiving brought forth giants,
- Whose stature was each three hundred cubits. These devoured all which the labour of men provided; until it became impossible to feed them;
- When they turned themselves against men, in order to devour them;
- And began to injure birds, beasts, reptiles and fishes, to eat their flesh one after another, and to drink their blood.

The Book of Enoch characterizes the *Nephilim* as cannibals, vampires, or demons, while the *Watchers* are maligned as teachers. 1 Enoch Chapter 8 lists the division of labor that took place:

- Azazyel taught men to make swords, knives, breastplates,…
- Amazarak taught all sorcerers, and dividers of roots;
- Armers taught the solution of sorcery;
- Barkayal taught the observers of the stars;
- Akibeel taught signs;
- Tamiel taught astronomy;
- And Asaradel taught the motion of the moon.
- And men, being destroyed, cried out; and their voice reached to Heaven.

This description would be consistent with our knowledge of the Aryan "sons of God" with one flagrant exception — the last line — which states

78 The Hebrew term *Irin* is borrowed from the Book of Daniel 4:13-17 where reference is made to the *Irin* as vigilant or watchful angels of Yahweh who decree in judgement.

that men were "being destroyed" rather than blessed with the knowledge of Heaven. This final line item conflates the mathematics and science taught by the sons of God, with the greatly exaggerated evil erroneously attributed to their *Nephilim* offspring (sons of the "sons of God"). Unfortunately, certain Torah commentary tries hard to remain consistent with the Book of Enoch, and speaks about the *Nephilim* as "giants" who were among the evil "sons of Cain." However, it must be emphasized that the Torah never actually states that the *Nephilim* were evil. It must be emphasized that the most authoritative translations of the word *Nephilim* renders: "heros of old" or "men of renown," translations that are consistent with the Sanskrit term *Aryan* as "Noblemen."

Christianity casts a great stigma upon learning the "heavenly secrets" of mathematics and science. This is the same mathematics and science that began civilization in Sumer, Egypt and Harappa. When the Emperor Constantine convened the First Ecumenical Council at Nicea, in 325 AD, ancient science officially became gnostic heresy. The Church appears to have equated knowledge of Heavenly secrets with Adam's sin of knowing too much. Unfortunately, that perspective turns its back on the Aryan/ *Nephilim* legacy of an integrated science and religion that began civilization and still holds the key to unlocking the secrets of Scripture.

Once the ancient science became heresy, it began a long history of enmity between the scientific community and the Church's Orthodox religious community. The characterization of *Nephilim* as cannibals, vampires, and demons in the Book of Enoch, has literally demonized the Aryan founders of civilization, and seriously distorted Christianity's notions of Hell. As a result, Christian demonology has been grossly exaggerated into a nightmarish fantasy, all beginning with the Book of Enoch's exaggerations and misinterpretations regarding the *Nephilim.*

Mainstream Christianity's notions of Satan as a synonym for the Devil began with the 1st Book of Enoch as the Watcher *Satariel,* and in the 2nd book of Enoch as *Satanael.* The Book of Enoch seriously conflicts with Abraham's writings in the area of demonology, as well as with the intended meaning of the Hebrew Scriptures. Christianity's concept of evil spirits grew into its exaggerated notions of Hell, based on the Book of Enoch's misrepresentations of "*Sheol.*" [79]

> *Now the giants, who have been born of spirit and of flesh, shall be called upon earth evil spirits, and on earth shall be their habitation. Evil spirits shall proceed from their flesh, because they were created from above; from the holy watchers was their beginning*

79 Sheol is a term used in the Books of Ecclesiastes and Job to describe Hell or *Hades* as the abode of both pious and wicked souls who "lie in sleep together."

and primary foundation. Evil spirits shall they be upon earth, and the spirits of the wicked shall they be called. The habitation of the spirits in Heaven shall be in Heaven; but upon earth shall be the habitation of terrestrial spirits, who are born of earth.

Abraham's theology, as described in the *Sefer Yetzirah,* does not differentiate terrestrial spirits from Heavenly spirits in this manner. In other words, every man's immortal soul incarnates in a physical body, and then is liberated either through death or through the sacred practice, but only man's soul is able to travel between Heaven and Earth. Abraham's writings, therefore, contradict any notions of demons or bodily resurrection, and they clarify that people who die before purifying their body have pure souls that live in bodies tainted by sin. However, we certainly would not call them demons, since that would imply that most, if not all of mankind, is demonic. Adam is the archetype of sinful man, but how can we apply Christianity's exaggerated notions of Hell to Adam, since Adam symbolizes the common man. The freakish and cannibalistic "Giants" who drank the blood of birds and reptiles in the Book of Enoch, does not, in any way, represent the plight of the common man. And further, it is completely inconsistent with the Hebrew Scriptures. Describing a race of cruel and evil giants is a problem rooted in the mistranslation of the word *Nephilim* based on unauthoritative, non-Canonical Enochian fantasy.

The Book of Enoch was excluded from both the Hebrew and Christian Canons, and thus, cannot be considered authoritative from the perspective of Orthodox religion, and rightly so.[80] It might be a useful exercise to consider what the world might have become if the *Nephilim* were remembered as "men of renown" or "heros of old." What if the Book of Enoch's "Watchers" and their offspring were valued for all they taught mankind, rather then degraded as cannibalistic, vampire demons. One unfortunate result of this text's influence is the Church's long-standing opposition to the advances of mathematics and science. I believe the wedge between Christianity and the other two monotheistic religions began here.

Without the Book of Enoch, we can speculate that Christianity might not have been so quick to condemn Gnosticism and *Moksha* as the Gnostic and Arian heresies, respectively. Instead, the Church's exaggerated notions were further influenced by such imaginative writings as Dante's *Inferno* and Milton's *Paradise Lost.*[81] In this tradition, the demonology in today's movie theaters reflect an other-worldly science-fiction imagination that boggles the mind and bombards the senses. Religion may have begun as a meditation practice to purify the body and liberate the soul, but Christianity has become dominated by a moralistic fervor driven by distorted notions of Satan and Hell.

80 There is one exception. The Book of Enoch is part of the Ethiopic Canon.
81 Dante Alighieri, *The Inferno*, trans by John Ciardi (New York: New American Library, 1954).

God punished Adam by banishing him to wander the cursed Earth in the path of the cursed serpent, man's alter-ego. Adam was in Hell as he wandered the Earth in exile from Heaven. It required no further embellishment. Christianity's "Hell" has become seriously distorted by man's active imagination. Clarifying these distorted ideas requires the Biblical mathematics described in Chapter 14. Hebrew notions of *Sheol* as the "abyss of the serpent" describes "the greatest possible distance from Heaven" (Job 11:8). The Bible borrows a bit from Egyptian notions of *Hades* as navigable rivers under the Earth, where the dead descend, and the revived ascend. It is from this perspective that David recites Psalm 30: "O LORD, you brought me up from Sheol, preserved me from going down into the Pit."

The serpent's abyss finds the serpent coiled 3½ times at the base of the spine. It is the unrealized Self in the dormancy of Hades often associated with death and darkness. Meditation uncoils the serpent energy, "awakening" the meditator as it climbs out of the abyss and up the spine. It vitalizes our Soul, saving us from sinful distractions and spiritual blindness. As man continues this spiritual practice, the abyss of Hell (unrealized dormancy) is ultimately transformed into "Enlightenment" at the Gates of Heaven. Thus, *Sheol* ambiguously defines the Gates of both Heaven and Hell — sin and salvation — and both are associated with the *ayanamsa* as the precessional gap or portal. From Abraham's perspective, we experience Hell whenever we are not One with the Divine energies that live within us. We are all tormented souls until we stop our mind's distracted wanderings and allow the sacred meditation practice to return us to the Paradise that has long been equated with the soul's liberation. The mathematical prototype of Heaven and Hell has ancient Aryan origins. The oldest extant writings articulating these concepts can be found among the numerous Sumerian and Babylonian cuneiform clay tablets. The Hebrew Scriptures never considered Adam or mankind evil or cursed, just inherently sinful, and morally obligated to find his way back to Heaven by learning to open the "gate" to the spiritual "path" known as Jacob's Ladder.

Kramer tells us that the pre-Sumerian tribes were the true founders of civilization who should be credited with the invention of writing, mathematics, science, and religion. With this historical background under our belt, we can now turn our attention to understanding the mathematical and scientific details of the Aryan legacy. In order to accomplish that, we must first solve two ancient mathematical riddles: "the Riddle of the Sphinx" and "a Circle and the Square Within."[82] In the following chapter, *Mastering the Elements*, we will see how the Aryan fathers addressed the first riddle, and in the subsequent chapter, *Mastering Time*, we will see how they addressed the second.

82 Zohar Prologue 5b -6a.

Chapter 3: Mastering the Elements

The Riddle of the Sphinx

Most people became aware of the Riddle of the Sphinx in the writings of Homer. Oedipus, the mythical Greek King of Thebes, became the protagonist in the epic literature of Homer, in a play by Sophocles, and in variations by other ancient Greek authors and poets. During this period, the "Riddle of the Sphinx" took the following basic form: "What walks on four feet in the morning, two in the afternoon and three at night?" Oedipus answered: "Man: as an infant, he crawls on all fours; as an adult, he walks on two legs and; in old age, he relies on a walking stick." Oedipus answered the riddle correctly causing the Sphinx to throw itself into the sea, freeing Thebes. Of course, the Egyptian Sphinx was constructed long before Homer lived (circa 850 BCE). And, although "man" is the correct answer, we need to understand the derivation of the myth in order to properly understand its mathematics and meaning.

Vedic astronomy divides the celestial dome of stars into four quadrants. All Mesopotamian ziggurats (Figure 9), and later, all Egyptian pyramids (Figure 32), were similarly constructed to align with four "fixed" constellations and the four cardinal directions on the first day of spring (vernal equinox). These constellations symbolize the four primordial elements: Earth, Water, Wind, and Fire, that were considered the building blocks of the cosmos:

- Taurus (Bull/Cow/Ram/Lamb): Earth sign
- Leo (Lion/Leopards): Fire sign
- Aquila/Opiuchus (Eagle/Vulture): Originally the Wind sign, was later replaced by Aquarius as the Wind sign
- Aquarius (Man): Originally the Water sign, was later replaced by Scorpio as the Water sign

Like all of Creation, man is a hybrid of these four elements, while the technology of *Moksha* uniquely empowers man to integrate these elements in a way that purifies the body and liberates the soul. Those who were able to master the elements with their mind became the stuff of legend — the so-called "gods on the mountain." These enlightened and wise "masters" included priests, wizards, magicians, healers, prophets, kings, and gods.

Figure 9 - Mesopotamian Ziggurats & Early Step Pyramids of Egypt

Figure 10 - Göbekli Tepe's Inner Pillars: the Oldest Monumental Architecture (10,000 BCE) Adorned with Lions, Bulls, Snakes, and Vultures, symbolizing Fire, Earth, Water, and Air

Göbekli Tepe contains the oldest archeological examples of monumental architecture (Figure 10); specifically, monoliths with carved reliefs that prominently featured vultures, eagles, snakes, bulls and lions, thus mapping to the four "fixed" constellations. We can safely assume that Aryan astronomer/priests understood how the cyclical nature of their observations defined the year, linking the elements in a seasonal rotation of Spring (Earth), Summer (Fire), Autumn (Wind), and Winter (Water). During the

Neolithic period, farming methods depended on the four seasons. As noted within many spiritual traditions, the cycle of four seasons metaphorically applies to the cycle of a man's life, including: birth, growth, aging, and death, followed by rebirth into a new cycle.

From today's perspective these four elements might best be understood as the four states of matter. For example, Earth would not have been thought of as limited to the dirt we can run through our fingers. The earliest concept of Earth would have taken on the meaning of a solid, i.e. materiality. Similarly, the body's various liquids would have been associated with the primordial element Water, such as: blood, semen, and urine. The ancient element of Air represented the air we breath, the winds of fall, and the subtle winds of Spirit. The Hebrew word *ruach* translates to either breath, wind or spirit. The concept of Fire was not limited to flames. When we heat gas it ionizes, freeing electrons that were bound to an atom or molecule. The mobility of positive and negative charges make it electrically conductive. Modern science calls this plasma. It is the most prevalent phase of matter in the universe. Saint Elmo's fire, for example, falls into this category. It has been explained as an electric field surrounding an object causing ionization that produces a faint glow. During an electrical storm this luminescence can be seen at the tips of ship masts or a bull's horns. At various times it has been called "St. Elmo's Fire," "the Candles of the Holy Ghost," or "the Candles of David." Since prehistoric times, man's thought separated him from other creatures, and early science described those thoughts in terms of man's "inner Fire." In 1791, Luigi Galvani first described bioelectricity in more modern terms. Today, we know that man's thought processes, and indeed his entire nervous system, is driven by a complex flow of electrical signals.

The science of polytheism is based on the Riddle of the Sphinx as a hybrid of the four primordial elements (Figures 11a - e). Similarly, the science of the Bible is based on these same four elements coming together as a *Cherubim,* i.e., the four-headed *Seraphim* that pulls Ezekiel's Chariot. This would become the template for the Creation of four "worlds" within the Jewish Kabbalistic tradition. These same four "worlds" are described in the Rig Veda's "Hymn of Man," where Primal man is a composite of creatures that are "three-quarters" immortal in heaven, and one-quarter earthbound.

> *Such is his greatness, and the Man is yet more than this. All creatures form a quarter of him; Three-quarters are what is immortal in Heaven. With three-quarters the Man rose up on high, and one quarter of him still remains here. From this he*

spread in all directions, into that which eats [the physical body] and that which does not eat [the soul]. From his navel arose the atmosphere, from his head the sky evolved, from his feet the earth, and from his ear the cardinal points of the compass: so did they fashion forth these worlds.[83]

Figure 11a - Four "Fixed" Signs in the Clock of 12 Zodiac Constellations Defines a Sphinx

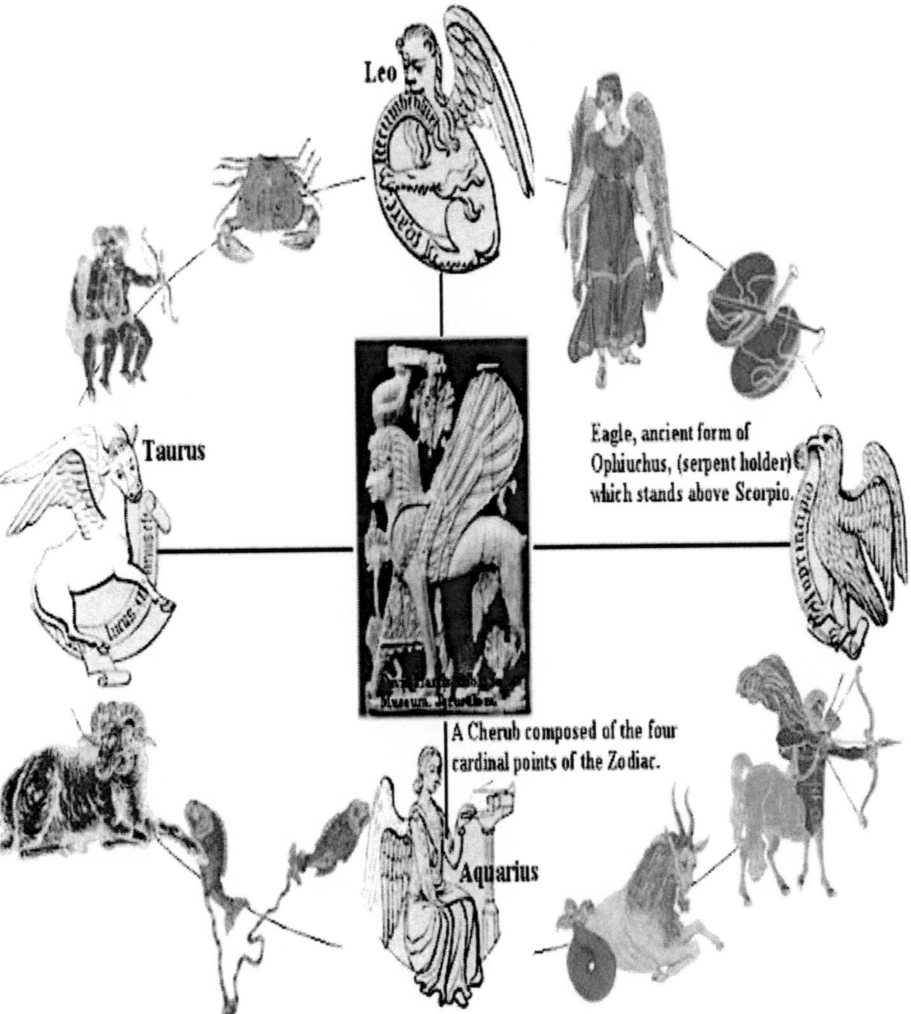

Within the ancient scientific lexicon, Fire (heat) was understood to be the catalyst between ice, water, steam and plasma. Man's meditation harnessed his "inner Fire" and transformed the primordial elements from one state to another. At birth, man was tied to the Heavens through his umbilical

83 Rig Veda, Op.Cit., 29-31.

cord, while at death, he would shed his Earthly skin, the body, in the manner of a molting snake. The meditation practice of *Moksha* harmonizes and transforms the soul's remaining three elements, which empowers it to liberate from its Earthly container in order to find its way "home." A High Priest, who mastered the elements in this manner, could liberate his soul at will while still very much alive. Man's most ancient and sacred priestly practice was always mankind's most guarded secret because one could acquire "divine gifts," i.e., the legendary powers of the Aryan fathers. The main goal of Eastern faiths is, to this day, rooted in meditation, guided by the unquestioned belief that it can bring man to a perfected state of Enlightenment. Indeed, since the dawn of civilization, the great goal and meaning of life has been to acquire knowledge, wisdom, and the "divine gifts" of healing and prophecy by using meditation to master the primordial elements.

The baseline for the entire mythological landscape in the Middle East can be generalized as a "harmonization" of the four primordial elements. And, any syncretistic matrix of "gods on the mountain" must begin with each culture's divine embodiments of these four elements. Ancient man viewed himself as a complex amalgam of these elements, and the primary goal of the pre-Sumerian meditation practice would have been to master them in order to "cross over" from the material to the spiritual world.

Figure 11b - Sumerian Goddess Inanna as a Sphinx *Figure 11c - Assyrian Sphinx*

Figure 11d - Four "Fixed" Banners Representing the 12 Tribes at the Tabernacle Encampment

Figure 11e - The 12 Tribes of Israel in Four Camps

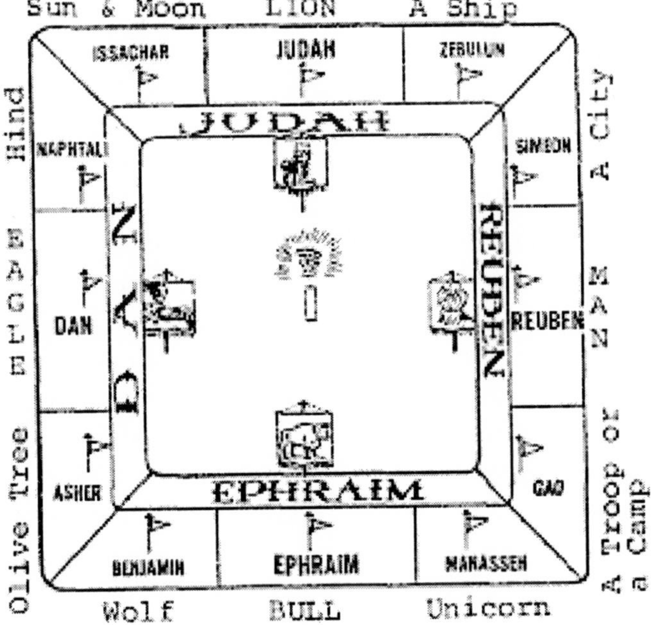

Comparing Wisdom Traditions

To get some perspective on what it means to master the four primordial elements, it might be helpful to get a closer look at the core religious practices of Buddhism, Hinduism, Taoism, Jainism, etc., since mastering the elements through meditation is still the mainstay of these faiths. Among the first things a new practitioner is taught is how to breath properly. There is Taoist breathing, Buddhist breathing, Hindu *Pranayama*, etc., but, all of these ancient faiths share the belief that mastering the primordial element of Air, or Wind, is a crucial step in establishing a "sitting" practice. Each of these faiths share in the belief that the primordial element of Water, as it relates to meditation, is associated with the seminal fluids. Mastering the element of Water through celibacy or infrequent ejaculation (varying with age) is the second powerful resource for establishing an effective daily practice. Mastering the primordial element of Fire implies thought control. Just as seminal fluid can be wasted during sexual contact, a distracted mind undermines one's ability to harness one's inner Fire because the brain's electrical activity is the main catalyst required to transform the other elements. Early religion was based on the idea that mastering Fire, Water, and Wind in this manner, vivifies and strengthens man's inner energies, ultimately empowering the practitioner to liberate their soul. The human body was the eternal soul's temporal container within the material realm.

In the West, we sometimes speak about death as "giving up the ghost." Buddhist monks and lamas tell us that their deep meditation practice is a simulation of death, because the "illusory body" — what the New Testament calls Christ's "Heavenly body" — is "liberated" as in death. Taoism calls it liberating the "immortal foetus." In the West, meditation has evolved into prayer. Western prayer might derive from the ancient meditation practice, but, generally speaking, it is considerably more dilute and much less exacting as a method. If we could learn to pray like the Biblical prophets, our meditation would be focused on learning to maintain the hypnagogic state for long periods of time.

Dramatic physiological characteristics, such as a dolichocephalic skull, suggests to me that the "Aryan" EMH cavemen had perfected their meditation technique across tens of thousands of years, and there is no telling how advanced their capabilities actually were. The Bible's patriarchal birthright was also defined by this practice, and thus it became precious knowledge granted only to the "anointed one" of each generation, to Aaron's lineage of High Priests, and to the Biblical prophets. Within any of the Eastern religions, people of faith take their meditation practice very seriously, but, generally speaking, only yogis, lamas, and monks are dedicated enough to devote the time required to master the practice.

When a member of the Aryan community died, their funery rites would be officiated by a priest who would have mastered this practice. He would pray to ensure the safe passage of the man's immortal soul, and then cremate his mortal remains. This explains the recent discovery of cremation remains at Stonehenge in England. Reconstructing ancient funery practices from Vedic hymns suggests that mortal remains were cremated on an altar, and the remains scattered nearby. Stories of the "gods on the mountain" appear in legend and myth within the art, architecture and literature of the various ancient cultures. In ancient Sumer, only one man was granted immortality by the gods. That man was Noah's Sumerian counterpart, king Ziusudra, who was the sole survivor of the "great flood" and preserver of the seed of mankind. He was given "life like a god" and "breath eternal" just as Noah was said to have "walked with God."

One of the most significant Sumerian and Babylonian myths is the search for a "magic elixir" of immortality that the Vedas call Soma juice or *Amrita* nectar (Sanskrit: immortality). Scholars still search for the mysterious Soma plant of the Rig Veda said to cause an ecstatic altered state of consciousness. But, a comparison of meditation practices across different cultures implies that Soma was more than a plant. Within Tibetan Buddhism there is an "ambrosia" of "Kundalini drops" that results from meditation. The New Testament speaks about "a true Baptism of the spirit" in contrast to a "Baptism by water." Biblical allegory "anoints" the patriarch or king's head with oil. The Hebrew word *Meshiach* means "Anointed One," which translates into English as Messiah, and into Greek as *Christos*.

The Rig Veda describes man's partial divinity as the reason for his continual search for immortality. In many Rig Vedic hymns, including: *This Restless Soma*, and *Soma Pressed in the Bowls*, Soma juice is a liquid said to heal all who are sick. It is a sage and a seer, a crusader of truth, a King, a God. Soma is associated with the male Bull and the Sacred Cow's milk. The hymn "Soma Pressed in the Bowls" describes Soma in metaphor as: "the pouring of the juices through a filter"; "the milking of rain out of the clouds"; "the pouring of seed into a womb"; "the downpouring of torrents upon the earth"; "the bull who rules over the rain"; "from the *Navel of Order*, the ambrosia is born."[84] According to the Rig Veda, the mathematical schematic of the cosmos also functions as a schematic describing the microcosm of the soul and its liberation (Figure 25).

Within the Vedic origins of Hinduism, Soma is interchangeable with Agni, the god of Fire. Tibetan Buddhists say that their "Inner Fire" practice, known as *tummo,* melts the Kundalini (Serpent) energy stored as Bodhicitta substance at the "Crown." This substance melts at the Crown and white Bodhicitta drops flow down

84 Rig Veda 8.79, 9.74; Op.Cit., 121-123.

the central channel (spinal cord) when exposed to man's "Inner Fire." The practitioner is harmonizing the primordial elements of Fire and Water with Wind.[85]

I can share one personal anecdote with respect to this phenomenon as a result of my doctor hearing me "drip" as he entered the examining room while I was meditating. He asked me what that clicking sound was? I replied, "You're the doctor, you tell me." After ruling out reflux and post-nasal drip, he sent me to a Harvard educated specialist, who naturally inquired why I was there. I responded that Dr. Gerdis wanted me to drip for you. He looked puzzled so I waved him over to listen. He then accused my watch of ticking loudly, which struck me funny, so I gave him my silent watch to listen to. He then asked me to do it again while he looked down my throat with a scope to observe. After asking me to start and stop at least four times, he said: "You made my day." He then explained that the medical term for what he observed was called *palatal myoclonus,* which is simply a spasm of the soft palate. But, he added that it was the first time in his career that he had ever observed someone who could control it at will.. Usually, he said, it was a condition that resulted from a brain lesion or epilepsy. To my great relief, he finally mentioned that it also occurred in healthy people when they were falling asleep. It is also called *hypnagogic myoclonus*. So, even with a Harvard medical education and many years practicing medicine, the doctor had no idea that an experienced meditator can quickly put themselves into a hypnagogic state. Although this explanation took a bit of the mystique out of the Soma plant for me, it should explain things perfectly for a modern scientific audience. The Tibetan Lama Thubten Yeshe used more of a traditional Buddhist vocabulary to describe his *tummo* practice of "flaming and dripping":

> *Inner Fire meditation is far more effective than ordinary deep meditation. It quickly grows into an explosion of nonduality wisdom, an explosion of telepathic power, an explosion of realizations. It is the key to countless treasures... In inner fire meditation the approach is made through the navel chakra... igniting the inner fire, blazing the inner fire, blazing and dripping, and extraordinary blazing and dripping.*[86]

"Blazing and dripping" explains why the god of fire, Agni, was considered interchangeable with Soma juice. In the Rig Veda's "Funeral Hymn," the hymn distinguishes between levels of spiritual attainment. For some, the Soma juice has already been purified, but for others, they must use a "sitting" practice and "sing" to invoke the "inner heat" for the "butter" to "flow like honey."[87] "*With a heart longing for cows [the milk of cows, or Soma] they sat down while with their songs they*

85 Lama Thubten Yeshe, *The Bliss of Inner Fire* (Somerville, Massachusetts: Wisdom Pub., 1998) 135.
86 Ibid., 132.
87 Rig Veda 10.154; Op.Cit., 54.

made the road to immortality."[88] We have yet to discuss details of the "*song*" of the practitioner, as described by the mathematical discipline of music.

There has always been an Eastern tradition of meditating in the quiet seclusion of caves. When we think of Himalayan monks, we often think of them meditating in caves. In the hymn, "*The Cows in the Cave,*" we are reminded of the sacred "cave practice" as a legacy of early man's time spent in caves during the Ice Age.

> *The wise ones struck a path for those who were in the cave; the seven priests drove them on with thoughts pressing forward. They found all the paths of the right way; the one who knew was the one who entered them, bowing low.*[89]

Within the Abrahamic and Vedic traditions, as well as the Tibetan Bon and Buddhist traditions, liberating the soul is a direct result of perfecting a "sitting" practice to simulate death. A man must "bow low" as he meditates, metaphorically surrendering one's ego and all attachments to the material world if liberation is to occur. The Jewish tradition takes this simulation of death very seriously. An oath is recited to bind the soul to the body "for those traveling to the highest realms."

- *For some, the Soma is purified; others sit down for butter. Those for whom the honey flows—let the dead man go away straight to them.*
- *Those who became invincible through sacred heat, who went to the sun through sacred heat, who made sacred heat their glory—let him go away straight to join the immortal fathers.*[90]

The Hindu Sun god, *Sūryā,* drives his chariot through Heaven harnessed by seven horses (the seven *chakras* of the soul). *Sūrya* represents both the sun and the soul. In the Vedic hymn, "The Marriage of *Sūryā*" (Sūrya's daughter), we learn that the moon is Soma (it retains its identity as the sacred elixir, but appears only this once in the Rig Veda as the moon). The Aryans were known for their great chariots. Sūrya's Chariot, like Ezekiel's Chariot, is a vehicle for meditation that "presses the Soma" and liberates the soul for its journey through the Heavens.

> *Soma became the bridegroom... The two luminaries [Sun and Moon] were your wheels as you journeyed; the outward breath was made into the axle. Sūryā mounted a chariot made of thought as she went to her husband.*[91]

88 Rig Veda, 3.31: Ibid., 153.
89 Rig Veda, 3.31: Ibid., 152.
90 Rig Veda, 10.154: Ibid., 54.
91 Rig Veda 10.85; Ibid., 268.

In the Vedic hymn *Yama and the Fathers* "This funeral hymn centers upon Yama, king of the dead, the first mortal to have reached the other world, and the pathmaker for all who came after him."[92] The priesthood was eternal insofar as three-quarters of each man was an immortal hybrid of "divine creatures," while the fourth creature was mortal. By 1500 BCE, the Babylonian legend of Gilgamesh describes the hero as two thirds divine, and one third human.[93] Christianity's First Ecumenical Council was convened in 325 CE at Nicea by the Emperor Constantine for the express purpose of discussing exactly how the two natures of God and man were conjoined in Christ. Without degrading Christ by imposing a fraction of divinity, the Church's orthodox position stated that Christ was both "true God and true man" simultaneously. Since the dawn of religion, the measure of man's divinity was determined by the four fixed signs of the zodiac. Joseph Campbell elaborates on this mythology as a function of Mesopotamian astronomy:

> The winged lion-bull with human head combines in one body those four signs of the zodiac that in the earliest period of Mesopotamian astronomy marked the solstices and equinoxes: the Bull (spring equinox and eastern quarter), Lion (summer solstice and southern quarter), Eagle (later Scorpio: autumn equinox and western quarter), and Water Carrier (winter solstice and northern quarter).[94]

The Eagle and Serpent Holder as Primordial Wind

Ophiuchus (or Serpentarius), the Serpent Holder, was the 13th constellation of the Zodiac. It appears directly above the 12th constellation, Scorpio. In Greek mythology, Ophiuchus is identified with Asclepius, the Greek god of medicine and healing, who had the power to bring people back to life. Asclepius was always depicted as an older man with a beard carrying a walking stick entwined with a wooden serpent (Figure 12b). Hades, the god of the Underworld, complained to Zeus that Asclepius threatened his trade in dead souls, and asked him to strike him down with a thunderbolt. Asclepius had already brought victims of Zeus's thunderbolts back to life, so Zeus was afraid Asclepius would teach the healing arts to mankind. Zeus then killed him with a thunderbolt and set him in the sky as Ophiuchus, holding Serpens (the Serpent) for eternity, just as he carried his pole-serpent walking stick staff. To this day, it is the pole-serpent that is the symbol of medicine (Figure 12b), rather than the *Caduceus* (Figure 12c: the staff of Hermes within Greek Mythology). Next to Opiuchus in the sky is Aquila, the Great Eagle, that carried and retrieved the thunderbolts of Zeus (Figure 12a).

92 Rig Veda 10.14; Ibid., 43.
93 Kramer, Op.Cit., 183.
94 Campbell, Op.Cit., 285.

Worshipped in Sumer as Aquila: the Golden Eagle, it was later adopted into Hindu and Buddhist mythology as Garuda: a half-man, half-eagle hybrid, and the mount of Vishnu, the Great Dreamer of the world illusion. The Garuda exists in rivalry with *Nagas* (serpentine sea creatures). The Vedas provide the earliest reference to Garudas, calling them *Syena* (Sanskrit: Eagle), which fetches Soma juice (*Kundalini*: Serpent Energy) from Heaven.

Figure 12a - The Golden Eagle Holding the Thunderbolts of Zeus and the Roman God Jupiter. Holding a Banner (Serpent) in its Beak was Inspiration for the Great Seal of the United States

Figures 12b & c - The Staffs of Asclepius and Hermes as Medical Symbols

Predynastic Egyptian mythology also pairs a bird of prey with the serpent. Nekhbet, the white vulture, was the symbol of Upper Egypt (Figure 13a). She is one of the earliest images in predynastic Egypt, and her white color symbolizes purification and fertility. In the *Book of the Dead*, Nekhbet is said to be: *Father of Fathers, Mother of Mothers, who hath existed from the beginning; and is Creatrix of this world.* She clutches a *shen* (a symbol of the all; eternity; infinity) in both talons. Upper Egyptian Pharaohs wore a white (conehead) crown in homage to Nekhbet (Figure 13b).

Figure 13a & b- Nekhbet, the White Vulture, and the White Crown as Symbols of Upper Egypt

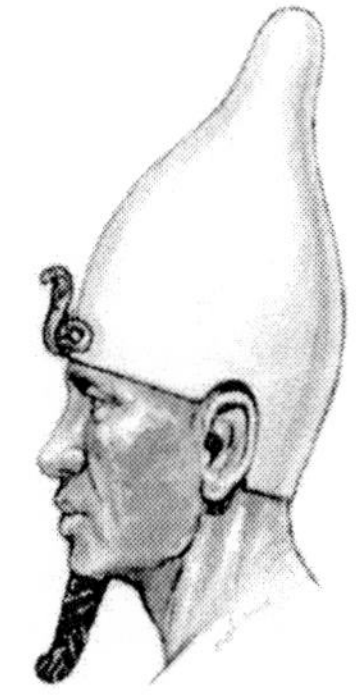

Wadjet, the cobra (as symbolized by Uraeus, an upright form of an Egyptian spitting cobra) was the symbol of lower Egypt as was the Red Crown (Figures 13c & d). Wadjet is also one of the oldest predynastic images in Egypt. Egyptians believed that Wadjet would spit fire at their enemies. These "Two Ladies" were joint protectors of a unified Egypt, enabling the pharaohs to wear the double crown of white and red, the crown depicting both Nekhbet and Wadjet (Figure 13e).

Figure 13c & d - Wadjet the Red Cobra and the Red Crown as Symbols of Lower Egypt

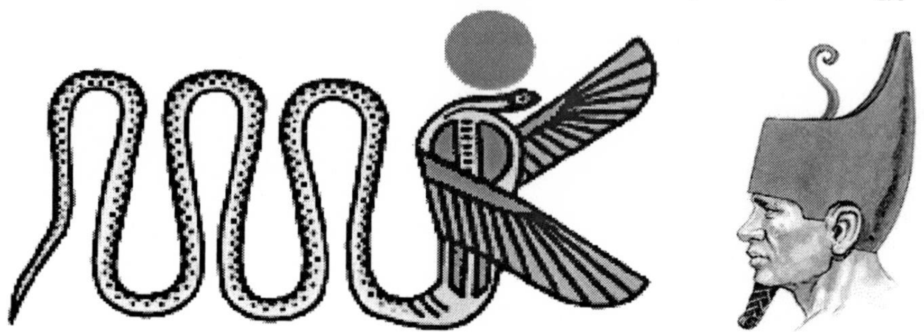

The vulture and cobra symbolize the unification of Upper and Lower Egypt during the life of the Pharaoh as well as in the Afterlife. This unification also takes place at a deeper spiritual level. Mastering Wadjet's "fiery serpent power" (Kundalini) implied "raising it up on the Wings of Nekhbet"; and when a pharaoh died, the priest would utter spells and incantations intended to empower the King's Ba (man's soul — half-man, half-bird) to rejoin his Ka (spiritual essence — close to the Chinese concept of *Jing,* which manifests in semen), harmonizing them in the Ib (man's metaphysical heart) for eternity in the Afterlife. Egypt's union of the white vulture and the red cobra is also reflected in Tibetan meditation as white *Bodhicitta* drops unite with red seminal fluid drops within the "heart drop of Dharmakaya," since the unified seat of the soul is said to exist in the heart (Figure 42b). With this unification, the adept's eternal "Buddha-body" can be liberated from its physical body.

Figure 13e - Nekhbet: the White Vulture
Wadjet/Uraeus: the Cobra as Third Eye of Ra

There is a similar unification between the white eagle and the red serpent within Hebrew Scripture. The tribe of Dan adopted the white and red standard of the Eagle (Figure 11d) to replace its former association with the Serpent and Scorpion. Some rabbinical sources often treated Dan as the archetype of wickedness. Christianity associated the tribe of Dan with the serpent and the Devil, which explains why Dan was omitted from the Book of Revelation. According to Jewish folk lore, it was Ahiezer (Numbers 2:25), a prince of the tribe of Dan, who substituted the eagle as the destroyer of serpents, giving the tribe a more upright image.

When Jacob was about to die, he gathered his 12 sons together as leaders of the 12 tribes and prophesied "*what will befall you in the End of Days*."[95] Jacob said that Judah would be like the lion (Figure 11d), the king of beasts, while: "*Dan would avenge his people, [and] the tribes of Israel will be united as one. Dan will be a serpent on the highway, a viper by the path, that bites a horse's heels so its rider falls backward.*"[96] This passage echoes God's curse on the serpent in Eden, when God declares: *I will put enmity between you and the woman [Eve] and between your offspring and her offspring. He will pound your head, and you will bite his heel.*[97] The Hebrew word "Dan" translates into English as "Judgement," and the tribe of Dan embodies Divine Judgement between Good and Evil. Therefore, the Bible describes its symbolism ambiguously, as both the Serpent and the Eagle, to be inclusive of both Good and Evil. The mission statement of the tribe, according to Jacob, was to enforce justice and unity by "biting at the heels of the unjust.[98]

Dan's role as "Judge" has been misunderstood, forgotten or ignored. Samson, who was from the tribe of Dan, was the last judge in the Book of Judges, leading Israel for 20 years. After Delilah cut seven locks of his hair, the Philistines seized him, gauged out his eyes, and made him a mill slave. When they put Samson between the pillars of the temple he prayed to *Yahweh* for the strength to push apart the pillars and bring down the temple to smite his enemies. The rabbis tell us that Samson remained pure in judgement, but adopted the treacherous tactics of the serpent in order to "bite at the heels" of the Philistines.

This same dichotomy is embodied within the twin pole serpents of the Caduceus (Figures 14d & e). When viewed from a horizontal perspective, their embodiment of Fire and Water causes them to ascend like Fire, and descend like Water, along the polar axis. From an aerial perspective, however (Figures 14a,b & c), the serpent circles around in a spiral, giving the appearance of swallowing its tail. The Great Serpent constellation, Draco, is circumpolar, revolving in a great circle in the northern sky around the polar star (Figure 14b). Like Ouroboros

95 Genesis 49:1
96 Genesis 49:16-17
97 Genesis 3:15
98 Christianity associated the tribe of Dan with the serpent and devil,

within ancient Greek and Egyptian mythology, Draco appears to swallow its tail (Figures 14a & b). The ancient mathematics that describes this —the *Navel of Order* (Figure 25) — is a mathematical description of the sun's path measured against the stars. The Caduceus, ascending and descending to and from God, is the go-between, or "messenger" between God and man, i.e., man's soul.

There is a profound mathematics at the heart of all religion that is symbolized by the tightly coupled mythologies of the eagle and the serpent. Solving the mathematics of the "circle and the square within"[99] reveals the great religious significance of the body's purification, as symbolized by the serpent "swallowing its tail." What each of these different myths share is a story of how a divine bird of prey somehow lifts the serpent, a symbol of libidinous energy and temptation, into the sky (the 12th constellation is effectively "swallowing up" the 13th constellation). Within this same purification tradition, on the Eve of the New Year, Jews would cast their sins onto a goat — a scapegoat — and then exile it from the town. Animal sacrifice (Hebrew: *korban*) was an important part of the purification rite. In the New Testament, the 12th disciple sacrificed Christ, the *lamb of God*, the 13th member of the group. Similarly, YHVH Himself slays "the Leviathan, the Elusive Serpent" in order to vanquish evil (Figure 14f).

Figure 14a & 14b - Draco: the Great Circumpolar Dragon

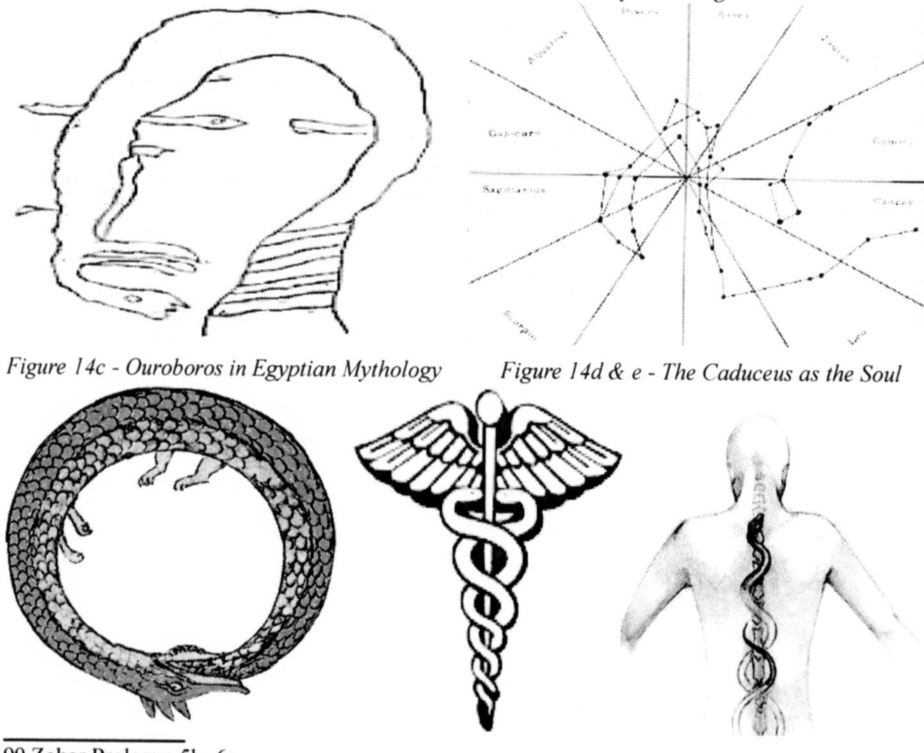

Figure 14c - Ouroboros in Egyptian Mythology

Figure 14d & e - The Caduceus as the Soul

99 Zohar Prologue 5b -6a.

In that day Yahweh will punish, With His great, cruel, mighty sword Leviathan the Elusive Serpent — Leviathan the Twisting Serpent: He will slay the Dragon of the sea...[100] *And in that day, Yahweh will beat out the peoples like grain from the channel of the Euphrates to the Wadi of Egypt; and you shall be picked up one by one, O children of Israel! And in that day, a great ram's horn shall be sounded; and the strayed who are in the land of Assyria and the expelled who are in the land of Egypt shall come and worship Yahweh on the holy mount, in Jerusalem.*[101]

Figure 14f - Gustave Dore's Slaying of Leviathan

100 Isaiah 27:1
101 Isaiah 27: 12-13

The story of *Yahweh* and the Leviathan has a long history in Middle Eastern myth. In Egypt, the pharaohs would journey to the afterlife with Ra, the Sun god, on his nightly 12 hour journey through the rivers of the Underworld. Ra was protected by the storm god Set. Each night Set would slay the serpent of chaos, Apep, allowing the sun to rise each day, often bloodied from battle (Figure 14g). The annual "banishing of Apep," an ancient rite of Egyptian priests, became the prototype for the actions of the Jewish High Priest of Israel on Yom Kippur. This ancient rite included an effigy of Apep built to contain all of the evil and darkness in Egypt. It would then be burned to protect the people for another year. The Egyptian Tuat derives from the Sumerian Apsû. It was both the waters that the boat of the Sun God Ra traversed during the night, and the place where mortal souls journeyed to after death.

The significance of "slaying the Great Serpent," is symbolic of mastering the seminal waters that lead us toward sexual distraction and away from Enlightenment, thus the need for Abraham's Covenant of Circumcision. In the Biblical version of this allegory, *Yahweh* metaphorically "slays" the evil serpent to save Israel (Figure 14f):

Figure 14g- Set slaying Apep the Evil Serpent in the Waters Below

The Bull of Heaven as Primordial Earth

Aurochs were very large bulls, now extinct, that were worshipped in Egypt and depicted in Paleolithic carvings and cave paintings discovered in Lascaux, France (Figures 15a & b) and *Çatal Höyük* (Figure 15c). Bulls and cows have been worshipped in India and the Middle East as a reflection of the constellation, Taurus, symbolizing Earth: The dense, opaque matter comprising the body contains the soul's divine light, the way a bucket contains water. It is "Mother Earth" that protects and nurtures the spiritual foetus. The Bull of Heaven plows the furrows that hold divine seed, while the gentle, nurturing Sacred Cow of India (Figure 15d) was the matriarchal goddess, Hathor of Egypt. "Finding the great secret [of immortality] is to find the cows, or their milk [Soma]." The Aryans longed for cows, because their utters symbolically contained the elixir of immortality. Indra slew the dragon Vrtra, (lit: the blocker), a stone serpent slain by Indra to liberate the rivers, while Vrtra's brother, Vala is a stone cave, similarly split by Indra to "liberate the cows." Vrtra and Vala symbolized the dense physical matter of the body blocking the flow of Soma, the Divine Elixer.

Figure 15a - Egyptian Bull god Apis

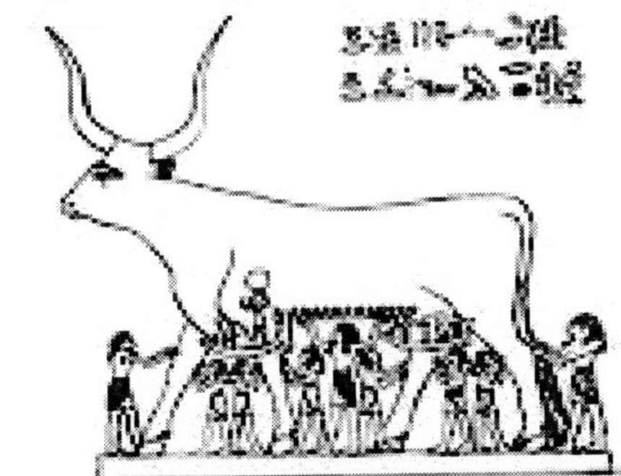

Figure 15b - Hall of Bulls
Lascaux France (circa 30,000 BCE)

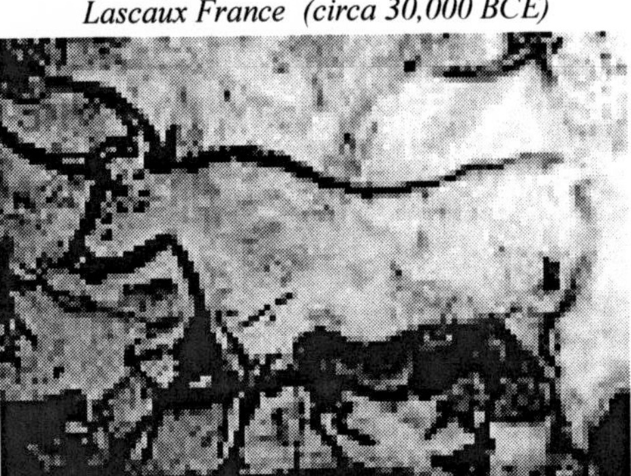

Figure 15c - Çatal Höyük (Circa 6500 BCE)

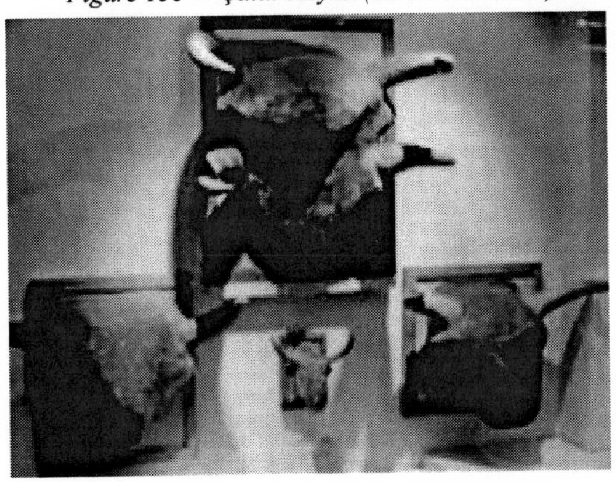

Figure 15d - Sacred Hindu Bull

The Lion as Primordial Fire

Lions and Leopards could still be found in Egypt until the rain belt moved south (circa 3500 BCE). They were "conquerors of death," and fierce protectors of royal tombs and thrones (Figures 16a & c). Just as a lion is "king of beasts," Fire held authority over the other primordial elements. Within monotheism, Heaven and the Throne of Glory were fashioned from the primordial Fires, while the Fires of Heaven purged away all impurity, freeing the Divine sparks from a *korban* sacrifice on the altar. Ariel, which literally means "altar," or "Lion of God," is one of the seven archangels mentioned in Jewish and Christian mythology. Jacob, who was renamed Israel by God, referred to his son Judah as a young lion. Judah was the dominant tribe of ancient Israel, the tribe of King David, and tribe of the anticipated Messiah.

Vishnu, within his dream of world-illusion, incarnated as a Man-Lion (Figure 16b) in order to devour the entrails of an atheistic king named "Golden Garment" who, through the power of yoga, had become sole sovereign of the universe, overthrowing even the gods."[102]

Figure 16a - Leonine Body of Egyptian Sphinx Guarding the Pharaoh's Tomb

Figure 16b - Man-Lion Altmuhl Caves (ca. 28,000 BCE)

Figure 16c - Çatal Höyük Leopard Throne (ca. 6500 BCE)

102 Campbell, Op.Cit., The Mythic Image, 117.

Man's Source of Wisdom as Primordial Water

Aquarius, the Water Bearer, is considered an Air sign within modern astrology, but in ancient times it was considered a Water sign, as its etymology suggests. Its Latin meaning is "water-bearer," symbolized by water spilling from the water pot of Aquarius. In the Babylonian calendar, the freshwater of the apsû spilling from the urn of Aquarius (Figure 17a) represented the purging rains from above, as well as the underground freshwater of the Apsû (Underworld or Hades), which flooded the world from below through springs, rivers, lakes, and wells. Genesis 2:8 describes a similar scene: "*On that day, the fountains of the great deep burst forth; and the windows of the Heavens were opened.*" In ancient Greece, Aquarius poured water from the Heavens for days on end, inundating the Earth.

In Greek mythology, Zeus fancied the handsome shepherd boy Ganymede, and had him abducted by Aquila, who carried him to off to Mount Olympus to be his lover and "cup-bearer," pouring the "nectar of the gods" ("magic elixir") from a jug. He was given a place in Heaven as Aquarius. The Egyptians associate this constellation with Khnum, the god of water, who caused the Nile to overflow when he dipped his water bucket into the river. The astrological symbol for Aquarius (Figure 17b) corresponds to a splitting of the spiritual waters from the material waters, "dividing the waters from the waters," as within Scripture.

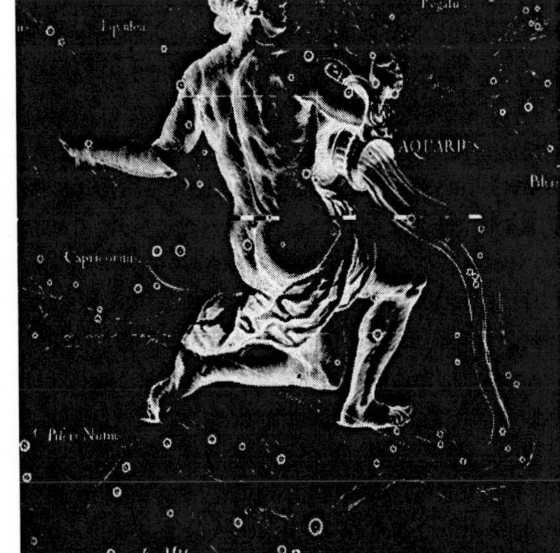

Figure 17a - The Water Bearer

Figure 17b - the Sign of Aquarius Separating the waters from the waters is also the Egyptian Hieroglyphic

Chapter 4: Mastering Time

Choosing a Metric

If the four primordial elements determine Creation's repetitive cycle of seasons: birth, growth, aging, and death; and, if the four fixed constellations of the Zodiac serve as seasonal markers in the sky; then, how would mankind measure the passage of time between each annual cycle, and between each of the four seasons within each annual cycle? Early science further explored the cyclical paths of the various heavenly bodies in search of a way to add more granularity to this annual and seasonal metric.

Telling time might appear to be as fundamental to prehistoric civilization as the discovery of fire. A clock enables us to measure our progress through life. But, imposing the metric of time on our lives might also be seen as a psychological constraint that demands an answer to "when" we did something or intend to do something. It brings more relevance to both the past and future. What about the spiritual ideas of eternity and immortality? If a clock simply counts to 12, where does eternity and divinity fit in? Evidence will be presented suggesting that the Aryan fathers believed it was possible to transcend the constraints of time and materiality through their meditation practice. Indeed, the central point of the entire religious exercise throughout history has been *Moksha*: meditation that results in the purification of the body and the liberation of one's immortal soul from the body's finite constraints of time and space.

The Aryan fathers attempted to understand their experience of *Moksha* as a real phenomenon that occurred within the fabric of cosmos. The apparent motion of the sun, moon, planets, and stars, all occur at different rates of speed, carving out different blocks of time from an observer's perspective. To track these cycles, priestly astronomers measured the changing angles created between the horizon and various orbiting objects (see Appendix D: A Primer on Astronomy). The sun's cycle differentiated days and nights; the moon's cycle delineated months, the solstice and equinox determined the seasons, while the stars came full circle every year. Early astronomers who first tracked these heavenly cycles needed to standardize on an effective metric to quantify them.

Any sort of measurement requires a numerical system and the ability to count within that system. Counting can be defined as the process of enumerating how many objects there are within a given finite set of objects.

There is archeological evidence to suggest that counting began as far back as 50,000 years ago."[103] It is logical to suggest that counting may have begun as a result of the one-to-one relationship between a material object and each of our fingers. Perhaps our decimal system (Base-10) began by counting small flocks of sheep on our fingers and toes. A decimal system can be defined by 9 unique digits plus zero.[104] Any *linear* measurement of space's three dimensions would require us to count a ruler's numbered increments. *Logarithmic* measurement also helps us count. Within Base-10, once we finish counting 9 objects, the very next object would require a change by an order of magnitude. We would indicate a high order 1 and add zero as place holder. Each change in order of magnitude would create a 1:10 ratio with its predecessor, that is, between the 1's column and the 10's column, between the 10's column and the 100's column, between the 100's column and the 1000's column, etc. Generally speaking, when we speak about a *ratio* we are comparing two things or ideas (known in ancient Greek thought as *analogy*). This can be expressed by the formula *a:b,* for example, 1:10 or 1:60. This last ratio describes the orders of magnitude within sexagesimal place holder notation, analogous to the ratios in a decimal system:

	0-9	10^1	10^2	10^3	10^4	10^5
***Decimal*:**	ones	10's	100's	1000's	10,000's	100,000's
***Sexagesimal*:**	0-59	60^1	60^2	60^3	60^4	60^5
	ones	60's	3600's	216,000's	12,960,000's	777,600,000's

What is most important here is that we understand the difference between linear and logarithmic numbers. We can see this difference clearly if we compare an arithmetic progression of like quantities 2,4,6,8,10,12, to a geometric progression of like ratios 2:4:8:16:32:64. With this information we will be better equipped to choose the most appropriate numerical system for whatever we hope to measure. For example, a computer might be simplistically thought of as a bunch of connected electrical switches, and each of these switches can either be "off" or "on." If a numerical system only has two states, 0 and 1, we call it a *binary system* (Base-2). If we need to count a small herd of sheep, the decimal system is perfectly suited, since we can make good use of our fingers and toes. But, what if we have to count a lot more than small herds of sheep? In ancient Sumer and Babylon, they decided on a sexagesimal system (Base-60), implying the use of 59 unique digits plus zero. As we can see in Figure 18, Sumer and Babylon counted unique digits from 1 to 12, but then used a modified decimal system as a kind of shorthand for expressing larger numbers.

103 Howard Eves, *An Introduction to the History of Mathematics* (Philadelphia: Brooks Cole, 1990) 9.
104 Zero functions as a numeric place holder, replacing the positional notation of ancient sexagesimal mathematics.

Just as Base-2 is tailor-made for describing a two-state switch within computer systems, Base-60 is arguably the best numerical system for modeling nature. The number 60 creates a very flexible system, primarily because there are twelve factors of 60, including: 1, 2, 3, 4, 5, 6, 10, 12, 15, 20, 30, and 60.

- Lunar tides, which alternate about every 6 hours.
- Days and nights, which take roughly 12 hours each.
- Lunar months, with a lunar cycle completing in roughly 30 days.[105]
- 12 lunar months of 30 days each approximate a 360 day solar year.[106]

Figure 18 - Decimal and Sexagesimal Counting

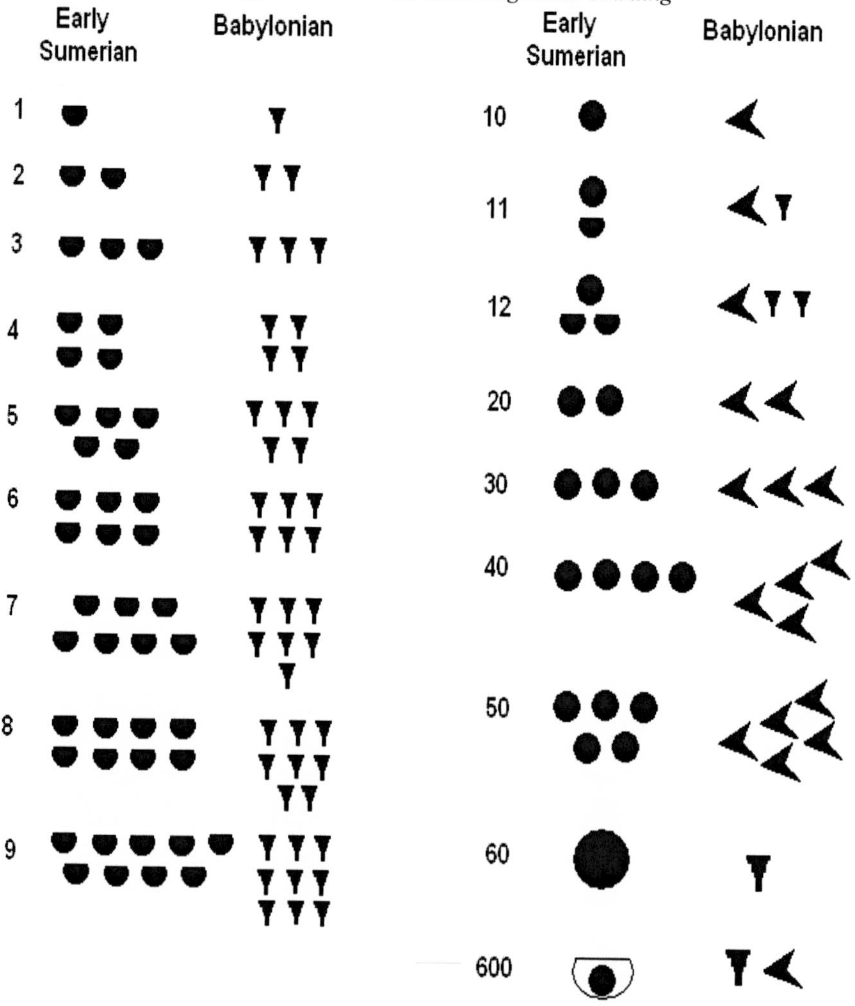

105 Closer to 29 1/2 days if we measure from New Moon to New Moon.
106 To compensate for ~5 extra days per year, a leap month was added every 6 years.

Telling Time

Within sexagesimal mathematics, the circle symbolizes time, with no beginning and no end. The Sun's 360° path across the zodiac takes approximately 365 days to complete, with a difference of 5 festival days. The clock goes about its business with no regard for whether or not the world actually runs in integer multiples or divisions of 12, but Base-60 provides a reasonably close approximation to natural phenomena.

Figure 19 - Triangulating Against the Heavenly Bodies

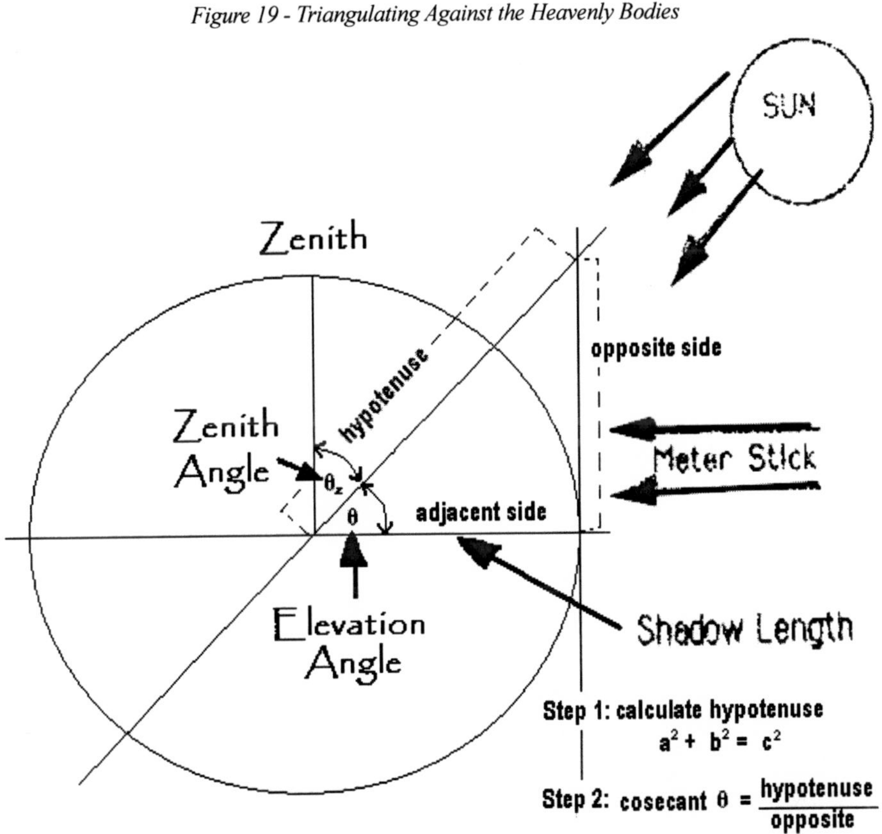

Sumerian and Babylonian astronomers measured the passage of time by triangulating on the sun's daily, monthly, and annual position, noting that position in relation to the background stars. They learned to calculate the sun's changing angle by using various trigonometric functions; like the tangent function that compares the length of a measuring rod, with the length of the shadow it casts (Figure 19). The oldest trigonometric table ever discovered (Figure 30a) used the Pythagorean theorem to determine the length of the third side and then used the cosecant function to determine the angle θ (see Figure 29). In Chapter 5, we will examine indisputable archeological evidence that trigonometry and the Pythagorean theorem existed long before the birth of Pythagoras.[107]

Imagine yourself as part of a race of vastly superior pre-Sumerians who had recently emerged from the shelter of cave life. The celestial dome would certainly have been much more interesting than the dome of your cave. But, even as part of an advanced race you would have taken a considerable amount of time to simply observe the heavens before understanding how and why to construct the first star observatory. The first religious temples were archeoastronomical devices used to measure cyclical events in the sky. The most well known temple/observatory of this genre is Stonehenge, built in England around 3,000 BCE (Figure 20a). But, what is religious about Stonehenge? How can telling time by observing the sun's position in the sky possibly relate to religion?

Figure 20a - Stonehenge in England (circa 3000 BCE)

The oldest of these, *Göbekli Tepe* (literally: *Navel Mountain;* circa 10,000 BCE), was discovered in 1994 during excavations in southeast Turkey by German and Turkish archeologists (see Figure 20b); a few hundred miles from Mount Ararat, where Noah and his family were said to emerge from the Ark.

107 Jöran Friberg, *Plimpton 322, Pythagorean Triples, and the Babylonian triangle parameter equations,* Historia Mathematica 8: 277-318.

Figure 20b - Göbekli Tepe (lit. Navel Mountain)
Concentric Circles in the World's Oldest Temple (circa 10,000 BCE)

Until the 1994 discovery, the oldest temples discovered had also been circular temple/observatories. There were ten circular stone foundations dating to the Halaf period (circa 5500 BCE) at Tell Arpachiya, which archeologist Jack Finegan suggests were "the earliest structures in northern Mesopotamia to have been erected for religious purposes." Finegan also considered 18 circular shrines unearthed in Eridu as "the earliest shrines in southern Mesopotamia."[108] Temple/observatories were also discovered at *Karahundj* in the Armenian highlands (circa 5000 BCE; Figures 20c - f), and in *Nabta Playa,* Egypt, as well as a number of other important archeological sites.

Think of Aryan priestly astronomers observing the skies from the ancient stone circle of *Karahundj* in the Armenian Highlands, ca. 5000 BCE. After constructing a device with the accuracy of a gun sight (Figure 20f), it would be much easier to quantify their observations. Of course, there are no written records going back this far, so we need to imagine what a race, possibly superior to our own, might have accomplished through careful observation? Figures 20b - f suggest that quantifiable observations of the heavens could have occurred 2000 years or more before the invention of writing. In the following passage, however, even noted scholar Joseph Campbell seems to accept the notion that sophisticated mathematics could not have come into existence before the invention of writing:

108 Jack Finegan, Op.Cit., 7-9.

Figures 20c - Karahundj: Armenia's Stonehenge (circa 5000 BCE)

Figure 20d, e & f - Stones Line Up Like a Gunsight

> The most important and far-reaching cultural mutation of this kind in the history of the human race was that which occurred in Mesopotamia about the middle of the fourth millennium B.C., with the rise in the lower reaches of the twin rivers Tigris and Euphrates, of a constellation of city-states governed by kings according to a notion of cosmic order and law derived from a long continued, systematic observation of the heavens ... members of a new type of highly specialized , heavenward gazing priesthood invented, ca. 3200 B.C., writing, mathematical notation (both sexagesimal and decimal), and the beginnings of a true science of exact astronomical observation.[109]

The existence of *Göbekli Tepe* and *Karahundj* as star observatories suggest the possibility that the origins of geometry and trigonometry were earlier than most scholars are prepared to acknowledge. Neugebauer admits that he expends little effort to explore the ancient origins of the fully developed science found within Old Babylonian period cuneiform tablets (circa 1800 BCE). There are other scholars, however, like Jöran Friberg, who search for the beginnings of mathematics in 4th millennium Sumerian script during the transition period between pictographs and cuneiform phonetics.[110] As we have already mentioned, Kramer goes so far as to credit the superior pre-Sumerian race with all of the great advances of Sumerian civilization. In light of Kramer's observations, perhaps we should at least reexamine our prejudice regarding the IQ and accomplishments of prehistoric man. We should take care not to underestimate the capabilities of a race that may well have been more biologically evolved than our own. Is it possible that mathematics and science preceded writing? Perhaps time will tell.

The Path to Heaven

Like most science, the science of religion developed from a need to understand man's place in the cosmos. And, after many thousands of years meditating in caves, our premise suggests that the Aryan fathers had perfected and experienced the sacred practice of *Moksha* as a liberation of the soul from the material constraints of time and space. We can surmise that the earliest scientific observations of the heavens may have been driven by the need to provide a rational explanation for Aryan "out-of-body" experiences. How did

109 Campbell, Op.Cit., 72.
110 Jöran Friberg, ed. by J.W. Dauben, *Mesopotamian Mathematics* (American Mathematical Society, 2000).

the framework of cosmos support the Aryan experiential reality? And, how did the mathematics of time describe the scientific framework of religion?

As ancient astronomer-priests studied the different cycles of the sun, moon, and stars circling around them, they found special significance in what was revealed to them on the first day of spring, the vernal equinox. As the name implies, day and night were equal in length, and, for a fleeting moment around noon, the sun was highest in the sky for the entire year. As the early astronomers observed the skies at the Eastern horizon before dawn, they would have taken note of the last stars they saw. In a few days, they would have noticed how the stars were slowly drifting across the dome of the sky while new stars took their place. In Figure 21a, we can get some perspective on the apparent motion of the stars across the celestial sphere during a solar year of ~365+ days by tracking their motion as they come full circle (360^0) to the next vernal equinox.

Figure 21a - The Precession of the Equinox

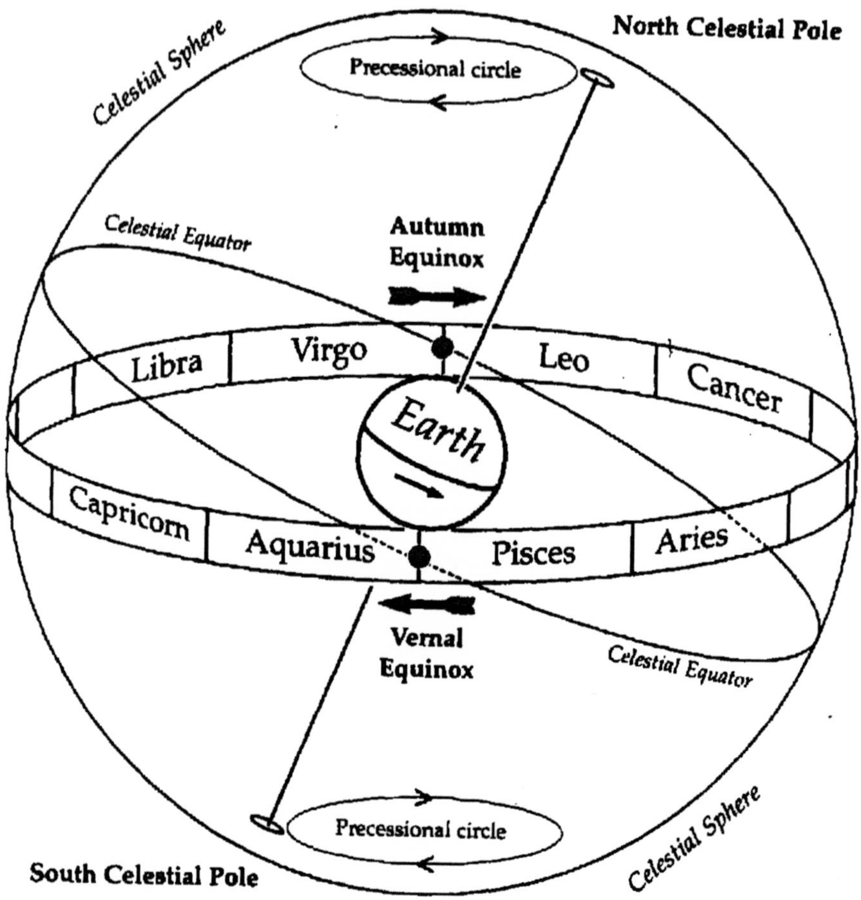

When the sun finally came back to its starting position on the first day of spring, the background stars were not exactly in the same place, as they intuitively should have been. They appeared to drift by a very tiny distance, and that same tiny distance accumulated each year. The annual drift of the stars came to be known as the Precession of the Equinox (Figures 21a & b). This phenomenon could easily have been observed through a gunsight-like device, like the one at *Karahundj* (Figures 20c - f) at any point in time between 10,000 and 3,200 BCE.

Figure 21b - The Sun's Spiral Around the Precessional "Axis Mundi"(Center of the World)

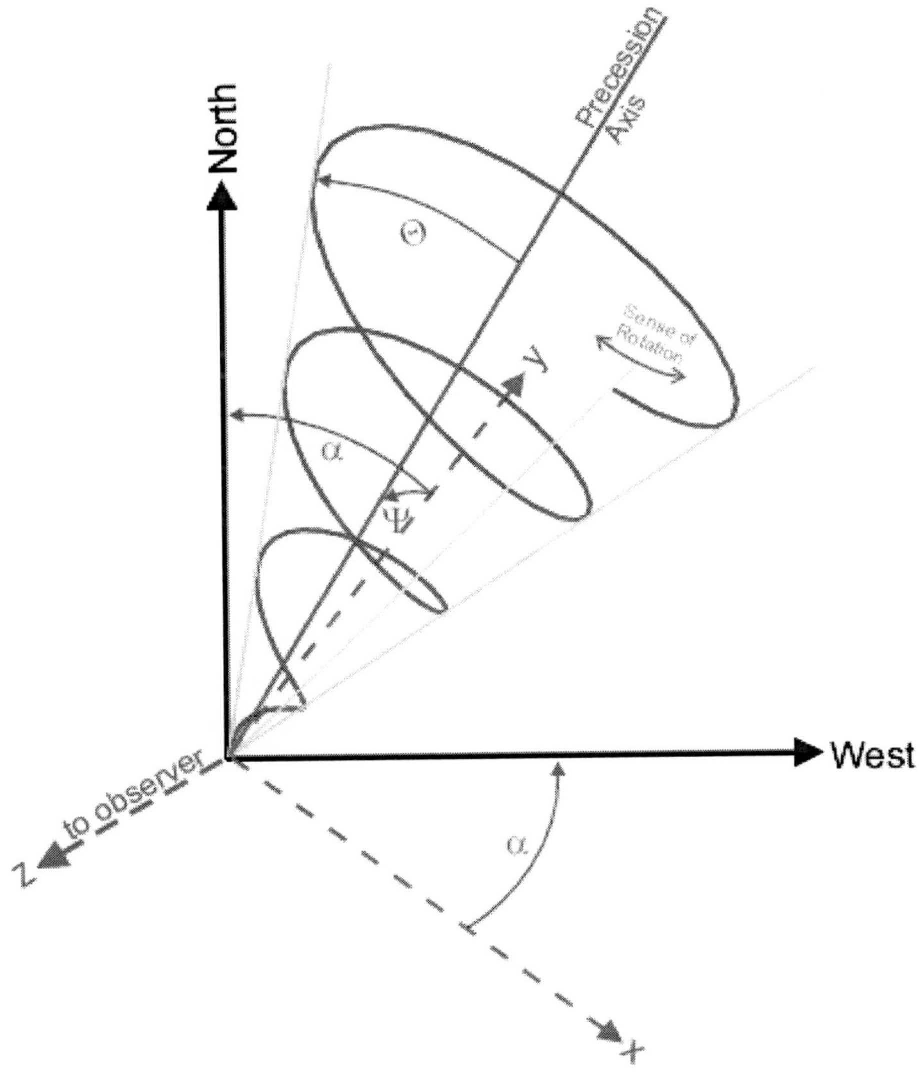

Within the Aryan conception of the universe, early astronomers understood the motion of the Sun and visible planets to be circular (Figure 22a). This Aryan concept of the macrocosm would have presaged Ptolemy's geocentric conception by thousands of years.

Figure 22a -Ptolemy's Geocentric Concentric Orbits May Have Neolithic Origins

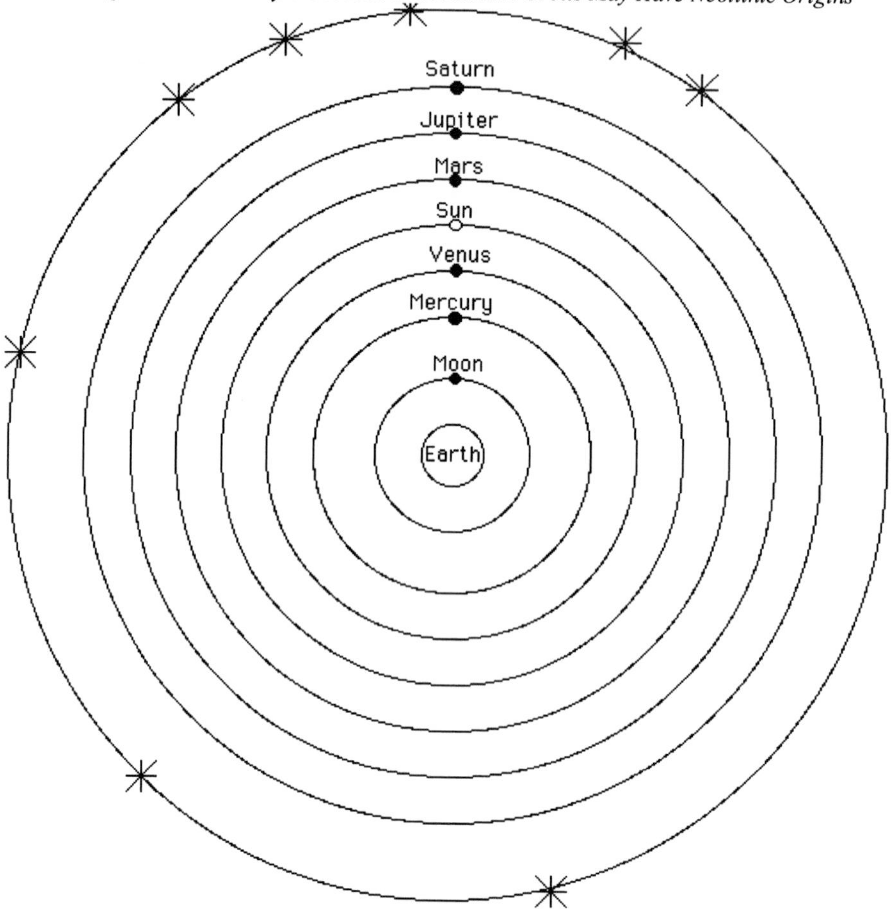

Aryan astronomers realized that the sun's annual circular path never completed its circle, but rather, formed a spiral that crossed the concentric circles of the planetary orbits (Figure 22b). Could Aryan astronomers have stumbled upon the path of man's disembodied soul as it followed the sun's transformational energy across the 6 other orbital layers of Heaven to form 7 Heavens? This "discovery" became the cosmological context for mankind's liberation practice. At birth, man's soul would first pass from Heaven to Earth through a "serpent-like" birth-tether — the umbilical cord. Upon death, or during *Moksha,* man's soul would be "ferried to the other side" as it spiraled across the concentric circles of the heavenly bodies until the soul reached Heaven — the dwelling place of immortals.

Figure 22b -The Sun and Man's Soul "Ascending" Through Ptolemaic Concentric Orbits to Heaven

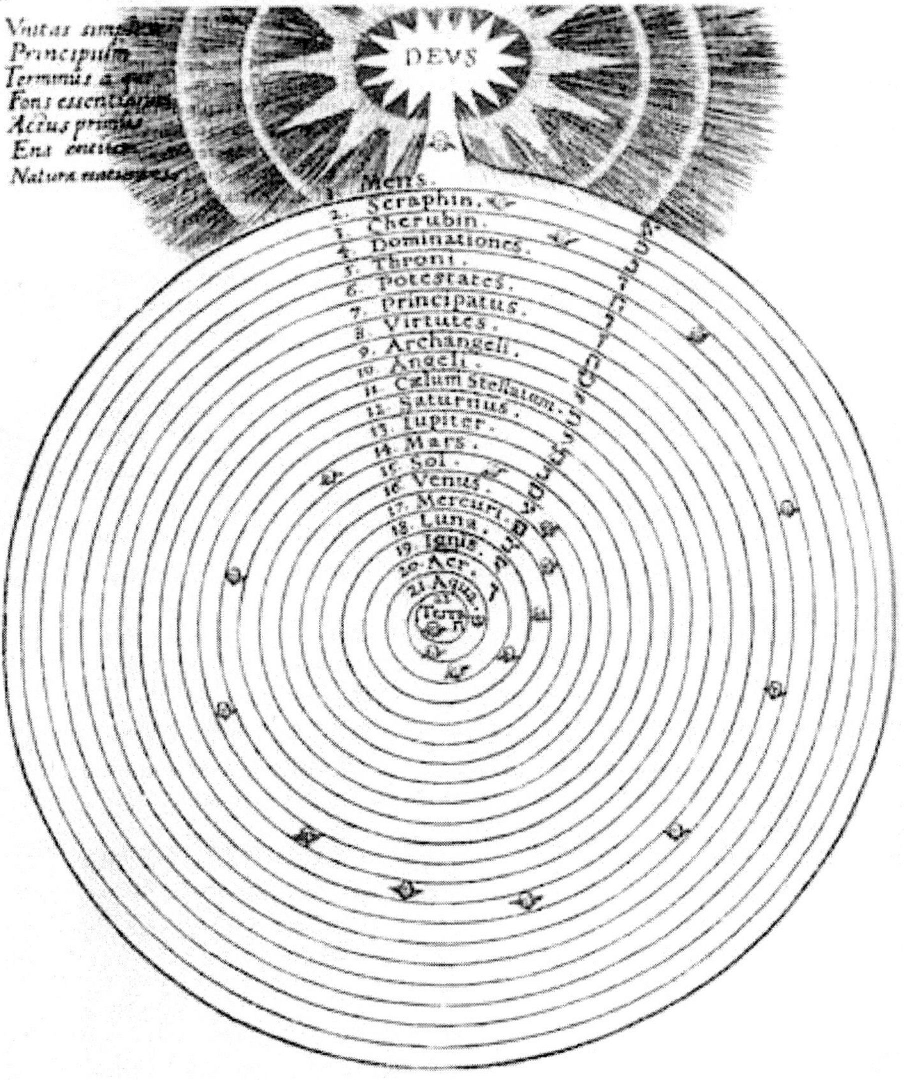

The Sun's spiral across the heavens would later become "Jacob's Ladder" within the Hebrew Scriptures. Its first appearance, however, could be found in the concentric circles enshrined within the architecture of *Göbekli Tepe* (Sanskrit: Navel Mountain; Figure 20b). These concentric circles also depict a "Navel of Order" within the navel of *Çatal Höyüks* sacred figure (Figure 22c) — a precursor to the Hindu diagram in Figure 22d. Both diagrams identify the figure's Navel "Wheel" (Sanskrit: *Chakra*) that is understood to be the seat of divine energy during meditation. Like the Sun, the inner Fires of man's meditation practice integrates 6 concentric *Chakras* into a transcendent, all-inclusive 7th *Chakra*.

-------- In the Microcosm ------

Figure 22c - Çatal Höyük (circa 6500 BCE) *Figure 22d- Hindu Descendants of Indo-Aryans*

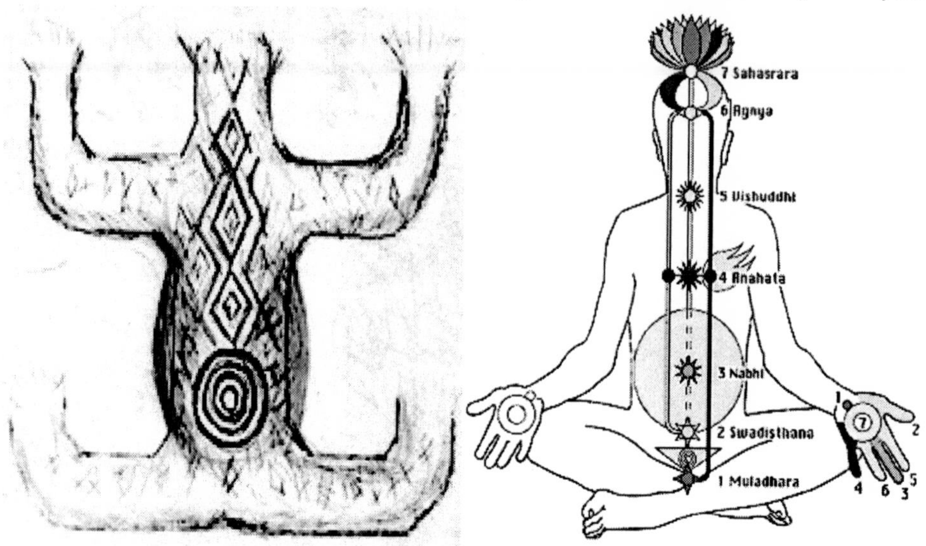

The genderless god in Figure 22c appears throughout many shrines at the important site of *Çatal Höyük* (circa 6500 BCE). James Mellaart, who discovered and excavated the site, remarks: "As is normal at Çatal Höyük, there is no indication of sex, but the navel was always shown."[111] Within the *Rig Veda*, this spiral pathway through the Heavens was defined by the mathematics of the *Navel of Order* (see Figure 25) that connects man's esoteric "inner" order to his exoteric "outer" order. Man's serpent-like umbilical cord was the thread energetically linking these two parallel and quantifiable orders. The lumbar-sacral plexus at the navel (Figures 22c & d) is considered the source of man's "life-force."

Meditation is sometimes called "navel-gazing." Navel-gazing from the temple of *Göbekli Tepe* implies a "gazing within" to the microcosm of the Soul, and an "outward gazing" toward the *Navel of Order* that organizes the Heavens. Astronomer-priests established this connection based on a theory that liberating their Soul through a simulation of death during deep meditation (*Moksha*) would send their Soul along the Sun's Precessional spiral which crosses the fixed geocentric planetary orbits. The link between macrocosm and microcosm (Heaven and Earth) marked the birth of religion. This cosmology connected *Göbekli Tepe* inhabitants (ca. 10,000 BCE) to *Çatal Höyük's* inhabitants (ca. 6500 BCE) to the articulated mathematics of the precessional spiral described by the Navel of Order (ca. 1800 BCE). However, even the *Navel of Order* mathematics (Figure 25) proves to be a subset of a still larger scale "divine design" that we will explain in Chapter 5.

111 James Mellaart, *Çatal Höyük* (New York: Thames & Hudson Ltd: 1967) 115.

In summary, our thesis describes the origins of religion based on a deep meditation practice that liberates the Soul within the fabric of a cosmos defined by the Precession of the Equinox. All that remains is for us to describe the mathematical and scientific details. The word "precession" refers to a change in the direction of the axis of a rotating object as it spins like a top or gyroscope. The Precession of the Equinox was first quantified using a sexagesimal system that measured 50 seconds of arc per year, which accumulates to 1 degree of arc every 72 years (50 seconds * 72 years = 3600 seconds = 60 minutes = 1^0). I hope I have at least raised some doubts as to when this quantification first took place. Determining precisely when these numbers were first understood is important to the history of mathematics and science. However, the initial conceptualization of the Path to Heaven probably antedated any accurate quantification of these numbers by thousands of years — a consideration that is important to the history of religion.

The discovery of this tiny gap in the Sun's ecliptic, measured against the background stars, was a great revelation that captured man's imagination. Following the Sun's path across the heavens offered an explanation for where man's liberated Soul traveled when a person died or when they simulated death through *Moksha*. The metaphysics of polytheism described how the essence of man's Being could transcend time and space to preview the Soul's Heavenly abode. Death would eventually transform each person into an immortal god who lived within this eternal dwelling. The undiscovered dimensions that are components of modern Superstring and M-Brane Theory provide us with a more up-to-date theory for locating Heaven within hidden dimensions. In the final analysis, the "Path to Heaven" remains as the main inspiration for all of the world's major religions.

The Clock of Heaven and Earth

Mathematics, music, and meditation informs our knowledge of the science of religion, which, in turn has implications for tracking Aryan migrations across the ancient world. It therefore behooves anthropologists, archeologists, scholars, and clerics to master its mathematical details as an investigative tool, just as a detective must learn to "follow the money." Understanding the science of religion makes it possible to recover the intended meaning of civilization's great religious and philosophical writings, as well as their art, architecture, etc.

As we begin to delve a bit deeper into these mathematical details it will become evident that we are solving the riddle of "the circle and the square within"[112] (Figure 26b). This ancient riddle encrypts the astronomy of the "Clock of Heaven and Earth" (Figures 24a-d) as a function of the Precession of the Equinox. Within religious writings, the Precessional axis (Figure

112 Zohar Prologue 5b -6a.

21a & b) has been called the *Axis Mundi* (Center of the World). Figure 21a provides us with a modern perspective of the Axis Mundi unavailable to ancient astronomers. It is an imaginary axis drawn through the center of the earth. In Figures 21a and 103, we can see the Earth tilted on its axis. The axis extends from the North and South Poles out to the polar stars, while circumpolar stars and constellations appear to swirl around that axis once per year.[113]

The Sun's orbital path weaves an invisible thread linking the Clocks of Heaven and Earth. Within Vedic astronomy, called *Jyotisha,* we tell time within the Clock of Heaven by gazing up at the *ayanamsa;* where *ayana* means "yearly degree" and *amsha* means "component." It is the ancient equivalent of our modern term for the precessional gap. It takes 72 years for the background stars to drift by 1° = 1 Day in Heaven. Each Heavenly month would take 30° x 72 Earth years = 2160 Earth years = 1 astronomical "Age" (such as the Age of Pisces, the Age of Aquarius, etc.). Traveling the full circle of the clock's 360° would indicate a "Great" or "Platonic" Heavenly year of 360° x 72 Earth years = 25,920 Earth years = 12 Ages x 2160 Earth years = 1 Heavenly Year.[114]

Closed Gate or Open Path?

The idea of an Aryan "Pathway to Heaven" was interpreted by invading Semitic tribe's as a "Gateway to Heaven." A gate would need to be opened in order to reveal a path. This book hypothesizes that the Aryan tribes were practicing *Moksha* for tens of thousands of years, and through meditation's impact on the natural selection process, became a vastly superior race.[115] We can speculate that the Semitic invaders struggled mightily to learn the yoga of *Moksha,* but probably met with little success. They needed to learn from the Aryan fathers how to master their unruly inner life by opening the "Gate" that leads to the "Path." The "Gateway to Heaven" was closed to neophytes.

One can imagine great skepticism as the first invading Semitic tribes learned about Aryan accomplishments. We can only surmise that the invading Semitic tribes tried to realize their own liberation and enlightenment, but history suggests that their initial efforts met with limited success. The frustration of Semitic tribes may have become a significant driving force in their application of a new and rigorous mathematics; a mathematics that scrutinized every detail of Heaven's Gate in order to open that Gate and begin on the spiritual "Path." Along with this new mathematics, a new Semitic attitude emerged, incorporating Semitic frustration into the notion

---

113 Today, we know that the stars don't actually swirl around the Earth, it just appears that way to an observer on Earth. The Earth rotates on its axis as it revolves around the Sun.

114 Campbell, The Mythic Image, Op.Cit., 74.

115 Meditation has been the point of the entire religious exercise since the dawn of civilization. A "gnostic hypothesis" tightly coupling the Quadrivium to meditation does not hinge on speculation about meditation's impact on the natural selection process and the origins of dolichocephalic skulls. The ancient texts speak for themselves.

of an inherent imperfection within man, i.e., "original sin." Unless and until man's sinful nature was atoned for, Semitic Souls would be blocked from entering the Path of spiritual salvation. The word "salvation" replaced "liberation." Thousands of years later, Christianity would forgo any expectations for the spiritual ascension of its parishioners, opting instead to focus on sin and morality. This line of reasoning culminated in Christianity's concept of mortal sin, in which sinners, unless forgiven and fully absolved, would be condemned to eternal damnation. Of the three monotheistic faiths, Christianity became the most passive faith, waiting for Christ to return and sit in judgement at "The End of Days," presumably to save "believers" who sinned the least. In Chapter 5, we will focus on the mathematical framework of sin and salvation. But, for now, suffice it to say that the Semitic beneficiaries of the Aryan legacy had come to believe that the manifest cosmos, like their own state of being, was imperfect.

The Aryan-Semitic dynamic fostered a world view that became increasingly divisive between the Eastern "Path" and the Western "Gate." Abrahamic monotheism culminated in Biblical allegory that attributed all imperfection to Adam and his crime against God. Since *Yahweh* embodied perfection, Adam's sin accounted for mankind's sinful and imperfect nature. "Inherent sin" would perpetuate man's exile from the Grace of God, and materiality itself absorbed Adam's imperfection once he was exiled. This gave rise to the Bible's moral imperative and struggle toward redemption. Within this context, mankind does not struggle merely for his own redemption, but for the salvation of the material world as well. The Eastern religious tradition considered purification a natural part of the Aryan Path, and meditation always focused on "the Path."

The *Navel of Order* (the *Nabhi Chakra*) was shared between East and West, weaving the Soul, Time, and the Universe together into a cosmic fabric. Semitic tribes were at least partially responsible for the rigor of the analytical and mathematical scrutiny applied to Aryan theology and cosmology. The Aryan approach was later recorded in the *Rig Veda;* while the Semitic approach was recorded in the *Sefer Yetzirah,* which I believe is the oldest monotheistic text. The *Rig Veda* is the foundation text of Hinduism, Buddhism, Jainism, Zoroastrianism, etc., while the *Sefer Yetzirah* is the seminal text of Semitic monotheism, as well as the scientific and theological basis of Judaism, Christianity, and Islam.

Integrating Knowledge

In the Introduction we mentioned the Renaissance ideal of integrating the liberal arts and sciences into a coherent framework of knowledge. We also mentioned civilization's growing need for subject matter experts, suggesting that an interdisciplinary approach may have become a thing of the past. The Aryan-Semitic conception of the universe is anchored in the mathematics of integer ratios that correlate sound with arithmetic, geometry, trigonometry, and astronomy as a function of the uniform circular motion of the sun. In the next chapter, we will carefully examine Sumerian and Babylonian cuneiform tablets that describe the sun's path plotted against the constellations as a periodic wave (Figures 23a & b). When following the circular motion of point "P" around the circle in Fig 23a, we can plot its location along the sine or cosine function as a one-dimensional projection of uniform circular motion. These sine and the cosine functions define the structure of simple harmonic motion, known in ancient Greece as "the Music of the Heavenly Spheres." The Music of the Spheres defines three important clocks (Figures 24a-d):

1. A Daily Clock helps guide the affairs of man on Earth (Figure 24a).
2. A Yearly Clock tracks the changing seasons and constellations (Figures 24c & d and 106a)
3. A Heavenly Clock measures the "eternal life" of man's immortal soul (Fig 24b)

Figure 23a - The Sun's Circular Motion Projects the Sine and Cosine Waves of Simple Harmonics

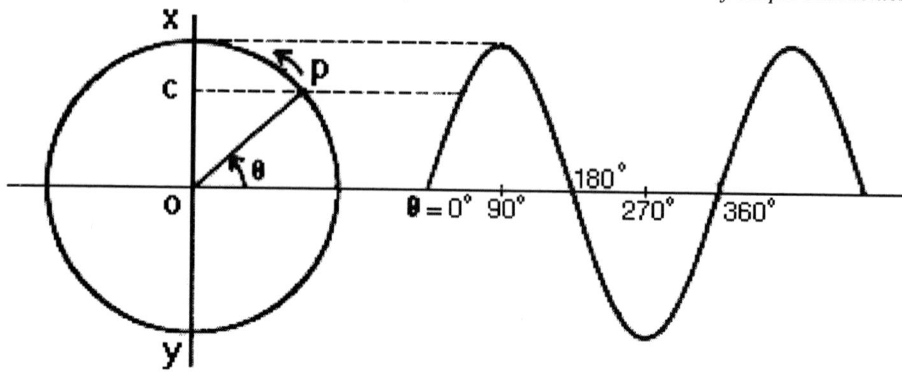

Figure 23b - Graphing the Projected Circular Motion of the Sun Against the Background Stars

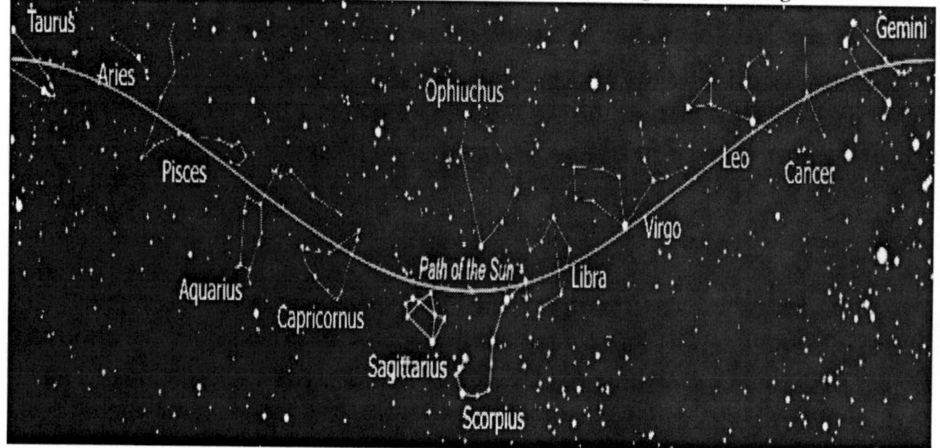

Figure 24a - The Daily Clock of Man is Defined by the Navel of Order as 12 Double-Hours

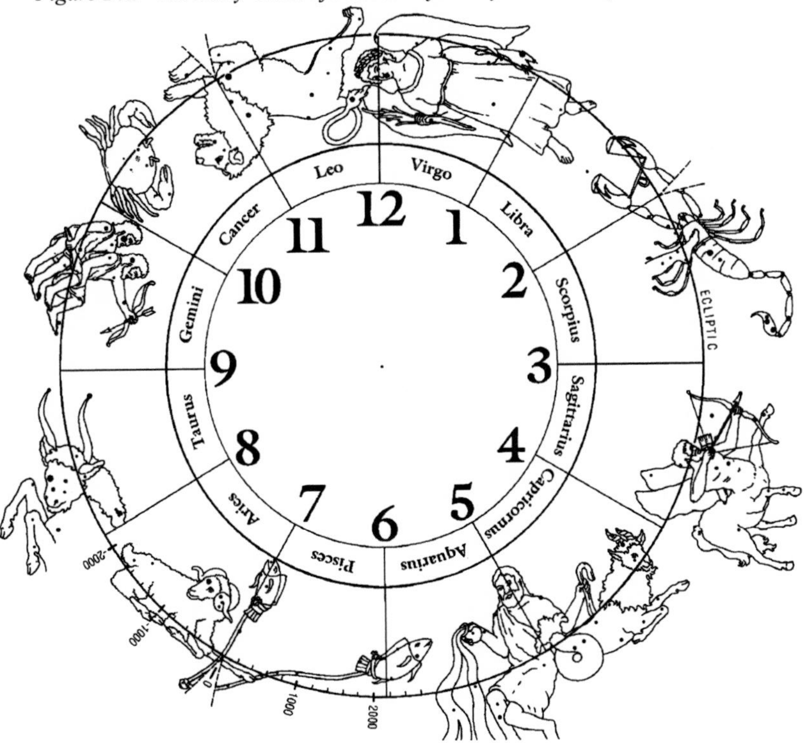

Figure 24b- The Clock of Heaven is Defined by the Navel of Order
Heaven is the Dwelling Place of the Immortal Soul

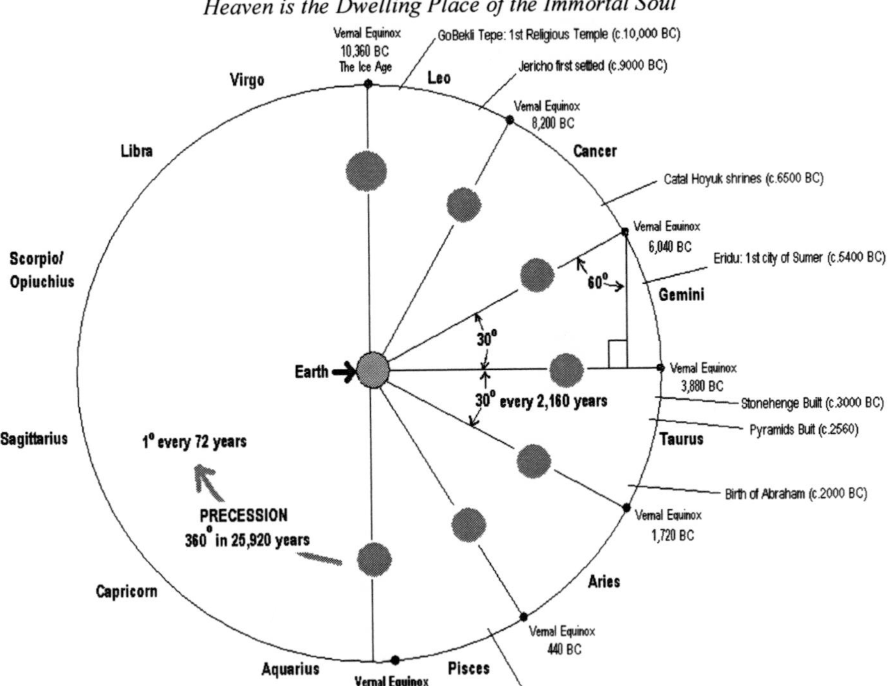

Figure 24c - The Navel of Order Defines the Annual Cycle of Vedic Astronomy

Figure 24d - The Navel of Order Defines Concentric Orbits as the "Music of the Spheres"

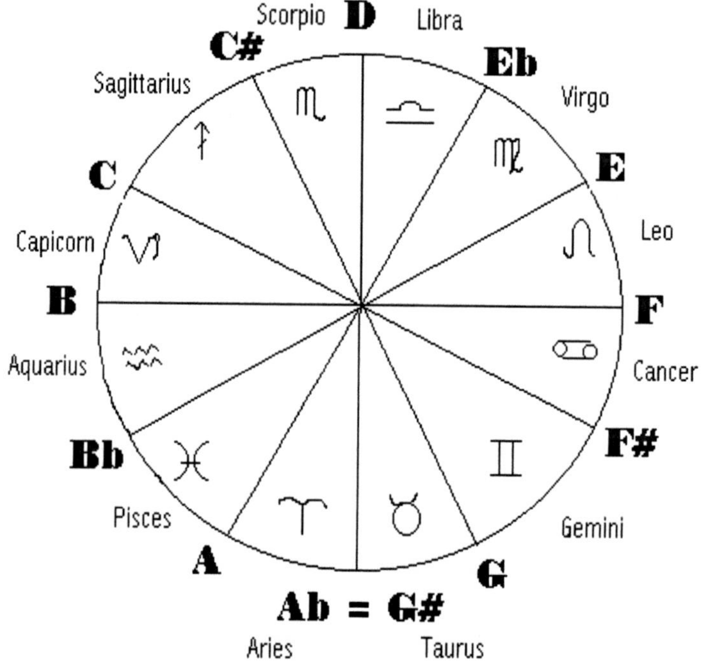

The written version of the Rig Veda was begun ca. 1700 BCE, and after an Aryan migration to the Indus Valley, it was completed around 1100 BCE. The *Vedic* hymn entitled “The Riddle of the Sacrifice” describes the precessional circle as the *Navel of Order* (Figure 25) in the following passage:

> *The Twelve-spoked wheel of Order rolls around and around the sky and never ages. Seven hundred and twenty sons in pairs rest on it, O Agni...Twelve Fellies, one wheel, three naves — who has understood this? Three hundred and sixty are set on it like poles that do not loosen.*[116]

Figures 25 - The Twelve-Spoked Wheel of the Zodiac as “720 Sons in Pairs” & “360 are set on it” that “rolls around the sky” [in a Precession of the Equinoxes]

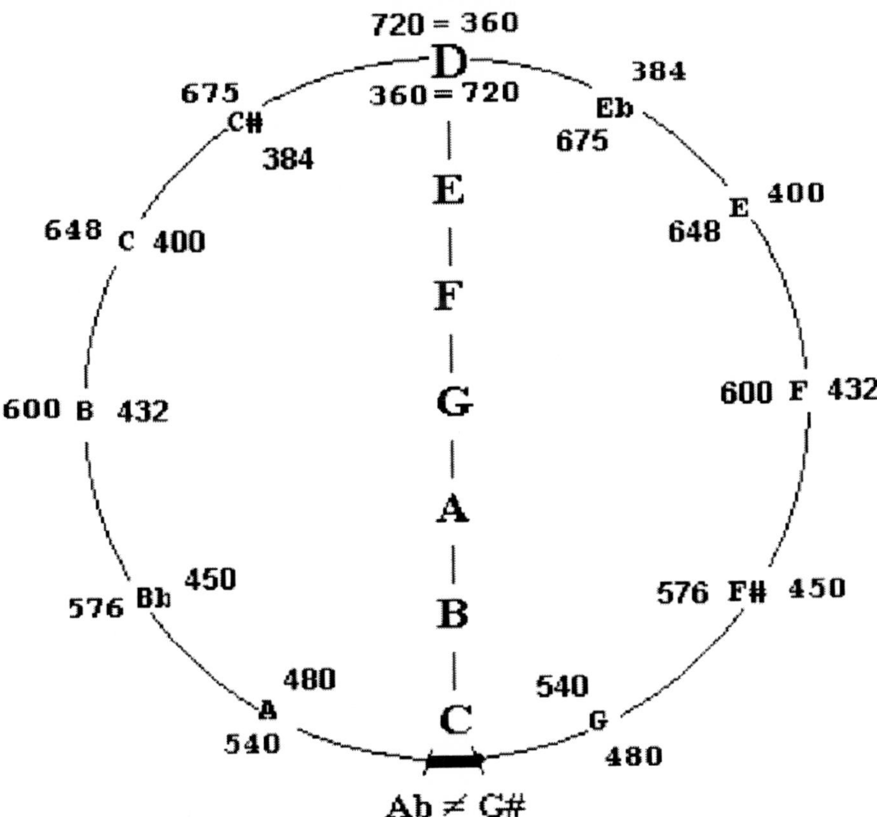

Three Channels of the Mind
Seven Aspects of the Soul
Twelve Aspects of the Body

116 Rig Veda 1:164, trans. By Wendy Doniger O’Flaherty (New York-London: Penguin Books, 1981) Op.Cit., 76 -81.

Chapter 5: The Gods in the Clock

The Sumerian King List

The Aryan fathers believed it was possible to transcend the constraints of time and space through the practice of *Moksha.* If man's liberated soul transcended the material constraints of time and space, and, if man's liberated soul was thought of as an immortal god dwelling in Heaven, then how could the finite increments of a clock measure eternity and the unlimited expansiveness of divinity? Today, when we think of Heaven we look skyward, because the Soul is experienced as traveling up and out of the body during liberation. In Chapter 4, we discussed how astronomer-priests studied the relationship between time and space to discover a "wormhole" to another dimension, suggesting the belief that man's Soul followed the Sun's path toward its Heavenly realm. The Precession of the Equinox defined a clock that linked two parallel realms — Heaven and Earth — where time could be measured proportionally by the integers 1 to 12. The existence of these realms implied that the well-known timeline of man's material existence on Earth as a mortal was proportional to an elongated timeline in Heaven, believed to be the final abode of man's liberated and immortal Soul. The discovery of a mathematical link between man's inner and outer world captured man's imagination, and marked the birth of religion.

The riddle of "the circle and the square within"[117] encrypts the astronomy of the clock as a function of Precession. The solution to this riddle solves the greatest mysteries of religion. It accounts for the scientific framework of epic Sumerian and Babylonian literature, as well as the scientific framework of the Bible. It also describes the shared mathematics of polytheism's gods and monotheism's God. Polytheism and monotheism turn out to be two sides of the same coin (in this case, the same clock). Even before the development of Vedic India's "Wheel of Order" (Figure 25), we will demonstrate that Sumerian cuneiform writings described a mathematical superset that was encrypted in the Clock of Heaven and Earth.

If we read the Sumerian King List table, as Kramer suggests, in terms of the "reigns of Kingship that descend from Heaven," then each of the Sumerian Kings, like each of the Egyptian pharaohs, was a "Son of God." The Daily, Yearly, and Heavenly Clocks (Figures 24a-d) were not just telling time, they were theorizing about what happened to a man's Soul after death. The 12 Ages of Man that structured the Clock of Heaven were inhabited by 7 tutelary

117 Zohar Prologue 5b - 6a.

gods, who, before they became deified, were just men living on Earth. From their newly acquired Heavenly perch they could astrologically guide "Kingship" on Earth. Eight Sumerian kings reigned over 5 different cities during a pre-dynastic period often considered mythical. This period is thought to have occurred before the great flood described in Mesopotamian literature. Each of these first 8 Kings was a "son of god" who reigned over one of the cities from Eridu to Shuruppak. However, these kings could not have antedated the great flood associated with the end of the Ice Age (circa 14,000 - 7,000 BCE). But, carbon dated sediments provide some evidence that a local flooding of the Euphrates River inundated early Sumerian cities, ca. 2900 BCE, which probably accounts for the legend of antediluvian kings.[118] Gilgamesh was contemporary with a 1st Dynasty king whose reign was verified by archeology (ca. 2600 BCE). Lugal-zage-si (ca. 2359–2335) was the last King of Sumer.

The early King List on the following page is attributed to a scribe from the Old Babylonian period (ca. 1800 BCE). Kramer believes it was first compiled in the last quarter of the 3rd millennium BCE.[119] To properly decipher this document, I believe it needs to be juxtaposed against two cuneiform tablets from the same time period: YBC 7289[120] and Plimpton 322.[121] Taken together, they form a single integrated *oeuvre* — a divine triptych — that elegantly marries arithmetic, music, geometry, trigonometry, astronomy, astrology, and theology, into a comprehensive science of religion that defines polytheism and sets the stage for monotheism.[122]

The invention of the clock involved much more than just telling time. "The circle and the square within" was symbolic of man's religious striving to reconcile the finite material realm (symbolized by the square) with the eternal spiritual realm (symbolized by the circle). When the diameter of a circle is also the diagonal of a square, these two distinct geometric shapes were juxtaposed and thus "harmonized" around the diameter/diagonal of the *Axis Mundi* in both the microcosm and macrocosm. The divine triptych of *Heaven*, *Sheol*, and *Moksha* mathematically encrypts this construction. And, when those details are revealed, the solution to the world's great religious mysteries becomes clear.

The long-standing debate between Creationists and Evolutionists pits the Bible's concepts of Time and Creation against scientific notions of Time and Evolution. Prehistoric concepts of time appear to be far more sophisticated than previously understood. Is the world really 6000 years old?[123] And, does this really imply that

118 Finegan, Op.Cit., 25-26.
119 Ibid., 224.
120 YBC 7289 refers to the tablet's Yale Babylonian Collection catalog number.
121 Referring to number 322 in the G.A. Plimpton Collection at Columbia University.
122 The Clock of Heaven and Earth would later evolve into the "Sacred Mystery" of "Three Hypostases in one Ousia" (Christianity's Holy Trinity). The King List describes the Kingdom of Heaven associated with "The Father"; YBC 7289 defines Sheol as the point of spiritual transfiguration usually associated with "The Son"; while Plimpton 322 defines Moksha as the "deification process" that purifies the body and liberates one's embodied Soul (The Holy Ghost) through meditation.
123 *Tanya*, Igeret Hakodesh 10; *Talmud*, Sanhedrin 97a: "Six thousand years shall the world exist..."

the "End of Days" is at hand, as evangelical Christianity would have us believe? The answer to that question will become clear once we gain some insight into how the Sumerians measured time. Perhaps it is finally justifiable to invoke the old cliche and tell the reader "exactly how the watch was made."

The Kingdom of Heaven

Biblical Creationism's 6000 year timeframe implies that the "End of Days" should have occurred around 2000 CE, since Adam was created circa 4000 BCE. From a scientific perspective, a 6000 year old world would not account for the anthropological record, the archeological record, nor the geological record. This challenge to common sense has long been a stumbling block in reconciling science and religion. Religion and science have different concepts of time, and it is important that we understand the difference between them. The unrealistic ages of Adam (930 years), Enoch (365 years), Abraham (175 years), and Jacob (147 years), suggest that they should be understood logarithmically, as "vibrations of spirit." The apostle Peter wrote, "With the Lord one day is as a thousand years, and a thousand years as one day."[124] What Peter was referring to — whether or not he understood it — was a linear conception of time measured quantitatively on Earth, as compared to a logarithmic conception of time measured qualitatively in Heaven.

What is so famously mysterious about the King List is the unrealistic length of each king's reign. I would suggest that these unrealistic reigns, like the unrealistic ages of the Biblical patriarchs, should be thought of qualitatively rather than quantitatively. Man's "window" into the spiritual realm can be found on the fringes of material reality, in the subtle and almost imperceptible drift of the stars. The previous chapter should have made it clear why the number 72 was so important to Sumerian astronomer-priests — because astronomy's Precession of the Equinox defined man's "window" into Heaven. That window was described by the 72 years it takes for the stars to drift 1^0 given an annual drift of 50 seconds of Arc (50 seconds * 72 years = 3600 seconds = 60 minutes = 1^0). In algebraic terms, each kingly reign (= x) is the product of an integer multiple (= y) in which $x = 72y * 10^2$ and $3 \leq y \leq 6$. In simpler terms, all the kingly reigns in the early King List turn out to be multiples of integers 3, 4, 5 and 6; the number 72; and the number 100. But, how do we extrapolate on integers 3, 4, 5 & 6 to include all 12 integers of the clock? The answer to that question is a critical part of solving religion's central mystery: "a circle and the square within (Figure 26b)."

The 12 integers of a clock measures 12 hours per day and 12 hours per night; which accumulates to 12 months per year; and 12 Ages of Man within each "Heavenly Year." A common, everyday clock measures and guides the affairs of men, while the Heavenly Clock was thought to measure and guide the affairs of the gods. The

---

124 II Peter. 3:8

"gods" were mortals who's immortal Soul was liberated to a parallel, but proportional reality. The simple integer ratios of the clock describe the harmonic vibrations of astrological emanation. Sumerian tutelary deities guided their "son" the King through these emanations, so the King could then guide his subjects.

The Sumerian King List [Kali Yuga]

Early Sumerian Version (ca.1800 BCE)			Berossus Version of List [125]	
1) Alulim	28,800		1) Aloros	36,000
2) Alalgar	36,000		2) Alaparos	10,800
3) Enmenlu-Anna	43,200		3) Almelon	46,800
4) Enmengal-Anna	28,800		4) Ammenon	43,200
5) Dumuzi	36,000		5) Amengalaros	64,800
6) Ensipazi-Anna	28,800		6) Dsonod	36,000
7) Enmendur-Anna	21,000	[21,600]	7) Euedoranchos	64,800
8) Ubar-Tutu	18,600		8) Amenpsinos	36,000
			9) Otiartes	28,800
			10) Xisuthros	64,800
			Kali Yuga Age	432,000

Original 7 Annunaki Tutelary Deities (72:144...864) ***Early Sumerian Version***

1) Anu: Sky = 60⁰ = Base 60 "Big One" was "Father of the gods"
2) Utu: Sun= 90⁰ = Zenith during vernal equinox
3) Sin: Moon = 30 day lunations for 31 luni-solar "Great Years" 31* 600 = 18,600
4) Enki: Water — 3 * 72 years * 100 = 21,600
5) Ki: Earth — 4 * 72 years * 100 = 28,800
6) Enlil: Wind — 5 * 72 years * 100 = 36,000
7) Inanna: "Integration" of Clock — 6 * 72 years * 100 = 43,200

The Early King List's Precessional 72 Years = 1⁰

Clock Logarithm	Years on Earth
1 * 72 = 72 * 30⁰ =	2160
2 * 72 = 144 * 30⁰ =	4320
3 * 72 = 216 * 30⁰ =	6480
4 * 72 = 288 * 30⁰ =	8640
5 * 72 = 360 * 30⁰ =	10,800
6 * 72 = 432 * 30⁰ =	12,960
7 * 72 = 504 * 30⁰ =	15,120
8 * 72 = 576 * 30⁰ =	17,280
9 * 72 = 648 * 30⁰ =	19,440
10 * 72 = 720 * 30⁰ =	21,600
11 * 72 = 792 * 30⁰ =	23,760
12 * 72 = 864 * 30⁰ =	25,920

The Berossus List's Wheel of Order (360:720)

Inanna:	15 x 720 =	10,800
Enki:	30 x 720 =	21,600
Sin:	31 x 600 =	18,600 (lunar deity)
Ki:	40 x 720 =	28,800
Enlil:	50 x 720 =	36,000
Anu:	60 x 720 =	43,200
	65 x 720 =	46,800 (sidereal year)
Utu:	90 x 720 =	64,800

125 Finegan, Op.Cit., 24-25

If 1 Day in Heaven = 1° takes 72 years on Earth, then 2 days in Heaven = 2° = 144 years on Earth, 3 days = 216 years on Earth, etc.... 30 Days in Heaven = 30° = 2160 years on Earth, which is an astronomical "Age" (such as the Age of Taurus, the Age of Aquarius, etc.— compare Figures 24a & b). In man's daily clock 60 seconds = 1 minute and 60 minutes = 1 hour. But, in the Clock of Heaven, each Earth year becomes the second hand; every 72 years becomes the minute hand; each Age of Man becomes the hour hand; and every day in Heaven becomes a Great Year that takes 25,920 years on Earth. Also, each Age of Man takes 2160 years * 360 days[126] = 777,600 days on Earth.[127] The Age of Aquarius would therefore take 777,600 Earth days; which, to immortals in Heaven, would be analogous to watching the clock move for a only one hour.

In Figure 26a, we can see that 7 of the 8 reigns in the early King List reduce to integer multiplications of 72, listing the kings within integer columns 3, 4, 5 or 6:

3 * 72 * 100 = 21,600 lists 1 King
4 * 72 * 100 = 28,800 lists 3 Kings
5 * 72 * 100 = 36,000 lists 2 Kings
6 * 72 * 100 = 43,200 lists 1 King

The factor of 100 is explained by McClain's observation that Vedic Hymn XXX refers several times to Indra as Lord of 100 powers. This is one of many Vedic examples, suggesting that "factors of the form 10^n are part of the essential arithmetic."[128] Factoring the kingly reigns by Precession's number, 72, is prerequisite to successfully deciphering the King List. But, how do integer multiples 3, 4, 5, 6 transform into the musical ratios necessary to construct a complete clock from the Sumerian King List, in which counting from 1 to 12 around the clock's circumference defines a harmonic series that astrologically emanates through the "7 gods who decree."

If we examine Quadrant I of Figure 26b we will see the solution for the great religious mystery: "a circle and the square within." The square is comprised of two back-to-back isosceles right triangles, in which the diagonal of the square is also the diameter of the circle. Music theory teaches us that the ratio 3:6 generates an octave tone circle, just like the one circumscribing the square in Quadrant I. Also within Quadrant I, in addition to the back-to-back $45^0 45^0 90^0$ right triangles forming the square, there is a 30^0 60^0 90^0 right triangle. In Figure 26b, we know that twelve of these 30^0 triangles would fit into the larger 360^0 circle. What the 30^0 60^0 90^0 right triangle and the 45^0 45^0 90^0 right triangles have in common is one irrational length side with ratios: 1, 2, √3 and 1, 1, √2, respectively. We should not be too surprised to

126 Disregarding the sidereal year which was approximated by 360 + 5 festival days.
127 We will see this number again, in Part II, in relation to monotheism's God, Yahweh. .
128 Ernest McClain, The Myth of Invariance: The Origins of the Gods Mathematics and Music from the Rig Veda to Plato (New York: Nicholas Hays: 1976) 73-75.

find out that the ratio of side lengths in these two types of right triangle are not characterized by the finite distances known to mortals, but by irrational distances known to gods who have transcended time and space within the ether of Heaven and *Sheol*.

The gods in the clock don't exist in the physical, exoteric world, they live in the esoteric realm of immortals. The 7 Annunaki live in the clock insofar as 6 gods embody 3 angles and 3 sides of the 12 replicating 30^0 triangles. Within YBC 7289, the spiritual energies of all six are "integrated" in sexual Union with Inanna, as each of her "legs" also opens 45^0 to inscribe a square that reaches down into the material realm of kingship on Earth. Inanna's circle of spirituality transforms her lover, the King, awakening his Soul along the diameter/diagonal of the circle/square. Thus, the ambiguity of Death and Nirvana are juxtaposed within the "Gates of Sheol."

As the Precessional "window" increments, it subtly alters astrological emanations from the gods. The center angle incrementally changes from 30^0 to 45^0, and the sides change length accordingly, as the imaginary hands of Heaven's Clock. Cuneiform tablet Plimpton 322 (Figure 30a) is acknowledged as the first trigonometric table. This third cuneiform component of our Divine Triptych measures the Precessional window, tracking the Sun's march through space and time. As each Age passes, the 3, 4, 5 triangles of Plimpton 322 (called Pythagorean triples[129]) utilizes 3, 4, 5 integer multiples to determine the center angle from 31^0 to 44^0, incrementally transitioning each King from 30^0 tutelary guidance to their own 45^0 Enlightenment.

A revised version of the King List was created by the legendary historian and astronomer/astrologer, the Babylonian priest Berossus (ca. 300 BCE). He formalized the modernizing of the 3rd millennium Sumerian King List's precessional metric unit of 72 years = 1^0 by transforming the King List with a more modern metric describing the Sun's incremental motion of 15^0 / hour * 12 double-hours = 360. With this revision, the King List depicted in Figure 26b would essentially be replaced by the subset described in Figure 25 — the Old Babylonian Period's Wheel of Order (15^0 * 12 hour days) + (15^0 * 12 hour nights) = 360:720. Elements of both versions of the King List would be incorporated into the mathematics of the *Sefer Yetzirah* and the *Rig Veda* to articulate the scientific basis of religion.

Berossus Tutelary Deities (360:720)	***Berossus Version***
1) Inanna	100 * 1.5 * 72 years =10,800
2) Enki	100 * 3 * 72 years = 21,600
3) Ki	100 * 4 * 72 years = 28,800
5) Enlil	100 * 5 * 72 years = 36,000
6) Anu	100 * 6 * 72 years = 43,200
(The sidereal year adds 60^2 = 3600 years)	100 * 6.5 * 72 years = 46,800
7) Utu	100 * 9 * 72 years = 64,800

129 Pythagorean triples describe three sides of a right triangle in which all three sides are integers that satisfy the Pythagorean theorem, $a^2 + b^2 = c^2$. For example, $3^2 + 4^2 = 5^2$ or $9 + 16 = 25$.

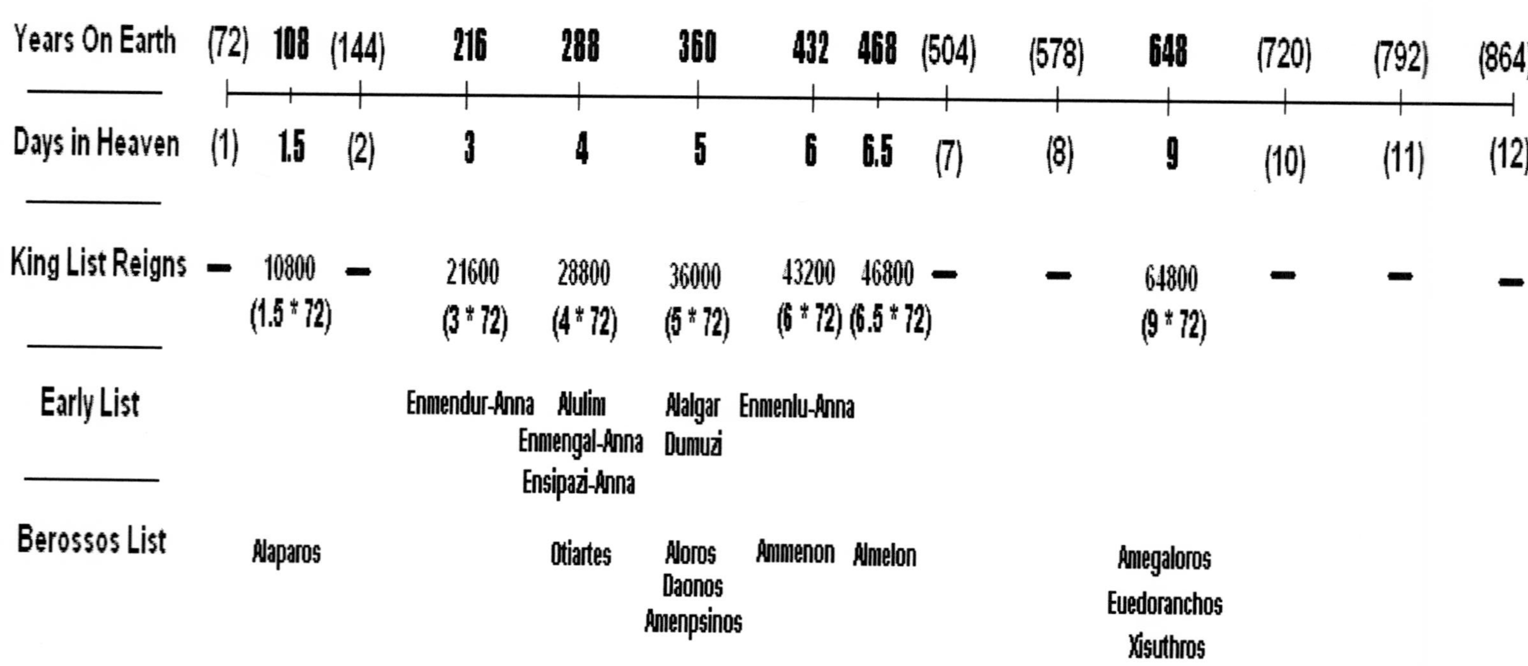

Figure 26a - The Sumerian King Lists Deciphered Defines the Clock as a Harmonic Series

Figure 26b - The Circle & Square Inscribed Within the Clock of Heaven & Earth

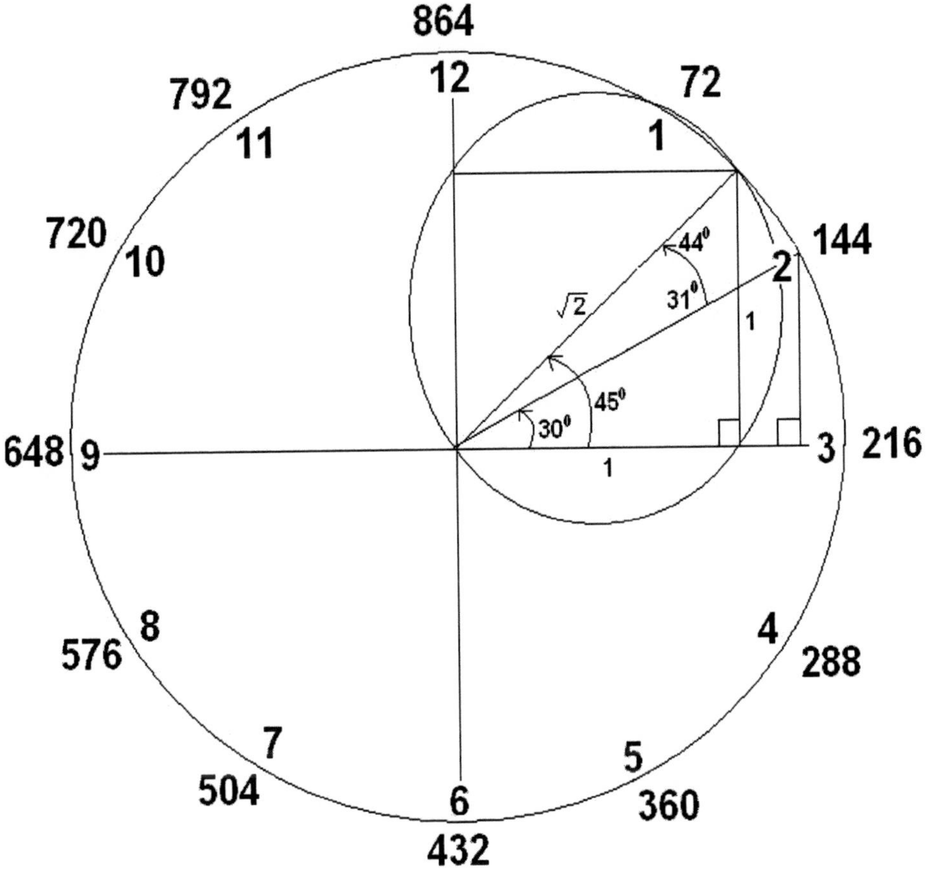

Figure 27 - "Gods in the Clock" Emanating Across 12 Ages as History's First Astrological Chart

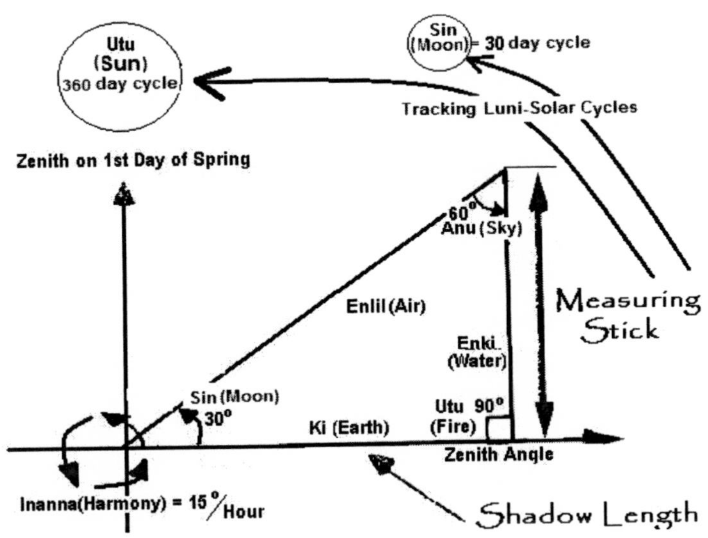

Berossus retrofit his change to derive a slightly modified version of the King List in which Inanna could easily be associated with the Sun's 15^0/hour metric, thanks to place holders and floating point arithmetic. Within the Hindu metrics of floating point arithmetic described in the Vishnu Purana, we can see how the Ages of Man varied according to how many times Vishnu or Brahma would blink: 1000 times, 100 times, etc. Each Yuga sinned more than the last, and the 10 Sumerian Kings of Berossus' 432,000 year combined reigns was meant to reflect the Kali Yuga Age of 3 parts sin and only 1 part virtue. "Modernizing" thus gave Berossus the flexibility to have Inanna integrate all 7 tutelary gods and 10 kings into the Kali Yuga Age of 432,000 years.

In his changes, Berossus included 1.5 and 6.5 as non-integer multiples of 72, the first number arithmetically bisected integers 1:2 as 1:1½:2, but harmonically bisected the octave tone circle 1:2 as 1:√2 :2. Later in this chapter, we will see the great significance of dividing the circle and square exactly in half. The number 6.5 adds 3,600 years to Ammenon's reign within the "modern" astronomy of the sidereal year.

The only numeric anomaly in the early King List is Enmendur-Anna's reign of 21,000 years.[130] Perhaps it is an archeological transcription error, but the number 21,000 is clearly inconsistent with the harmonics of the Clock depicted in Figures 26a & b. The 1 digit difference between 21,000 and 21,600 (3 * 72 * 100 = 21,600) is the only missing integer multiple from King List's 3, 4, 5, 6 harmonic pattern. The validity of 21,600 is confirmed by Vedic tradition's 10,800 "solar" breaths by day, 10,800 "lunar" breaths by night, with 21,600 breaths in a daily cycle.[131] The Hindu rosary also has 108 beads, enabling the faithful to pronounce Vishnu's name 10,800 times per day. If we could pronounce Vishnu's name at night as we sleep (with each breath), there would be a nighttime equivalent of 10,800, implying that day and night combined would again complete a 21,600 daily cycle.

King Ubar-Tutu is not represented in Figure 26a because he is the only lunar guided king among the solar astrological forces of Heaven. The ancient Jewish historian Flavius Josephus speaks about a Great Year as equivalent to 600 years on Earth.[132] Since a solar Great Year takes 25,920 years on Earth, we can assume he was talking about a lunar Great Year. In 600 years plus 1 day there are 7421 lunations ((600 * 12 months) + 221 intercalations), when the New Moon and the Sun's equinox correspond within a single hour.[133] This suggests Sumerian knowledge of

130 Finegan, Op.Cit., 24.
131 Satapatha Brahmana XII 3.28
132 Flavius Josephus, *The Antiquities of the Jews*, trans. By William Whiston (Virginia: IndyPublish.com) Book I 2:9.
133 Rev. F.A. Jones, *The Ancient Year and the Sothic Cycle,* Proceedings of the Society of Biblical Archeology (PSBA), Vol. XXX, London: 1908, 95-106.

the Sothic cycle, which states that every 19 solar years contains 235 lunar months (12 ordinary lunar years plus 7 intercalary lunar years of 13 months each). Therefore, (235 lunar months * 600 solar years)/19 = 7421. The combined action of the Sun and the Moon is called luni-solar precession, and the length of Ubar-Tutu's reign is therefore the only reign given in terms of 31 lunar Great Years or 31 x 600 = 18,600 years. This lunar cycle correlates with the Moon's orbit precessing around the Earth in 18.6 year cycles with respect to the tides on Earth.

There is still much to be learned by integrating the Sumerian King List, Plimpton 322, and YBC 7289. Understood as a single *oeuvre*, these three documents comprise the earliest written evidence of what Campbell describes as a "mathematically structured astronomical system." The reconciliation process between the circle and the square, describing the Clock of Heaven and Earth, is the first historical record of what modern science calls a harmonic series. Its discovery is as old as the Sumerian King List, which is generally believed to antedate the Old Babylonian period. In the first four chapters of Part I we discussed thousands of years of archeological evidence that suggest a long period of historical development for this material among the pre-Sumerian Aryans.

The harmonic series is a recognized empirical phenomenon that mathematically describes the Soul, the Cosmos, and Time in terms of how the Clock's 12 sequential integers structure the diversity of the 6 Annunaki within the unity of a 7th — the goddess Inanna. The early Sumerian King List, ca. 3rd millennium BCE, marks the first historical appearance of the harmonic series, about 4000 years before either Nicole Oresme (ca. 14th c.) or Joseph Saveur (ca. 18th c.) contributed to its scientific "discovery." Abraham's *Sefer Yetzirah* later transformed the Sumerian sexagesimal system's harmonic series into its decimal equivalent — counting from 1 to 10 within the decimal framework of monotheism's *10 Sefirot of Nothingness.* This became the Torah's *pnimiyut* (Hebrew: inner vibrational essence) of the Ten Commandments. Within the modern physics of Superstring and M-Brane Theory, the harmonic series describes the "deep structure" of Time and the Cosmos. We will now take a look at the mathematical details of the Soul within both polytheism and monotheism.

How the Clock of Heaven Structures the Soul

We have seen how the early King List was based on 100 divine "blinks" in order to facilitate its floating point arithmetic. Epic Hindu literature allegorizes this musical construction within Hymn 82 of the Rig Veda, which states that the primal seed rested on the "Unborn's navel." This was the source for the later Puranic version that depicts Creation starting with the birth of Brahma. A snake-like umbilical chord is depicted as the root of a flowering Lotus that rises from Vishnu's navel.[134] And, the "World Soul" of Brahma emerges from within that Lotus while Vishnu lies floating on a coiled "serpent bed" on the cosmic sea dreaming the "world illusion" that is Creation. Once we understand the clock in terms of the sequential integers that comprise a harmonic series, we can see exactly how man's Soul arose as a subset of that harmonic series.

If 1 Day in Heaven takes 72 years on Earth, then a sexagesimal Work-week in Heaven would take 6 * 72 = 432 years on Earth. The *Rig Veda* describes the tonal basis of *śruti* as "seven tones in symmetric scale order — symmetrically rising or falling — bounded by the 432:864 octave double that dominates Hindu cosmology.[135] We can find this octave double (432:864) within Figures 26a & b as component parts of the Clock of Heaven and Earth's harmonic series. The World Soul is contained by this 432:864 octave double, generating seven *śrutis* from successive powers of 3. The 1st tone "integrates" the diversity of the other 6 tones into a sonorous body, while the 8th tone duplicates the 1st, thus "containing" the scale.

The World Soul Arising From Vishnu's Navel

Ratios	432	486	512	576	648	729	768	864
Rising	D	E	F	G	A	B	C	D
Falling	D	C	B	A	G	F	E	D
Powers of 3	3^3	3^5	3^0	3^2	3^4	3^6	3^1	3^3

At the close of each 100 Brahma years, Brahma and all of Creation dissolves into the body of the cosmic dreamer, until Vishnu dreams again and Brahma can be reborn from Vishnu's navel: "Every day of a Brahma's lifetime of 100 Brahma years, Vishnu's eyes open and close 1000 times. When they open a universe appears..."[136] Within this slightly revised version of early King List numerology, Vishnu's 1000 "blinks" creates the "Ages of Man," while integer multiples still define harmonic ratios: 1+2+3+4 = 10 (see table that follows).

The learned Babylonian priest Berossus attempted to integrate the sexagesimal reigns of the original 8 Sumerian Kings into the decimal "shorthand" of 10 Kings to define the Kali Yuga Age.[137] Maha Yuga sums the Four Ages of Man based on integer multiples of 432 and Vishnu's 1000 blinks. The harmonic whole was considered a divine being that embodied the cosmos. From this perspective, the earliest Vedic conception of a Creator was monotheistic, and the various Ages were considered an illusory part of Brahma as dreamed by Vishnu.

---

134 Vishnu rules over the highest heaven, and within Vedic astronomy, the snake-like umbilical chord rising from Vishnu's navel identifies him with the pole star, or *Axis Mundi*. Similarly, the Biblical symbolism of a serpent winding around the Tree of Knowledge of Good and Evil depicts monotheism's *Axis Mundi* at the center of the Garden of Eden.
135 McClain, Op.Cit., 61.
136 Campbell, Op.Cit., 143.
137 Parallel allegories exist within the Torah as 8 Kings of Edom who reigned before any King (God) and His 10 Commandments, ruled over Israel.

Ages of Man		Integer Ratio		Years in Heaven [138]
Kali Yuga (432 * 1000 years)	=	1	=	432,000 years
Dvapara Yuga (432 * 2000 years)	=	2	=	864,000 years
Treta Yuga (432 * 3000 years)	=	3	=	1,296,000 years
Krta Yuga (432 * 4000 years)	=	4	=	1,728,000 years
Maha Yuga (432 * 10,000 years)	=	10	=	4,320,000 years

In the early King List, tutelary deities were the energetic components of 12 right triangles establishing the first astrological chart (Figure 27). These "gods" each guided their "son" the king from within the Clock of Heaven's 12 triangles. As time progresses, the King's prayers, and ultimately his Soul, would ascend toward Heaven, while tutelary guidance and blessings astrologically emanated from the gods in Heaven and descended to each Earthly King, each of whom was considered the son of a god. As the King's Soul gradually ascended, Plimpton 322 (later section in this chapter) lists precessional angles that gradually increment. As described within YBC 7289, the King did not simply die and "give up his ghost" during this process. The King's Soul ascended in Nirvanic bliss with his lover Inanna, and his success at attaining Enlightenment was understood to greatly enhance his abilities as a ruler.

YBC 7289 - Sheol: the Gates of Heaven and Hell

The Akkadian Empire began with Sargon of Akkad who reigned from 2270 to 2215 BC after defeating Lugal-zage-si, the last King of Sumer. Akkad preceded Babylon (Akkadian *Babilli* : "Gateway of the Gods"; Hebrew *Babel*: "to confuse")[139] the capital of Babylonia. Some scholars suggest that Sargon was portrayed by Noah's great-grandson Nimrod, civilization's first "mighty man." Nimrod was the King said to have built the Tower of Babel in *Shinar* (Sumer) dedicated to the glory of man, rather than to the glory of God. This type of idolatry was outlawed in Mosaic Law. It was considered evil, giving God reason to confuse language and disperse the nations. The Aryan holy men Enoch and Noah knew only one proto-language.[140] Each of 70 nations would be dispersed to the "four corners of the earth" due to the evil of Nimrod's idolatry.

The city of Babylon began as a small 3rd millennium town, located about 50 miles south of modern day Baghdad. By the 21st century, the Akkadian Dynasty fell to King Ur-Nammu, ushering in the dynastic period known as Ur III (in contrast

138 McClain, Op.Cit., The Myth of Invariance, 73-74; also cites Berossus' commentary on 432,000 as the Babylonian "Great Year."
139 Akkad is mentioned in Genesis 10:10
140 Jews generally assume the first language to be Hebrew, while Hindu's assume it to be Sanskrit.

to the archeological periods: Ubaid and Uruk). Ur III marked a cultural renaissance. The Tower of Babel may portray the Ziggurat of Ur, known in the Sumerian language as *Etemenanki* (literally: "Temple of the Foundation of Heaven and Earth").

Within the context of Semitic contributions to the mathematics of sin and salvation — King Ur-Nammu wrote the Ur-Nammu Code. This was the first set of cuneiform laws, predecessor to the most famous codifications of law: Hammurabi's Code and Mosaic Code. The science and theology of sin and salvation gave rise to many codified cuneiform laws, including Elamite Code, Hurrian Code, Hititte Code, etc.. The Ur III Dynasty fell to an Elamite eastern invasion in 1940 BCE, and Babylonia soon fell under Amorite influence after a western invasion from Martu, "the land of the Amorites." These were Semitic tribes from Syria and Canaan, and the great patriarch of monotheism, Abraham, would probably have been born to a Canaanite family in Ur during this period.

In order to understand YBC 7289 we should first examine Da Vinci's "Vetruvian Man" (Figure 69), which symbolizes man's imperfect material existence as a two dimensional square, and his perfect spiritual existence as a circle. Da Vinci regarded the mathematical problem of "squaring the circle" as a sacred riddle based on the writings of Marcus Vetruvius, Rome's first architect. Vetruvius became known for using harmonic proportions in his designs. However, just as the real "Riddle of the Sphinx" was lost, the real riddle for "the circle and the square within" was misinterpreted as "squaring the circle" by constructing a circle with the same area as a square. The solution to the correct riddle does not require knowledge of the golden ratio, the Fibonacci series, Pascal's triangle, nor **π**, as some would have us believe.[141]

The riddle of "the circle and the square within" describes the mathematical context for sin and salvation with respect to ratio and proportion. A *ratio* is a comparison of two things or ideas, known in ancient Greek thought as *analogy.* This can be expressed by the formula *a:b,* for example, 2:3. A proportion, however, is a comparison of two ratios of four related items, expressed in formula as *a:b :: c:d,* for example: *2*:4::3:6. A *continuous proportion* can be defined using three related terms *a:b::b:c*, where the *extremes* are bound together by a *mean* term, for example: 2:4::4:8. The ancients compared spirituality and materiality by reconciling opposites with their mean in this manner. The observer (b) experiences the external objective world (a) through the lens of subjective perception (c). In other words, man must continually reconcile the external material world with his internal spiritual world.[142] A three term proportion was therefore the model for an observer comparing a circle and a square, as well as an observer reconciling materiality and spirituality within his own being. YBC 7289 is an inscribed stone depicting "a circle and the square within,"[143] in which the square's diagonal becomes the circle's diameter, creating

141 Including Vetruvius and the important Indian music theorist Pingala (300–200 BCE).
142 Robert Lawlor, *Sacred Geometry* (London: Thames & Hudson, 1982) 44-45.
143 Zohar Prologue 5b -6a.

two opposing shapes reconciled by a mean: the diagonal/diameter. In other words, a continuous proportion that mathematically defines man's relationship to the divine.

Figure 28a & b - YBC 7289

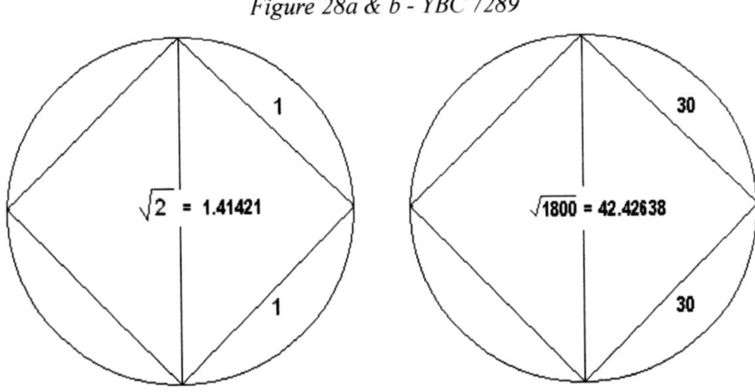

YBC 7289 demonstrates the earliest use of the Pythagorean Theorem. Since we know the length of two sides of the right triangle, the Pythagorean Theorem can be used to determine the length of its hypotenuse. YBC 7289 describes a special case of right triangle that we call isosceles, in which two sides and two angles are equal. A square is created from back-to-back isosceles triangles. If each side has a length of 1, the Pythagorean Theorem determines that the length of the hypotenuse will never be a whole number integer — it is an irrational number: 1.41421.

Figure 28c - Bisecting the Octave Tonecircle of YBC 7289

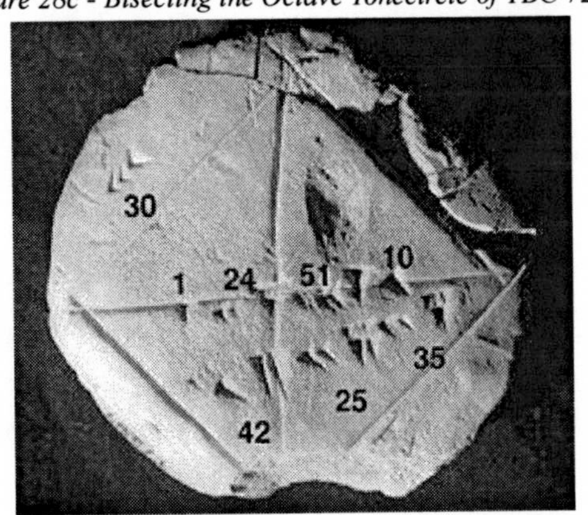

This tablet is evidence that Old Babylonian astronomers had knowledge of the Pythagorean Theory more than 1000 years before the birth of Pythagoras:

> In any right triangle, the area of the square whose side is the hypotenuse (the side opposite the right angle) is equal to the sum of the areas of the squares whose sides are the two legs (the two sides that meet at a right angle).

Cuneiform numbers are engraved along this diameter/diagonal as: 1, 24, 51 and 10. The length of the hypotenuse is $\sqrt{2}$ correct to five places: 1.41421. This solution can be converted from sexagesimal to its decimal equivalent as follows:

$$1 + 24/60^1 + 51/60^2 + 10/60^3$$

$$\text{or} \quad 1 + 24/60 + 51/3600 + 10/216{,}000 = 305{,}470/216{,}000 = 1.41421+$$

The number 30 appears along one of the tablet's triangle sides implying that we apply the Pythagorean Theorem once again to calculate yet another hypotenuse. We know this because there is a 2nd diagonal of the square carved into this tablet immediately below the first hypotenuse as sexagesimal 42, 25, 35 which can be converted to decimal as follows:

$$42 + 25/60^1 + 35/60^2 = 42.42638+$$

Taking the cosecant function (hypotenuse over the opposite side), we can see that the ratios of the sides didn't change — still approximating $\sqrt{2}$.

$$1.41421 / 1 = 1.41421 \quad \text{and} \quad 42.42638 / 30 = 1.41421$$

A continuous proportion $1:\sqrt{2}::\sqrt{2}:2$ compares the body (symbolized by the square) and the soul (symbolized by tone circle ratio 1:2), harmonized by the Axis Mundi that bisects both the tone circle and square. Having an irrational mean of $1:\sqrt{2}:2$ does not imply that the number is "without reason," but rather, "without numerical ratio." Since the calculated length was not the expected whole number ratio, many among the Semitic tribes viewed this as evidence of a closed Gateway, rather than as the Aryan Pathway to liberation. In either case, one's perspective could generally be determined by one's cultural orientation and ancestry. This mathematics suggested that the spiritual and the material realms were out-of-sync, and this would have a profound effect on the history and development of monotheism.

We can speculate that the Aryan founders of Sumer would have understood this "imperfection" in a positive experiential way, as the Gateway to the Soul's liberation, ascending along the Sun's path through the 7 Heavens. The Semitic tribes, however, came to see this Gateway as closed and inaccessible — blocked by imperfection in a Universe that echoed with man's sinful, imperfect nature. Imperfection could never be ascribed to Abrahamic notions of a perfect God. Therefore, in Scripture, this imperfection was ascribed to Adam's Fall from Grace, which provides the mathematical context for the Semitic concept of inherent, or original sin.

Plimpton 322 - Moksha: the Soul's Liberation

The final tablet in the triptych is Plimpton 322 (Figure 30a), which lists fifteen sets of Pythagorean triples within history's first trigonometric table (ca. 1800 BCE). It is a cuneiform tablet containing four columns and 15 rows of "Pythagorean triples." Each triple forms a right triangle, but, unlike YBC 7289, all side lengths are whole number integers. And, each angle is determined by the cosecant function (the hypotenuse over the opposite side: Figure 29) approximating fifteen one degree increments where $30^{\circ} < \theta < 45^{\circ}$.

The divine emanations that "ascend to" and "descend from" the tutelary gods in the clock are a function of the Sun's Path during a Great Year. Plimpton 322 provides a degree by degree tracking of that energy beginning with Heaven's idealized 30^{0} right triangle (Sumerian King List), and culminating in Nirvanic Union within Inanna's "Gates of Sheol" (YBC 7289). As this spiritual and cosmic drama plays out, the "sons of god" are in-sync with a universe astrologically predisposed to facilitate the king's spiritual progress, while Plimpton 322 tracks that progress.

A Pythagorean triple is defined as three sides of a right triangle in which all three sides are integers that satisfy the Pythagorean theorem, $a^2 + b^2 = c^2$. For example, a 3, 4, 5 right triangle is a Pythagorean triple that can be written in the form $3^2 + 4^2 = 5^2$ or $9 + 16 = 25$. Mathematician Erik Zeeman noticed that there should be 16 triples in this table.[144] However, the motion of the Sun at a rate of 15^{0} per hour provides a plausible reason for why there are 15 sets of triples included in the table.

Figure 29 - The Cosecant Function within a Pythagorean Triple

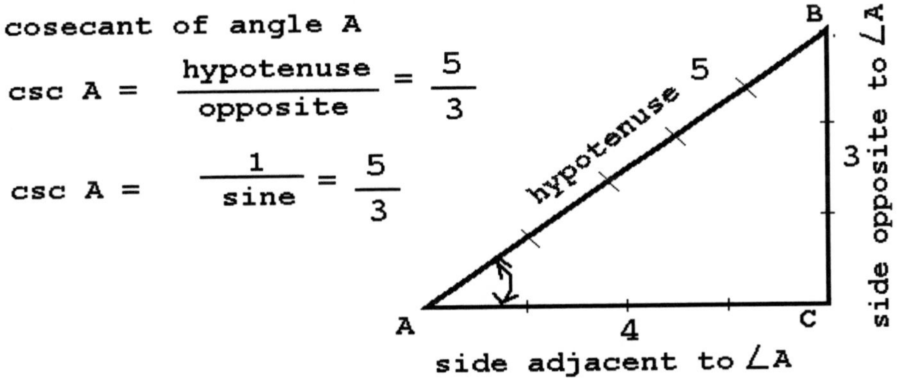

cosecant of angle A

$$\csc A = \frac{\text{hypotenuse}}{\text{opposite}} = \frac{5}{3}$$

$$\csc A = \frac{1}{\text{sine}} = \frac{5}{3}$$

B
5
hypotenuse
3
side opposite to ∠A
A
4
C
side adjacent to ∠A

144 If the Babylonians generated triples using the formulas: side a = p2 - q2 ; side b = 2pq; and side c= p2 + q2 then there should be exactly sixteen 5-smooth triples in this table satisfying $n \leq 60$, $30^{\circ} \leq \theta \leq 45^{\circ}$, and tan2t = b2/a2. The term "5-smooth" implies that a number like 360 can be completely factored by 2, 3 and 5. Modern terminology states that a positive integer would be considered B-smooth if B is the upper limit. A superparticular number can be defined as any integer which factors completely into prime numbers (see Appendix: Primer on Music for a discussion of superparticular numbers and music)

Figure 30a - Plimpton 322

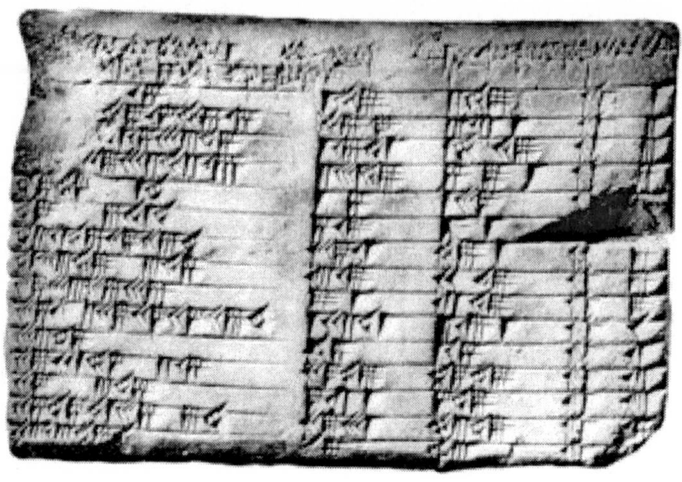

	Sexagesimal	....		Decimal	....	
angle	length (squared)	width	diagonal	length(sqrt)	width	diagonal
44.76	1:59:00:15	1:59	2:49	120	119	169
44.25	1:56:56:58:14:50:06:15	56:07	1:20:25	3456	3367	4825
43.79	1:55:07:41:15:33:45	1:16:41	1:50:49	4800	4601	6649
43.27	1:53:10:29:32:52:16	3:31:49	5:09:01	13500	12709	18541
42.08	1:48:54:01:40	1:05	1:37	72	65	97
41.54	1:47:06:41:40	5:19	8:01	360	319	481
40.32	1:43:11:56:28:26:40	38:11	59:01	2700	2291	3541
39.77	1:41:33:45:14:03:45	13:19	20:49	960	799	1249
38.72	1:38:33:36:36	8:01	12:49	600	481	769
37.44	1:35:10:02:28:27:24:26	1:22:41	2:16:01	6480	4961	8161
36.87	1:33:45	45	1:15	60	45	75
34.98	1:29:21:54:02:15	27:59	48:49	2400	1679	2929
33.86	1:27:00:03:45	2:41	4:49	240	161	289
33.26	1:25:48:51:35:06:40	29:31	53:49	2700	1771	3229
31.89	1:23:13:46:40	56	1:46	90	56	106

The sun travels 15 degrees every hour, so in a 24 hour day, $15^0 * 24$ hours $= 360^0$. In the clock of Heaven, the 7th “God who decrees” is Inanna. In Heaven, each of Inanna’s legs spans 15^0. Her two legs span the 30^0 required to “integrate” the 12 component triangles into a coherent whole. Opening her legs to 45^0 reaches into the material realm of the square, implying sexual rites with the mortal King.

> It was the Sumerian religious credo that the ritual marriage between the king of Sumer and this fertility goddess [Inanna], full of sexual allure, was essential for the fertility of the soil and

the fecundity of the womb, and of its people. The first Sumerian ruler who celebrated this rite, was the shepherd-king Dumuzi (the Biblical Tammuz) who reigned in Erech, one of Sumer's great urban centers, early in the third millennium B.C."[145]

Joseph Campbell equates Inanna with the Semitic Ishtar, and the Greek Aphrodite.[146] With the passage of each hour, day, month, year and Heavenly Age, each triangle in its turn emanates its divine forces. The "Gods in the Clock" are always in motion, continually emanating divine energy from their ever-changing Heavenly position. Within this dynamic astrological landscape, Inanna channels sexual desire as the bliss of salvation (Sanskrit: *Nirvana*).

The relevant trigonometric functions result from taking the ratio of a right triangle's line segments within time's unit circle as we track the angles of the Sun's path (Figures 29, 30a). This ratio determines the angle θ and locates point "P" on the circle, which can be plotted over time as a one-dimensional sine wave projection of uniform circular motion (Figure 30b). The cosecant function is a reciprocal of the sine function that defines simple harmonic motion. Greek tradition has labeled this mathematical musical system the "Music of the Spheres."

Figure 30b - Projected Circular Motion Defines the Sine and Cosine Waves of Simple Harmonics

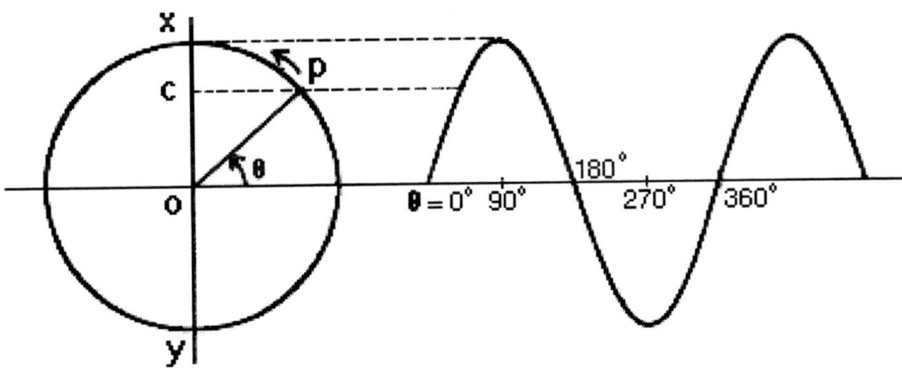

The heavenly body being tracked here is, of course, the Sun, and the Sun's perceived uniform circular motion "engraves" an orbital circle that never closes. It therefore traces a spiral path for the liberated soul to travel as "messenger" between Heaven and Earth. As the serpent circles the *Axis Mundi*, point "P" spins and marks off incremental degree approximations along the way. Capturing this motion requires all three pieces of this sacred cuneiform puzzle (Figure 31):

145 Kramer, Op.Cit., 305.
146 Joseph Campbell, *The Masks of God: Occidental Mythology* (New York: Viking Press, 1964) 73.

1. The Sumerian King List as the idealized 30^0 angle of the Tutelary deities
2. Plimpton 322, which tracks the Sun's hourly motion across the sky using degree increment approximations between 30^0 and 45^0
3. YBC 7289 encrypts Inanna's sexual embrace as the King looses his material self in the spiritual bliss of Nirvana. This Aryan-Semitic "Rorschach test" epitomizes the duality of Good and Evil, Heaven and Hell, and the ambiguity of liberation and death.

Figure 31 - The Sumerian-Babylonian Triptych Measuring the Journey of the Sun & Soul

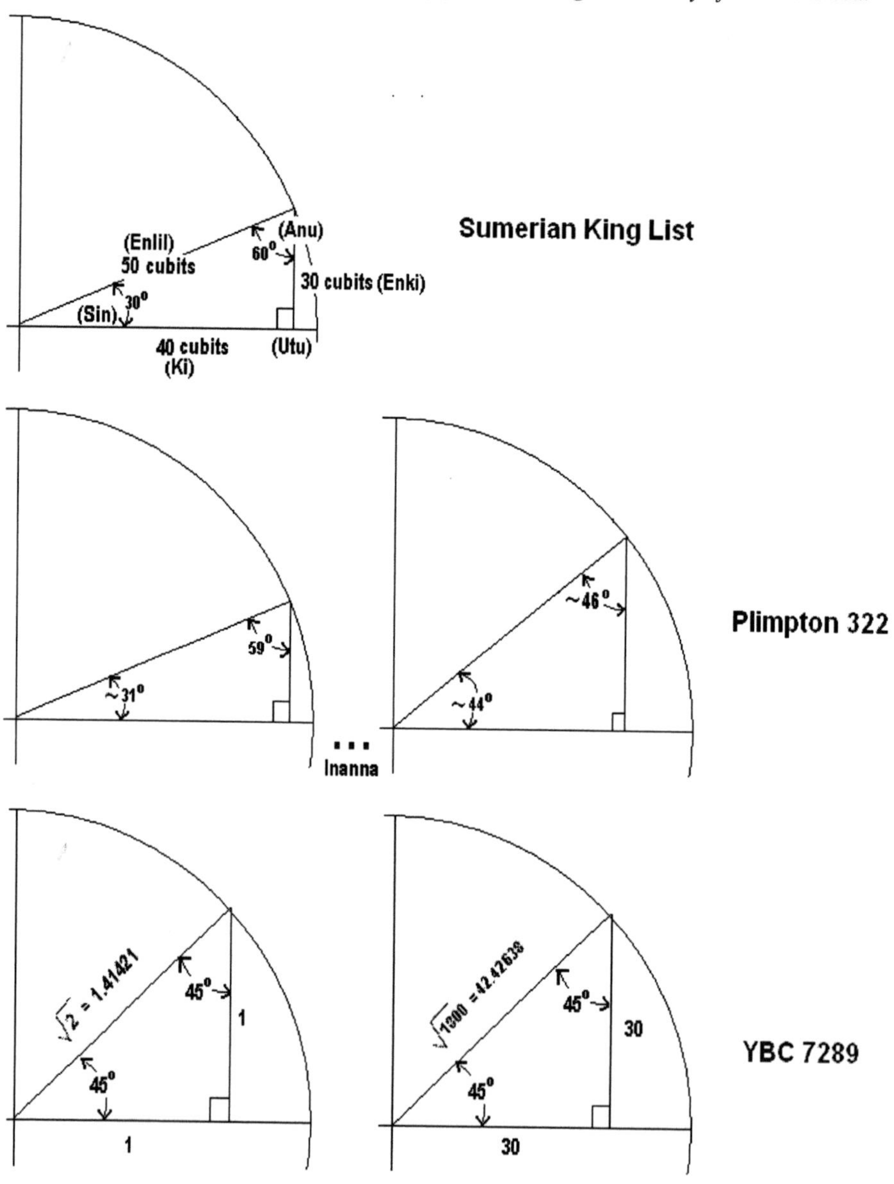

Ancient astronomers had a limited ability to peer into the Heavens. They certainly had no perspective like the one depicted in Figure 21a. They could only watch the sun rise and set in the sky and measure its path against the background stars during the Vernal Equinox. Each Heavenly Age forms 1/12 of the whole, and as Time passes with each new Age in Heaven, each new locus forms a "tonecircle and square within." The stone circle's snapshot of the sky on the Vernal Equinox might be thought of as a clock with stationary hands (as observed from within the stone circle), while the 12 numerals of the clock (the celestial dome of constellations) swirls around its stone "hands." Astronomers could "tell time" as the constellations slowly revolved around their archeoastronomical window.

The Sumerian interpretation of YBC 7289 as the mathematics of Inanna's Heavenly Union was generally interpreted as sin within the Semitic culture, thereby rendering *Moksha* and prophecy a great secret, restricted to the High Priests. The Aryan fathers of civilization made a sincere effort to explain their esoteric spiritual world within the context of exoteric material phenomena. Aryan priestly astronomers, who may well have mastered the art of liberating the soul, were no doubt excited by their discovery of a "wormhole" in the Heavens connecting the material and spiritual realms of Heaven and Earth. This slender thread to Heaven was connected to man as his Soul passed through the umbilical chord at birth, and "rose up" during *Moksha* or death.

When Semitic tribes first invaded the Aryan founders of ancient Sumer, a new Aryan-Semitic dynamic began to develop a fully articulated written record of the science of religion, rooted in the exact sciences of antiquity. The Aryan genetic predisposition for spirituality joined forces with the rigor of a skeptical and analytical Semitic mind, to produce ground-breaking progress for civilization — true progress — in which the Aryan-Semitic dynamic exhibited a balanced utilization of man's frontal lobes and limbic system. Discovering a detailed written explanation of the clock's integer harmonic ratios, even as late as 1800 BCE, should have no bearing on the likelihood that Ice Age priests were the earliest masters of space and time.

This new science of religion explains how to open the Gateway to Heaven by requiring the practitioner to transcend the duality of the "circle and the square within" in order to liberate the Soul. Aryan astronomers at *Göbekli Tepe* and *Karahundj* measured the Sun's progress from their vantage point on Earth. Plimpton 322's incremental tracking of a man's liberated soul, degree by degree, ascends along the sacred spiral engraved by the Sun's ecliptic across the 7 Heavens. Once a practitioner experienced the bliss of liberation associated with the goddess Inanna, the Gateway to the Gods was opened to them. The practice of *Moksha* leverages these sexual energies as they travel up the microcosm of man's Axis Mundi, the spinal chord. Attaining *Nirvana* in this manner implies the divine judgement to locate the mean between materiality and spirituality that manifests in the diameter/diagonal of the circle and the square inscribed within. Thus, the 12 harmonic aspects of polytheism's divine order were brought to life by the 7 Gods in the Clock. These "gods" were the liberated souls of the earliest Aryan priests to reach Heaven through *Moksha,* thus becoming the spiritual guides of the Sumerian Kings.

As the science of religion migrated from Mesopotamia to Egypt, it is significant to note that the Great Pyramid was located on the 30th parallel (30° North latitude), and, as archeoastronomical devices, the Pyramids were aligned to angles relevant to the Sumerian-Babylonian triptych just described. Perhaps, we should not be too quick to disparage early science, nor too quick to write off prehistoric man as primitive. The founders of civilization were very close to the mark being set by today's crop of theoretical physicists who seek to empirically establish a Theory of Everything based on the harmonic series — the same harmonic series that first defined the clock as the structure of the cosmos sometime between 4,000 and 1800 BCE, and possibly as early as 10,000 BCE.

The Holy Mountain as a Moment in Time

The Sumerian Ziggurats and Egyptian Pyramids were Holy Mountains. Egyptian Pyramids were also archeoastronomical devices, constructed in such a way that each pharaoh (considered an incarnation of the falcon god, Horus) could continue to engage in "navel gazing" even in death. As already mentioned, the Great Pyramid was located at 30* north latitude, and was aligned to angles relevant to the Sumerian-Babylonian triptych. Further down the Nile, the Egyptian stone circle, *Nabta Playa* (circa 4000 BCE) was exactly aligned with the solstice.

Robert Bauval and Graham Hancock suggest that the great monuments at Giza map the Heavens as they were when the vernal equinox was about to enter the constellation of Leo [ca. 10,360 BCE]. They also determined that the King's Chamber at 45^0 and the Queen's chamber, at 39.5 degrees (Figure 32), would have targeted the stars Zeta Orionis (Osiris) and Sirius (Isis).[147] This is consistent with the determination that the three pyramids at Giza correspond to the stars in Orion's belt: Zeta, Epsilon, and Delta Orionis. After the appropriate precessional adjustments are made, the southern shaft emanating from the Kings Chamber aligned with the brightest star of the Orion Belt, Zeta Orionis, while the northern shafts aligned to the ancient pole star Alpha Draconis (Kings Chamber) and to Beta Ursa Minor (Queens Chamber).[148]

---

147 Graham Hancock and Robert Bauval, "The Message of the Sphinx, A Quest for the Hidden Legacy of Mankind" (New York: Three Rivers Press, 1997).
148 Paul A. LaViolette, *Earth Under Fire: Humanity's Survival of the Ice Age* (Inner Traditions/Bear & Company, 2005)107.

The pyramids at Giza were completed around 2551 BCE, and if Bauval and Hancock are correct, the Egyptians would also have had knowledge of precession long before Babylon. This would be consistent with the historical migration of the science of religion as it has been presented here. The earliest Egyptian pyramids were, in fact, stepped ziggurats, designed by the Egyptian polymath ("Renaissance man") named Imhotep. The four sides of their base, like the Mesopotamian ziggurat, were aligned with the four fixed constellations and directions during the vernal equinox. The Egyptologist, Flinders Petrie, was Giza's first accurate surveyor of "the circle and square within." He found that the ratio of its perimeter to its height was 1760/280 cubits, which equated to 2π (with $\pi \sim 22/7$) with an accuracy of ~.05%. Petrie concluded: "The relations of areas and of circular ratios are so systematic that we should grant that they were in the builder's design."[149]

Figure 32 - The Great Pyramids as Archeoastronomical Devices

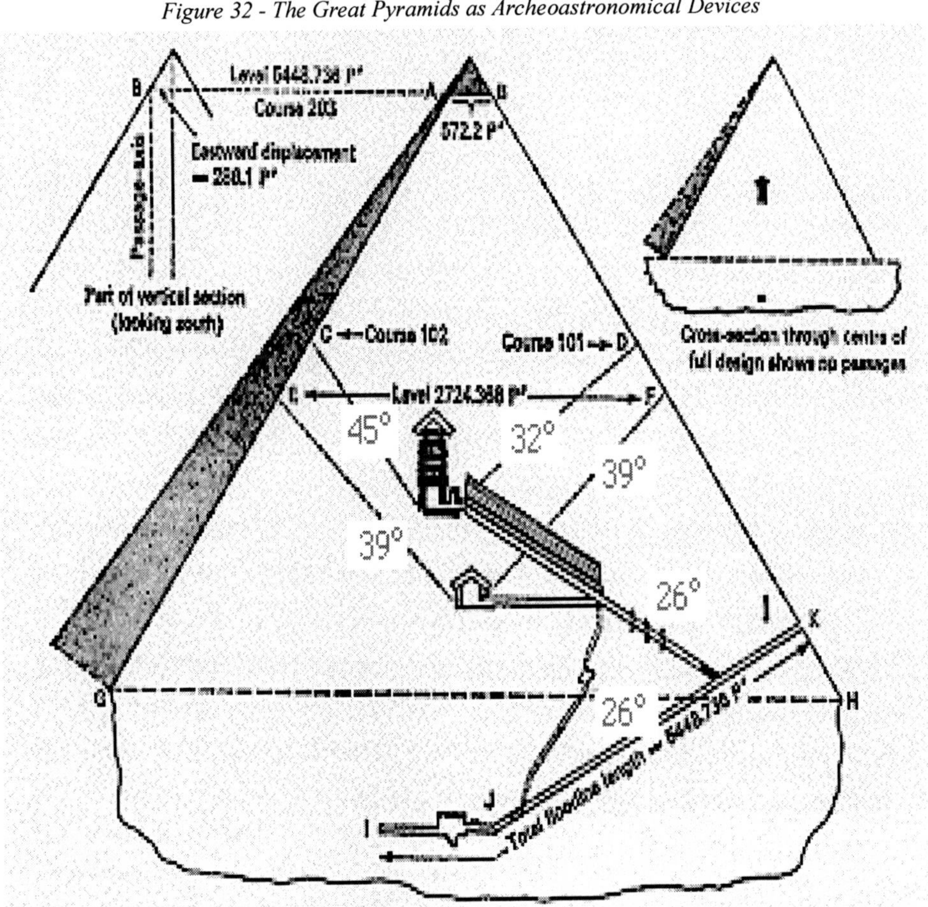

149 Flinders Petrie, Wisdom of the Egyptians (London, British School of Archeology in Egypt and B.Quaritch ltd., 1940) 30.

The Science of Religion

The Sumerian King List's is history's first record of the clock as a harmonic series — the scientific framework of all religion. Each of the various octave-double subsets within the Clock of Heaven: 72:144, 360:720, 432:864,... became significant as the transposed musical framework of the world's religious cultures and allegorical contexts. It is critical to recognize that all such subsets derive from the harmonic series as defined by the early King List.

For example, modern Kabbalah is largely based on the work of Isaac Luria (the *Ari*), who described the 72 Names of God as the root of a system that he called *Tzimtzum* (Contraction of Divine Light).[150] The octave double 72:144 also describes the Kabbalah of Christianity as encrypted within the Book of Revelation.[151] We have already discussed the Hindu World Soul (Brahma) that arises from Vishnu's navel as 432:864; as well as the Navel of Order within the 360:720 octave that was common to the *Rig Veda* and the *Sefer Yetzirah*. The various octave doubles must all be understood as important subsets of the clock's integer ratios 1 - 12 that define the following harmonic series.

72:144:216:288:360:432:504:578:648:720:792:864
1 2 3 4 5 6 7 8 9 10 11 12

We have presented the case for considering three cuneiform tablets as a single *oeuvre*. They form three distinct components that track the Sun's apparent motion[152] across the heavens and through the Ages. And, when this numerology was sightly revised to reflect the Sun's 15° hourly increments and 360° orbit, its circular motion projects the sine and cosine waves of simple harmonic motion that structures Figures 23a, 26b, and 31.

We have presented arguments suggesting that this "Divine Triptych" is the founding document of religion, and precursor to the Holy Trinity. Theologically, it describes the gods who inhabit the Kingdom of Heaven (the Father); it describes *Moksha* as the process of "giving up the ghost" and tracking the Holy Ghost's ascent (i.e., the Soul's ascent) toward the Gates of *Sheol*; and, finally, it describes any "Son of God" who passes through the Gates of *Sheol* in order to conquer death and attain divinity. In Chapter 14, we will see that the heart of the Torah is the Sabbath. And, according to the Jewish Kabbalistic tradition described in the Zohar: "My Sabbaths, God

150 Schatz, Op.Cit., 83-84.
151 McClain, Myth of Invariance, 109-110.
152 It doesn't hurt to remind ourselves that the Sun's apparent motion is an amalgam of the Earth's daily rotation on its axis, and its yearly orbit around the Sun.

said, denotes the circle and the square within."[153] As religion's foundation document, this ancient triptych completes religion's defining puzzle.

The invention of the clock, as documented within the Divine Triptych, is the high point of Sumerian culture as a comprehensive integration of the Quadrivium's mathematical disciplines: arithmetic, music, geometry, and astronomy. This early Sumerian version of the Greek "Music of the Spheres" defines the structure of sound as integer multiples of what today's scientists call a harmonic series. For the ancients, these integer multiples integrated the structure of sound and light to define the "substance" (Greek: *ousia*; Hebrew: *pnimiyut*) of polytheism's gods and monotheism's God. This divine substance was then used to construct the Soul, Time, and the Universe. The mathematical and scientific details of this divine "Blueprint" has been lost to civilization for thousands of years — until now.

Divine emanations are "musical" (or rather, sonic) vibrations, that are tightly coupled to the geometry and trigonometry of circles and spheres, squares and cubes, triangles and pyramids — none of which exists in a static state. It is time, as measured by the Clock of Heaven and Earth, that sets the geometry in motion as a function of astronomy. Within monotheism, the primary focus was shifted away from astronomy and the "gods in the clock." Monotheism de-emphasized the external astrological influence of multiple distant gods. Instead, these divine energies manifest as a unified divinity within each man.

The Torah's 12 tribes of Israel were "Sons of Heaven" in the same manner that the first 8 Sumerian Kings were considered "Sons of Heaven." Abraham brilliantly retained the harmonic series as the mathematical Blueprint of God and Creation, but switched the ancient sexagesimal focus from 12 to a decimal focus of 10 emanations; which became the *pnimiyut* (inner vibrational essence) of the Torah's Ten Commandments and Ten Plagues. In other words, the oldest sexagesimal artifact, the clock, is religion's predecessor to the Ten Commandments. In the next chapter we will study the mathematical details of how these 10 emanations originated in the "Voice of God" as the essence and sustenance of Creation (see Appendix: Primer on Music).

Abraham was apparently successful in helping civilization switch from Sumer and Babylon's sexagesimal system to Egypt and Israel's decimal system. Civilization has retained the clock, but it is no longer thought of as a religious artifact. Since telling time has become such a frequent and mundane task, perhaps we should keep it in mind that the divine forces of Heaven originally emanated from Heaven's Clock, introducing both science and religion to civilization. What is most significant about the science of religion is that both the Eastern and Western approach are based on the harmonic series as the "divine and eternal truth," and thus all religions share this empirical common ground with modern physics.

---

153 Zohar Prologue 5b -6a.

PART II:

THE HISTORY & SCIENCE OF MONOTHEISM

Figure 33 - Abraham's Journey

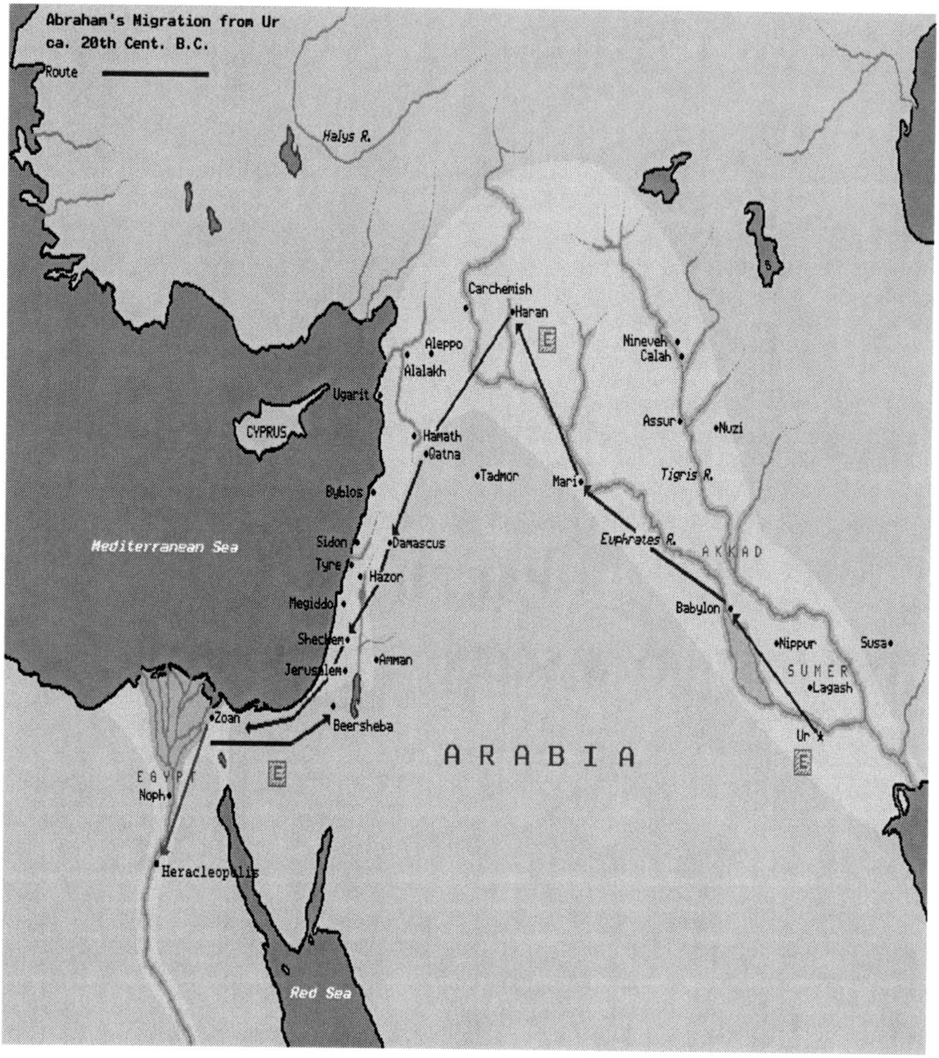

Chapter 6: The Great Patriarch of Monotheism

The Lost Word of God

Abraham's *Sefer Yetzirah* defines the "Living God" as the first theory of everything. It synthesizes a new numeral system based on the sexagesimal mathematics of ancient Sumer and Babylon (Base-60); on the decimal mathematics of ancient Egypt and Canaan (Base-10); and, on the septenary mathematics (Base-7) of Mitanni. Abraham's scientific observations of sound and light verified this integration of forces as a natural phenomenon, stressing the unity of the one God over the diversity of many gods. From a mathematical perspective Abraham's monotheism would be called a "mixed-base" numeral system.

Whether or not Abraham actually lived is a valid question. Whoever actually wrote this important sacred text is the man we have come to know as the great patriarch Abraham. This short treatise transformed religion from a homage to the golden age of "gods on the mountain" into the science of a "Living God" who is accessible to all men through the ancient and sacred meditation practice of the Aryan founders. The *Sefer Yetzirah* has been slow to yield its secrets, because scholars and clerics have never understood that music theory is necessary to integrate the separate mathematical axioms of the Quadrivium into a comprehensive cosmology, cosmogony, and ontology.

Today, religion and science are often considered mutually exclusive. But, we have seen that a form of monotheism originally developed from the astronomy and astrology of Inanna's sexual cult, guiding mankind through Heavenly emanations from the 7 gods in the clock. Abraham's great contribution to science and religion is based on his observation that light and sound are complex emanations that harmonize together into the Unity of a *Living God*. Ernest McClain points out that "the Indian tradition also emphasizes the 'luminous nature of sound' in the similarity between *svar* (light) and *svara* (sound)."[154] He also quotes Marius Schneider, who affirms that "sound represents the original substance of the world."[155] From a modern scientific perspective, we are aware of the close mathematical relationship between light and sound, since they are both examples of wave phenomena.

154 McClain, *The Myth of Invariance*, Op.Cit., 7.
155 Marius Schneider, "Primitive Music," *The New Oxford History of Music*, vol. I (London: Oxford University Press, 1957) 43.

What distinguishes Abraham's text is its stress on mathematical unity over its diverse energetic components. In other words, One God became more important than many gods, and the diversity within divine unity became the "Blueprint of Creation." The dualism between unity and diversity is embodied by the harmonic series — the "rainbow principle" — a natural phenomenon that defines the God of Abraham. God and His Blueprint are encrypted within the Ineffable Name (**יהוה** = YHVH). Abraham's text encrypts mathematical instructions on how to "pronounce" YHVH in order to liberate one's Soul from the container of one's body.[156]

Joseph Gikatilla, in his *Sha'arei Orah* states, "The entire Torah is like an explication of, and commentary on, the Ineffable Name of God."[157] Since the time of Solomon's Temple, the High Priests of the temple and the Jewish population must say the word *Adonai* (**אדני**) instead of YHVH (*Jehovah* or *Yahweh* to the English speaking world). The three faiths each believe that their holy book is the "Word of God," but before these holy books existed there was only one Word of God, YHVH. The last High Priest of Solomon's Temple died protecting its sacred mysteries:

- Only Abraham's text explains the transcendental meaning and "pronunciation" of YHVH, the secret of secrets within monotheism.
- Only Abraham's writings explicitly instruct mankind in a non-verbal "pronunciation" of YHVH. By this I mean that Abraham provides step-by-step instructions on how to articulate the deep meditation practice of Biblical prophets that purifies the body and liberates the soul in order to enter what the New Testament's *Epistle to the Hebrews* calls the "everlasting priesthood."[158]
- Abraham's writings explain Christianity's "Sacred mystery of the Holy Trinity," based on the "Holy Trinity" of letters, **יהו** – YHV, within the Holy Tetragrammaton.[159]

Abraham passed knowledge of the Word to his heirs as the birthright of Israel's patriarchs, who became the "Anointed One" of each generation, including Abraham's descendants Isaac, Jacob, and Joseph. The Book of Genesis tells us that Jacob's son Joseph was sold into slavery by his brothers, and taken to Egypt, where he soon rose to prominence as Viceroy of Egypt by interpreting the pharaoh's dream and saving the country from famine. Joseph, as magistrate, sent for his father Jacob (who God renamed Israel) and his brothers, and saved them all from famine.

The Biblical timeline of these events roughly corresponds to the historical timeline when invading Hyksos tribes took control and reigned in the

156 Schatz, Op.Cit., *The Lost Word of God*, 187-199; Provides a detailed mathematical analysis of the Word of God, YHVH.
157 Scholem, Gershom, Kabbalah (New York-Jerusalem: Keter Publishing House, 1974) 171.
158 Hebrews 8:24.
159 Robert Macoy, *General History, Cyclopedia and Dictionary of Freemasonry* (New York: Masonic Publishing Company, 1869) 554.

delta region of what was called lower Egypt during the 15th and 16th Dynasties (circa 1800 - 1550 BCE). A lack of Egyptian records during this period makes it difficult to verify whether ancient historians Manetho and Josephus are correct in identifying the Israelite Exodus with the Hyksos "shepherd kings" who ruled and ultimately left Egypt and returned to Jerusalem. The Canaanite origin of the Hyksos, however, has been well established by archeological connections.[160]

The Bible's version of these events, in Exodus 1:7-8, states: "The children of Israel were fruitful, teemed, increased and became strong – very, very much so; and the land became filled with them. A new king arose in Egypt, who did not know of Joseph. He said to his people, "Behold! The people, the Children of Israel, are more numerous and stronger than we. Come, let us outsmart it lest it become numerous and it may be that if a war will occur, it, too, may join our enemies, and wage war against us and go up from the land." During the next three generations, the Book of Exodus tells us that Israel was enslaved and oppressed, and knowledge of the Word of God was lost.

Once knowledge of the Word of God was lost, it had to be revealed to mankind once more. This became the revelation of Moses on Mount Sinai. Jewish tradition tells us that Moses was given the "Written Law" (the Torah) on Mount Sinai, as well as the inner meaning of the Written Law, which is called the "Oral Law." The Oral Law was the scientific framework of religion that was transmitted orally from generation to generation. After Solomon's Temple was destroyed (ca. 586 BCE), most of this knowledge was, once again, lost. What remained of the Oral Law was first written down around 200 CE by the rabbinical establishment,[161] and it was called the *Mishnah.* After several more centuries, this preservation effort began anew, resulting in the *Gemara*, circa 500 CE. Collectively, the *Mishnah* and *Gemara* form the Talmud, Judaism's second most important set of books after the Torah.

Jewish Orthodox tradition maintains that the *Sefer Yetzirah* is the seminal work of Kabbalah, and the only text attributed to Abraham. It is generally considered the mystical key to the Oral tradition that describes the deepest meaning of the Torah. The inner meaning of the Written Law does not easily lend itself to the type of legalistic discussion or debate that characterizes the Talmud. To be authentic, the *Sefer Yetzirah* would have to be older than the oldest pages of the Torah. However, the oldest extant version of Abraham's text has been dated by philologists to somewhere between the 2nd and 6th century CE, approximately 2000 years after Abraham would have lived. The dating of this ancient text is generally accepted by the secular academic community, however, the methodology used to date this text appears to be fundamentally flawed.

160 The Oxford History of the Bible, ed. by Michael D. Coogan (New York: Oxford University Press, 1998) 74.
161 The rabbinate began with the elder sages of Sanhedrin led by Hillel (ca. 1st century BCE).

The Book of Creation was written in mathematical riddles, and since rabbis, secular scholars, and philologists, have never understood the ancient music theory that is necessary to decipher the meaning of these riddles, the text could never be properly understood; therefore, the true origin of this text has never been determined. It is also significant that any date offered up by linguists ignores the important role of the Jewish oral tradition in transmitting ancient religious texts through time. The conclusions, therefore, of those who study form rather than content, must be considered highly suspect. As a direct result of my own efforts to decipher the meaning of this text, it is clear to me that the mathematical framework of the *Sefer Yetzirah* determines the very nature of monotheistic theology, just as it shapes all Biblical allegory — and, not the other way around — as some would suggest, in which an imagined Neo-Platonist retrofit the mathematics to Biblical allegory. The complexity of the mathematics, and how it is interwoven into the entire warp and woof of the Torah, precludes that possibility. My own expertise in Biblical music theory (i.e., Kabbalah) convinces me of the book's antiquity, as well as its authenticity as the scientific and theological foundation of the Torah and Tanakh — which in turn, became the model for both the New Testament and the Koran.

Without implying that the revelation on Mount Sinai was anything less than holy, there may be have been a practical reason for writing the Torah. The authors of the Torah understood Abraham's work, but they also realized that the genius of this great sage would be lost to posterity unless it was recorded in a more accessible form. That momentous decision resulted in the creation of the *Torah,* which, as I will demonstrate, is based on Abraham's mathematical framework.

The Word of God, *YHVH*, like the Torah itself, attempts to communicate the origins of the universe, and teach mankind how to pray like the prophets portrayed in the Bible. The real difference between the two texts is that the *Sefer Yetzirah* teaches the mathematical complexities and meaning of *YHVH*, as well as how to "pronounce" it; while the Torah allegorizes and codifies that information into an actionable set of *do's* and *don'ts* that mathematically derives directly from *YHVH.* As civilization's first "Theory of Everything" (TOE), both the *Sefer Yetzirah* and the Torah encrypt the same "eternal truth," but the Torah introduces a "yoga" of 365 prohibitive commandments to purify the body, and 248 positive commandments to liberate the Soul; while the *Sefer Yetzirah* explains the mathematical derivation and underlying science of the numbers 365 and 248, as well as the details as to why and how the commandments work.

As the patriarch of Judaism, Christianity, and Islam, Abraham is said to have lived seven generations before the Commandments were revealed to Moses, yet rabbis tell us that Abraham understood the essence of these Commandments better than anyone. It is for this reason that Saint Paul made Abraham the model of Christian faith — because he was in God's Grace before the Law was ever revealed to Moses. Paul believed that God's Law was inscribed in Abraham's heart. Similarly, before Mohammed wrote the Koran, he was a *Hanif* who sought "the true religion of Abraham" as it existed before Judaism and Christianity came into being. Abraham understood the truth of God's Law because, in a real sense, he was the author of the Torah insofar as his scientific framework shaped it in all its aspects and layers of meaning. Abraham communicated knowledge of *Yahweh* within the mathematical and scientific framework of 10 *pnimiyut* (the essence of the Ten Commandments) and 613 derived *pnimiyut.*[162] It is important to recognize that the mathematical context of the Quadrivium was couched within the ambiguity of language and culture. Nevertheless, it can always be reduced back to its mathematical form in order to clarify any theological ambiguities, misconceptions, or conflicts.

Da Vinci used mirror writing to encrypt his notebooks, but his method pales in comparison to how just four Hebrew letter symbols could encrypt the essence of the entire Torah. Perhaps a more accurate analogy might be the complexities encrypted in *YHVH* versus the complexities encrypted in the symbols: $E=mc^2$. In Part III, arguments will be presented suggesting that *YHVH* and $E=mc^2$ are conceptually analogous mathematical "formulas," but *YHVH* actually includes the mathematical core of Superstring Theory, which was first presented in 1984, almost 70 years after Einstein presented his Theory of Relativity.

Over the centuries, none of the great rabbis and scholars who have written translations and commentaries on Abraham's text have ever learned the music theory necessary to integrate the separate disciplines of the Quadrivium. As a result, the great patriarch's writings have remained a great mystery, even to the likes of such legendary rabbis, scholars, and Kabbalists as Saadia Gaon, Joseph Gikatilla, Chaim Vital, and Isaac Luria (the Ari). There is, however, some evidence that Abraham Abulafia may have appreciated the importance of music theory to a proper understanding of Scripture.[163]

Training in the axioms of the separate mathematical disciplines: arithmetic, music, geometry, and astronomy, does not go far enough. Even the vast knowledge of Judaism's foremost expert on "the wise men of Athens," Moses Maimonides (the Rambam), has never been able to synthesize a comprehensive scientific framework capable of reconciling the *Sefer Yetzirah's* Word of God (YHVH) with the Torah. The last High Priest's of Solomon's Temple died protecting their knowledge of deep meditation as the key to prophecy. The 10 Commandments defines the structure of sound and light that resonates within us (often referred to as our "mantra" and "aura," respectively). These 10 vibrations integrate the Quadrivium's separate disciplines, while deep meditation empowers our consciousness to embrace them. Thus, the harmonic series describes the "first principles" of both science and religion.

162 The rabbis tell us that all 613 Commandments derive directly from the original 10, but they have no idea what that mathematics actually looks like.

163 Gershom Scholem, Kabbalah (New York- Jerusalem: Keter Publishing House, 1974) 180.

The ancient Greek philosopher Plato may have been the last person to fully grasp the significance of music theory as the key to the science of religion. Philo of Alexandria (20 BCE - 50 CE) believed that both Pythagoras and Plato learned their theology from the Torah, while the Church father and Platonist, Clement of Alexandria, regarded Plato as an "Attic Moses," i.e., a Greek version of Moses.

The Bible tells us that Abraham was born in the city of Ur (circa 1800 BCE), traveled to Canaan, and then sojourned in Egypt, almost 1000 years before the oldest pages of the Hebrew Scriptures were written. Discontent with the inaccuracies and cumbersome nature of the Sumerian/Babylonian mathematics that he inherited, the author of the *Sefer Yetzirah* began by observing nature; specifically, the behavior of light and sound. Abraham mathematically defined the *Living God* as a harmonic series: the essence and sustenance of the manifest world. Since the formulation of Superstring Theory in 1984, theoretical physics has acknowledged the central role of the harmonic series as the scientific basis for a theory of everything.

This implies that the God of Abraham did not originate out of man's psychological need for a father figure, nor from man's desire to control the weather or defeat his enemies. The Torah adopted Abraham's concept of God directly from the *Sefer Yetzirah's* scientific framework. The authors of the Torah, taking their cue from Abraham's anthropomorphic description of God as a *Living God*, describe Him as having appeared to Abraham in human form — as a house guest. It is the Torah's dramatic personalization of God that would have filled the public's psychological need for a father figure. It portrays God in anthropomorphic terms, as someone who mankind could talk to, confide in, and pray to; a being who was capable of taking sides in a dispute. However, Abraham's *Living God* was mathematically and scientifically conceived as a transcendent and ethereal "Being."[164] Giving God human traits made Him more accessible to mankind, and contributed to making the Bible popular, but the Torah's anthropomorphic personalization of God does not accurately reflect Abraham's original definition of the Living God. It is from this distorted anthropomorphic perspective that Christ became a personification of YHVH[165] within Christian doctrine. Becoming "One with the LORD" is not the same as being the LORD. For Christians, Christ is the LORD. This dogmatic notion demonstrates a serious disconnect with Abrahamic monotheism.

The *Sefer Yetzirah* is a mathematical and theological treatise. Like the Sumerian King List, it explains natural phenomena through mathematics. It is important to note that the Sumerian gods and the Semitic God were both defined by a harmonic series. The transcendent unity of the rainbow principle of light and sound is a natural phenomena structured by the harmonic series. This Omnipresent *Living God* transcends any material instantiation of those harmonics, and the

---

164 A concept consistent with Aristotle's "Unmoved Mover" and the "Five Proofs" of St. Thomas Aquinas.
165 The King James version of the Bible translates YHVH to *Jehovah*, but today, Christian tradition commonly uses the Septuagint's translation of the Hebrew *Adonai* ("My Lord") as Kyrios ("Lord"). Due to the ambiguities of the Holy Trinity, Christ has become personified as the LORD Himself.

complex vibrations that emanates from this transcendent Source is the essence and sustenance of each object and being in Creation.

Abraham's writings were revolutionary, insofar as his concept of the One God absorbed the entire pantheon of ancient Mesopotamian and Egyptian gods and goddesses, both logically and theologically. This was parodied in the Biblical story of how Moses' staff became a serpent that swallowed up the serpent's of Egyptian magicians. It is from this perspective that we begin our study of Abraham's science and how it rigorously shaped the Bible's rich allegorical narrative.

According to Kabbalistic tradition, the four mathematical disciplines of the Quadrivium were recorded on the "Pillars of Seth" when "God destroyed the world by flood and flame."[166] Unfortunately, the rabbinical tradition has never understood how Kabbalistic number (Hebrew: *gematria*) extends into the mathematics of the Quadrivium. The purest form of Abrahamic monotheism derives from that mathematics within the Sefer Yetzirah. And, within that mathematical context, musical harmonics describes the "language of God" capable of correcting any historical distortions imposed by language, culture, and the variations of religious dogma.

Breaking with Aryan Tradition

Some within the Jewish Orthodox community might fear that the advances of modern science implies a diminishing of the miracle at Mount Sinai as the authoritative foundation for fulfilling God's Commandments. Much to the contrary, by staying true to Abraham's writings ,we are able to explain the mystery behind the miracle of revelation with an unprecedented empirical understanding of God and the Commandments. Scientific understanding may be even more compelling than blind faith. Only the *Sefer Yetzirah* explains how to achieve the meditative intent (*kavanah*) necessary to fulfill all the Commandments. What is being presented here should not be considered a modern interpretation of the Torah, but rather, a rediscovery of the Torah's source material that explains the original intent of its authors.

Abraham's legacy taught the patriarchs, the prophets, and the High Priests how to "conquer" death. The writings of Abraham provide access to the most sophisticated meditation methods of the Aryan fathers. It is a methodology that can also be found in the *Sefer Yetzirah's* Eastern counterpart, the *Rig Veda*. Both texts and cultures share the sacred deep meditation practice, as well as the "Navel of Order" that defines time as a subset of the original Sumerian Clock (Figures 26a & b). What differs most dramatically between East and West are their respective notions about sin and morality that derives from their philosophical differences about how

166 Seth was Adam's third son. Josephus tells us that the Pillars of Seth were still to be seen in his day. In the works of Manetho, 300 years prior to Josephus, Manetho declares that he had seen them, but that they were engraved by Thoth. Thoth, Hermes, Seth and Enoch, essentially fulfilled the same functions in their respective cultures. A syncretistic approach suggests that there may have been different names used by distinct cultures to represent the same divine beings..

to reach Heaven. Over the centuries, monotheism and polytheism appear to have evolved into mutually exclusive theologies, but, they did not begin that way.

Before the God of Abraham became the embodiment of Divine Unity, the ritual marriage between the King of Sumer and Inanna was the great unifier of spiritual energy and the material world. It is no wonder that the moral sensibilities of invading Semitic tribes parodied these sexual rites within a Garden of purity in which the shame of Adam and Eve was awakened by knowledge of what was Good and what was Evil. The invading Semitic neophytes morally struggled with the Aryan concept of channeling their sexual energies into the bliss of liberation through Moksha. The invading Semitic tribes had trouble ascribing lofty spiritual goals to either ceremonial or tantric sex. Perhaps it is not that they were unable to harness their sexual energies, but they were clearly unwilling to do so. Sumerian sexual practices seemed morally wrong. For them, there had to be a better way to reach Heaven. A Semite whose moral compass became a psychological barrier could not easily envision their future in Heaven as an immortal. Thus, Aryan Moksha was not embraced as a way of life. About 2000 years later, during the time of Abraham, the Semitic focus would finally switch from the immortal gods in Heaven to the moral divinity within each of us on Earth. Liberation of the Soul was no longer limited to the sexual rite of Kings. It could now be attained by all righteous and chaste Children of Abraham who inherited a knowledge of the Word. However, the holy books of a developing monotheism would depend on the birthright of the "Anointed Ones," a handful of patriarchs, who, like the Sumerian Kings, were taught to "travel the Heavens."

The Semitic preoccupation with sin may well have been a significant factor in driving the development of mathematics and science throughout the Old Babylonian period. And, the evolution of the exact sciences must certainly be considered great progress for civilization. However, the Semitic preoccupation with sin has influenced the Western psyche to operate from a baseline of inherent sin and moral dilemma. Moralistic judgement and self-judgement, along with the accompanying guilt and recrimination, creates inner turmoil and stress that characterizes a great deal of Western life. Generally speaking, the monotheistic faiths do not meditate, and, as a result, high levels of stress have contributed significantly to their "warring nature." To quote Christopher Marlowe: "Nature that framed us of four elements, warring within our breast for regiment, doth teach us all to have aspiring minds."

This basic difference between the Eastern and Western theological self-image has had a profound effect on all aspects of civilization, and perhaps, on our evolution as a species. In Vajrayana Buddhism, deity yoga empowers the practitioner to imagine that they are in essence, the same as the Buddha. If Westerners primarily see themselves as sinners, rather than as inherently divine, it becomes impossible to follow in the footsteps of spiritual leaders like Moses, Christ, or

Mohammed. Their holiness is seen as unique and unattainable by lowly sinners, therefore the Gateway to Heaven remains closed. The virtues of knowledge and wisdom, and the "divine gifts" of prophecy and healing, require a strengthening of the limbic system through deep meditation.

God prophesied to the Israelites: "You shall be to Me a kingdom of priests and a holy nation" (Exodus 19:6). Based on these stated intentions, all the "Children of Abraham" should feel compelled to learn Abraham's sacred meditation practice; a practice that the Bible tells us will empower Israel to become a nation of prophets. Studying the Bible "through the eyes of Abraham" will teach us that returning to Jerusalem from "the four corners of the earth" does not necessarily imply that Jews must return to the geographical Israel. We must learn to recognize metaphor when we see it. Israel must finally be understood as it was originally conceived — as a spiritual destination. To fulfill the prophecy of building a Third Temple within the spiritual high ground of a New Jerusalem, all the Children of Abraham are obliged to follow his teachings on how to construct that Temple within, thus becoming an integral part of the New Jerusalem in the prophesied "world to come."

The *Sefer Yetzirah's* message was intended for all Abrahamic faiths. In Part II, we will carefully examine Scripture with an eye toward what Karen Armstrong elegantly described as "the kernel of truth that lay at the heart of all the various historical religions."[167] The 12 divine harmonic emanations that form the Aryan Clock of Heaven and Earth evolved into Abraham's 10 divine harmonic emanations that are the essence of the Ten Commandments. This provides us with a profound mathematical and scientific common ground describing the objective and empirical foundation of religion, to which all can subscribe. It provides the world with a comprehensive scientific framework for interfaith discussion, reconciliation, and peace.

With the treasure of the Aryan and Abrahamic legacies in hand, we can better appreciate meditation as religion's sacred practice. Our hypothesis has suggested that meditation was the driving force that shaped pre-historic civilization from the end of the Last Ice Age, circa 10,500 BCE, through the beginnings of recorded history (circa 4000 BCE), to the present time. Meditation has always been mankind's inner compass, pointing him toward true North.

The Jewish Orthodox tradition tells us that the author of the *Sefer Yetzirah* was the Biblical patriarch Abraham. Whoever wrote this ancient and sacred text would have been born in the right time and place to absorb the great mathematical, scientific and spiritual advances of Sumer, Babylon, Mitanni, and Egypt. Biblical allegory describes "Abraham's Journey" (Figure 33) as a chronological record of those influences. Similarly, seven generations after Abraham, his direct descendant Moses was raised as an Egyptian prince. This provided Moses with the opportunity for a similarly auspicious education in the mathematics and science of his time.

167 Armstrong, Op.Cit., 173.

Chapter 7: How to Read the Bible

Three Layers of Meaning

The authors of the Bible never intended it to be taken literally. Its content goes much deeper than that. Scripture relies on symbolism, metaphor and allegory, accompanied by enough historical and geographical information to blur the line between myth and reality. Unfortunately, through the centuries, it has left the reader to his or her own devices to discover more than the simple morality of "Do Good and Refrain from Evil." Finding revelation in Scripture requires some knowledge of mathematics and music theory. It will be demonstrated that the entire Hebrew Scripture — as well as the meaning and pronunciation of the Word of God, *YHVH* — derives from the *Sefer Yetzirah*, the only text attributed to Abraham. Therefore, the Bible can only deliver on its great promise of knowledge and wisdom if we can learn to read it "through the eyes of Abraham." After many years spent deciphering the mathematical allegories in Abraham's text, it has become clear to me that the author(s) of the Torah remained true to the framework of mathematics and science set out by Abraham in his seminal work. In other words, the Torah was written to bring Abraham's "theory of everything" to the world, or, at least to his descendants, the "Children of Abraham."

In the first Stanza of the Hebrew text, Abraham instructs us about Creation's three layers of meaning:

And He created the universe
with three books (Sepharim),
with text (Sepher)
with number (Sephar)
and with sound[168] *(Sippur)*

Abraham's approach reveals its meaning in the mathematical and scientific layer that lies beneath any literal, allegorical, or numerological interpretations. It is the third layer of Abraham's approach that reveals its true meaning. The "gnostic hypothesis" being presented here focuses on understanding this content at its deepest level. It asserts that Wellhausen's "Documentary Hypothesis" is limited by the principles of philology, which, by definition, stresses form over content.[169]

168 Literally: "*and with telling*"; The *Sefer Yetzirah* describes God's "*Ten Sefirot of Nothingness*" that Created the universe. Jewish tradition calls them "*10 Utterances.*"

169 Julius Wellhausen, *Composition des Hexateuch* (Verlag Classic Edition, 2010); Wellhausen's "documentary hypothesis" may be the most significant development in Biblical literary criticism in

It may be surprising to discover that Plato's writings must also be read using Abraham's method. Philo suggested that Plato got his metaphysics from the Hebrews, which implies that Plato's multi-layered approach found its precedent in the mathematical allegories of the Torah. Chapter 6 attempted to explain in general terms, how Abraham's treatise structures monotheistic theology and shapes all Biblical allegory, but the remaining chapters of Part II will describe the mathematics and science of Scripture in detail. Abraham's writings teach us that the universal language of mathematics and music defines and explains God and Creation.[170] His writings accomplish this task eloquently, comprehensively, with no ambiguity — and with considerably less dependence on geometry and astronomy than Abraham's Sumerian and Babylonian predecessors.

Throughout history, religion has been a highly subjective topic. Most people are born into the context of a particular faith and culture, and, generally speaking, they are provided with guidelines and parameters for what to think and how to behave within that context. There are also many who reject religion entirely, for any number of reasons, and, there are many of us who have come to believe in a personalized God that they can speak to and pray to. They ask Him to comfort them when they are afraid, and to heal them when they are sick. They ask Him to win their wars, and to find their house keys when they are lost. Once people grow comfortable with their own subjective views about God, whatever they might be, they tend to become highly resistant to change, or to any suggestion of change. Each person's concept of God may have taken years to develop, but that concept is often transformed into the "ground" we walk on. In that figurative sense, Abraham's three layers of meaning rudely shifts the ground beneath our feet, by revealing, in the words of monotheism's most authoritative source, that the roots of religion are empirically-based rather than faith-based.

There may even be a need to mitigate the powerful impact of explaining God from an objective, scientific perspective — especially since it would be difficult for even the great prophets to quibble with the father of their faith. Modern science has had religion on the defensive for quite a long time. However, Abraham's text completely levels the playing field among clergy, scientists and atheists. Many may need time to adjust and assimilate this information, but, on the whole, religious traditionalists can breath a sigh of relief that science has not come to bury religion, but to empirically prove God's existence. Abraham's three layers of meaning also establishes him as a pioneer of modern science. His methodology included careful observation of natural phenomena, experimentation, and extensive mathematical calculations to verify various aspects of the "theory of everything" that Abraham called the "*Living God.*"

---

the past 200 hundred years. It assumes that the Torah has at least four identifiable authors that predate its compilation into the Hebrew Canon by centuries. It was developed in 1877.

170 Schatz, *The Lost Word of God*, Op.Cit.,

Layer 1 - Text

The textual layer of the Bible can be thought of as a garment — like an overcoat — that insulates the reader from its deepest meaning. The innermost layer of mathematics and sound is what actually defines the essence of God and Creation. If God's Light is metaphorically "blinding," we might also say that Scripture wraps God's Light in text, so we are not overwhelmed. Understanding God in the empirical terms that He was originally conceived of is not a trivial thing, but it is certainly possible, as long as we attempt to master all three layers of meaning.

Historically, it has been difficult for man to think about God in logical terms, let alone mathematical and scientific terms. However, most of us can bear witness to the fact that even the most well articulated verbal description of God falls short of being able to adequately define or describe God. How then, could the average rabbi even imagine that a single Word, YHVH, was able to explicate the entire Torah — as Abraham Abulafia, Joseph Gikatilla, and other Kabbalists believe.

In the Middle Ages, the 7 Liberal Arts included the ancient Quadrivium's four mathematical disciplines, as well as the Trivium's language disciplines: grammar, logic, and rhetoric. However, no language expert, past or present, is up to the task of explaining God; partly because of the vague and ambiguous nature of language, and partly because of the anthropomorphized or highly personalized conceptions about God. One of the world's leading religious scholars, Karen Armstrong, in her book: *The Case for God,* addresses this issue in her description of the *Brahmodya* competition among 10th century Brahmin priests:

> Its goal was to find a verbal formula to define the Brahmin, in the process, pushing language as far as it could go, until it finally broke down and people became vividly aware of the ineffable, the other. The challenger asked an enigmatic question, and his opponent had to reply in a way that was apt but equally inscrutable. The winner was the contestant who reduced his opponents to silence — and in that moment of silence, when language revealed its inadequacy, the Brahman was present; it became manifest only in the stunning realization of the impotence of speech.[171]

I wholeheartedly agree with Ms. Armstrong regarding the inadequacy of language to describe God. Why then, do most of us go through life in search of a better explanation for God? And, why do many of the most ardent spiritual seekers ultimately abandon their search, and turn to agnosticism or atheism. From an experiential perspective, I must agree that God can be found amidst the silences, however, those silences must be an integral part of a sacred deep meditation prac-

171 Karen Armstrong, *The Case for God* (New York - Toronto: Alfred A. Knopf, 2009) 13.

tice, as they were for Ms. Armstrong's Brahmin priests. Experiencing God, in the manner of the ancient High Priests and Biblical prophets, requires the cultivated silence of deep meditation. The Aryan-Semitic tradition has a long history of experiencing the divine through meditation, however, understanding God is an entirely different matter. We don't need to understand God in order to meditate, but, if we do want to understand God, then we must come to realize that everyday language, whether spoken or written, is simply not up to the task.

Layer 2 - Number

The idea that God can be defined by something as mundane as number is blasphemous to some, but text and number are two important components of Abraham's approach. If we hope to penetrate to the third and deepest layer of meaning, then we must first realize that Hebrew letters of the alphabet are also Hebrew numerals, and that reciting the Hebrew alphabet is basically equivalent to counting.

Text		Number
Alef	א	1
Bet	ב	2
Gimel	ג	3
Dalet	ד	4
Heh	ה	5
Vav	ו	6
Zayin	ז	7
Chet	ח	8
Tet	ט	9
Yud	י	10

We become aware of the relative importance of certain Biblical numbers, based on their frequency of use within allegory. For example, we read about 12 tribes of Israel, 12 stones carried across the Jordan, 10 Commandments, 10 Plagues, 10 generations from Adam to Noah, 10 generations from Noah to Abraham, 7 lights on the Temple Menorah, 7 generations from Adam to Enoch, 7 generations from Abraham to Moses, 40 days and forty nights fasting, Israel's 40 years wandering in the desert, etc. Generally speaking, what Biblical scholars and clergy do not realize, is that the Torah's numbers have been predetermined by Abraham's mathematical constructions. Abraham's mathematics defines specific monotheistic theological concepts that shapes even the subtlest nuances of Biblical allegory. In other words, the Bible is completely structured by number and mathematics.

For example, Abraham's music theory routinely pre-determines something as seemingly unrelated as why Noah's wife and Abraham's mother would both give birth to triplet sons (Chapter 14). It is Abraham's music theory that required Four Wheels of Ezekiel and Four Rivers of Eden (Chapter 8). Abraham's writings also explain why the Torah put two trees in the Garden of Eden, as well as what mathematical function each "Tree" fulfills (also Chapter 8). The *Sefer Yetzirah* is also the only text to define the Christian "sacred mystery" of the Holy Trinity,[172] once again, based upon Abraham's mathematical/musical/theological constructs.

The Jewish rabbinical tradition, beginning with Hillel in the first century BCE, has always been well aware of the relationship between Hebrew letters and numbers, although they have never accurately recreated any of Abraham's mathematical tables and diagrams. In fact, the centuries have produced countless volumes of Kabbalistic interpretation that exploit this relationship in a discipline known as *gematria.* But, since the beginnings of the rabbinate, the rich Kabbalistic tradition of the Jewish people has never even scratched the surface of the Bible's third layer — the layer of "sound" — with God's "Voice" speaking (*Sippur* literally translates as "telling") Creation into existence. In over 2000 years of rabbinical writings there has been a severely limited understanding of Kabbalistic *gematria*, with no mention of the ratios, proportions, nor any musical mathematics, implying that the rabbinate's understanding of the Torah is incomplete at best. In recent history, only Leo Baeck (1873-1956) and Gershom Scholem (1897-1982) have suggested that the Pythagorean tradition (i.e., "The Music of the Spheres") may be necessary to understand the *Sefer Yetzirah.* Scholem also cites Abraham Abulafia (1240-1291) as the only renowned Kabbalist to state that music theory was necessary to facilitate a proper understanding of Scripture.[173]

Here are some of the allegorical contexts in which the Torah's numbers take on both mathematical and spiritual significance:

- The *gematria* of a righteous patriarch's name.
- The age of a patriarch when historically significant children are born.
- The age of a patriarch at death

To master this layer of meaning we must learn how to read these numbers. As we might expect, our explanation begins with the number 1 as a symbol of the Monad — the "One." The most ancient and renowned Hebrew prayer, the *Shema*, declares "Hear, Oh Israel, the Lord is God, the Lord is One." Once the One is extended into 1 thing, it becomes capable of division into 2. The Living God, the Monad, instantiates from the transcendent spirituality of the "One" into a material object of "1" something. However, even after this instantiation, we might say that God's essence (=1) can be found within every object and being's numerical essence. This is reflected by the fact that "1" is the only common factor of all numbers.

172 Schatz, *The Lost Word of God*, Op.Cit., 189.
173 Gershom Scholem, Kabbalah (New York- Jerusalem: Keter Publishing House, 1974) 180.

The numbers 1, 2, 3 and 5 are the only prime number factors of 60. A prime number can only be divided by itself and 1. Composite numbers are numbers that can be "reduced" to a product of primes. For example:
\

- $6 = 2 \times 3$
- $10 = 2 \times 5$
- $12 = 2 \times 2 \times 3 = 2^2 \times 3$
- $60 = 2 \times 2 \times 3 \times 5 = 2^2 \times 3 \times 5$

Abraham noticed that the only prime number factors of 60: 1, 2, 3 and 5, occurred within the first six integers. This is significant because Abraham had discovered a unique formative principle embedded within these first six numbers. In their book on acoustics, called *Tone*, Ernest Levy and Siegmund Levarie provide some insight into what Abraham had stumbled upon:

> The first six numbers are known as the senarius. There is a special formative power inherent in the senarius — a force that sets limits and thereby shapes the given elements... Crystallography operates primarily with ratios based on the senarius. Snowflakes that deviate from the norm of the hexagon are rare exceptions. The senarius becomes manifest again and again in affinity calculations of chemical elements, in chromosome numbers, in plant structure, et cetera. The number of faces, edges, and vertices of the five regular polygons, which are the perfect forms in three dimensional space, are all determined by senaric values.[174]

We can safely assume that Abraham did not understand crystallography. However, he saw the Hand of God manifest within the first six numbers, defining the structure of sound, light, and the phenomenal world. He also saw the limitations of Base-60, and focused his energies on understanding exactly how and why it was a bit "out of sync" with nature. These incongruities appear to be hard evidence of "flaws" in nature, and the numerical system of Mesopotamian mathematics was not equipped to account for those flaws.

The complex sexagesimal mathematics of the Sumerian/Babylonian "Gateway to the Gods" was interpreted in the Semitic tradition as the "Abyss of Hell." This Aryan-Semitic dynamic had created an apparent paradox that mapped both Good and Evil to the same tiny *ayanamsa* (precessional gap). As already stated, the Biblical story of Adam and Eve in the Garden of Eden suggests that Inanna's cult of sexuality was not an acceptable way to "reach Heaven." The unification of Shiva and Shakti within the Hindu Tantric tradition is still misunderstood in the West as

174 Ernest Levy and Siegmund Levarie, *Tone: A Study in Musical Acoustics* (Kent, Ohio: Kent State university Press, 1968) 30.

sexual, rather than spiritual in nature. Sumer's goddess Inanna became Ishtar in Babylon, and the cult of "sacred prostitution" within Babylon's "Houses of Heaven" was described by YBC 7289's mathematics of sin.

If the great goal of religion is for man's soul to thread the *ayanamsa's* tiny needle, then Abraham was faced with a complex and unique mathematical problem. It is clear that reaching Heaven inspired him to seek the truth using a scientific methodology that included observation, speculation, experimentation, and calculation. Abraham knew he would have to adapt the sexual cult of Ishtar and the Clock of Heaven to a theology that was morally acceptable to Semitic sensibilities. If possible, he would also need to improve on the flaws and complexities of sexagesimal measurement with a numerical system that would be much simpler for calculations. This new synthesis would require a morality backed by a mathematics of salvation that did not require fornication as part of the antidote. In retrospect, we know that Biblical allegory took the form of Adam's bite from the fruit of the Tree of Knowledge of Good and Evil, while the antidote required a bite from the fruit of the Tree of Life. Abraham's mathematics would support sexual restraint as a means to accomplish the moral purification of man's body and liberation of his soul, while remaining true to the sacred Aryan meditation tradition. Abraham's mathematics needed to reflect spiritual success by describing exactly how a man's sinful "imperfections" could be overcome, while enabling the prophet/priest to "walk with God."

Abraham integrated Sumerian Base-60 components, Egypt's Base-10 components, with his observations of how a Base-6 mathematical template "contains" sound and light within a complex fractal of Creation described as the "Hand of God" within Base-7. [175] The mathematics of the *Sefer Yetzirah* ties it to Old Babylonian period mathematics (circa 1800 BCE).[176] This corroborates the time of Abraham's birth in the city of Ur according to Genesis. The Torah was careful to provide the correct historical context, carefully naming the right time and travel itinerary to establish Abraham's education credentials. The Biblical story of Moses continues the patriarchal line seven generations after Abraham. And, it describes a similarly auspicious historical context for Moses, enabling him to learn the scientific disciplines appropriate for an Egyptian prince.

In order to reveal the deepest meaning of Scripture, we must begin our study of the crucial third layer of meaning. We will see exactly how and why certain critical passages must be interpreted numerically. And further, how these Kabbalistic numbers extend into the mathematics of the lost "first principles" of Abraham's science of religion — the harmonic structure of light and sound.

---

175 A fractal is a reduced size miniature of the whole. In this case "the whole" of Creation can be described by the tone-generating aspect of the harmonic series, i.e., prime numbers 2, 3 and 5.

176 Neugebauer, Otto, *The Exact Sciences in Antiquity* (New York: Dover Pub., 1969) 29.

Layer 3 - Sound

We would expect a revolutionary treatise from the great patriarch of monotheism. Unfortunately, neither the clergy nor the academic establishment has ever understood Abraham's third layer of meaning as the science of sound. Once we make that leap, it becomes clear that the Bible is essentially a book of music theory. Every word of the Torah has a numeric value in Hebrew, while any two numbers form a numeric ratio that generates a sound. The *Zohar* states: *From a word of Torah is formed a sound ... that sound ascends and breaks through the Heavens.*[177] Music theory defines Kabbalistic gematria and empowers us to accurately decipher the *Sefer Yetzirah* and tie it directly to Scripture. The *Sefer Yetzirah*'s short,[178] complex, and comprehensive presentation of the Bible's scientific framework, provides the only substantial evidence (other than Jewish tradition) that the man we have come to know as Abraham was an actual person. His text establishes him as the great patriarch of monotheism and science.

Sound is the key to unlocking the great Biblical mysteries. The harmonic series integrates arithmetic, geometry, trigonometry, and astronomy, into a "theory of everything." The Quadrivium's mathematical disciplines define a comprehensive cosmological framework, and once we understand God and Creation in terms of that framework, we are also in a better position to understand the role of mankind and the purpose of life.

When viewed through the prism of a raindrop, Abraham observed a rainbow of six colors as components of sunlight. His research into the structure of sound enabled him to describe the Hand of God in terms of simple counting. He theorized that this "rainbow principle" harmonized 6 components into a transcendent 7th, all-inclusive "One" — the transcendent "White Light of God."

The number 7 is normally a tone generating prime number, but Abraham did not allow it to fulfill its usual tone generating function, because he wanted to model nature's rainbow more accurately as a container of what the other 6 colors pour into it. Thus, it was given special treatment as a day of rest — the Sabbath — to contain what the other 6 days pour into it. The number 7 functions as a proxy for the number 1 — it is God's number. Since 7 was not a factor of 60, Abraham found reason to expand his numerical scope from Base-6 to Base-10. Base-10 could be thought of as the intersection of Base-6 and Base-60, while Base-7 can be thought of as the union of all Base-6 components.

Within the context of Abraham's science of religion, we can finally understand the inner substance of God (Hebrew: *pnimiyut;* Greek: *ousia*), by observing the complexity of natural light as it passes through a raindrop or

177 Zohar, part III 31b, 121b.
178 The *Sefer Yetzirah* is only about 2000 words long.

prism (Figure 34a). Similarly, there is a "rainbow of sounds" that structures every complex natural sound. When we direct any natural sound through a prism-like device called a harmonic analyzer, we input a natural sound, and we output its component sine waves, i.e., a "rainbow of sound," that harmonizes into the Unity of "the One" (Figure 34b &c).

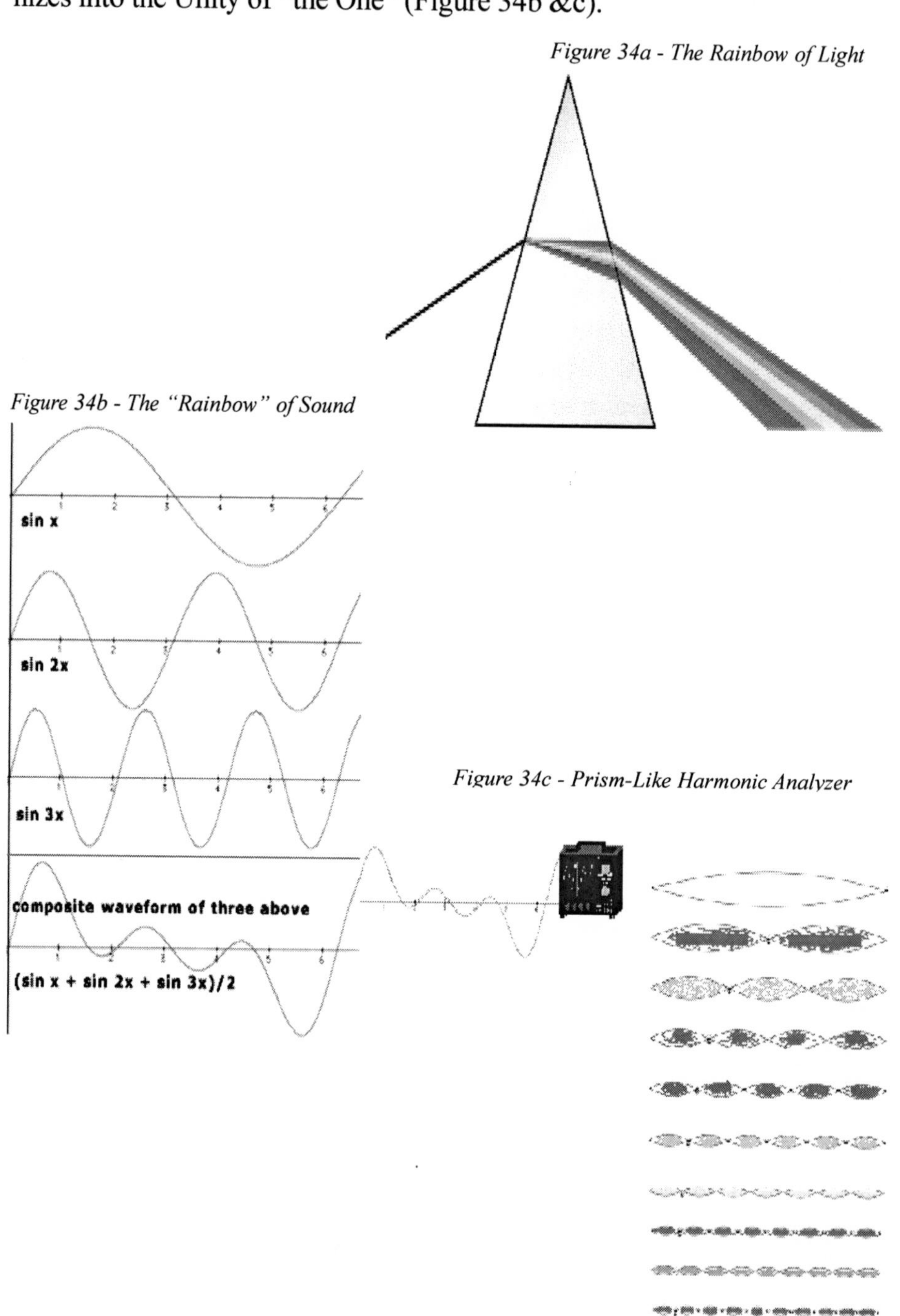

Figure 34a - The Rainbow of Light

Figure 34b - The "Rainbow" of Sound

Figure 34c - Prism-Like Harmonic Analyzer

It is no coincidence that God's Covenant with Noah was sealed with a rainbow. Within Abrahamic mathematics, this rainbow principle: *E Pluribus Unum* (From Many, One), is not only the American motto, but it is also a simple yet profound way to think of prayer as a derivative of Abraham's sacred meditation practice. The inverse of this principle, "From One, Many," describes God and the Creation process.

All vibrations of God's "Voice" embody the inner essence of Creation — which can be understood by looking at the component vibrations of a vibrating string. As it vibrates, the foundation vibration of the Monad leaves the transcendent realm and enters the material realm of the mundane. In other words, the number 1 becomes capable of extension, and the string's motion causes it to divide into 2 vibrating parts; 3 parts, 4 parts, *ad infinitum* — all vibrating at the same time. Physical limitations prevent a violin string from creating an infinite number of harmonics. In that respect, the vibrations of a violin string should not be thought of as resembling the actual Voice of God, but rather, as a single instantiation that is stamped from the Blueprint of God's vibratory essence. The human ear is limited to about 16 of these harmonic resonances. Within modern acoustics, the limiting factors of a classic Newtonian vibrating string are its material constraints.

Figure 34d - Classic Newtonian String [179]

$$f = \frac{1}{2L}\sqrt{\frac{T}{m}}$$

The formula in Figure 34d relates the fundamental frequency f, the length of a string L, its mass m, and its tension T. The use of sound to explain the universe was clearly not limited to audible everyday sounds. Audible sound helps us understand the laws that govern the entire spectrum of vibration that is the essence of energy and matter in the universe. John Keats expressed this idea in his poem "Ode on a Grecian Urn":

Heard melodies are sweet, but those unheard
Are sweeter; therefore, ye soft pipes, play on;
Not to the sensual ear, but, more endear'd,
Pipe to the spirit ditties of no tone.

The *Sefer Yetzirah* speaks to us in a "language of God" that marries music and mathematics as a universal language capable of eliminating the di-

179 Peat, 53.

visiveness that results from the ambiguities of spoken language and traditional culture. Abraham rejected polytheism's "gods on the mountain" in favor of monotheism's Living God. He saw God as a universal energy that permeates our own essence, as well as the world around us — all organized by the same harmonic series. God's complex unity and rainbow diversity are "flip sides" of the same coin. Within Abraham's world view, man, like the rest of Creation, was an instantiation of the harmonic Blueprint of Creation, and man could never become the transcendent Blueprint itself. The formula for a harmonic series is: "integer multiples of a fundamental sine wave," which tells us that if the first harmonic has a frequency of 1 cycle per second (1 sine wave per second), then the 2nd harmonic will vibrate at 2 cps, the 3rd harmonic at 3 cps, etc., *ad infinitum*. And, all these separate vibrating harmonics become components of a single vibrating string. Similarly, if the 1st harmonic vibrated at 110 cps, then the 2nd harmonic would have a frequency of 220 cps, then 330 cps, etc.. Each harmonic being a different mode of vibration of the same string.

Music theory is a very ancient science. Abraham was able to deduce the basic principles of light by studying the behavior of sound. He manipulated number as a function of frequency and string length, and he recognized the common properties of light and sound as the unseen "Hand of God." He described the source of all vibration as the Living God who's "Voice" became the essence and sustenance of Creation. God's "Voice" created the world through *Sippur* (literally: Telling). Of course, the rabbis believe God spoke Hebrew, so the exact nature of God's 10 Utterances would be Hebrew letter/numerals that count and stack individual vibrations one on top of the other; all of them vibrating simultaneously, and harmoniously together, according to the physics of vibrating strings known in ancient times. Within the original context of the *Sefer Yetzirah* the inner vibrational essence (*pnimiyut*) of the Ten Commandments was called the *Ten Sefirot of Nothingness*.

Text		***Number***	***Sound***
Alef	א	1	C
Bet	ב	2	C
Gimel	ג	3	G
Dalet	ד	4	C
Heh	ה	5	E
Vav	ו	6	G
Zayin	ז	7	Bb
Chet	ח	8	C
Tet	ט	9	D
Yud	י	10	E

Chapter 8: The Ten Commandments

The Ten Sefirot of Nothingness

Abraham transformed the Sumerian/Babylonian harmonic model from a Base-60, 12 integer "Clock of Heaven," to the *Ten Sefirot of Nothingness* within Base-10 that became the vibrational essence (Hebrew: *pnimiyut*) of the Ten Commandments. *Yetzirah's* mathematical account of Creation begins as God "Counted" (Hebrew: *Sefirot*) in a sequential line (Hebrew: *Kav*), starting with the numeral 1 ("the One"). God extended his divine light with His next sequential Utterances: 2, 3, etc., until all 10 Utterances were spoken. This was the model for God's statement in Genesis: "Let there be Light," an ancient version of the "Big Bang." Both versions of Creation occur within the same harmonic framework, but its mathematics was first described almost 4000 years before Galileo established the reciprocity of frequency and wavelength, and before Nicole Oresme and Joseph Saveur contributed to modern science's understanding of the harmonic series.

God's "Voice" Uttered the vibrational essence of all beings and things in the universe. Thus, He created the universe with *Sippur* (Telling). The following Abrahamic riddle unlocks the meaning of the *Sefer Yetzirah* and the Bible, but, it has never been properly understood by either rabbis or scholars.[180]

> ***2.5*** *How? He permuted them, weighed them, and transformed them,*
> *Alef with them all*
> *and all of them with Alef*
> *Bet with them all*
> *and all of them with Bet*
> *They repeat in a cycle*
> *and exist in 231 Gates.*
> *It comes out that all that is formed*
> *and all that is spoken*
> *emanates from one Name.*

The *Sefer Yetzirah*'s "Secret of the Torah" first tells us to combine *"Alef with them all,"* which should be interpreted as combining the Hebrew letter *Alef* with all the Hebrew numerals of the *Kav*. *Alef* (= 1), is representative of God Himself, *Alef* is "The One" who utters *The Ten Sefirot of Nothingness*. The resulting fractions

180 Schatz, *The Lost Word of God*, Op.Cit., 24; The "Secret of the Torah" (Hebrew: Raza d'Oraita) is also known as the "Secret of the Twenty-Two Letters" or the "Secret of Knowledge."

can then be understood as the divisions of a vibrating string that defines a harmonic series, in the manner of "Egyptian unit fractions," known in ancient times.[181] These are Arabic numeral translations of Hebrew numerals.[182]

Figure 35a - The Kav: God's 10 Utterances as a Harmonic Series

1/1 1/2 1/3 1/4 1/5 1/6 1/7 1/8 1/9 1/10 1/20

Once we have taken *"Alef with them all,"* we are then instructed to take *"all of them with Alef."* Taking our cue from the text, as well as our knowledge that musical ratios can be taken "either in direct or reverse order,"[183] in keeping with the reciprocity of frequency and wavelength. During the Creation process, the ratios of frequency defined by God's harmonic series of Ten Utterances descends into matter through the "22 Foundation Letters" of the Hebrew alphabet, reflecting God's 10 root frequencies into a reciprocal arithmetic series of wavelengths (Figure 35b).

Figure 35b - God's Ten Utterances "Descending" as an Arithmetic Series

1/1
2/1
3/1
4/1
5/1
6/1
7/1
8/1
9/1
10/1
20/1
30/1
40/1
50/1
60/1
70/1
80/1
90/1
100/1
200/1
300/1

181 McClain, "A New Look at Plato's Timaeus," *Music and Man* (1, no. 4 (1975)), 351.
182 The Arabic number 11 doesn't exist as a Hebrew numeral (Figure 35a). The next sequential Hebrew numeral after 10 would be 20. The numeral 20 does fall within the harmonic series, and it servers a unique function — to define the upper limit of God's 6000 (logarithmic) year universe (=300 * 20).
183 Schneer Zalman, *Likutei-Amarim-Tanya* (New York-London:Kehot Publication Society, 1973) 287.

We then add the next layer to this construction by combining "*Bet with them all and all of them with Bet*" as follows:

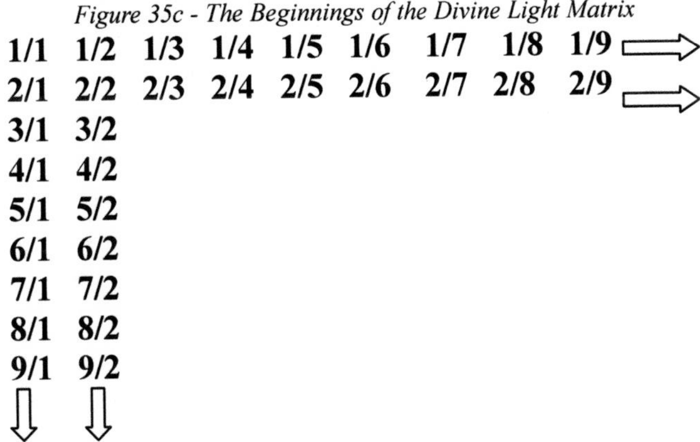

Figure 35c - The Beginnings of the Divine Light Matrix

1/1	**1/2**	**1/3**	**1/4**	**1/5**	**1/6**	**1/7**	**1/8**	**1/9**
2/1	**2/2**	**2/3**	**2/4**	**2/5**	**2/6**	**2/7**	**2/8**	**2/9**
3/1	**3/2**							
4/1	**4/2**							
5/1	**5/2**							
6/1	**6/2**							
7/1	**7/2**							
8/1	**8/2**							
9/1	**9/2**							

Figure 36 - "Let There be Light": Science's First Harmonic Conception of the Big Bang

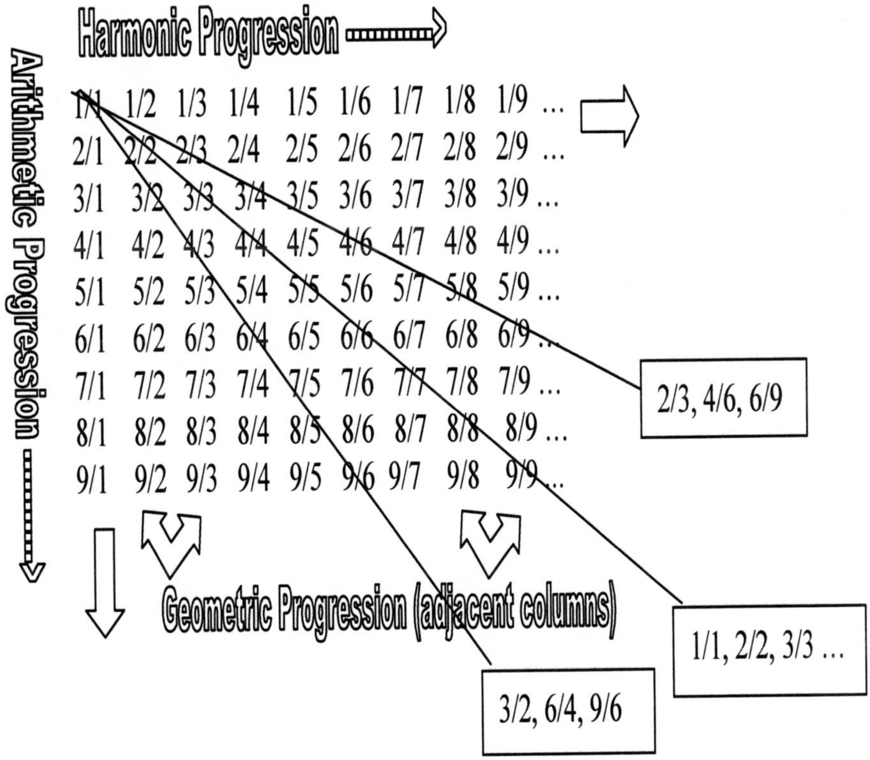

Harmonic Progression
Arithmetic Progression
1/1 1/2 1/3 1/4 1/5 1/6 1/7 1/8 1/9 ...
2/1 2/2 2/3 2/4 2/5 2/6 2/7 2/8 2/9 ...
3/1 3/2 3/3 3/4 3/5 3/6 3/7 3/8 3/9 ...
4/1 4/2 4/3 4/4 4/5 4/6 4/7 4/8 4/9 ...
5/1 5/2 5/3 5/4 5/5 5/6 5/7 5/8 5/9 ...
6/1 6/2 6/3 6/4 6/5 6/6 6/7 6/8 6/9 ...
7/1 7/2 7/3 7/4 7/5 7/6 7/7 7/8 7/9 ...
8/1 8/2 8/3 8/4 8/5 8/6 8/7 8/8 8/9 ...
9/1 9/2 9/3 9/4 9/5 9/6 9/7 9/8 9/9 ...
2/3, 4/6, 6/9
Geometric Progression (adjacent columns)
1/1, 2/2, 3/3 ...
3/2, 6/4, 9/6

Nineteenth-century music theorist Albert von Thimus discovered the three main types of mathematical progression: geometric, harmonic and arithmetic, encrypted within Plato's writings. Von Thimus called it a "lambdoma table" (Figure 36), because lines drawn from God =1 form a Greek letter lambda, emanating divine light from a point source, to propagate harmonic waves that are defined by the three types of mathematical progression (see Appendix: Primer on Arithmetic). Plato used it to explain the World Soul in his Timaeus,[184] and I have discovered it within the *Sefer Yetzirah,*[185] which is arguably the oldest extant manuscript that makes use of it (also, see Appendix: A Primer on Music).

Figure 37 - Opening 231 Gates (Fig. 98a) Requires 462 Integers to Reveal 231 Musical Paths

1:1=d	1:2=d	1:3=a	1:4=d	1:5=f#	1:6=a	1:7=c	1:8=d	1:9=e	1:10=f#	1:20=f#
2:1=d	2:2=d	2:3=a	2:4=d	2:5=f#	2:6=a	2:7=c	2:8=d	2:9=e	2:10=f#	2:20=f#
3:1=g	3:2=g	3:3=d	3:4=g	3:5=b	3:6=d	3:7=f	3:8=g	3:9=a	3:10=b	3:20=b
4:1=d	4:2=d	4:3=a	4:4=d	4:5=f#	4:6=a	4:7=c	4:8=d	4:9=e	4:10=f#	4:20=f#
5:1=bb	5:2=bb	5:3=f	5:4=bb	5:5=d	5:6=f	5:7=ab	5:8=bb	5:9=a	5:10=d	5:20=d
6:1=g	6:2=g	6:3=d	6:4=g	6:5=b	6:6=d	6:7=f	6:8=g	6:9=a	6:10=b	6:20=b
7:1=e	7:2=e	7:3=b	7:4=e	7:5=g#	7:6=b	7:7=d	7:8=e	7:9=f#	7:10=g#	7:20=g#
8:1=d	8:2=d	8:3=a	8:4=d	8:5=f#	8:6=a	8:7=c	8:8=d	8:9=e	8:10=f#	8:20=f#
9:1=c	9:2=c	9:3=g	9:4=c	9:5=e	9:6=g	9:7=bb	9:8=c	9:9=d	9:10=e	9:20=e
10:1=bb	10:2=bb	10:3=f	10:4=bb	10:5=d	10:6=f	10:7=ab	10:8=bb	10:9=c	10:10=d	10:20=d
20:1=bb	20:2=bb	20:3=f	20:4=bb	20:5=d	20:6=f	20:7=ab	20:8=bb	20:9=c	20:10=d	20:20=d
30:1=eb	30:2=eb	30:3=bb	30:4=eb	30:5=g	30:6=bb	30:7=db	30:8=eb	30:9=f	30:10=g	30:20=g
40:1=bb	40:2=bb	40:3=f	40:4=bb	40:5=d	40:6=f	40:7=ab	40:8=bb	40:9=c	40:10=d	40:20=d
50:1=gb	50:2=gb	50:3=db	50:4=gb	50:5=bb	50:6=db	50:7=fb	50:8=gb	50:9=ab	50:10=bb	50:20=bb
60:1=eb	60:2=eb	60:3=bb	60:4=eb	60:5=g	60:6=bb	60:7=db	60:8=eb	60:9=f	60:10=g	60:20=g
70:1=c	70:2=c	70:3=g	70:4=c	70:5=e	70:6=g	70:7=bb	70:8=c	70:9=d	70:10=e	70:20=e
80:1=bb	80:2=bb	80:3=f	80:4=bb	80:5=d	80:6=f	80:7=ab	80:8=bb	80:9=c	80:10=d	80:20=d
90:1=ab	90:2=ab	90:3=eb	90:4=ab	90:5=c	90:6=eb	90:7=gb	90:8=ab	90:9=bb	90:10=c	90:20=c
100:1=gb	100:2=gb	100:3=db	100:4=gb	100:5=bb	100:6=db	100:7=fb	100:8=gb	100:9=ab	100:10=bb	100:20=bb
200:1=gb	200:2=gb	200:3=db	200:4=gb	200:5=bb	200:6=db	200:7=fb	200:8=gb	200:9=ab	200:10=bb	200:20=bb
300:1=cb	300:2=cb	300:3=gb	300:4=cb	300:5=eb	300:6=gb	300:7=bbb	300:8=cb	300:9=db	300:10=eb	300:20=eb

The rabbis[186] tell us that all of Israel heard God recite the Ten Commandments, but only Moses heard them individually, because only he had risen to the level of prophecy. The Israelites could not distinguish the Commandments from one another, so God's Voice sounded to them like thunder.[187] Because of the deep meditation practice of the prophets, Moses "heard" the rainbow-like components of God's 10 Utterances. When we learn to pray like the prophets, we "open" the 231 Numerical Gates (Figures 98a & 37) to transform integers into superparticular ratios (Figure 98b; See Appendix: A Primer on Music). God's 10 Utterances (in the

184 Levarie and Levy, *Tone*, Op.Cit. 40; adapted from "Pythagorean Table."
185 Schatz, Op.Cit., 30-40.
186 Rashi and Ramban, as well as the *Mechilta* and *Gur Aryeh,* tell us that all Ten Commandments were communicated in a single instant. - Exodus 20 (Chumash: Stone Edition commentary)
187 "You were hearing the sound of the words" [but not recognizing them] - Deuteronomy 4:12

first row) "descend into matter" (through 20 additional rows), any of which lead us back to God, the Divine Source (1:1 = D), along a musical Path. In this table (Figure 36), we see three types of mathematical progression: harmonic, arithmetic and geometric. We can begin to understand the difference between them by comparing a geometric series of like ratios 2:4:8:16:32:64 (logarithmic) to an arithmetic series of like quantities 2,4,6,8,10,12 (linear). In the equation $8 = 2^3$ the exponent 3 is called the logarithm of 8 on the base 2, or $\log_2 8 = 3$. A logarithm is the power to which a number called 'base' had to be raised in order to obtain a third number."[188]

Musical tones are defined by their frequency and wavelength of vibration. Musical intervals consist of two or more musical tones. If we look at our vibrating strings in Figure 97a of the Appendix, we can see that a frequency of 3 vibrating waves requires 1/3 the wavelength for each cycle; a frequency of 4 has a wavelength of 1/4, etc. It was Galileo who proved that frequency and wavelength were reciprocals of one another, but somehow, Abraham already knew that. When we look at this set of numeric ratios and see how they are situated on a piano keyboard (Figure 97b in the Appendix) we might get a better idea of what a musical interval is and how it might sound on a piano. We can interpret them musically in terms of frequency as the number of vibrations per unit of time, or as wavelength, a measure of distance, since sound travels across both time and space.

Four Subsets of Divine Light

The "6 Days of Creation" in Genesis is allegory based on the *Sefer Yetzirah's* description of the first six integer "Utterances" of God (the senarius). Within monotheism, God only needed 6 numbers for Creation, rather than 60 numbers, because the prime number factors of both 6 and 60 are 2, 3, and 5. Prime numbers are important in music theory because it takes prime numbers to generate new musical tones and intervals, while composite numbers stack groups of prime number tones and intervals one on top of the other, like building blocks. The essence of each object and being in Creation corresponds to a number that can be factored into its prime number factors of 2, 3, and 5.[189] Each base vibration was raised to the appropriate exponent as the essence and sustenance that defines each object and being in Creation. For example: $12 = 2^2 \times 3$ and $90 = 2 \times 3^3 \times 5$. Squared numbers are planer; cubed numbers have volume, etc. When these "regular" number bases are extended, by raising them through a series of exponents, they were thought to form the primordial building blocks of Creation: Earth, Water, Wind, and Fire, which God then harmonized into the substantive essence of each being and thing.

188 Ibid., 220.
189 Called "5-smooth" in mathematical parlance; also called "regular" numbers, which are integers in the form $2^p \cdot 3^q \cdot 5^r$.

Here is how it works: let's say that a fundamental frequency of 440 cycles per second (today's "concert A") was doubled to form the octave interval 880:440 cps. Since the ratio of 2:1 defines an octave, 2 will become the "base" which can then be raised through several powers (the exponent). In this manner, we can generate several musical octaves (2:1), repeating the same musical pitch across several octaves, so that each "C" is double the frequency of the previous "C" in a geometric progression of 1:2:4:8:16 ...

Rising Octaves:	C	C_1	C_2	C_3	C_4
Duple Progression:	$2^0 = 1$	$2^1 = 2$	$2^2 = 4$	$2^3 = 8$	$2^4 = 16$

The reciprocal of *frequency* is *wavelength*, which is a function of string length. The octave ratios of ascending frequencies (see table above) travel in pairs with their reciprocal wavelength component (see table below).

C .... C_1 .... C_2 .... C_3 .... C_4
1/1 .... 1/2 .... 1/4 ....1/8 ...1/16

With regard to string length, these octaves are not equidistant from one another, even though they sound that way to our ear. That is because humans hear logarithmically.[190] In the equation $1/2^4 = 1/16$, the exponent 4 (the logarithm) is what we hear, because it is easier for the ear to track four equivalent logarithmic musical distances then it is to track the linear length of a string that has been shrinking exponentially in size with each new octave.

Multiplying the frequency of a vibrating string by 3 also reduces its wavelength to 1/3 the length (Figure 97a), which generates a second note that is 5 tones away from the first. For example, if we start on the note "C" then five notes up (C, D, E, F, G) gives us a "G." Conversely, dividing a frequency by 3, would be five notes down in pitch from the starting note; so, by starting with "C" we would generate an "F" five notes down (C, B, A, G, F).

We have already looked at Base-2 raised to the 4th power, to ascend through four octaves; here is Base-3 raised to the 4th power, to ascend through four perfect fifths:

Rising Fifths:	C	G	D	A	E
Triple Progression:	$3^0 = 1$	$3^1 = 3$	$3^2 = 9$	$3^3 = 27$	$3^4 = 81$

190 Levarie & *Levy, Tone*, 220.

We can do the same thing for Base-5. A quintuple progression would create a cycle of musical thirds, with each pitch three notes away (= two wholetones) from the one before it, ascending through four major thirds.

Rising Thirds:	C	E	G#	B#	D##
Quintuple Progression:	$5^0 = 1$	$5^1 = 5$	$5^2 = 25$	$5^3 = 125$	$5^4 = 625$

Since God "rested on the 7th day," He did not create any new objects or beings on the Sabbath, and that is why the Torah commands mankind to refrain from work on that day. If we can acknowledge the possibility that the Ten Commandments were originally based on Abraham's *Ten Sefirot of Nothingness*, then those first 10 sequential integers includes a fourth prime number, the number 7, to represent the Sabbath. Although 7 is not a 5-smooth prime number factor of 60, like 2, 3, and 5, it is, nevertheless, a prime number. And, as a prime number, it is capable of generating new musical tones and intervals. Because the number 7 has the capability to "Create" tones in a harmonic sense, Genesis must explicitly tell us to rest on the 7th day, and only create tones on the first 6 days (from the first six integers). By sticking to the prime factors of 60 (2, 3 and 5), Abraham yielded to the constraints of Base-60, as described by Babylonian mathematics and science. But, he might have also learned a great deal about the spirituality of the number 7 during his sojourn in Haran within the Aryan Mitanni empire.[191] Abraham modeled nature's light and sound using the number 7 as a container for the rainbow of 6 lights and 6 sounds. It receives a unique spiritual treatment in Abraham's text, and therefore in the Bible. Although no new objects or beings were created with 7, here is a septenary progression (Base-7) similar to the previous duple, triple, and quintuple progressions:

Rising Sevenths:	C	Bb	Ab	Gb	Fb
Septenary Progression:	$7^0 = 1$	$7^1 = 7$	$7^2 = 49$	$7^3 =343$	$7^4 = 2301$

Other than God's number = 1, there are four prime numbers that exist within God's Ten Utterances: 2, 3, 5, and 7. Abraham defined the vibratory essence of the four primordial elements as extensions of these four prime number bases: 2, 3, 5, and 7, each of which manifests as musical progressions: octaves, fifths, thirds and sevenths, respectively. And, these musical progressions correspond to the vibrational essence of Earth, Water, Wind, and Fire, respectively. Within the Bible, the first three primordial elements become the basic building blocks of Creation, while the element of Fire functions as a catalyst that purifies and transforms matter into its spiritual reflection.

191 There was a 2nd millennium migration of Aryan tribes out of the Armenian Highlands. They conquered the Hurrians to begin the Mitanni Empire in today's northern Iraq. Abraham sojourned in Haran on the Euphrates during this period and appears to have had contact with the Aryan spiritual tradition.

The Evolution of Music Theory

These four logarithmic progressions, and the musical intervals that they form, have driven the evolution of Western music theory from ancient times until the modern era.[192] For example, the early Middle Ages philosopher, Boethius (ca. 480-524) was instrumental in bringing knowledge of Greek philosophy and music theory into the Christian world. In his work *De Musica,* he introduced Pythagorean "perfection," as embodied by the first four integer harmonics (1, 2, 3, and 4). Within the Semitic tradition, the duple progression embodied the female principle of the "perfect octave" as "womb" and Biblical "Heavenly Firmament," "giving birth" to all other numbers and tones. The female octave was "impregnated" by the male principle of "perfect fifths" (triple progression), The Early Church had no theological place for major and minor thirds (quintuple progressions),[193] and certainly no place for progressions of "sevenths" (septenary progression).

For 1000 years, the Church held the line against allowing "imperfect intervals, i.e., musical thirds (quintuple progression) and musical sevenths (septenary progression) into the musical vocabulary. The musical third finally made its appearance in the English "gymel" as the Renaissance began, and soon found its way onto the European Continent. The musical seventh (septenary progression) was added to the music of Johann Sebastian Bach; while prime number harmonics 11 and 13 were incorporated into the musical vocabulary of the time in the "tone paintings" of Claude Debussy, the father of "modern" music.

Of the "Big Four" tuning systems that define the history of Western music theory, only Pythagorean tuning (Log $2^p 3^p$) and Just tuning (Log $2^p 3^q 5^r$) can be considered true tuning systems, because they are based on the natural integers that define the harmonic series. Pythagorean tuning is based on duple and triple progressions, while the Biblical version of Just tuning harmonizes duple, triple and quintuple progressions. By definition, a Just tuning system could include all integers within the harmonic series, but within the Bible it is synonymous with the "Tree of Life," and it is limited to the 5-smooth subset (Log $2^p 3^q 5^r$). The other two significant tuning systems in the history of Western music theory are Meantone Temperament and Equal Temperament, both of which "temper" or alter natural tuning to some non-integer variant.

192 Howard Schatz, "The Chord of Nature and the Evolution of Music Theory" in *Music in Human Adaptation,* eds. Daniel Schneck and Judith K. Schneck (Blacksburg: Virginia Tech, 1997) 423-436.
193 Ibid., 423-436.

Four Rivers and Four Wheels

We have just explained the four geometric progressions that are of primary interest. Mathematically, they can be exponed in a single row, or bent around into a tone circle mandala, as described in Genesis (see below), and as my geographical depiction suggests (Figure 38). My effort to locate the Four Rivers of Eden as depicted is based upon archeological and geological information already discussed in Chapter 2. This mathematics has been encrypted within Hebrew Scripture as the "Four Rivers of Eden" and the "Four Wheels of Ezekiel" (Figures 39a & b).

Figure 38 - The Four Rivers of Eden

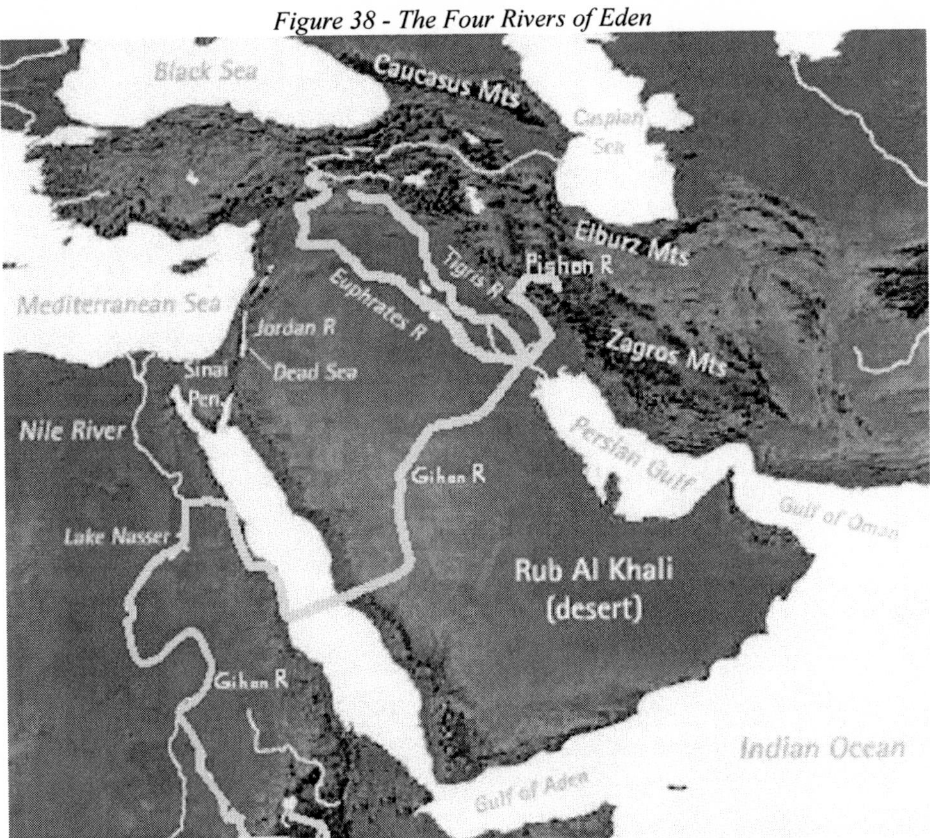

A river issues forth from Eden to water the garden, and from there it is divided and becomes four headwaters. The name of the first is Pishon, the one that encircles the whole land of Havilah, where the gold is. The gold of that land is good; the bedolach is there, and the sholem stone. The name of the second river is Gihon, the one that encircles the whole land of Cush. The name of the third river is Hiddekel, the one that flows toward the East of Assyria; and the fourth river is the Euphrates. [194]

194 *Genesis 2:10-14, Stone Edition*

Like the Four Rivers of Eden, the Four Wheels of Ezekiel is a complex mathematical riddle. Ezekiel's vision allegorizes Abraham's acoustical constructions as the *Merkavah* (Chariot) and the Divine Presence (*Shechinah*) that sits on the Throne of Glory pulled by four-headed creatures. Abraham describes these creatures as angels called *Seraphim,* (the heavenly choir). *Seraphim* derive from the Sumerian, Babylonian and Egyptian sphinx (see Figure 11a - c). Each creature had the head and hoofs of a bull (the Earth element as powers of 2); the head and hands of a man (the Water element as powers of 3); the head and wings of an eagle (the Wind element as powers of 5); and, the head and torso of a lion (the Fire element as powers of 7). The great secret of the *Merkavah* is that a holy man is a *Seraphim*, "singing" his soul to God, and liberating it during meditation; riding in Ezekiel's fiery chariot, sitting on the "Mercy Seat," the "wellspring of prophecy," and hovering above the "Throne of Glory." Man's soul arises from within him and hovers above him as the "cloud" of the Divine Presence that guides the prophet in truth — like the cloud over Moses' tent.

In addition to the *Seraphim*, the *Sefer Yetzirah* describes two other types of angels: *Ophanim* (Hebrew: "wheels" or tonecircles); and *Chayot*, the tiny flames of ascending and descending light and sound that carry our consciousness, "riding on the Winds" of the Holy Spirit (*Ruach Hakodesh*). It is extremely important to realize that the entire pantheon of angels (and demons), including all archangels, were written into Scripture subsequent to the writings of Abraham. In *Yetzirah*, only the musical concepts of tonecircles (*Ophanim*), musical notes (*Chayot*), and a Heavenly choir (*Seraphim*), were elevated to the functional role of Heavenly angel. It may be fair to say that all other angels are anthropomorphized allegorical embellishment.

Figure 39a - The Four Wheels of Ezekiel "Cutting Through One Another"

Figure 39b - The Four Wheels of Ezekiel as Four Ophanim

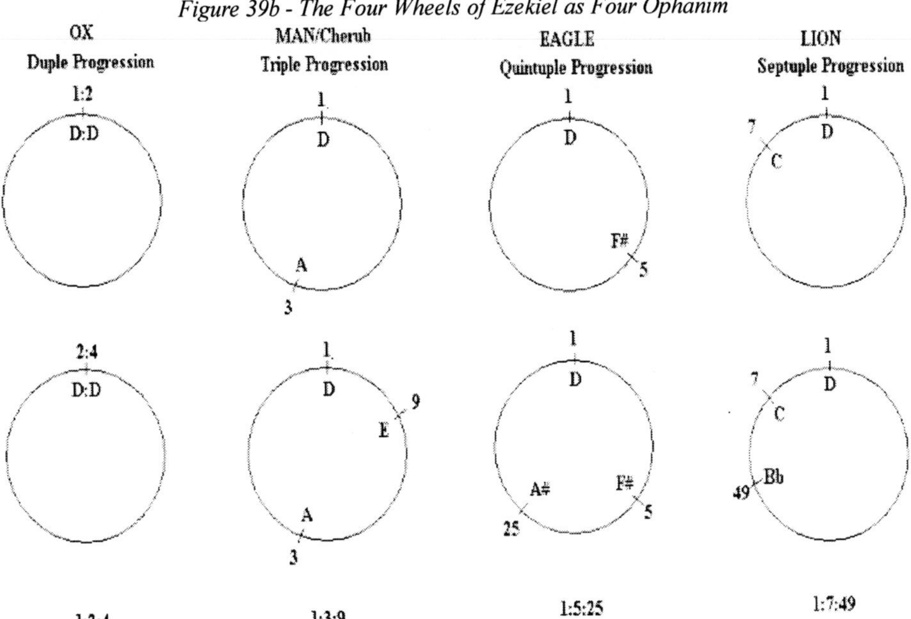

Ezekiel tells us that "the spirit of the creatures was in the wheels." In the second step of Creation, God's 10 sequential harmonic Utterances were "reordered" (Hebrew: *Tikun*). During the reordering process, the prime numbers: 2, 3, 5 and 7 were extended into the four subset building blocks of Creation: Earth, Water, Wind, and Fire, respectively. In Figures 40a & b, we can see how this allegory utilizes three of the Four Rivers of Eden as "irrigation" for the two trees in the Garden: The Tree of Knowledge of Good and Evil and the Tree of Life. These three rivers, the duple, triple, quintuple harmonic progressions extend the Heavenly waters into the roots and branches of each tree, with each tree "watered" by two rivers — mirroring the construction of the "wheels of Ezekiel that were "cross-cut" two at a time.[195] The opposing triangles of the two "trees" in the Garden resembles a Greek letter Chi or "X" as a side-view, similar to what the Book of Ezekiel called "cross-cut" wheels (see Figures 39a & b and 40a & b).

We now know of two tuning systems based on prime number integers: Pythagorean Tuning (based on powers of 2 and 3) and "Just" tuning (based on powers of 2, 3 and 5). These are the two "trees" in the Garden of Eden. There are also two hidden tree constructions that derive from the *Sefer Yetzirah*, based on powers of 7, that were not revealed to Adam and Eve in the Garden, but were revealed to the 7th generation holy man, Enoch, and to all subsequent holy men. The first of these, "cross-cuts" powers of 3 with powers of 7, while the second

195 With one exception — powers of 7 (Fire) receives a special acoustical and allegorical treatment that will be addressed in Chapter 14: The Mathematics of Salvation.

cross-cuts powers of 5 with powers of 7 (see Figures 71a & b). The number 7 is considered God's number, and the musical construction it generates refers to "7 circuits around the sacred cube," Abraham's sacred meditation practice. These hidden "Sabbath Trees" describe the Fires of Heaven and Hell that becomes a crucible to purge impurities from man's Body and corrupted Soul.

Figure 40a & b Pythagorean Tuning (the soul) and Just Tuning (the body "containing" the soul)

Tree of Knowledge of Good & Evil **Tree of Life**

1/729 1/4861/324 1/216 1/144 1/96 1/64 1/15625 1/9375 1/5625 1/3375 1/2025 1/1215 1/729
1/243 1/162 1/108 1/72 1/48 1/32 1/3125 1/1875 1/1125 1/675 1/405 1/243
1/81 1/54 1/36 1/24 1/16 1/625 1/375 1/225 1/135 1/81
1/27 1/18 1/12 1/8 1/125 1/75 1/45 1/27
1/9 1/6 1/4 1/25 1/15 1/9
1/3 1/2 1/5 1/3
1 1
2 3 3 5
4 6 9 9 15 25
8 12 18 27 27 45 75 125
16 24 36 54 81 81 135 225 375 625
32 48 72 108 162 243 243 405 675 1125 1875 3125
64 96 144 216 324 486 729 1215 2025 3375 5625 9375 15625

<u>Two "Cross-Cut Wheels" Form the Tree of Knowledge of Good and Evil</u>

- Diagonal numbers from to top right to bottom left define a duple progression with ratios of 1:2, such as 2:4, 4:8, 3:6, etc.
- Diagonal numbers from top left to bottom right define a triple progression with ratios of 1:3, such as 3:9, 9:27, etc.
- All horizontal numbers define a ratio of 2:3, such as 4:6, 6:9, 8:12, 12:18, etc.

<u>Two "Cross-Cut" Wheels Form the Tree of Life</u>

- All diagonal numbers from top right to bottom left define a triple progression with ratios of 1:3, such as 3:9, 5:15, etc.
- All diagonal numbers from top left to bottom right define a quintuple progression with ratios of 1:5, such as 3:15, 5:25, etc.
- All horizontal numbers define a ratio of 3:5, such as 9:15, 15:25, 27:45, etc.

The Musical Scales of Creation

For Abraham, the harmonic series defined the substance of both God and Creation. Once the *Ten Sefirot* of the harmonic series was Uttered by God, then Creation entered its second phase of construction. Abraham logically theorized that the four primordial elements (Earth = powers of 2 =octaves; Water = powers of 3 = fifths; Wind = powers of 5 = thirds; Fire = powers of 7 = sevenths) harmonized together to Create the main composite structures of Creation from various subsets of the harmonic series. For example, the first four harmonics defines the spirituality of Divine Light (which includes primes 2 and 3). The fifth and sixth harmonics defines the vibratory essence of all material forms that contained Divine Light (primes 2, 3, and 5). The seventh harmonic functions as the crucible of sin and salvation that defines Biblical morality (primes 2, 3, 5, and 7).

Biblical allegory describes Four Rivers of Eden as four "rivers" of prime number tone generators that "irrigates" the two trees in the Garden (Figures 40a & b), and then flows out to the farthest reaches of Eden, emanating three of the four primordial Elements throughout Creation. In Figure 42b, God "engraved" the World Soul directly from Divine Light (octaves and fifths) to form a special type of musical scale called the Phrygian mode. In Figure 41a, He harmonizes octaves, fifths, and thirds to Create two material "containers" of Divine Light: the Diatonic and Chromatic scales. The fourth primordial element, Fire's powers of 7, raises the numerosity of all 6 sounds and 6 colors, transposing the Day 6 Chromatic scale into a Day 7 Sabbath scale (which is also a Chromatic scale, but higher in frequency). Abraham referred to the Biblical "Fires of Heaven" as a "Crown." He described it as the Divine Influx that binds to one's Body and Soul through deep meditation (Hebrew: *Tardemah;* literally: "deep sleep"), purging away all imperfection and sin "upon the altar." Man was unique among all the creatures of Creation to be able to "wear" this Crown of Heaven. The Sabbath scale was "sung" by God to create the Fires of Heaven, and it must be "sung" by man in order to reenter Heaven.

Within the monotheism of the *Sefer Yetzirah* and Torah, these four scales define the *ousia* or *pnimiyut* of all material and spiritual objects and beings. They were "Sung" by God to create the Soul, Time, and the Universe (Figures 41a & b and Figure 42b). Similarly, the Indo-Aryan Vedas are considered *Apauruseya* (Sanskrit: "unauthored," implying divine origin). They are also considered *mantras* (transformational sounds) that reveal the inaudible essence of Creation through *śruti* ("what is heard"). Within the Bible, here are the mathematical-musical constructions for "what is heard":

- The 7-note Phrygian mode (modern Dorian) describes the root vibrations of man's soul. To approximate[196] this on the piano, start with the note "D" and then play all 7 white notes until the next D. It is the only mode that retains the same pattern of tones and semitones both ascending and descending.
- Diatonic major scale (also called the Ionian mode) is considered the *pnimiyut* (essence) of all "moving creatures." It is the animal counterpart to the human soul. To approximate this on the piano, start with the note "C" and then play all 7 white notes until the next C. This describes the divine essence of animal sacrifice that rises up to God, but does not symmetrically descend.
- The 12-note Chromatic scale provides the root vibrations of man's body as a container of his soul. It was created on Day 6 of the Creation allegory. To approximate this on a piano,[197] start with the note "D" and play all 12 notes, including black notes, until the next D. It is the ancient Navel of Order, completely symmetrical both ascending and descending.
- Man's spiritual goals can only be reached by sounding the 12-note Chromatic scale of the body, with the same pitches as the Day 6 construction, however, purified by the Fires of the Sabbath (multiplied by powers of 7; Figure 77). The Sabbatical and Jubilee constructions utilize additional powers of 7 to raise man's vibration, ultimately empowering liberation along the Pathway to Heaven .

Thirty years ago, describing the universe in the harmonic terms of simple counting might seem primitive and laughable, but today, theoretical physics is highly focused on proving it true. The harmonic series is the empirical core of today's "theory of everything" in theoretical physics. It is also the mathematical and physical basis of the *Sefer Yetzirah's* "Living God." We must recognize that Abraham's 2nd step of Creation reorganizes the harmonic components in a purely speculative and theoretical way. Abraham's embrace of the Base-6 senarius as a subset of Base-10 (within his 10 *Sefirot of Nothingness*) was a way to simplify sexagesimal calculations that resulted from Sumer and Babylon's focus on the number 12 as a factor within Base-60 (within the Clock of Heaven and Earth). From Abraham's reductionist perspective, God constructed musical subsets from the only prime number factors of 60, which were 2, 3 and 5, which were then extended exponentially into matter as primordial Elements. Using a "rainbow principle" to define monotheism's God was a significant scientific discovery describing how 6 colors and 6 sounds poured their energies into a transcendent and all-encompassing 7th element.

The Heavenly Firmament musical octave is the beginning of nature's complexity. It embodies the concept of duality, in which opposites coexist as the

196 It can only be approximated because a modern piano is not tuned to integers, but to equal temperament.
197Equal temperament divides the octave into 12 notes, therefore each musical step would be equivalent to $\sqrt[12]{2}$ which is an irrational number. Therefore, within equal temperament each note must be approximated and therefore it is slightly out-of-tune with nature's harmonic series.

musical complements of frequency and wavelength that "fit together" within a musical container. This duality then becomes the mathematical model for Creation, manifesting as Heaven and Hell, spiritual and material, good and evil, day and night, etc. They are all polar opposites that derive from frequency and wavelength. Holy men in the angelic choir of *Seraphim* "sing" God's Name to purify the body's 12 outer lights, while integrating and liberating the soul's 7 inner lights, ultimately transcending duality in the Unity of a "7th Heaven."

If we were to continue adding integers to the Creation Week we would, of course, finally come to the 7th Day of Creation, "container" of the other 6 Days. Normally, the number 7 would form a ratio with the number 6 that immediately precedes it as a musical interval of ratio 7:6. However, Abraham's treatise instructs us that the number 7 functions as a container that is not to be used to generate any new musical ratios or intervals. It behaves like a simple multiplier, to raise the vibration (i.e., transpose the frequency ratio) of the Day 6 construction to a higher octave. To communicate all this Abraham uses a teaching metaphor that instructs us how to build "houses" from "stones":

Two stones build 2 houses
Three build 6 houses
Four stones build 24 houses
Five stones build 120 houses
Six stones build 720 houses
Seven stones build 5040 houses
From here on go out and calculate that which
the mouth cannot speak and the ear cannot hear.

This passage and the following two diagrams (Figures 41a & b) demonstrate how the "pebble arithmetic" of the *Sefer Yetzirah* became the prototype for the Bible's Creation allegory; Divine Light emanated on Day 1. On Day 2, God created the Heavenly Firmament (2:1) that would "give birth" to all beings and things in Creation. On Day 3, God gathered the Waters together to reveal dry land, and then created vegetation. On Day 4, God created the Heavenly lights (sun, moon, and stars) as arithmetic and harmonic means. Abraham's mathematical template informs us that by Day 4 God had sufficient musical material to create the World Soul (traditionally called Supernal Man or Adam Kadmon) as an extension of the sun, moon, and stars (see Figure 42b). On Day 5, God utilized powers of 5 to create sacred cubes; each cube with 12 edges to contain the Divine Light. These edges expanded with the Divine Light to the 12 boundaries of the universe, within which it manifests as the 12 months of the year and the body's "12 Directors of the Soul." On Day 6, God breathed Adam's soul into his nostrils.

Figure 41a – The Sefer Yetzirah's Mathematics and Music *41b - As the Framework of the Bible*

							D
							1
							x 2 =
D							D
1							2
x 3 =							x 3 =
D			G				D
3			A				6
			4				
x 4 =			x 4 =				x 4 =
D			G	A			D
12			A	G			24
			16	18			
x 5 =			x 5 =	x 5 =			x 5 =
	e^b	f	G	A	b^b	c	
D	c#	b	A	G	f#	e	D
60	64	72	80	90	96	108	120

x 6 =	x 6 =		x 6 =		x 6 =	x 6 =	x 6 =		x 6 =		x 6 =
	e^b	e	f	f#	G	A	b^b	b	c	c#	
D	c#	c	b	b^b	A	G	f#	f	e	e^b	D
360	384	400	432	450	480	540	576	600	648	675	720

x 7 =	x 7 =	x 7 =	x 7 =	x 7 =	x 7 =	x 7 =	x 7 =	x 7 =	x 7 =	x 7 =	x 7 =
	e^b	e	f	f#	G	A	b^b	b	c	c#	
D	c#	c	b	b^b	A	G	f#	f	e	e^b	D
2520	2688	2800	3024	3150	3360	3780	4032	4200	4356	4725	5040

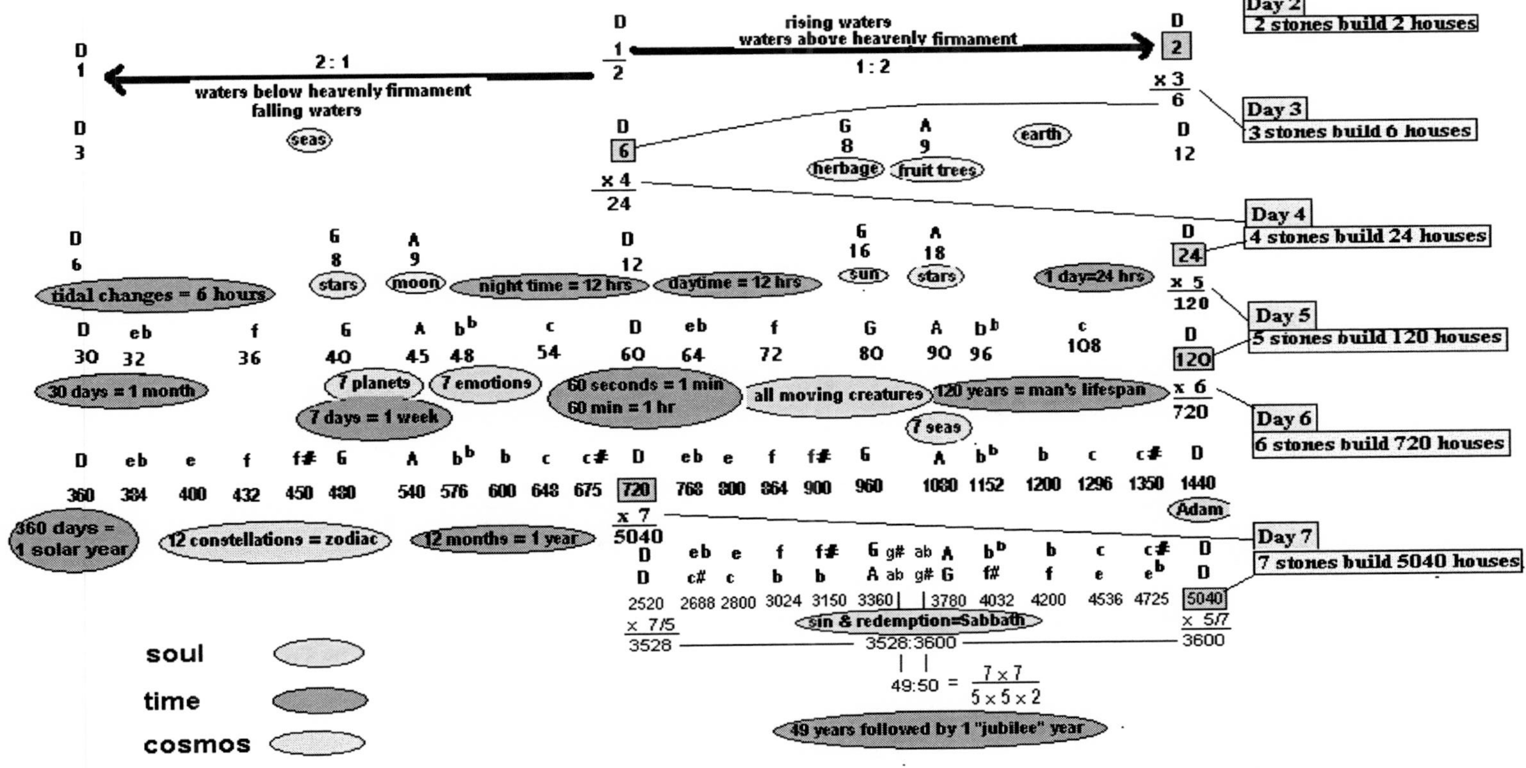
Day 2
2 stones build 2 houses
rising waters
waters above heavenly firmament
1 : 2
2 : 1
waters below heavenly firmament
falling waters
seas
herbage
fruit trees
earth
Day 3
3 stones build 6 houses
x 4
24
Day 4
4 stones build 24 houses
stars
moon
night time = 12 hrs
daytime = 12 hrs
sun
stars
1 day=24 hrs
tidal changes = 6 hours
x 5
120
Day 5
5 stones build 120 houses
30 days = 1 month
7 planets
7 emotions
7 days = 1 week
60 seconds = 1 min
60 min = 1 hr
all moving creatures
120 years = man's lifespan
7 seas
x 6
720
Day 6
6 stones build 720 houses
Adam
360 days =
1 solar year
12 constellations = zodiac
12 months = 1 year
x 7
5040
Day 7
7 stones build 5040 houses
sin & redemption=Sabbath
x 7/5
3528
3528:3600
x 5/7
3600
49:50 = 7 x 7 / 5 x 5 x 2
49 years followed by 1 "jubilee" year
soul
time
cosmos

Figure 42a - Harmonic Marriage of God (1), Woman (powers of 2) & Man (powers of 3)

1

2 3

4 9

8 27

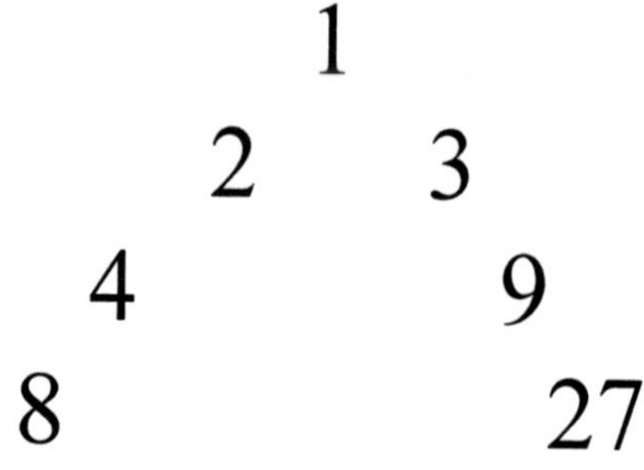

Figure 42b - The Construction of Man's Soul from Powers of 2 and 3 with Means Inserted

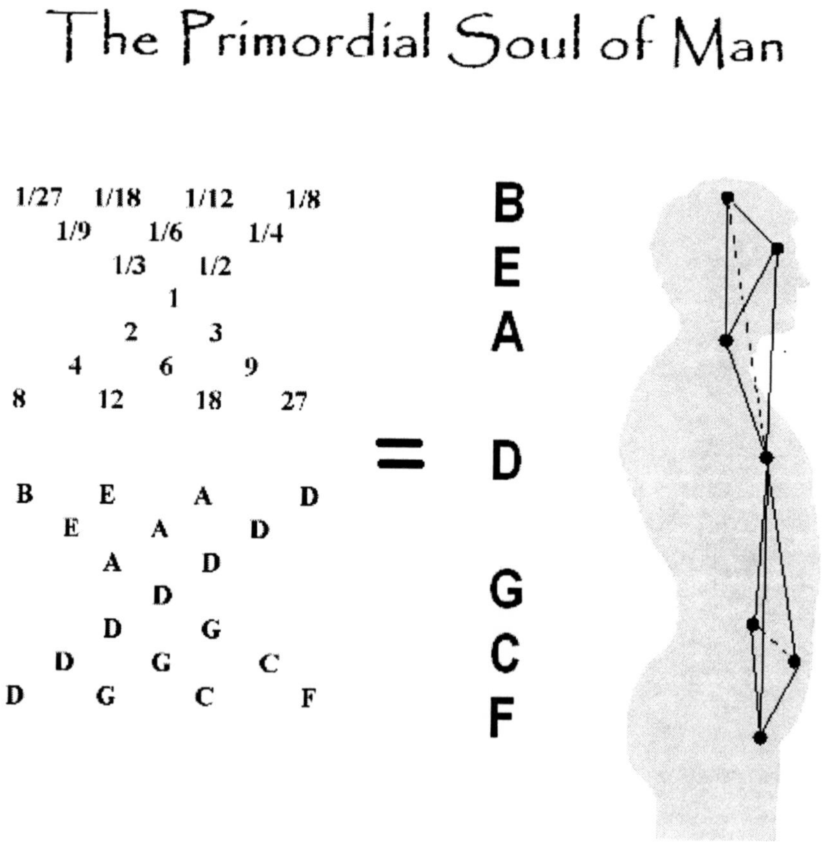

The Primordial Soul of Man
1/27 1/18 1/12 1/8
1/9 1/6 1/4
1/3 1/2
1
2 3
4 6 9
8 12 18 27
B E A D
E A D
A D
D
D G
D G C
D G C F
=
B
E
A
D
G
C
F

Creating the Soul

The subset 1, 2, 3, and 6 is used to construct the soul, not from polytheism's 12 Emanations, but from *Yahweh's* 10 emanations. The numbers 2 and 3 are prime factors of the number 6; this is the "substance" of the Divine Presence (Hebrew: *pnimiyut*; Greek: *ousia*) that lives within us as our soul (Figure 42b). It is the essence of our being and driving force of our character that manifests in our thoughts, emotions, and actions. Abraham first defined the "inner light" of the soul by harmonizing prime factors of 2 and 3, and embedding the composite Hebrew letter/numeral, "*Vav*" (2*3=6), into the third letter of the Word of God, YHVH (Figure 43).

Figure 43a - The Senarius & its Prime Factors

Alef	א	1	
Bet	ב	2	prime factor
Gimel	ג	3	prime factor
	ד	4	
	ה	5	
Vav	ו	6	
	ז	7	
	ח	8	
	ט	9	
	י	10	

In Figure 42b, the masculine aspect of man's soul is characterized by the number 3. If we start at the center of "His Holy Palace" (= 1), then longer string lengths lower pitches while shorter lengths raise them. String length ratios of ascending and descending musical fifths (1/3 : 1 : 3) are "cross-cut" with the feminine aspects of man's soul, generating ascending and descending octaves from the center (1/2 : 1 : 2). The female number "2" therefore harmonizes with the male number "3", and their 2:3 ratio replicates throughout adjacent female-male pairs. This mathematical relationship shapes the Biblical allegory of Eve being taken from Adam's side.

On Day 4, the number 4 "extends" the octave number 2, implying a further extension of prime numbers 2 and 3 through additional powers of 2 and 3, which are also taken with their reciprocal, with geometric means inserted (see Figure 42b). We should take note that Abraham's construction of man's soul is a subset of the Bible's Tree of Knowledge of Good and Evil. Figure 51 describes the music theory of Adam's bite from the forbidden fruit, and how his newly acquired Knowledge added the *pnimiyut* of Good and Evil to his soul, incorporating the vibrational essence of the entire Tree.

Creating the Body

The brilliance of Abraham's mathematics is in its reduction of Sumerian and Babylonian sexagesimal numerosity (Base-60) to smallest integers (Base-6), but he became a pioneer of science by realizing that God's mathematics of the "rainbow principle" was all-pervasive. Modern science was born in the harmonic structure of God and Creation. Abraham could scientifically explain the universe, and man's role in that universe, in terms of a harmonic series defined by God's *Ten Sefirot of Nothingness*. He believed that all beings and things had their root vibration in the first ten sequential integers, and that the essence of all beings and things was a reorganization of vibrational energy. The function of the prime number 5 (and powers of 5) was to contain the Divine Light (Figure 44a) of the first four integers. Once it was contained, that Light could be raised back up to God, just the way one would contain water in a bucket and hoist it up out of a well.

Two occurrences of the Hebrew letter *Heh* (=5) within YHVH creates "two wings" that "contain" the *Vav* (=6). In Figure 45c, we can see how $2^p \times 5^q$ and $3^p \times 5^q$ "contains" $2^p \times 3^q$. Jewish Kabbalistic tradition graphically depicts YHVH as the bird-like (and cross-like) Metatron, God's highest ranking angel. *Yahweh* can be graphically depicted by the ancient symbol of a caduceus (Figure 44b). In the diagram below, the two occurrences of the Hebrew letter *Heh* (=5) within YHVH, become the two wings of Metatron surrounding the divine light of the soul that contains the letter Vav = 6 = ($2^p \times 3^q$). In allegory, the two *Hehs* become the "Wings of the Great Eagle" mentioned in both Exodus and Revelation. The inner light of man's soul ($2^p \times 3^q$) ascends to God on two "wings" ($2^p \times 5^q$).

Figure 44a - Base-10 & its Prime Factors

Hebrew		Base-10	Factors
Alef	א	1	
Bet	ב	2	prime factor
	ג	3	
	ד	4	
Heh	ה	5	prime factor
	ו	6	
	ז	7	
	ח	8	
	ט	9	
Yud	י	10	

Figures 44b - The 2 Wings (=2 x 5) of Metatron as a Caduceus

Within Genesis, the proper dimensions were specified by God in order to build an Ark of the Covenant to contain the Divine Light as an appropriately sized scalene cube of 6 faces, 8 vertices, and 12 edges. The spiritual proportions specified by God for the Ark of the Covenant is based upon the primordial elements as a function of musical prime numbers: 2, 3 and 5. In Exodus 25:10, God gives Bezalel specific instructions on how to build the Ark of the Covenant within the Holy of Holies: *"They shall make an Ark of acadia wood, two and a half cubits its length; a cubit and a half its width; and a cubit and a half its height."* Since all of Creation occurs within the Heavenly Firmament (an octave ratio of 2:1) musical ratios created by these dimensions generates a scalene sacred cube of 3:2 by 3:2 by 5:2 (Figure 44c), as a combination of Earth (duple progression), Water (triple progression) and Wind (quintuple progression).

Figure 44c –The Ark of the Covenant: A Sacred (Scalene) Cube

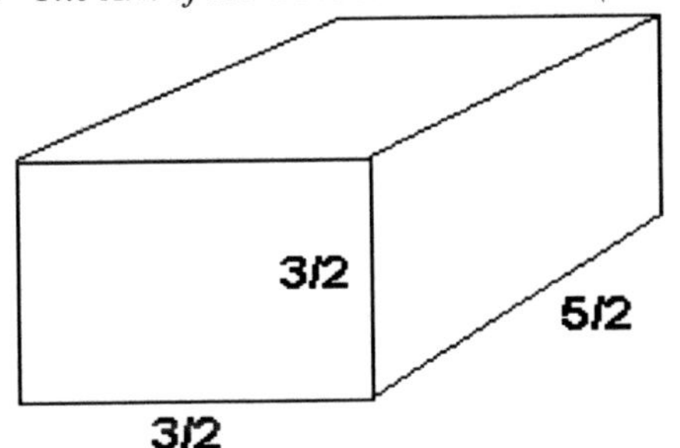

The prime numbers 2 (woman), 3 (man), and 5 (wind/wings) are given as the length, width, and height (or depth) of the sacred cube. It is important to realize that a vessel, created by powers of 2, 3 and 5 to contain divine light, was itself a vibrational essence and not a physical object. The essence of everything in the physical world that can be seen or touched is formed by the "outer light" of a sacred cube.

By Day 6 of Creation, God had uttered 6 integers, and on Day 6, God extended His Divine Light exponentially for all three prime numbers 2, 3 and 5 (Figures 45a & b). Thus, we can say that God constructed the "Outer Light" of the body from the letter *Heh* (= 5) in order to contain the "Inner Light" of the soul from the letter *Vav* (= 6). In Figure 45c we can see two Wings (2 * 5) that contain and elevate the Light of man's dualistic soul. This dualism begins with frequency and wavelength as the mathematical model of Creation, but it permeates throughout Creation, including "Supernal Man's" male and female aspects.

As the three primordial elements descend further into matter they manifest in the physical world of Earthly solids to form a dense physical body. In Figures 47a,b & c, the body's 12 chromatic tones within the 360:720 octave can be factored into prime numbers 2, 3 and 5. Powers of 5 empower the body to contain the soul's powers of 2 and 3.

Figure 45a - The Pnimiyut of the Star of David Figure 45b - Extending the Pnimiyut of the Star

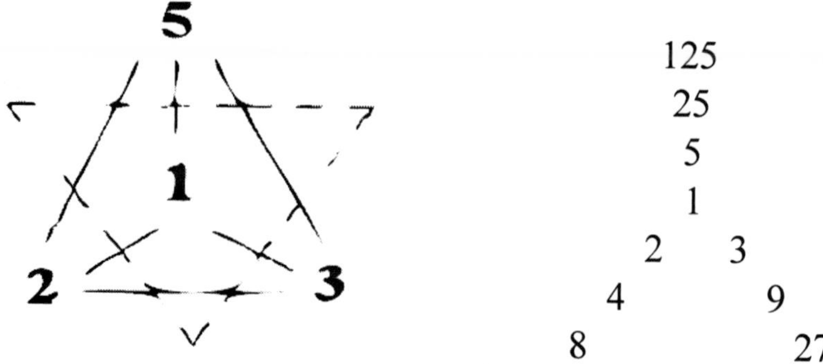

In Figures 45a, b & c, YHVH is represented by musical constructions that begin with God = 1, as the Source, then extending Light to Creation through "lambdas" of 2, 3, and 5, with geometric means inserted.

Figure 45c - Extending the Pnimiyut of YHVH with Geometric Means Inserted

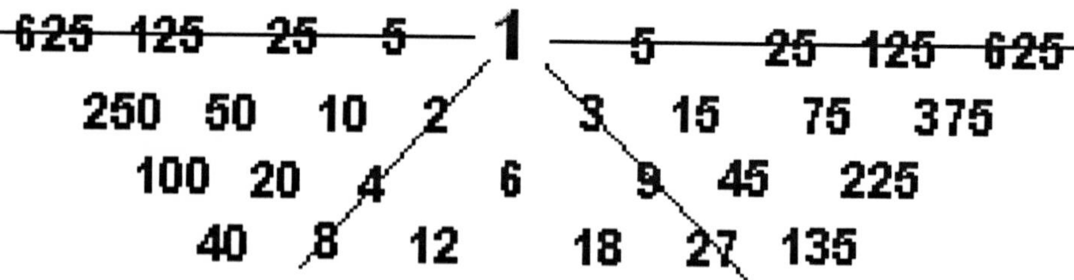

Figure 46 - The Three Paths of the Sacred Practice[198]

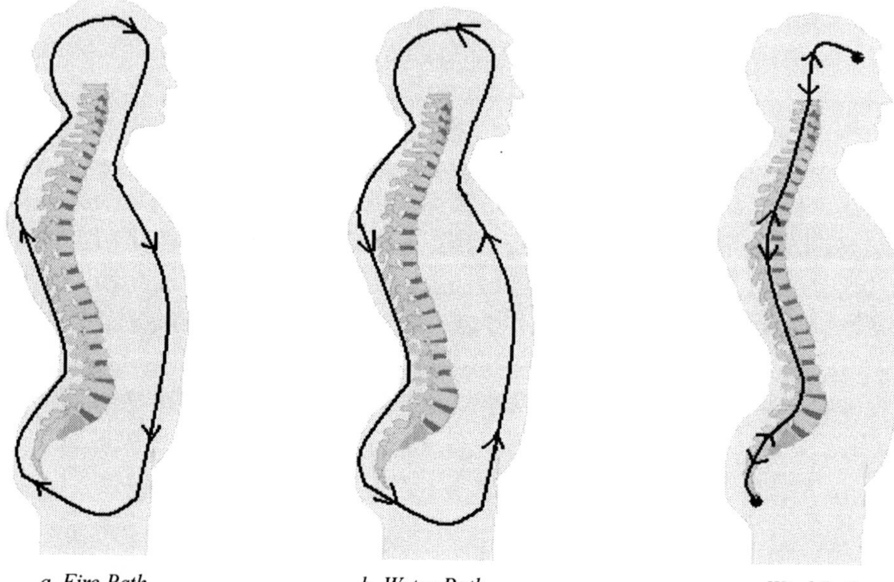

a. Fire Path b. Water Path c. Wind Path

198 Dr. Yang Jwing-Ming, Muscle/Tendon Changing & Marrow/Brain Washing Chi Kung (Jamaica Plain, Mass.: YMAA Pub., 1989) 60; Kaplan, *Sefer Yetzirah*, 1:10 - 1:12.

Figures 47a - The 12 Lights of the Body Encircling 7 Aspects of the soul

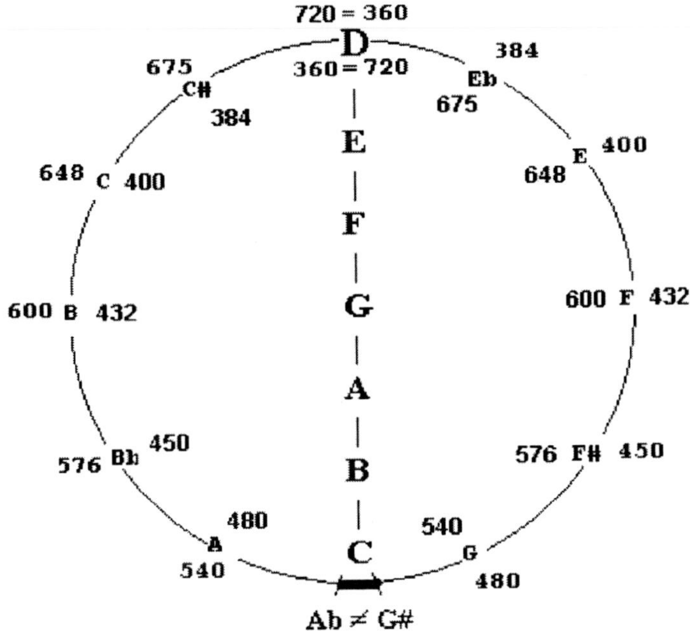

Three Channels of the Mind
Seven Aspects of the Soul
Twelve Aspects of the Body

Figures 47b & c - Making Peace within the Soul for the "12 Who Stand in War"

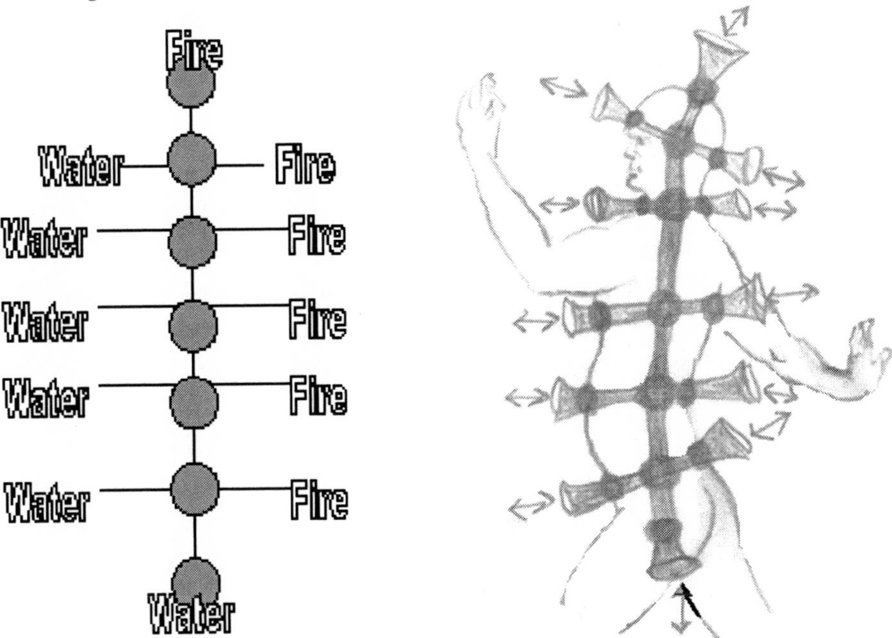

The Sacred Practice

The Torah articulates Semitic civilization's frustration with their inability to liberate their soul and "walk with God" in the manner of Enoch and Noah — two legendary Aryan holy men who were known to each culture by different names. The Semitic inability to liberate one's soul, in the manner of the Aryan fathers, has been inhibited by a seemingly insurmountable psychological barrier called inherent sin. A great wall, the metaphorical "Walls of Jericho," separates God from God's potential prophets. Before taking the Eucharist, Roman Catholics recite that they are "unworthy to receive it." In Genesis 18:27, Abraham states: ''I am but dust and ashes." Surrender of the ego empowers the possibility of ascension, but a healthy humility has often given way to culturally-ingrained guilt and self-loathing that is unable to acknowledge man's ability to transcend sin.

It was reasoned that since God was perfect, Adam's inability to return to Paradise had to be man's own doing or undoing. The Torah commands an action-based approach to God based on Abraham's mathematical precepts. The Bible begins with Adam's exile from the perfection of Heaven, followed by generations of wandering in sin in search of a way back to Heaven. Seven generations after Adam, a holy man was born named Enoch. He was a righteous man, who God deemed worthy of salvation from the evil that surrounded him. Similarly, seven generations after Abraham, another holy man was born. Moses wandered in exile for 40 years in the desert, to deliver the Israelites. But, even Moses was not worthy of metaphorically "crossing over" the Jordan River to the Promised Land[199]

Refraining from sin became the moral imperative of the Bible. Jewish tradition tells us that only 6 laws were given to Adam in the Garden of Eden, and that he did not have access to the Divine Wisdom (Hebrew: *Chochmah*) embodied by the number 7 to "permute them [the numbers], weigh them, and transform them..."[200] Enoch would have learned how to "calculate that which the mouth cannot speak and the ear cannot hear,"[201] as well as how the number 7 relates to the "pronunciation" of God's sacred name, *Yahweh*. Once Enoch learned to "pronounce" the Word, *Yahweh,* he would be saved. But, what exactly does salvation mean?

Deciphering the mathematical riddles of the *Sefer Yetzirah* explains the "pronunciation" of YHVH and describes the 7 Noahide Laws required

199 In the same manner that a High Priest would "cross-over" — by passing through the veil between life and death into the Holy of Holies— liberating the soul in order to pray for Israel during the Day of Atonement.
200 Kaplan, Aryeh, *Sefer Yetzirah* (York Beach, Maine: Samuel Weiser, 1990) verse 2:5; Schatz, Op.Cit., 30;
201 Kaplan, Op.Cit., verse 4:16; Schatz, Op.Cit., 114;

of all Jews and non-Jews alike. Noah, Enoch, and Abraham followed the same meditation practice,[202] but strictly speaking, Judaism really began with Moses at Mount Sinai, not with Abraham. Kabbalistic tradition suggests that knowledge of these 7 laws passed from Enoch to Noah, Shem, and ultimately to Melchizedek,who initiated Abraham into the sacred meditation practice of High Priests.[203]

Abraham recorded these 7 laws for posterity in the *Sefer Yetzirah by* encrypting them directly within the Word, YHVH, within a mathematical and scientific context.[204] The *Sefer Yetzirah,* and more specifically, the Word of God, YHVH, might appropriately be thought of as an instruction manual for the Bible. This encryption provides solutions to the greatest mysteries of Scripture, including the mysteries of the *Merkavah* (Ezekiel's Chariot) and Christianity's Sacred Mystery of the Holy Trinity. Knowledge of the meaning and pronunciation of the Word of God became the patriarchal birthright for the next three generations: Isaac, Jacob and Joseph.

Once Joseph's brothers sold him into slavery in Egypt, Israel began its exile, and three generations later, God was compelled to reveal the Word's meaning and pronunciation to mankind once more. This time through the prophet Moses — not coincidentally — 7 generations after Abraham, so that Israel could fulfill its prophesied destiny to become a nation of priest-prophets. Leading Israel out of bondage in Egypt is metaphor for liberating the soul from its bondage within the body to the "Promised Land." Israel is not a geographical place, but rather, a spiritual destination that is associated with the liberated soul or *Shechinah* (Divine Presence).

The number 7 takes on a very special and unique role within monotheistic theology and thus within Biblical allegory. It holds a special place in Abraham's "mixed-base" numerical system as the driving force of purification and the prelude to salvation (Figure 80). Within Jewish tradition, the spiritual aspect of the wedding ceremony describes how the mind's "7 tone circles" integrates the 6 lights of the soul into a 7th all-inclusive light to create the "White Light of God." The sacred practice enables man's soul to transcend the body, and once it ascends "on Wings," to stand before, and resonate with, the transcendent Unity of God.

Abraham's sacred practice of 7 circuits around the Axis Mundi teaches mankind how to pray like the Biblical prophets, i.e., how to pray like the Aryan fathers. Specifically, we will see how the mathematical model for Sab-

---

202 However, Jewish tradition is clear that Abraham somehow knew all the Commandments of God's Torah even before they became the Written Law. This text will explain exactly how this was possible, since the 365 prohibitive commandments and the 248 positive commandments of the Torah have their *pnimiyut* (inner vibrational essence) in the *kavanah* (meditative intent) of the sacred practice..

203 According to Jewish Kabbalistic tradition, Melchizedek was Shem's reincarnation.

204 Schatz, Op.Cit., 187-199.

bath prayer is 7 times the tonal frequency of weekday prayer. Weekday prayer gathers the soul's Divine energy, while the introspection and Divine Influx of Sabbath prayer attempts to purge sin that has become lodged within the mind and body. Three different "paths" enable us to purify the amalgam of primordial elements within us: Water, Wind, and Fire (Figure 46a, b & c). They enable us to harmonize the elements and "bind" the mind, body, and soul together in what is effectively a marriage ceremony. God, the Groom, is bound to His bride, in anticipation of man's purified and liberated soul (called the *Shechinah*). The Jewish wedding ceremony reflects this with the bride circumambulating her groom 7 times under a *Chuppah* (a sacred cube).

The Jewish practice of *Tefillin* wraps a leather strap 7 times around the arm, binding a small sacred cube opposite the heart and another on one's forehead (mind), to God. The 3 "channels" of the mind bind the 7 tonecircles of the soul and 12 tonecircles of the body to God. This describes weekday prayer. It redirects man's focus on the divine energy within by avoiding all distractions. The cumulative effects of those 6 days pour their energy into the Sabbath.[205] The Sabbath balances the energies with the Winds of the Holy Spirit (*Ruach Hakodesh*), transforming the body and vivifying the soul to empower liberation. "The adept who seeks to arouse the *Kundalini* [Sanskrit: serpent power] must be prepared to die, because this process [liberation of the soul], quite literally, anticipates the death process."[206]

The High Priest "pronounces" the Word of God on the Day of Atonement in order to liberate his soul. Liberation implies that the soul would pass through a "veil of palms and pomegranates," symbolic of the veil between life and death, in order to enter the Holy of Holies within Solomon's Temple, where the Ark of the Covenant was said to hold the tablets brought down from Sinai by Moses. Once in the Holy of Holies, the liberated soul of the High Priest would pray for the forgiveness of Israel's sins, with the intention of wiping the slate clean for each New Year.

The sacred practice is also symbolized in the Hebrew Scriptures by Joshua's 7 tone circles around Jericho. His generals were priests sounding trumpets that would bring down the walls to God's promised city on the 7th circumambulation. The sacred practice is also symbolized in the final scene of the New Testament's Book of Revelation, when the sacred cube of the New Jerusalem descends from Heaven, heralded by 7 angels blowing trumpets (7 tone circles). The sacred practice of 7 circuits around the sacred cube is also practiced by Muslims circumambulating the Kabah in Mecca during what is called the *Hajj.* Abraham's sacred practice defines the *greater jihad* (inner struggle), as compared to the *lesser jihad,* which tends to occur on the battlefield against perceived oppression.

Lighting the Temple Menorah is metaphor for performing Abraham's sacred practice. Lighting the seven candles of the Temple Menorah consecrates the

205 Just as the 6 Days of Creation poured their energy into 7th Day.
206 Feuerstein, Op.Cit.,178.

Temple that exists within us just as it consecrated Moses' Tabernacle in the desert, igniting the soul to rise up to God like a flame. Knowledge of this practice has been locked away in the *Sefer Yetzirah* since the destruction of Solomon's Temple 2500 years ago. Its secrets reveal that the "pronunciation" of *Yahweh* is not verbal at all, it is an articulation of the mind as it "engraves" seven circuits around the body. It enables a Jew to perform each of his 365 prohibitive commandments and 248 positive commandments with the proper level of *kavanah* (meditative intent) necessary to purify the body and liberate the soul.

Opening the Gate to Heaven

The Taoist meditation practice that became the foundation of Chinese martial arts and Traditional Chinese Medicine is essentially identical to the Abrahamic sacred practice described in the *Sefer Yetzirah.* And, they are both similar to Hindu Tantric and Buddhist Vajrayana meditation techniques. These similarities should not be too surprising if we consider that the original technique to purify the body and liberate the soul began with civilization's common ancestors, the Aryan fathers.

The mind leads the "life-force" in either direction around the body's "tone circle," depending on whether one is practicing a Fire Path or Water Path (Figure 46). Judicious use of these paths ultimately balances what Abraham called the "12 Directors of the Soul"—12 aspects of the body that have entry points located around the body's tone circle (Figures 47a, b & c). If a person is introverted and bookish, for example, they might require the Fire path to bring their energies into balance. Once a Kan-Li (Hebrew: *Chesed-Gevurah*) balance has been achieved, these energies begin to enter the central channel through the "Gateway to Heaven" at the base of the spine. At that point, man's breath can be transformed into the"Breath of God"—the subtle Winds of the Holy Spirit that harmonizes Fire and Water into a subtle life-force that rises like steam within the central channel during the hypnagogic state.

The "12 Directors of the Soul" are initially "12 who stand in War" until the sacred practice harmonizes the opposing Fire and Water elements. The Fires of non-conceptual thought heats the body's seminal Waters, which are made considerably more abundant if not wasted through the distraction of sexual release. The practitioner then "fans" the flames of non-conceptual thought with the "Winds" of breath, harmonizing the Fire and Water into a steam-like substance, which then rises up the central channel toward the top of the head. This initiates what Buddhist Vajrayana practice calls a dripping of "White Bodhi substance." This inner "flaming and dripping" purifies and heals the body from any and all illness or impurities that have become lodged within our mind and body as manifest sin. In this way, a Buddhist monk can purify or cleanse themselves through the sacred meditation practice of "flaming and dripping" (also known as *tummo*).

Chapter 9: Shaping Biblical Allegory

The Soul of the Bible

The Hand of God "engraved" the seven aspects of man's soul. The root vibrations of the soul are symbolized by the Temple Menorah (Figures 48a & b). Six rainbow colors blend into the "White Light of God" at the center of the Menorah: red, orange, yellow, white, green, blue, and violet.

Figure 48a & b - Base-7 - The Temple Menorah

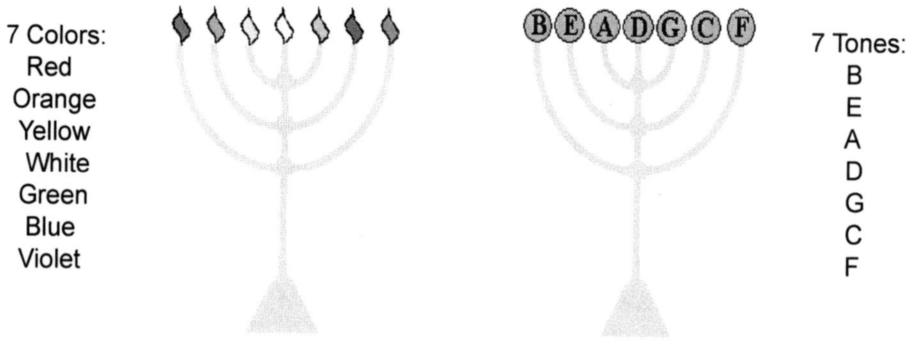

7 Colors:
Red
Orange
Yellow
White
Green
Blue
Violet

B E A D G C F

7 Tones:
B
E
A
D
G
C
F

The rainbow of lights within the divine harmony (Figure 48a) resonates as the ancient Phrygian mode[207] : D, E, F, G, A, B, C (Figure 48b). All notes in this musical scale gravitate toward the tonic note "D" ("God in His Holy Palace"). This corresponds to the Omnipresent, all-inclusive sound, the way white light corresponds to the all-inclusive light at the center of the Menorah. Once the body has been purged of sinful impurities, it becomes a vehicle to express the harmonized 6 color/sounds that naturally unite into the 7th all-inclusive white light of the Divine Presence. The Soul's energy takes up residence in man's spinal chord, and it is centered at the heart (Figure 42b).

In the same way that six colors and sounds harmonize as a 7th color/tone, this pattern is embedded directly in the Biblical text itself as the Bible's "chiastic structure." The term chiastic is most commonly used as a literary structure, in which ancient allegorical ideas are placed in a symmetric order, for example, B-E-A-D-G-C-F puts God ("D") in "His Holy Palace" at the center. A more detailed mathematical exposition of this structure can be found

207 The ancient Greek Phrygian mode is equivalent to the modern Dorian mode.

in the Greek letter Chi or "X" as reciprocal lambdas (Figure 42b). In my first book, *The Lost Word of God*, I compare the equivalent harmonic construction of Plato's "World Soul" within his Timaeus to Abraham's "Primordial Man" construction within the *Sefer Yetzirah.* They both describe the exact same mathematical "Blueprint" for realizing the divine within us through meditation (Greek: *theoria*; Hebrew: *tardemah*). In Figure 42b, the Greek letter Chi's symmetry derives from the reciprocity of frequency and wavelength and it reflects in a mirror-like image across the *Axis Mundi* of God (= 1).

In his recent book, *Nahum,*[208] Duane Christensen analyzes the Tanakh's Book of Nahum in terms of his own lifelong "study of word counts, chiastic structures, and the like, demonstrating that the Biblical authors used certain numbers as structural principles in the composition of their texts." Christensen's book can be considered a quantum leap for the field of "logo-prosodic analysis" —because — for the first time, a reputable and progressive scholar and theologian has been able to tie his detailed analysis of the Bible's symmetrical literary structures to Ernest McClain's analysis of the Bible's symmetrical harmonic structures. By integrating their respective approaches, Christensen and McClain have accomplished nothing less than definitively cracking the only real Bible Code, linking Biblical prosody to its mathematical/musical framework. The literary structures described in *Nahum* focus on the symmetrical harmonic structure of the Temple Menorah of ancient Jerusalem as already described. Their combined approach reveals a complex harmonic and literary integration of Biblical text and the science of sound that suggests an entirely new direction for Bible scholarship.

In an example taken from his book on *Nahum*, Christensen describes the prosodic structure of Hebrew cantos, strophes, verses, disjunctive accent marks, word and letter counts, and *mora* counting (syllable-counting), all of which reflect the harmonics of a symmetrical Temple Menorah pattern. Another of these published studies analyses three cantos in Genesis 1-2, once again, reflecting a Temple Menorah pattern.[209]

Although masterfully analyzing the prosodic and harmonic structures of the Hebrew Scriptures according to the chiastic structures of the Temple Menorah, Christensen and McClain never address my own hypothesized addendum to this thesis: that lighting the Temple Menorah is Biblical metaphor for vivifying the 7 aspects of the soul in order to purify the body and liberate the soul. From this perspective, the entire Torah becomes an explication of Abraham's sacred deep meditation practice. In Chapter 9, we will reexamine Christensen's *Nahum* passages from this slightly modified perspective, and hopefully, shed additional light on how the Temple Menorah relates to meditation as the core message and practice of the Bible.

208 Duane Christensen, *Nahum* (New Haven, CT: Yale University Press, 2009).
209 Duane Christensen, *Reading Genesis 1-2 in Hebrew* (Rodeo, CA: Bibal Corp., 2005) 60.

The Book of Genesis

Adam is symbolic of the common man whose soul was created to eternal life in Heaven, with his soul's 3 upper and 3 lower lights integrated into the One. God then "Breathed" the 7 "inner lights" of his soul into the 12 "outer lights" of his translucent and ethereal body. Adam was blissful in his ignorance, and he knew nothing of Good and Evil. However, Adam disobeyed God when he ate from the forbidden fruit, and acquired knowledge of right and wrong. We might consider the story of Adam and Eve as a parody of Inanna's sexual unification rites, and a Semitic critique describing the Aryan's apparent lack of self-awareness. The Semitic position, as stated in this allegory, suggests that Adam was unsuitable for Heaven, not for his bite from the fruit of the Tree of Knowledge, but for his acquisition of knowledge without wisdom, i.e., without also partaking of the fruit of the Tree of Life. Without the "wings" of wisdom, God was compelled to exile him from Heaven to a cursed Earth. His fall from Grace embodied the dissonance of greater knowledge, and as he "fell" further into matter, his physical body became more dense, incorporating the grosser aspects of the primordial elements. The Semitic position argues that the souls and ethereal bodies of mankind are created in Heaven, but then incarnate into the bondage of a physical body, with all its various appetites, driving man toward sin and distraction from God. Despite some later Kabbalistic commentary that attempts to portray Adam as wise and knowing,[210] Adam was no prophet, and he had no idea how to rise above his physical nature. Adam was the common man forced to choose between Good and Evil.

Spiritual completion would only be possible once mankind discovered the "Pathway to Heaven." Here are stories of the 7 holy shepherds in Genesis who learned how to spiritually transform the four elements in order to travel that path.

1. Seven generations after Adam there was much evil in the world, so God began mankind on a spiritual path back to Paradise by saving Enoch from his exile on the cursed Earth. God saved Enoch by teaching him how to "pronounce" YHVH, making him the first holy man to liberate his soul through the sacred meditation practice. Within Genesis, Enoch didn't die, he "walked with God," successfully liberating his soul from its bondage and exile within the body, a container that God fashioned from the dense matter of Earth.

2. By the time Noah was born, Adam was dead, and the Earth was no longer cursed. God then purged all the remaining Evil from the Earth with a

210 Zohar 37b and 55b: "God did indeed send a book down to Adam, from which he became acquainted with the supernal wisdom..."

Great Flood. He saved Noah from the Waters by teaching him how to build an Ark, which is metaphor for teaching him how to pronounce the Holy Name. Thus, the sacred meditation practice became known as the 7 Noahide Laws. The sacred practice requires the mind to "sound the trumpet" like Joshua's priest-generals, and utilize the mind's 3 pathways to make 7 circuits around the 12 aspects of the body. One of the mind's 3 pathways is called the Water Path (Figure 46b). Noah mastered "the Water Path," and, like Enoch, he successfully liberated his soul to "walk with God."

3. God saved both Abram, and his nephew Lot, from Fire. In a Midrashic backstory to Genesis, God saved Abram by sending the angel Michael[211] to rescue him from the fiery furnace into which he had been thrown by Nimrod. However, Abram's brother, Haran, did not survive Nimrod's furnace.[212] In the Torah, God makes reference to this when he tells Abram: "I am YHVH Who brought you out of the Ur Kasdim [Fire of the Chaldeans] to give you this land to inherit it." At Abraham's request, God then saved his brother's son Lot from Fire and brimstone that "cleansed" the sinful cities of Sodom and Gomorrah. Since Lot was a righteous man, he was led through the Fires of Heaven by angels, thus becoming a prophet in the Fire Path. God's first covenant with Abram, the Covenant of the Parts, describes Abram's Fire Path. Abram sacrificed 3 heifers, 3 goats, 3 rams, a turtle dove and a young dove. "He cut them in the center and placed each piece opposite its counterpart. The birds, however, he did not cut up… There was a smoky furnace and a torch of fire which passed between these pieces." God then put Abram into a "deep sleep" (Hebrew: *Tardemah*), in which his prophetic visions revealed Israel's future exile in Egypt and its liberation to the Promised Land.

4. God had another Covenant with Abram, the "Covenant of the Word," also translated as the "Covenant of Circumcision." The Hebrew word for circumcision is *milah,* which also translates from the Hebrew as "word" (meaning God's "Word"; Greek: *Logos*). This usage is confirmed for us in the Biblical phrase: "The spirit of God spoke in me, and His Word (*Milah*) is upon my tongue."[213] God tells Abraham that "my Covenant will be in your flesh for an everlasting Covenant.[214] Circumcision is a lasting reminder that any physical distractions from God due to one's lust or appetites must be "truncated." When Abram was initiated into the sacred practice by Melchizedek he was metaphorically climbing God's Holy Mountain, empowering him to transform his breath into the "Breath of

211 Tanya: Igeret Hakodesh 12: "Michael is the prince of water and Gabriel is the prince of Fire, yet they do not extinguish one another."
212 Midrash Genesis Rabbah xliv. 16.
213 II Samuel 23:2.
214 Genesis 17:13

God," which is synonymous with the subtle and holy Winds of *Ruach Hakodesh*[215] (the Holy Spirit). The Hebrew letter *Heh* was added to his name, imbuing him with the "Breath of God," and thus his name would be transformed from Abram to Abraham. Abram's circumcision had written the Word of God into his flesh, and he would no longer be distracted from God. He was One with the Holy Spirit, the spiritual Wind.

5. To test Abraham's devotion, God requested that Abraham kill his son Isaac as a sacrifice to God on Mount Moriah, God's Holy Mountain. This was called *Akeidah Yitzchak* (the Binding of Isaac). Torah commentary and Midrash tell us that upon realizing that he was to be the sacrifice, Isaac showed great inner strength and restraint (Hebrew: *Gevurah*) when facing immanent death. Within the Jewish Orthodox tradition, Isaac epitomizes *Gevurah*, the spiritual Fires of sacrifice. Isaac's soul ascended, as if he were actually sacrificed, and God said to Abraham: "All the nations of the earth shall bless themselves by your offspring, because you have listened to my Voice."

6. On Mount Moriah (Hebrew: "Seeing"), at the exact location of the *Akeidah*, Isaac's son Jacob dreamt of angels ascending and descending along a great ladder that reached into Heaven (along the unique inverse symmetry of the Sabbath scale). God then told Jacob that his offspring would spread out, powerfully westward, eastward, northward, and southward, and all the families of the earth shall bless themselves by you and your offspring. When he awoke, he called this spot the "abode of God" and the "Gate of the Heavens." Jacob vowed that a house of God would be built on that site. In later generations, the Holy of Holies of Solomon's Temple would be built on that precise spot. Jacob epitomized the seminal spiritual Waters of male effluence. He wrestled with an angel who renamed him Israel, and his 12 sons led the 12 Tribes of Israel.

7. Joseph symbolizes a spiritual transformation of Earth as the body of Egypt holding the soul of Israel captive. Joseph's own captivity in Egypt began when he was sold into slavery by his brothers. This began Israel's exile in Egypt, thus bringing the Book of Genesis to a close the way it began — in Exile. However, in clear contrast to Adam's exile, Joseph's birthright transformed Earth to spiritual Earth, enabling him to correctly interpret the Pharaoh's dream: after 7 years of bounty the Earth would be barren. Joseph was transformed from slave to chief magistrate, and he ordered grain to be stored over the 7 abundant years, which fed the country and neighboring countries during the 7 lean years.

215 The Hebrew word *ruach* translates into breath, spirit and wind.

Once the leaders of Egypt had forgotten Joseph, the Israelites became oppressed slaves. After several hundred years of captivity, the story of Moses and the Exodus from Egypt would begin a new 7-step process, once again structured by the spiritual transformation of the four primordial elements. This 7-step process, associated with the 7 shepherds of Genesis, comprises an instruction manual for Abraham's sacred practice. The secrets of prophecy embodied by the *Merkavah* (Ezekiel's Chariot) have been hidden before our eyes since the destruction of Solomon's Temple. These secrets were at least mentioned in the oldest passages of the Talmud, but by the time the rabbinate was founded by Hillel (110 BCE - 10 CE), prophecy was declared dead, and any knowledge of how to pray like the prophets had been lost for hundreds of years. That is why discovering the secrets of the *Merkavah* within Abraham's *Sefer Yetzirah* is so important.

Mount Moriah, the Temple Mount, has traditionally been the seat of prophecy. Climbing the Holy Mountain, and lighting the Temple Menorah is metaphor for the 7 steps of Abraham's sacred meditation practice. We must all look within ourselves to construct the anticipated Third Temple. *Yahweh* will reign over a New Jerusalem of prophets among all three faiths, once God's Name is "pronounced" in deep meditation by all the "Children of Abraham."

The Book of Exodus

The Torah's Book of Exodus states, and Jewish commentaries help to explain, how the "Voice" of God uttered Ten Commandments to all of Israel in a single moment. But, only Moses was at the level of prophecy necessary to "hear" the individual commandments. This defining moment in Exodus describes how God's simultaneous unity and diversity were originally conceived of as a harmonic series. The *Sefer Yetzirah*'s mathematics lays out the acoustics of Exodus as 10 distinct vibrating modes of a single string — almost 4000 years before that principle was discovered by modern scientists. Abraham further defines exactly how 10 vibrating modes of that single string generate 7 vibratory essences of the Soul, 12 vibratory essences of the Body, and the harmonic structure of Time and the Universe. Like all allegory in the Book of Genesis, the Exodus framework is defined by a 7-step process that transforms the four primordial elements into their spiritual counterpart — all of which emanate from God's primordial string — vibrating as a harmonic series and "emanating from one Name." Modern superstring theory echoes Abraham's string theory, and modern physics is on the cusp of proving it empirically true as a comprehensive cosmology.

That process was allegorized as the 7 lights of the Temple Menorah, including the 3½ steps required to ascend to the top of God's Holy Mountain, followed by the 3½ steps necessary to descend the mountain. It is no coincidence that the Kundalini serpent of Hinduism is coiled 3½ times at the base of the spine. The twin serpents of the Caduceus each make 7 spirals ascending like Fire and 7 spirals descending like Water, while the "two wings," riding on the Winds, symbolize the soul's liberation as divine messenger between God and man.

Abraham is the founding father of monotheism within the Book of Genesis, while Moses is the father of Judaism within the Book of Exodus. The Holy Mountain and the Temple Menorah reflect the same template for Biblical allegory based on mastering the four primordial elements through meditation:

1. Adam and Eve's exile was analogous to Israel's Earthly exile in Egypt. The Israelites were oppressed and suffering in bondage by the time Moses was born.

2. Since Hebrew infants were being killed, Moses' mother saved him by building, what was effectively, a tiny wicker ark, placing it among the reeds at the bank of the river. Thus, we can say that the Pharaoh's daughter saved Moses from the Waters. This story echoes God's salvation of Noah from the Waters in a much larger ark. So, instead of killing first-born Moses, the Pharaoh raised him like an Egyptian prince. He could therefore be well-educated in the liberal arts, which was necessary in order to become Judaism's most important prophet. As he grew to adulthood, he became increasingly aware of Israel's oppression and found reason to kill a cruel Egyptian taskmaster. Moses fled from the Pharaoh and found respite at the well of Jethro, a priest of Midian, where he encountered the priest's 7 daughters. The symbolism of both sexual and spiritual "Waters" are alluded to here. But, there was nothing sexually overt. Sexuality had been morally sanctified and allegorized to Semitic satisfaction. Like Isaac and Jacob, Moses found his bride at the well.[216] Having saved Jethro's daughters from rogues, their father sought to repay Moses by giving him his daughter Zipporah for a wife. Becoming a shepherd for Jethro was a training ground to become the great shepherd of Israel.

3. While herding Jethro's sheep on Mount Sinai, the Holy Mountain, Moses experiences his first prophetic vision, speaking to him from within the Fires of the burning bush. God spoke to Moses for the first time from amidst the bush.

216 The patriarchs meet their wives "at the well" — symbolizing a marriage to wisdom and prophecy through Abraham's sacred practice — matrimony between God as groom and a man's soul (*Shechinah*) as bride. Jethro's 7 daughters were symbolic of the 7 lights of the soul as the wellspring of prophecy and wisdom..

4. Once Moses removed his shoes, the final barrier was removed between Moses and the Ruach Hakodesh (Hebrew: Holy Spirit; Breath of God, Holy Wind) atop the Holy Mountain.[217] God introduced Himself as the God of Abraham, Isaac and Jacob, telling Moses that He would descend to rescue the Children of Israel from the oppression of their Egyptian taskmasters, and that he, Moses, was being dispatched to the Pharaoh, to shepherd the Children of Israel out of Egypt to the Promised Land. Atop the Holy Mountain, the Breath of God worked hard to transform Moses, "with signs and wonders," into the shepherd of Israel. When Moses was worried that the Israelites would ask who sent him, God instructed him to say *"Ehyeh* has sent me to you." It is important to note that the holiest Name of God, *Yahweh* (יהוה), has almost the same spelling and meaning as *Ehyeh (***אהוה**). The letter *Yud* (י = 10) of *Yahweh* becomes the *Alef* (א = 1) in *Ehyeh.* The point source and diversity of the letter *Yud* "י" of *Yahweh* defines both the unity and diversity of a harmonic series; but, the diversity that reaches down into matter as HVH הוה is emphasized in the letter *Yud* "י" whereas, the transcendent Unity of *Alef* "א" is stressed in *Ehyeh.* Although God reassured Moses that by using *Ehyeh*, the Israelites would heed his voice, Moses asked that his brother Aaron speak for him, even as he descended the Holy Mountain.

5. Deuteronomy 33:2 calls the Torah "eish da'at" (a fiery law). Midrash tells us that God engraved the tablets with "black fire on white fire."[218] The spiritual Fires of God's Ten Utterances are the Fires of Heaven and Hell that manifest as both the Ten Commandments, sent to guide Israel in purification and liberation; and the Ten Plagues, sent to defeat the hardened hearts of the Egyptians. The Ten Plagues were created from subsets of the four primordial elements in order to cleanse the "body of Egypt":

* 1-2 were Wind plagues: Locusts and Darkness.
* 3-4 were Fire plagues: Boils from furnace soot, and Fiery Hail.
* 5-6 were Water plagues: Frogs and turning the Nile to Blood.
* 7-9 were Earth plagues: Lice from dust, Wild Beasts swarmed the land, and an Epidemic of livestock in the field.
* 10 God descended to Smite the first born of Egypt as the 10th and final plague in response to Egypt's killing of first-born Hebrews, which precipitated the exile of Moses as an infant, bringing Moses full-circle in his personal journey

217 Genesis 3:5 (see commentary in Stone Edition)..
218 *Midrash Tanhuma, Genesis 1.*

6. a) God saved Israel by parting the spiritual Waters of the Red Sea just as God parted the spiritual Waters from the material Waters within the Heavenly Firmament during Creation. The Red Sea liberated the Good and long-suffering Israelites and drowned the "Evil" Egyptians.
b) Israel wandered in the desert just as Adam and Eve wandered in exile, the people cried out when there was no water. They came to the waters at *Marah*, but they were to bitter to drink. YHVH then showed Moses a piece of wood, which he threw into the water, transforming them into sweet spiritual Waters. There God decreed that as long as Israel followed His commandments, their needs would be fulfilled. To emphasize this bounty, Moses lead the people to *Elim*, where they camped beside 12 springs of water and 70 date-palms.
c) After more wandering in the desert, there was no food, and the people cried out, and God spoke to Moses and told him to speak to Israel, and make them aware that their God would fill their hunger. The spiritual Waters of manna then rained down to nourish Israel each morning, each taking nourishment according to their spiritual worth.

7. After forty years of wandering in exile like Adam, the children of Abraham arrived at the Promised Land, the spiritual Earth, Israel, which is symbolic of the *Shechinah*, the liberated soul. Moses, however, even after all his years as Israel's great prophet, was forbidden from crossing over the Jordan to the Promised Land to "walk with God" in the manner of Enoch and Noah.

When a man meditates in the manner of the ancient High Priests, his mind effectively "sings" the 7-note sacred scale of the Temple Menorah, metaphorically lighting its seven candles. Abraham's writings also reveal the principle of the Bible's Temple Mount as Axis Mundi, and that the high ground of the spiritual Israel is of much greater significance than any geographical location or piece of real estate. Israel, the Temple Menorah, and the Temple Mount, are merely symbols of the Bible's great purpose: to acquire knowledge and wisdom by mastering the four elements through deep meditation. It is only our ability to transform those elements into their spiritual reflection that empowers the children of Israel to end their exile and enter the Promised Land.

Comparing Two Traditions

Within Abraham's practice, the 4th and 5th steps are consolidated into one step, symbolizing a transition from the material to the spiritual realm, resulting in 7 sacred steps as compared to the 8-step Vajrayana Buddhist process:

1. The Earth element dissolves into the Water element as "Inner Fire" rises from the base of the spine causing a vision: a shimmering mirage-like image.
2. The Water element dissolves into Fire element in a vision of rising "smoke."
3. The Fire element dissolves into the Wind element in a vision of "fireflies."
4. The Wind element dissolves into Mind in a vision of "butterlamps."[219]
5. Inner Fire of the first four steps melts Kundalini white drops from the "Crown," creating the first bliss, called "white appearance."
6. The sexual Waters, heated by meditation's Inner Fire, are also fueled from above by the dripping of white Kundalini drops. Steam-like red drops then ascend the central channel to create the second bliss called "red increase."
7. The Winds of Breath harmonize the white and red drops in the "heart drop of Dharmakaya" (the seat of the soul), and the practitioner goes into a brief faint or swoon, called "black near-attainment," the third bliss.[220]
8. As the heart drop rises from the heart to the head, within the central channel, the practitioner wakes up from his swoon in the "clear light of death," the fourth bliss. Stabilizing one's practice in the clear light of death brings about a liberation of the heart drop's harmonized soul from one's Earthly body.

The four visions and four blisses attained during the Tibetan Buddhist deep meditation practice are functionally equivalent to the 7 steps experienced during Abraham's sacred practice. Theologian Elaine Pagels explains this commonality: "For the gnostics stood close to the Greek philosophic tradition (and for that matter, to Hindu and Buddhist tradition) that regards the human spirit as residing 'in' a body — as if the actual person were some sort of disembodied being who uses the body as an instrument but does not identify with it."[221]

219 In Potala, the hilltop palace of Lhasa, Tibetan monks light butterlamps at night, blowing horns; a welcome sight to the people below, and reminiscent of lightning and trumpets on the mountain with Israelites below.
220 Tanya, Igeret Hakodesh 12: "In the terminology of the Kabbalists, *tiferet* [literally: truth - the seat of the soul] is made up of the two colors white and red, which allude to *chesed* and *gevurah*."
221 Pagels, Op.Cit., 27.

The Storm on the Mountain

It is important to recognize the ascent of each prophet through the "Storm on the Mountain" as metaphor for engaging the four primordial elements that identify the sacred practice within both Testaments of the Bible. It is interesting to note how the sound of trumpets is always present, clearly depicting the significance of music to the entire process:

- Earth quakes
- Water rains down
- Fire of thunder & lightning
- Wind howls
- Trumpets sound

One of the most dramatic descriptions of the "storm on the mountain," other than Moses on Mount Sinai, occurs after Elijah fasted 40 days and nights during his walk to Mount Horeb (God's other mountain);

> *"Come out," He called, "and stand on the mountain before the Lord." And lo, the Lord passed by. There was a great and mighty wind, splitting mountains and shattering rocks by the power of the Lord; but the Lord was not in the wind. After the wind – an earthquake; but the Lord was not in the earthquake. After the earthquake —fire; but the Lord was not in the fire. And after the fire – a soft murmuring sound. When Elijah heard it, he wrapped his mantle about his face and went out and stood at the entrance of the cave. Then a voice addressed him...*[222]

The "soft-murmuring sound" that Elijah heard comes to us in the quietude of caves, after the "storms" of the body's physiology quiesce. In Isaiah 30:15 we read;

> *For thus said my Lord God, The Holy One of Israel,*
> *"You shall triumph by stillness and quiet;*
> *Your victory shall come about*
> *Through calm and confidence."*[223]

Abraham's ancient practice is also embedded in the allegories of the New Testament's Book of Revelation. In the "preparatory visions" before the peace and tranquility of the descent of the sacred cube from Heaven as

222 *Tanakh*, I Kings 19:11-12.
223 *Tanakh*, Isaiah 30:15.

the New Jerusalem, seven angels descended with 7 golden bowls, full of the purging wrath of God. In the prophecy, all seven bowls were poured out:

> *And there were flashes of lightening, rumblings and peals of thunder, and there was a great earthquake such has never been seen since men were first upon the earth, so great an earthquake was it…and great hail, heavy as a talent came down from Heaven upon men…*[224]

There were also seven angels with trumpets blowing seven tone circles. The seventh angel sounded the trumpet, heralding the New Jerusalem's descent from Heaven:

> *And the temple of God in Heaven was opened, and there was seen the ark of his covenant in his temple, and there came flashes of lightening, and peals of thunder, and an earthquake, and great hail.*[225]

Understanding the sound of horns or trumpets as "tone circles" was made more literal in the Hebrew Scriptures by the actual circles Joshua's "priests holding trumpets" made around the city of Jericho. Jericho within Hebrew Scriptures, is the prototype for the New Jerusalem within Revelation. The Lord had just cleared the way for Israelites to cross the Jordan River into the Promised Land after wandering in the desert for 40 years. He then delivered Jericho to the Israelites with these instructions to Joshua:

> *Let all your troops march around the city and complete one circuit of the city. Do this six days, with seven priests carrying seven ram's horns preceding the Ark. On the seventh day, march around the city seven times, with the priests blowing the horns. And when a long blast is sounded on the horn – all the people shall give a mighty shout. Thereupon the city wall will collapse, and the people shall advance, every man straight ahead.*[226]

Like Islam's "7 circumambulations around the Kabah" (a sacred cube); like Judaism's 7 wraps of a leather strap to bind the sacred cube of a *Tefillin*; like the 7 circumambulations around the *Sukkah* (a sacred cube) during Judaism's Festival of Tabernacles; and, like Christianity's 7 trumpet tone circles heralding the New Jerusalem's descent from Heaven as a sacred cube; Abraham's sacred practice of lighting the 7 lamps of the soul is able to tear down the walls separating man from God — impediments to the soul's liberation. With the

224 Revelations 16:19-21.
225 Revelations 11:19
226 *Tanakh*, Joshua 6:3-5.

Lord's instructions to Joshua "*people shall advance*" and, to use Saint Paul's words, "*reach behind the veil...*" of life and death by liberating one's soul.

When Moses descended from Mount Sinai with the *Tablets of the Testimony*,[227] he had not only "seen" God, but was physically transformed by God's Light, and each of the primordial elements within him: Earth, Water, Fire and Wind, had been transformed at the top of the Holy Mountain:

> *When Moses descended from Mount Sinai ...Aaron and all the Children of Israel saw Moses, and behold! — the skin of his face had become radiant; and they feared to approach him... [so] Moses placed a mask on his face. When Moses would come before Yahweh to speak with Him, he would remove the mask until his departure."*

Moses' use of a mask to hide his radiance when speaking to the Children of Israel, helps to clarify how the average man masks the bright light of his soul every day, blocked by his corporeal body. We might recall how Jesus frightened his Apostles when he walked toward them across the lake within his "heavenly body." Identifying Christ's "heavenly body" as he walked on water, and during his Transfiguration, is in direct conflict with the Western church's concept of bodily resurrection. The body and soul were originally intended to be understood as distinct, albeit tethered, entities. Liberating the soul into a "heavenly body" was something that Christ could do at will, demonstrating his skill at entering and returning from Heaven.

In the Book of Exodus, several chapters were devoted to the consecration of the Tabernacle in preparation for the anointing of High Priests into the sacred practice of the eternal priesthood. It was built by Bezalel, the Temple architect, who "knew how to permute the letters from which Heaven and Earth were created."[228] Once all its components were put in place, *Yahweh* spoke to Moses:

> *You shall bring Aaron and his sons near to the entrance of the Tent of Meeting, and immerse them in water... You shall anoint them as you had anointed their father and they shall minister to Me, and so it shall be that their anointment shall be for them an eternal priesthood for their generations*[229]*...*

The writings of Abraham strongly suggests that Jesus could only have become *Christos* (Greek: Anointed One) because the sacred practice of the eternal priesthood produces what Abraham called "snow." Christian-

227 Exodus 34:29
228 Kaplan, Sefer Yetzirah, 26.
229 Exodus 40:12-15

ity, however, describes it as a "true Baptism of the spirit" as one is initiated into the everlasting priesthood. For Hindus, it is "Soma Juice"; in Tibetan meditation, *tummo* is "flaming and dripping"; Buddhists and Taoists speak of an "ambrosia" of red and white "drops" that commingle at the heart.[230]

The expression "End times" must be reevaluated, and the meaning of "judgement" within the Bible must be carefully reexamined in light of Abraham's writings. A proper rendering involves a man's judgement as a harmonization or balancing of the mind's inner struggle between *accuser* and *advocate*.[231] It does not refer to an externally imposed judgement, in which Christ, or some third party judges mankind.[232] A man's judgement can be measured by his progress on the Holy Mountain, and whether or not he is in the light of the *Ruach Hakodesh*, the Holy Spirit. Armageddon is not a prophecy of World War III. It refers to man's internal struggle to achieve balance and harmony within, and then to seek divinely inspired judgement. In light of Abraham's writings, becoming a nation of prophets implies that the Children of Israel need to actively seek God through Abraham's sacred meditation practice, rather than passively wait for a deliverance that can only come through that practice.

Since a knowledge of prophecy lies outside of the rabbinic tradition, there may be a great reluctance to recognize the meaning and pronunciation of *Yahweh*. However, Abraham's perspective explains the significance of igniting the Temple Lamps as metaphor for embarking on Israel's journey to the Promised Land.

> *He [Moses] placed the Menorah in the Tent of Meeting, opposite the Table, on the south side of the Tabernacle. He kindled the lamps before Yahweh as Yahweh had commanded Moses[233]... The cloud covered the Tent of Meeting, and the glory of Yahweh filled the Tabernacle... When the cloud was raised up from the Tabernacle, the Children of Israel would embark on their journeys. If the cloud did not rise up, they would not embark, until the day it rose up.*[234]

By "lighting the Temple Menorah" the Temple is consecrated in holiness as the *Shechinah* (the Divine Presence of a liberated soul) hovers overhead like a cloud — just as the *Shechinah* of Moses hovered over the Tent of Meeting. The Divine Presence that rose up from the Tabernacle also hovered over the Ark of the Covenant. Theoretically speaking, the Divine Cloud in question might have been the *Shechinah* of Enoch or Noah that hovered over the Ark.

230 What may be producing this dripping sound and sensation is called *palatal myoclonus*, regular spasms of the soft palate, which can occur as an adept enters the hypnagogic state. It is also called *hypnagogic myoclonus*.
231 Kaplan, *Sefer Yetzirah*, Op. Cit., 250, stanza 6.5.
232 Abraham's writings internalized monotheism's notion of judgement since the days of mythic Egypt when Osiris weighed a man's heart against the white feather of truth and harmony.
233 Exodus 40:24-25
234 Exodus 40:34-37; note how close the image of a "cloud rising up" is to the Tibetan "smoke rising up."

Logoprosodic Analysis

Within the context of logoprosodic analysis, and in collaboration with Ernest McClain, Duane Christensen links *Nahum's* prosodic structures to its mathematical/musical structures, by focusing on the chiastic structure of the Temple Menorah (Figures 48a & b). Christensen creates detailed tables quantifying an array of literary measures used by the authors of Scripture, and known to the Masoretic scribes who transcribed the Torah from generation to generation

These quantified measures include counting verses, strophes, cantos, words, syllables, letters,... arranged in chiastic, symmetrical patterns, and organized according to a Temple Menorah template. Christensen's *Nahum* begins with his own translation of the Book of Nahum within the Hebrew Scriptures. He shows how the text forms 7 symmetrical "cantos" within the Temple Menorah pattern. He then drills down into each of these cantos with many details. For our purposes, we will limit ourselves to Canto I, which Christensen considers to be one of only two Hymns of Theophany that appear in the entire prophetic corpus. He describes the other within the Book of Habakkuk, as symmetrical "bookends" with Nahum, completing yet another Temple Menorah pattern.[235]

"The basic building blocks in each poetic *verset* are the *briques* (primary SAS units). These sub-units are delineated by the Masoretes (Torah scribes), who marked most of the boundaries..."[236] "The exact position of each of these disjunctive accent marks is indicated with either a single slash / (for any of the regular disjunctive accent marks) or a double slash // (for the two strongest disjunctive accents *atnah* and *silluq*)."[237] Within Canto I of Nahum, 7 successive strophes scan 9.4 SAS units; which then becomes part of a larger Temple Menorah pattern as follows:

[9.4] . [5.5] . [4.4] . [4.4] . [4.4] . [5.5] . [4.9]

A. ***Yahweh Takes Vengeance against His Enemies*** (1:1-2) SAS units [9.4]

1:1 The exposition / of Nineveh // 2
The scroll of the vision / of Nahum / the Elkoshite // 3
1:2 A zealous and avenging God (ʾEl) / is YHWH / 2
Avenging is YHWH / and a lord (Baʿal) of wrath // 2
Avenging is YHWH / against his foes / 2
And he rages / against his enemies // 2

The structure of Canto I has 7 strophes within 10 verses (1:1 - 1:10). This mirrors the harmonic template of 10 number ratios generating 7 musical tones.

235 For a logoprosodic analysis of Habakkuk refer to Christensen's BIBAL.net web site.
236 Ibid.
237 Christensen, *Nahum*, Op.Cit., xix-xxxiv.

Christensen focuses his attention on this symmetric 7 pattern. But, we have also discussed harmonic 3 and 12 patterns with respect to the mind and body, respectively. Cantos II and IV have 3 verses, while a 12-pattern container is the overall container of the Book of Nahum as the Tanakh's "Body" of Twelve Minor Prophets.

Christensen and McClain push the envelope of Biblical scholarship by linking prosodic analysis to Scripture's mathematical and harmonic framework. My own contribution focuses on the theological meaning of the Temple Menorah template: where the "7 lights of the soul," "lighting the Temple Menorah," and "the storm on the Holy Mountain" are metaphors for Abraham's 7-step meditation practice to transform the four elements through the Holy Spirit. We will continue using Christensen's translation, but from here forward, I will add my own interpretation. I will also superimpose the four elements and Holy Spirit within brackets to demonstrate the repetitive "storm on the mountain" theme.

There is a Temple Menorah structure embedded within the 10 verses of what Christensen describes as Canto I. Within the 10 *Sefirot* (Counting), the 7 aspects of the Soul arise from the four transformed elements. The serpent is said to sleep coiled 3½ times at the base of the spine and emerges from "the pit," ascending through 3½ circuits. In Nahum, *Yahweh's* "serpent-energy" sleeps during verse 1:3; awakens in 1:3½; ascends until verset 7; and descends for the next 3½ verses.

1:3 YHWH he is slow to anger but great in power
and the guilty he does not acquit
[1:3½] YHWH In the whirlwind and in the storm is his way [WIND]
and clouds are the dust of his feet
1:4 He blasts the Sea and he dries it up
and all the Rivers he desiccates [WATER]
They wither away (that is) Bashan and Carmel
and the green of Lebanon withers
1:5 Mountains quake before him
and the hills melt away [EARTH]
And the earth reels before him
and the world and all who dwell in it
1:6 In the presence of his fury who can stand?
and who can rise up in the heat of his anger?
His wrath is poured out like fire [FIRE]
and the rocks are broken asunder by him
1:7 Good is YHWH
indeed a stronghold in the day of distress [HOLY SPIRIT]
And he knows those who take refuge in him

1:8 And in the sweeping torrent
a full end he will make of her place
And his enemies he pursues into darkness
1:9 Whatever you devise against YHWH
a full end he himself is making
Distress will not arise a second time
1:10 For while like thorns matted together
And in a drunken state soaked with "drink"
Devoured they will be like dry stubble completely

The ascent and descent of *Yahweh's* whirlwind (i.e., tone circles) are symmetrical around *Yahweh* at the summit of the Holy Mountain." The four ascending verses, describing the primordial elements, have 4 versets each, while the 4 descending verses have been "transformed" into 3 versets each. Yahweh destroys Nineveh's "body of sin," transforming the four elements into their spiritual reflection. Nahum's prophecy is cast within the Temple Menorah/Storm on the Mountain template that we have been discussing. "In the whirlwind and in the storm" of 3½ circuits, experiencing the gross aspects of Wind, Water, Earth, and Fire, while the Holy Spirit (*Ruach Hakodesh*) transforms them as the prophet "takes refuge in him" at the summit of the Holy Mountain. In the final 3½ strophes, the prophet descends from the summit. "And in the sweeping torrent" the prophet is anointed, and all impurities ("his enemies...whatever you devise against YHWH") are purged. "And in a drunken state, soaked with 'drink'" (Soma juice, snow, ambrosia, true baptism of the spirit,...) the gross elements of the body have been destroyed. "Devoured they will be like dry stubble completely," empowering the soul's liberation.

Israel (the soul) was freed from Egypt's bondage (the body) with 10 Plagues that transformed Egypt's four elements. Like the Exodus from Egypt, Nineveh, the capital of Assyria, destroyed Israel's Northern Kingdom, capturing Israel's 10 tribes. However, time had passeed, and the metaphorical "Soul" to be liberated by Nahum's prophecies were not the 10 lost tribes, but the remaining 2 tribes of Judah still under Assyrian control. The "Body" of Nineveh would be transformed to bring forth Judah's liberation. In the 3 verses of Canto II, Nahum implies that the destruction of the Body of Nineveh would free the Soul of Judah:

1:11 From you [Nineveh] he has departed a plotter of evil against YHWH
(He is) the counselor (of) Belial [prince of Hell]
1:12 Thus says YHWH "Are they not strong and ever so numerous?
But even so they shall be sheared and they will pass on
though I afflicted you [Judah], I will afflict you no more
1:13 And now I will break his rod from upon you and your bonds snap apart"

Chapter 10: Music in the Garden of Eden

The Two Steps of Creation

In the beginning ... God said "Let there be Light" (Figures 36 & 37) and God's harmonic series extended to the boundaries of the universe. In step 2 of Creation, the harmonic series was "reordered" (Hebrew: *Tikun*), beginning with the creation of the Heavenly Firmament on the second day. A musical octave (2:1) subset of the harmonic series was created to contain all other tones. In Figures 41a & b Abraham's "2 stones" shaped the Biblical allegory of the 2nd Day of Creation by creating a Heavenly Firmament as the container of all that would follow.

- The next harmonic subset created the Earth's seas and plant life derived from the arithmetic and harmonic means within the Heavenly Firmament octave. This was rooted in the musical template for "3 stones" to shape the 3rd Day of Creation.
- Next, the Heavenly luminaries of the sun, moon and stars extended the arithmetic and harmonic means from Earth to the Heavens, using "4 stones" to shape the 4th Day of Creation.
- All living creatures were created from the diatonic scale using "5 stones" on the 5th Day.
- God created Adam from the chromatic scale with "6 stones" on the 6th Day. Adam was then put into a deep sleep (Hebrew: *Tardemah,* i.e. deep meditation). Within the hermaphrodite soul of man (Figure 42b)[238] woman's number is 2 and man's number is 3. Thus, the essence of woman was taken from one of Adam's many geometric "ribs" of ratio 2:3.
- God "rested" from any new Creations with "7 stones" on the 7th Day.

Tending the Garden

God planted two trees in the Garden of Eden (Figures 49a & b): the Tree of Knowledge of Good and Evil, and the Tree of Life. He then commanded Adam to tend the Garden, but forbade him from eating from the Tree of Knowledge of Good and Evil. We might recall that the Pishon and Gihon Rivers carry the elements of Earth and Water to sustain the roots and branches of the Tree of Knowledge (Log

238 Zohar 22b;

2^p x Log 3^q = Earth * Water), while the Tree of Life provides us with Abraham's formula for all containers of Divine Light (Log 3^q x Log 5^r = Water * Wind). The winding serpent that ascended and descended the branches and roots of the Tree of Knowledge was Adam's alter ego (Figure 50). The "Breath of God" (powers of 5), within the Tree of Life, raised up the serpent energy of man's soul "on wings."

Figure 49a & b Two Trees in the Garden of Eden

Tree of Knowledge of Good & Evil **Tree of Life**

1/729 1/486 1/324 1/216 1/144 1/96 1/64 1/15625 1/9375 1/5625 1/3375 1/2025 1/1215 1/729
1/243 1/162 1/108 1/72 1/48 1/32 1/3125 1/1875 1/1125 1/675 1/405 1/243
1/81 1/54 1/36 1/24 1/16 1/625 1/375 1/225 1/135 1/81
1/27 1/18 1/12 1/8 1/125 1/75 1/45 1/27
1/9 1/6 1/4 1/25 1/15 1/9
1/3 1/2 1/5 1/3

1 1
2 3 3 5
4 6 9 9 15 25
8 12 18 27 27 45 75 125
16 24 36 54 81 81 135 225 375 625
32 48 72 108 162 243 243 405 675 1125 1875 3125
64 96 144 216 324 486 729 1215 2025 3375 5625 9375 15625

Figure 50 - The Cunning Serpent as the Essence of Man

serpent ascending:

1 3 9 27 81 243 729
F C G D A E B

serpent descending:

729 243 81 27 9 3 1
B E A D G C F

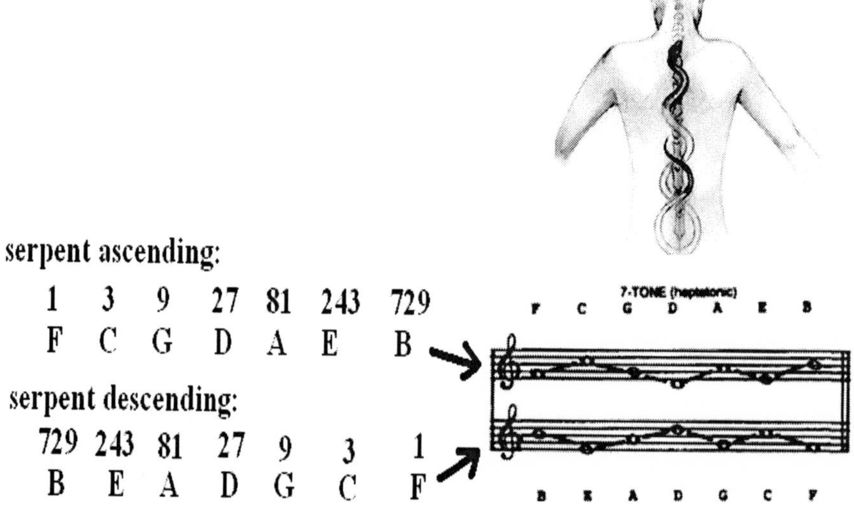

Figure 51 depicts the contrast between Adam as a pure and innocent soul as compared to his soul corrupted by knowledge — ascending the tree to know Good: F#, C#, and G#, and descending to know Evil: Bb, Eb, and Ab. The seven musical tones of Adam's pure soul are a subset of the Tree of Knowledge as derived from the prime factors 2 and 3. After Adam took a bite of the forbidden fruit (Figure 52a), his soul's essence was harmonically extended to "know" both Good and Evil .

Figure 51 - Adam Partakes of the Tree of Knowledge of Good & Evil

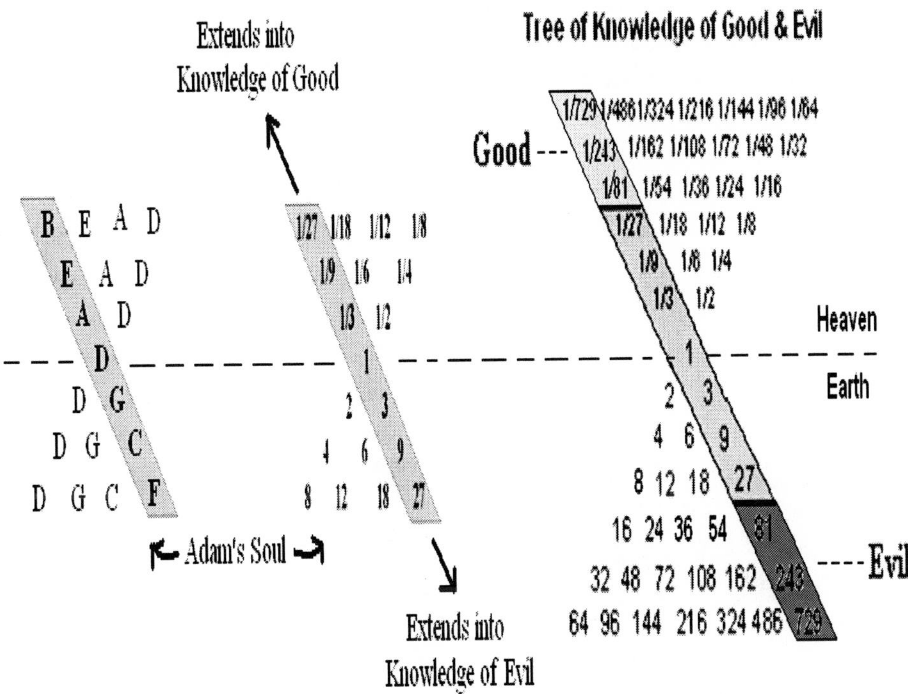

Adam's Fall from Grace

In Heaven, it would have been easy for Adam "to stretch out his hand and take also from the tree of life and eat, and live forever!" Therefore God banished Adam, Eve, and the serpent, from the Garden, and protected the Tree of Life by stationing cherubim East of the Garden with a fiery, ever-turning sword. Within a cross-cut of the triple and quintuple progression, the Tree of Life empowers the outer lights of Adam's body to successfully contain and harness the inner lights of his soul. But, Adam would never learn to harness his soul's divine energy. Adam, Eve and the serpent, fell from Grace without ever partaking of the fruit of the Tree of Life.

Adam's soul then became obscured within the exile of an even more gross container of matter, a dense physical body, created from an increasingly dense Earth element. The spiritual Earth element that exists within man's "Heavenly" or ethereal body, descended further into matter and became increasingly opaque, until none of Adam's inner light shone through. This dense physical body had appetites of its own that muddled and confused Adam's thoughts and emotions. At least Adam was not cursed like the serpent who had to crawl on its belly in the dust of the earth.

After God banished them from the Garden he cursed the serpent, and he cursed the Earth for as long as Adam lived (Figure 52b). It is important to note that he did not curse Adam and Eve. Mankind's life on earth was not Hell, per se, but neither was it a half-way house for less severe crimes. It was the final destination for those in exile from God and Heaven. Pain, suffering, and death is as bad as it got for the Torah's notion of exile from God. We have already mentioned how non-canonical works like the Book of Enoch, and literary works like Dante's *Inferno* and Milton's *Paradise Lost* have distorted Christian notions of Hell until they became quite different than what was theologically envisioned in the *Sefer Yetzirah* and the Book of Genesis.

Figure 52a - Adam & Eve Tempted

Figure 52b - Adam & Eve Exiled

From Adam's new perspective on Earth, Heaven's Tree of Life was transformed into a Holy Mountain that was missing its spiritual reflection. In other words, the upper triangle, i.e., the upper branches of the Tree of Life, were no longer evident to mankind after the Fall. The Holy Mountain's upper spiritual reflection would not be available to mankind until Enoch, in the 7th generation from Adam.

The Holy Mountain

Thus, the Tree of Life in Heaven was transformed into the Holy Mountain on Earth, as depicted in Figure 53a. The mathematical foundation of Biblical allegory would now be moved from God's Holy Palace at the center of the Tree of Life, to the lower left-hand side "cornerstone" of God's Holy Mountain (the 1 x 3 x 5 ziggurat depicted in Figures 53a & b). Mankind's spiritual progress would be based on incorporating progressively higher powers of 2, 3 and 5 into one's spiritual substance. The serpent wanders through powers of 3 along the base of the Holy Mountain to gain in knowledge, but to gain in wisdom, the Eagle must ascend through powers of 5, on the Winds of the Holy Spirit (see the ziggurat's left slope in Figure 55). The Torah chronologically progresses through Biblical allegory in Figure 56.

Figure 53a - After the Fall, the Tree of Life in Heaven Becomes God's Holy Mountain

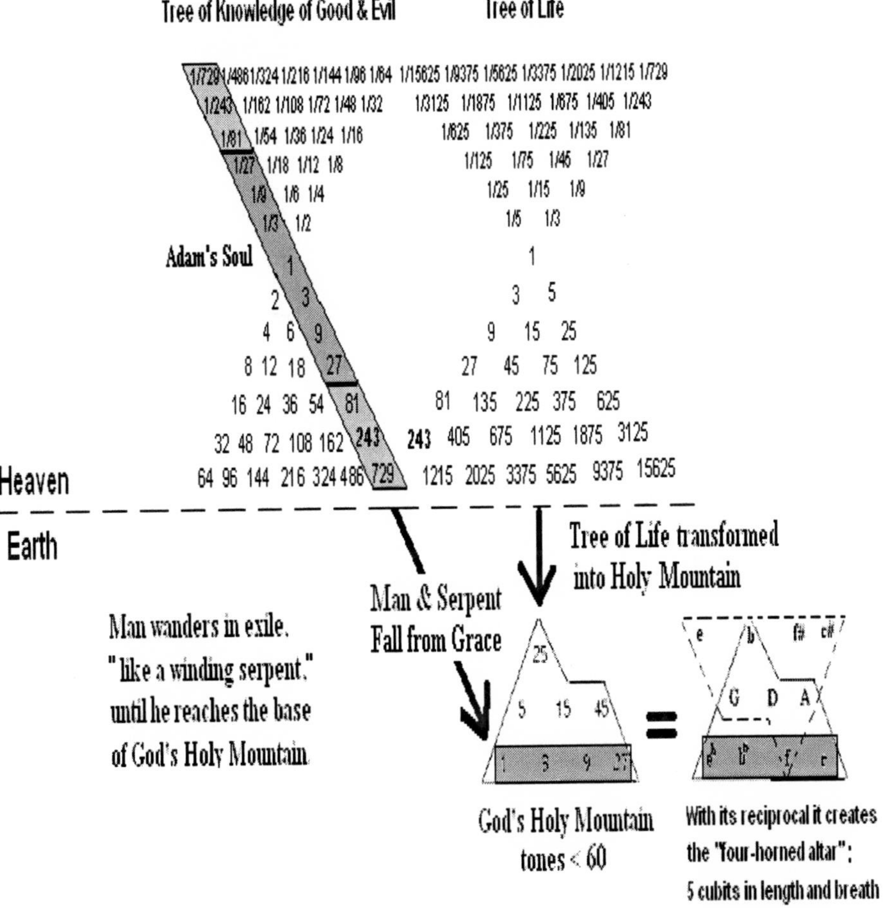

Figure 53b - God's Holy Mountain as the 3 x 5 Tree of Life "Lambda" Turned on its Side

15625	46875	140625	421875	1265625	3796875	11390625
3125	9375	28125	84375	253125	759375	2278125
625	1875	5625	16875	50625	151875	455625
125	375	1125	3375	10125	30375	91125
25	75	225	675	2025	6075	18225
5	15	45	135	405	1215	3645
1	3	9	27	81	243	729

The Tent as Holy Mountain

Spiritual progress didn't begin until seven generations after Adam, when Genesis 4:20-21 speaks about the first tent dweller as "brother" to the originator of music. The "tents" of these brothers can be understood in terms of miniature Holy Mountains which translate number to sound. As a wanderer, Adam was not considered a "tent dweller." If Adam were a tent sweller, then his tent would have been based on the mathematical model depicted in Figures 54a & b. The essential vibrations of the serpent lives within man as powers of 3. In the second row, above the level of the serpent, the gematria for Adam is אדם = 40 + 4 + 1 = 45, who's name contains two powers of 3, and, Adam did not have to crawl in the dust since he began life one power of 5 higher than the serpent ($3^2 * 5 = 45$).

Figure 54a & b - Adam's "Tent" as a Musical Subset of God's Holy Mountain

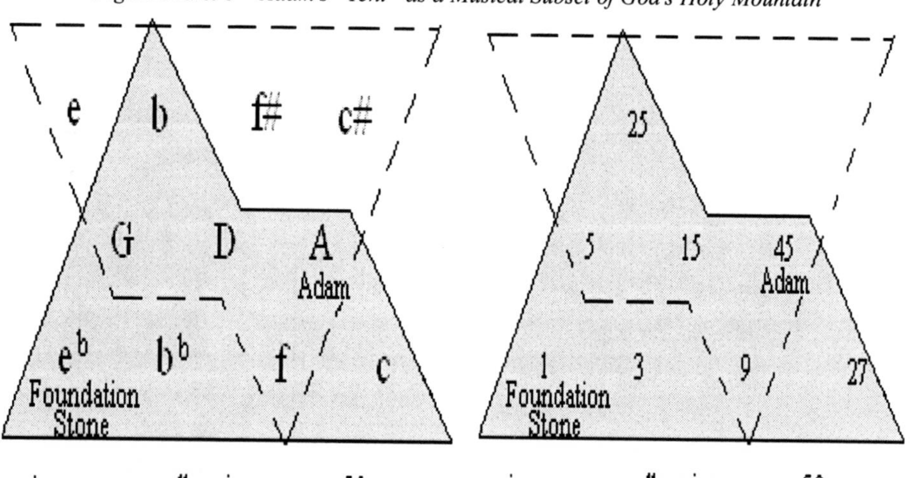

One cannot say that the divine light and sound of Adam's "tent" produced a sacred musical scale, because the tones of Adam's soul (i.e. his "tent") were scattered across several octaves, and in that form he could not "sing" the sacred scale of his Divinity, thus he could not join the Heavenly choir of angels that Abraham called *Seraphim*. There were no musical scales in Adam's tent, just stacked musical fifths and thirds. Being a tent dweller implied staying in one place within a single octave in the stillness of a meditation on God's Name. During this process, these scattered tones are musically transposed into the song of a soul, transposed to a scale within a single octave. Since Adam was in exile on Earth, his destiny, like the serpent's, was to wander across the wilderness, gaining in knowledge but not in wisdom. The high vibration and gradual descent of his divine sparks, degree by degree, spanned across all the generations of his descendants, and thus across many octaves.

In Biblical allegory, man's spiritual journey begins with God at the number 1, the lower left-hand base of the Holy Mountain, which is the "Cornerstone" of Creation. The first material substance that God created from Earth was the Foundation Stone. Today, monotheists believe that the Foundation Stone is located at the Temple Mount in Jerusalem within the 7th century mosque called the Dome of the Rock. This spot became monotheism's most precious piece of real estate, and a constant source of turf wars among the three monotheistic faiths. According to the Talmud, Adam, Eve, and the serpent, began their wanderings in exile at the Foundation Stone where the following events also took place:

- Cain and Abel made their offerings to God.
- Noah made his offerings to God
- Abraham tied Isaac to the altar of sacrifice
- Jacob dreamed of angels ascending and descending a great ladder to God
- The Holy of Holies was located, holding the Ark of the Covenant that contained Moses' tablets
- The Divine Presence hovered over the Ark as the "wellspring of prophecy"
- Mohammed ascended to Allah on his "Night Journey"

The Foundation Stone is the physical reflection of God in His Holy Palace. It is where the transcendent meets the mundane. Once the Monad was instantiated as one stone, it became capable of extension, and therefore divisible into two stones. Abraham speaks to us about "stones building houses" in terms of ancient pebble arithmetic. In this manner, Creation of the entire universe proceeds from God's "Cornerstone," which also became known as the "Philosopher's Stone" that brings enlightenment, rejuvenation and immortality — the great goal of religion. It embodies Creation's beginnings and the promise of a "World to Come." The site of the Foundation Stone, at the lower left of God's Holy Mountain, is the location of the "Tree of Life" (called the World Pillar; the Axis Mundi; the Center of the World).

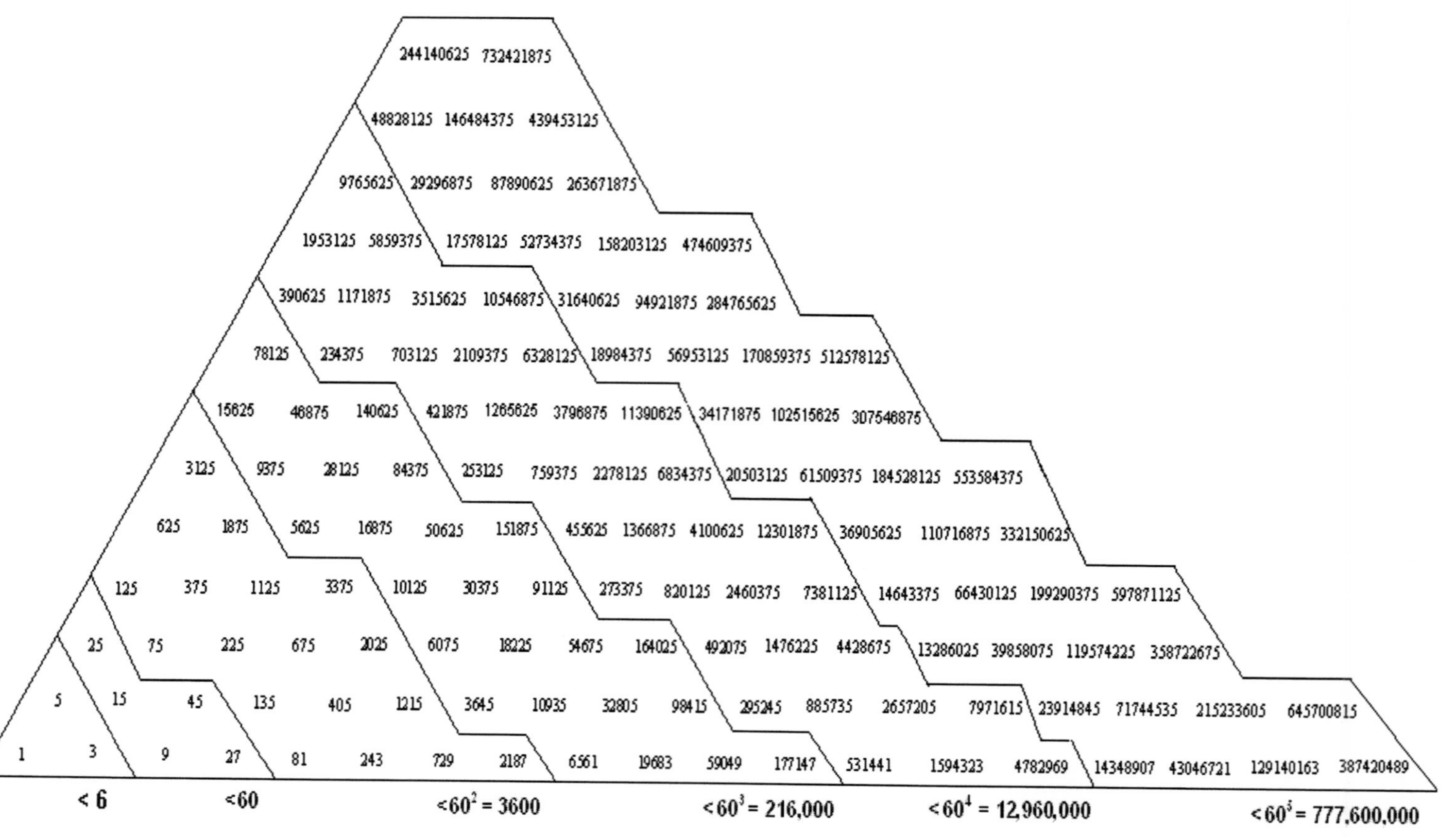

Figure 55 - Yahweh's Holy Mountain as Part of a Mixed-Base System Framed by Powers of 60

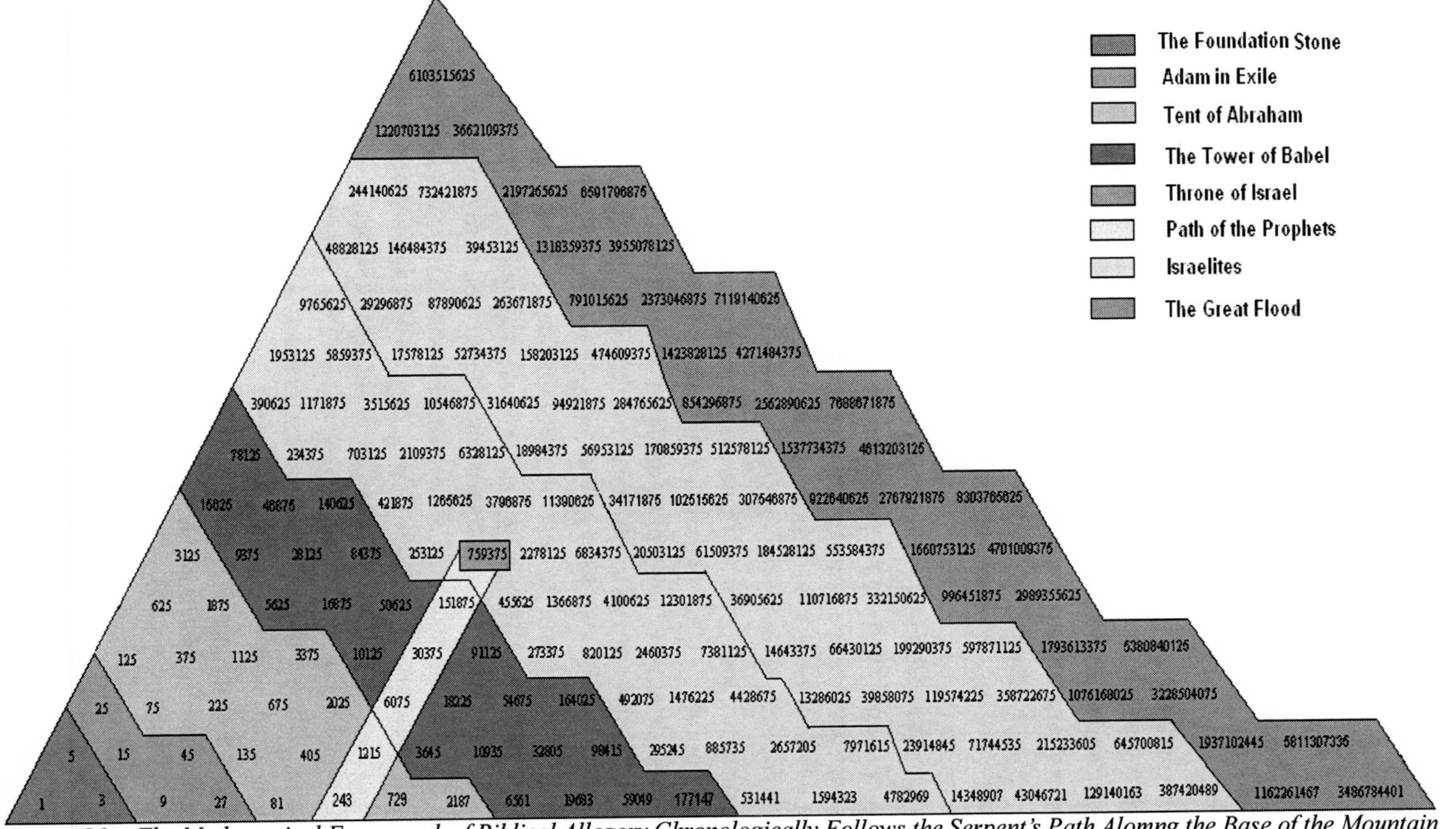

Figure 56 – The Mathematical Framework of Biblical Allegory Chronologically Follows the Serpent's Path Alomng the Base of the Mountain

From a modern scientific perspective, we know that the real Axis Mundi runs through the North and South Pole (Figure 21a), and extends to the North Star (within the northern hemisphere). All circumpolar stars seem to revolve around the Pole Star, but of course, they do not. The earth is really rotating on its axis making it appear that they revolve. Monotheism's first Axis Mundi was Mount Moriah in Jerusalem. Mohammed then switched the *Qiblah* (direction of prayer) for Islam from Jerusalem to the Kabah in Mecca, although Jerusalem always retained the unique status that was associated with the Foundation Stone. Every archeoastronomical device, every ziggurat, every pyramid, and indeed, every person, can be considered an Axis Mundi where the mundane physical world can be transcended through the sacred meditation practice. The first prophet to "pronounce" God's Name ascended the Holy Mountain "on wings" that were powers of 5.

It is important to note that there are no powers of 7 within the Earth's Holy Mountain, nor within Heaven's Tree of Life, only powers of 3 and 5. Once the prophet climbs to the summit of the Holy Mountain, he is transfigured by the number 5, the Wind element's Holy Spirit (*Ruach Hakodesh),* not by the number 7's Fire element. So, what role does the number 7 play in transforming the prophet as he ascends the Holy Mountain toward his God?

The practitioner would never have reached the holy ground of the summit if he did not already "bind a Crown" to his mind, body, and soul, as specified in the *Sefer Yetzirah*. During the Creation process, the first 6 Days poured their essence into the Sabbath. Similarly, the *Crown* describes the Unity of the soul's 6 Divine Lights as a harmonized and transcendent 7th Light. Binding a Crown to both our inner and outer lights purges sin and harmonizes the essence of one's entire being into Divine Unity. The "Wings of Metatron" could not lift the corrupted Soul of an impure, unharmonized Body. The story of Enoch, the first holy man, presents us with the opportunity to understand some of the mathematical details of salvation.

The exact sciences were still very young when the first Semitic patriarchs lived, and efforts to explain man's inner and outer worlds in scientific terms were revolutionary for their time. To a modern scientist they might appear naive, but, if we compare the work of the ancient Aryan-Semitic pioneers of science with their modern scientific counterparts, it is miraculous how much they got right — especially with respect to the harmonic series as the mathematical framework of the Living God as the first theory of everything.

Chapter 11: Enoch's Salvation from Earth

The First Holy Man

Figure 57 - Enoch Pronounces God's Holy Name and Ascends

There were ten generations from Adam to Noah. In the seventh generation after Adam, there was a righteous man named Enoch. God saved Enoch from the cursed Earth (Figure 57), because he was surrounded by the evil generations of Cain, and was liable to go astray. Biblical commentary suggests that the "sons of God" were born within the patriarchal lineage of the "sons of Seth," but were seduced by the "daughters of man," who, according to some commentators, were considered evil descendants of Cain. The *Nephilim* are usually portrayed within Jewish tradition as the evil offspring of this mismatch, and the Book of Enoch goes so far as to call them the evil demons that precipitated the Great Flood. The Book of Enoch seriously distorts Abraham's theology, and we must keep in mind that it is non-canonical, and therefore non-authoritative, for good reason. It was probably authored more than 300 years after Solomon's Temple was destroyed, which is long after the secrets of prophecy were lost, and the last canonized books were written. Even rabbinical commentary begins after this crucial period, and therefore the rabbinate cannot remain beyond reproach.

To remain consistent with both the Bible and the geological record, we can consider Enoch to be the first to "pronounce" God's Name to master the elements ca. 28,000 BCE at the latest, when the Last Glacial Maximum began, and when men had to retreat to the shelter of caves in order to survive. Reconciling the Bible with the anthropological record implies that Adam and Eve would have been dark-skinned Cro-Magnons (EMH) "out of Africa" (circa 70,000 - 60,000 BCE). Enoch would have been the first Aryan master within the patriarchal lineage (circa 28000 BCE), and Noah (circa 10,500 BCE) would have been the last of the Aryan fathers before the birth of Shem (circa 4000 BCE). The Semitic invasion of Sumer would therefore have begun 6000 years ago with Shem. And, Enoch is said to have lived three generations before Noah and Shem, suggesting that the world is considerably older than the Bible's accepted 6000 year timeline.

The Bible's 6000 year time limit prevents science from finding a reasonable way to compare Biblical chronology to the archeological and geological record. However, reading the Torah "through the eyes of Abraham," reveals that the Bible's 6000 year time limit is really a logarithmic subset of the Clock of Heaven that should not be misinterpreted as 6000 linear years spent on Earth. This approach opens up the possibility that the Torah's chronology may be one of mankind's best historical records of prehistoric events. A "loosening" of these Biblical time constraints makes reconciliation with science, archeology, and history, possible (see Chapter 5: The Kingdom of Heaven). It enables us to address many ancient religious mysteries, such as: Where and when was Eden? Where were the Four Rivers of Eden located? Who were the earliest patriarchs? When did the first holy man live? Et cetera.

We have speculated that Adam's journey out of Africa followed the path of the Gihon River (Figure 38) beginning at the headwaters of the Blue Nile in Ethiopia. It flowed into the Nile through the Sudan and Egypt, and through Egypt's Eastern wadis, crossing the Red Sea and entering a port near Mecca. It then flowed through Saudi Arabia all the way to Basrah. At the intersection of the four Rivers of Eden, Enoch would have ascended the Zagros Mountains in Iran (the Land of the Aryans), after following the Pishon (today's Karkheh River) toward its headwaters. He would have settled near the Neolithic site of Susa on the banks of the Karkheh. After Enoch's ascent, he would have discovered a karst or porous topology of caves that could provide him with the shelter and seclusion necessary to become the first great meditator, and father of the Aryan "Good Shepherds" who began civilization. The legend of this first scribe and wise man abounds across many cultures.

Within the Bible, the first important number associated with Enoch is his age, 65, when his son Methuselah was born. The second important number associated with Enoch is 365, the number of years that Enoch sojourned on Earth. The Bible does not state that he died at 365 years old, but rather, that "God took him" and then he "walked with God."[239] We might recall how the letter *Heh* = 5, the *Ruach Hakodesh* (Breath of God or Holy Spirit), was bound to Abram's name (= 243), changing it to Abraham (=248), and how 360 days in the solar year was also appended with 5 festival days, to create 365 total days in the solar year. If we were then to remove the Holy Spirit from the equation, we would see that the important *pnimiyut* defining Enoch's years on Earth were 60 and 360, before the Breath of God transformed him.

Man's unconscious mind is a reflection of his complete inner being (soul + etheric body). Meditation's hypnagogic state accesses this inner being and harmonizes the three channels of the mind, which are composed of Water, Wind, and Fire. The serpent within us (Water element) wanders and sins; the eagle (Wind element) redirects our serpent energies (our knowledge of Good and Evil) toward God; while meditation (Fire element) purges impurities from each of the other two components. Without wisdom, every man naturally follows the horizontal path of the serpent, gaining in knowledge of Good and Evil as he travels along the base of the tent/mountain. But, man's journey begins one step closer to God than the serpent, as if the eagle had air-lifted the serpent one power of 5 higher on the Holy Mountain. For purposes of comparison, we have included Adam's tent, as if he were a tent dweller. We can then compare Adam's and Enoch's tent, as a reflection of their inner being, and see exactly how Enoch's "tent" evolved spiritually (Figure 58).

In order to ascend on "Wings" (the two *Hehs* in God's Holy Name), Enoch had to "sing" God's Holy Name. In order to do that, the *pnimiyut* of Enoch's soul had to be reordered into an enlightened, stepwise and singable musical scale, rather than the smallest integer tones of musical fifths that are associated with the path of the serpent, and typical of Adam's soul wandering in exile. Adam's triple progression *pnimiyut* can be spread across the entire piano keyboard as a series of musical fifths — which is not very singable.

Wandering in Exile and Ascending in Grace

Enoch's sacred practice had to transform Adam's archetypal and unsingable progressions in Figure 58a (Water's triple progression and Wind's quintuple progression) into the singable harmonization in Figure 58b. In order to accomplish that, Enoch had to harmonize them both with the Earth element's duple progression in a way that would transpose all tones into a single octave as a singable musical scale.

239 Genesis 5:22-29

You will note that every number in the ziggurat on the left (Figure 58a) can be multiplied by some power of 2 in order to transpose that tone into the 30:60 octave within the ziggurat on the right (Figure 58b). This process transposes and harmonizes the Water element (man's blood, sweat and semen) with the Wind element (breath), with the Earth element (body). The body contains this divine energy within its octave container. By pronouncing the Name of God, Enoch brought the Fire element's septimal progression into play. In Chapter 14, we will see how Fire purifies, transforms, and harmonizes all the elements into a spiritual Unity.

Fig. 58a - Unharmonized Triple & Quintuple Progressions *Fig. 58b - Transposed and Harmonized*

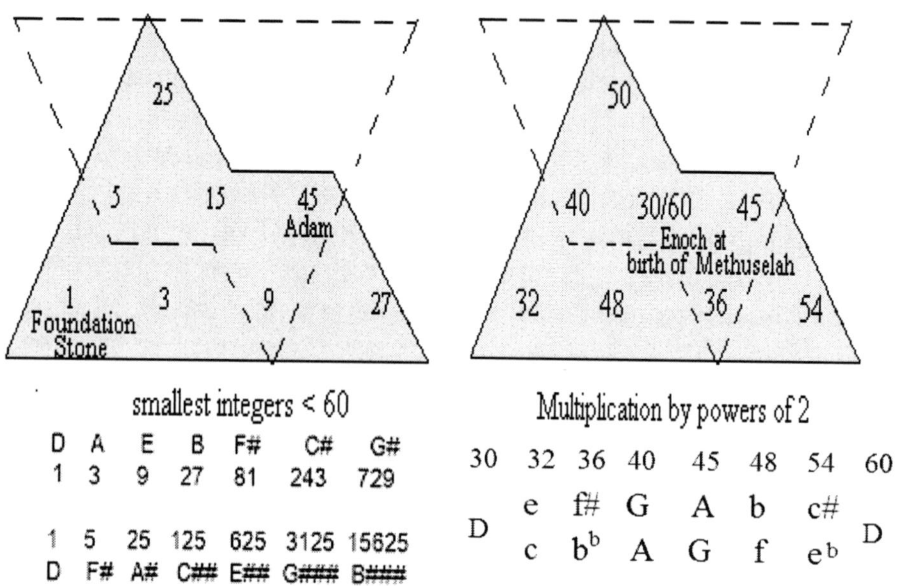

Enoch's spiritual journey had properly harmonized and reordered his being in preparation for the birth of Methuselah, who would continue in the patriarchal lineage. However, Enoch had still not reached the spiritual heights he was destined for. "Singing" God's praise (as a *Seraphim*) is metaphor for the inaudible mental articulation of vibration that ascends and descends the spinal chord. This has been allegorized as angels (*Chayot*) ascending and descending the spiral tonecircle to Heaven called Jacob's ladder (*Ophanim*).[240] In Figure 58b, Enoch's soul "sings" a 7-tone ascending and descending diatonic scale, marking his Sabbatical in 7 spiritual steps. A Sabbatical therefore defines "singable" tones on the Path to God. Musical steps occur in terms of frequency and wavelength ratios, rather than in terms of linear years. Enoch was 60 years of age when he completed his first Sabbatical. During the next 5 years Enoch was transformed by the *Ruach Hakodesh* (Holy Spirit = *Heh* = 5). This was in preparation for the birth of Methuselah after 65 years.

240 *Chayot*, *Ophanim* and *Seraphim* were the three types of angels specified by Abraham in the *Sefer Yetzirah*.

There is another, higher level of prophecy within the Torah only achieved by Enoch and Noah — the level of "walking with God." Even Moses was not permitted to "cross over the Jordan" to "walk with God" in the Promised Land. And, Enoch could not "walk with God" on the single "Wing" that he earned by completing his first Sabbatical. In order to earn his second "Wing" (the second "H" in YHVH), Enoch would have to live and meditate through his Jubilee Year, which required 7 Sabbaticals in Heaven — but 60 years for each Sabbatical on Earth — or, 60 x 6 = 360 Earth years. Finally, after 365 years, Enoch would epitomize *Gevurah* (Strength) within the Kabbalistic tradition, effectively accomplishing all 365 prohibitive Commandments that have been codified from the Torah. Internally "singing" the ascending and descending chromatic scale within the 360:720 octave is functionally equivalent to performing all 365 prohibitive commandments with the appropriate level of *kavanah* (meditative intent).

The octave doubles (30:60 and 360:720) contain two scales in the path toward God (Figures 58c & d). The latter construction is also recognizable as the mathematics of the Navel of Order (Figure 25). The 360:720 octave defines the only symmetrical chromatic musical scale that both ascends and descends across the same set of numbers and tones.

Figure 58c - First Singable Scale of Enoch *Figure 58d - Second Singable Scale of Enoch*

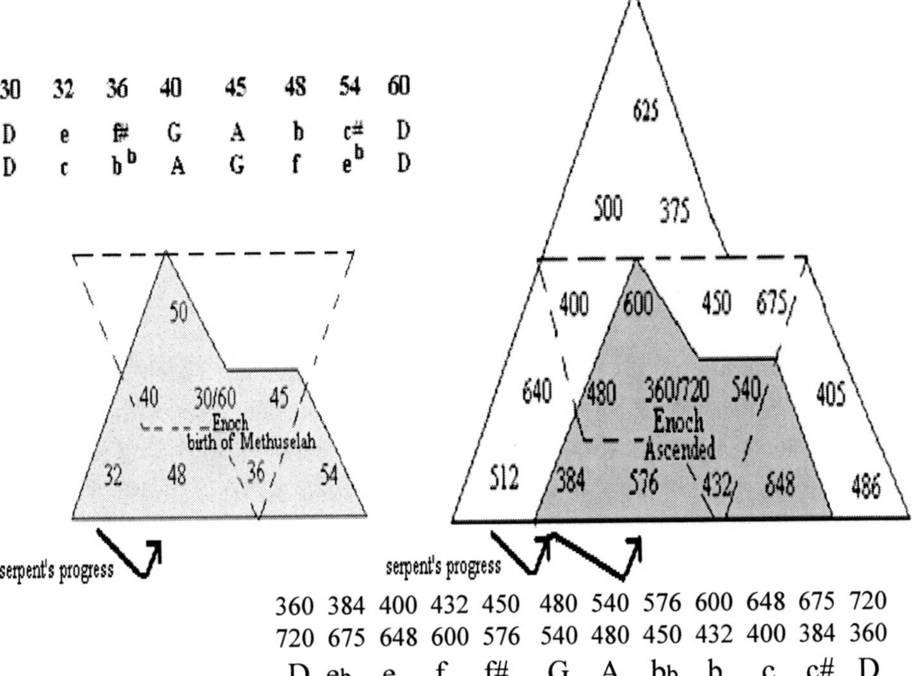

Chapter 12: Noah's Salvation from Water

Building the Ark

Figure 59 - Saving Noah and Repopulating the Earth

Ten generations after Adam, Lamech named his son Noah (נֹחַ) saying: "*This one will bring us rest* [נוֹח] *from the toil of our hands.*" God was intent on washing away the Evil that cursed the Earth during the life of Adam. A 7th Law was added to the 6 Laws originally given to Adam. With that 7th Law, God began anew with Noah and his descendants. God made a Covenant with Noah and sealed it with a rainbow. He wanted the 7 lights of the rainbow, obscured by man's knowledge of Good and Evil, to shine unencumbered. According to the Jewish Talmud, these 7 Laws were called the 7 Noahide Laws. It was not until the time of Abraham that this teaching would be recorded for posterity. The *Sefer Yetzirah* would teach the Children of Abraham how to make "7 circuits around the sacred cube." By building the Ark according to God's exact specifications, Noah learned how to construct a Holy Ark to contain and save all living creatures from a great flood. To build the Ark, Noah had to learn the proportions of the Word of God, YHVH, the ultimate sacred container of Divine Light. In Figures 61a & b we can see that the Arks musical construction is an elongated musical "Tent," much like the ones already discussed.

Man's sins would be washed way by the Great Flood, however Noah, and the seeds of future generations, would be saved from the primordial Waters. Noah was instructed to save 7 male and female pairs of each type of living Creature (Figure 59). The dimensions of Noah's Ark were 300 cubits x 50 cubits x 30 cubits. These sacred dimensions describe a higher vibration version of the multiplication table for God's Holy Mountain (Log 3^p 5^q), which happens to be the same dimensions that God would later specify to Moses in order to build a different type of Ark: the Ark of the Covenant (Figure 44). We can even assume that the Ark of baby Moses discovered in the reeds, like a musical leitmotif, would have been constructed from the same divine ratios and proportions as Noah's Ark and the Ark of the Covenant.

Noah's Ark, as well as the various tents already discussed, have been constructed 5-smooth, with regular prime number factors of 2, 3, or 5. In musical terms, they were built from octaves, perfect fifths, and major thirds. The full gamut of vibrations in Heaven and Earth was defined by the eagle's ascent in major thirds (powers of 5), and the serpent's wanderings across the base in perfect fifths (powers of 3).[241] Noah was the savior for all of this — from the farthest wanderings of the serpent, to the highest flight of the eagle — encompassing Heaven and Hell, Good and Evil (Figure 60).

The *pnimiyut* of past, present, and future prophets were also in the Ark, spanning all the generations of Adam within five octaves. The Ark contained octave doubles between 45 and 1440; beginning with Adam (45:90), followed by Sarah (90:180), Isaac (180:360), and Enoch (360:720), and book-ended with Adam (720:1440). All the generations of Adam spanned five spiritual octaves (45:1440). Also, within the Ark is Abraham (100 at Isaac's birth), looking on approvingly from his perch one level (i.e., one power of 5) spiritually higher.

- Adam (אָדָם) = 45 and 1440 (the upper limits of Adam's name can also be read as place holder values 1-4-40 or 1440).
- Noah = 64 as Cornerstone (In keeping with Genesis, Rashi, the foremost Biblical commentator, relates "Noah" (נֹחַ) to the Hebrew root for "rest" (נוֹחַ) replacing *gematria* 58 with a functional *gematria* of 64)

241 Transposed to the same octave by powers of 2 so that Noah could contain everything in his Ark.

- Enoch = 60 was filled with the Breath of God (60 + *Heh* = 65) completing his Sabbatical at the time of Methuselah's birth
- Isaac = 60 at the Birth of twins Jacob and Esau[242]
- Sarah = 90 at the birth of Isaac
- Abraham = 100 at the birth of Isaac
- Isaac = 180 at death[243]
- Enoch = 360 completed his Jubilee (360 + *Heh* = 5) and "walked with God" in Heaven.

Figure 60 - The Serpent and the Eagle Define Progress on the Holy Mountain

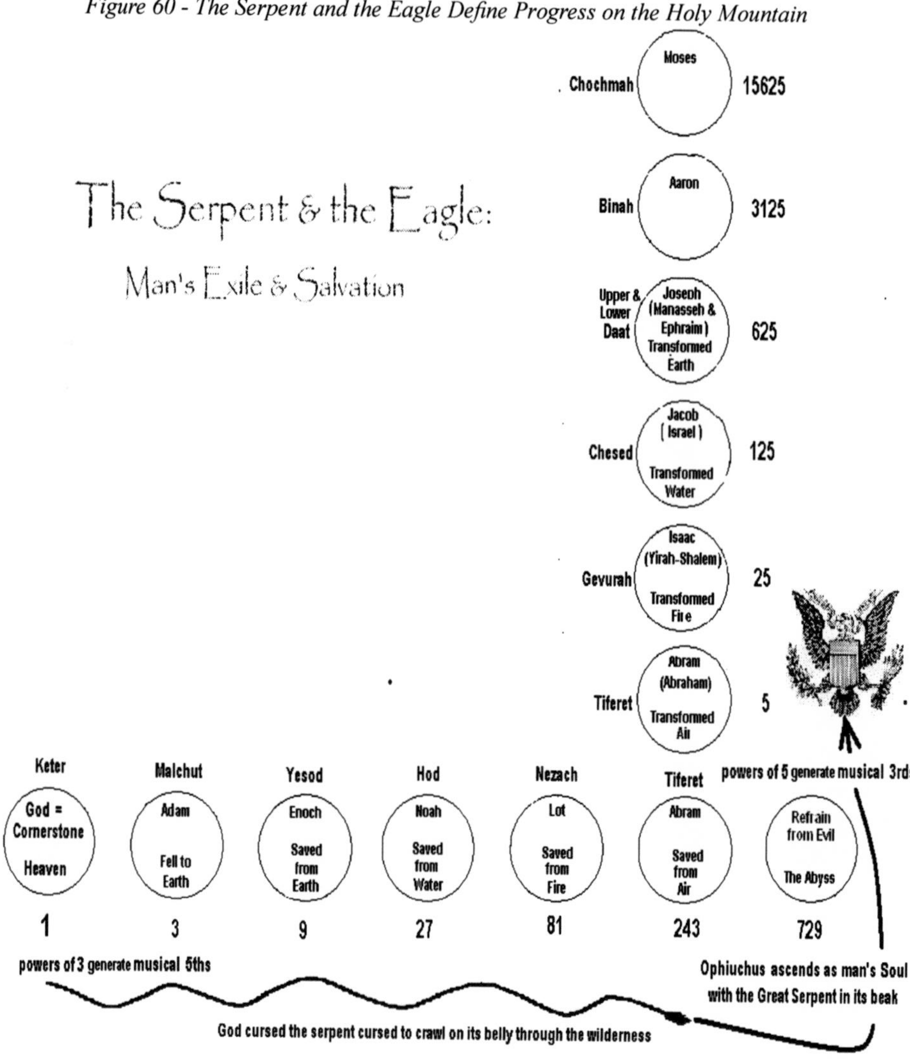

242 Genesis 25: 26
243 Genesis 35:28

Figure 61a & b - Noah's Ark as Savior of Mankind

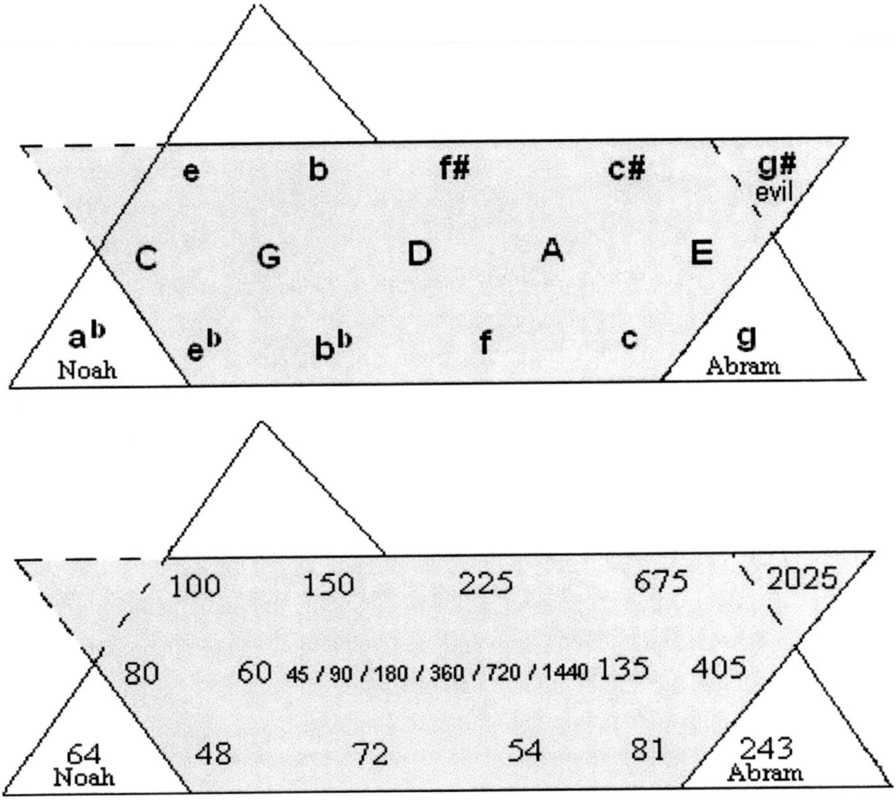

The First Savior

Noah's Ark carried more than animals. In Figures 61a & b, at the farthest corners of the Ark, separated by two stacked major thirds and four perfect fifths, sits the vibrations for Good and Evil. Noah, of course, epitomized Good (= 64) as the "Cornerstone" of the Ark, and it was up to him to find a way to deal with the Evil within the Ark. The way in which Noah saved his passengers from Evil is reflected in the lineage of High Priests that began with Aaron. These were the saviors of Israel. As part of the ceremonial ritual of the Day of Atonement, the High Priest would sacrifice one of two he-goats for his own sin-offering, and another goat on behalf of all Israel:

> *Aaron shall lean his two hands upon the head of the living he-goat and confess upon it all the inequities of the Children of Israel, and all their rebellious sins among all their sins, and place them upon the head of the he-goat, and send it with a designated man to the desert.*[244]

244 Leviticus 16:22

Animal sacrifice (Hebrew: *korban*) has been replaced in modern times[245] with the custom of casting off (Hebrew: *Tashlikh*) pieces of bread, symbolic of casting one's sins into the river. It derives from the passage recited at the ceremony: "You will cast all their sins into the depths of the sea."[246] Christianity has traditionally regarded Jesus as the *korban* symbol of a sacrificial lamb. Jesus, like the scapegoat, takes on the sins of humanity, but instead of being cast out into the wilderness, Christ was crucified. This is very ancient symbolism. Pre-historic cave drawings of eagles or vultures, serpents or scorpions, and lions or leopards, were often accompanied by drawings of goats or rams. There is evidence to suggest that the scapegoat made a very early appearance in mathematical harmonics deciphered on Egyptian archeologist's discovery of the Narmer macehead, along with graphic imagery on an accompanying palette, circa 3200 BCE.[247]

These customs are based on mathematical/musical models that acknowledge and forgive sin. In the Bible, the serpent is symbolic of sin, ascending and descending the Tree of Knowledge by spinning around the tonecircle in perfect fifths (forming a 3:2 ratio with the octave): D to A to E to B to F# to C# to G# and descending from D to G to C to F to Bb to Eb to Ab (as in Figure 62a).

Figure 62a - The Ascending and Descending Spiral Paths of the Serpent

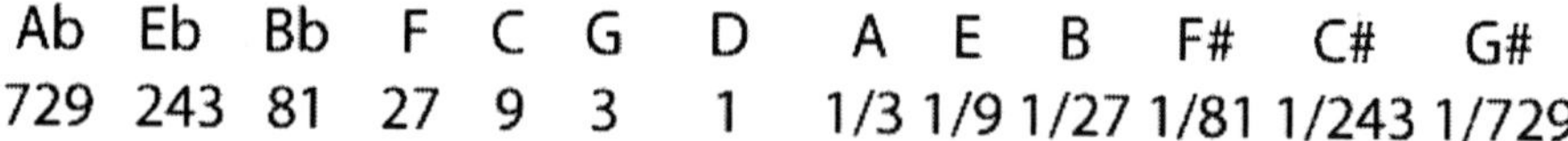

Ab	Eb	Bb	F	C	G	D	A	E	B	F#	C#	G#
729	243	81	27	9	3	1	1/3	1/9	1/27	1/81	1/243	1/729

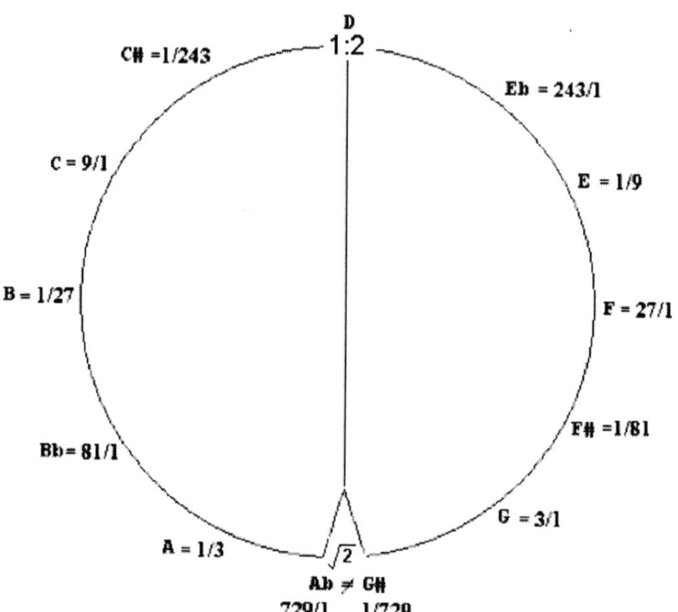

245 The Jewish Encyclopedia suggests that this more modern practice may have begun in 14th century Germany.
246 Micah 7:18-20
247 Ernest McClain, *Narmer*, unpublished.

Time is symbolized by Ouroboros (Figure 14c), the ancient symbol depicting a serpent or dragon swallowing its own tail and forming a circle – the cycle of time – with "no beginning and no end." The reason Ouroboros appears to be swallowing its tail is because we see an aerial view of it traveling in a spiral rather than a perfect circle[248] As a result, the circle's diameter cannot be accurately measured. When the diagonal of an inscribed square is equated with that diameter, as in "the circle and the square within," then a gap exists between the Ab and the G#, and we can only approximate the length of the diameter/diagonal line segment as an irrational number: √2. This line segment is irrational, implying that the circle (of the Sun's orbit) never closes.

The tuning difference between the "enharmonic" A♭ and the G# defines a Pythagorean comma as a triple progression of twelve perfect fifths $3^{12} = 531441$ which does not quite line up with a duple progression spiral of perfect octaves $2^{19} = 524288$. The resulting ratio is 531441:524288 = 1.01364 — two tones that should sound the same note, but wind up ~1/4 of a semitone apart from one another. It bisects the circle from God's "Holy Palace" (=D) at the apex of the circle to "the devil's workshop" opposite God at the bottom of the circle. We split the 2:1 octave down the middle, approximating √2 with 729/512 = 1.4238 (Figure 62a), which is a reasonable approximation of modern calculations: √2 = 1.41421356....

Noah, as Cornerstone of the Ark (64 = Ab), takes on the sins of his passengers that exist in the "abyss" between Noah's A♭ and Evil's G#. Like the scapegoat being sent into the wilderness, the Ark is cast out to sea with Evil in the boat. The Ark in Figures 61a & b is tuned differently than Figure 62a, because it includes powers of 5 (musical thirds). On the Ark, Evil is embodied by the G# = 2025, situated four perfect fifths and two major thirds away from Noah's A♭ = 64, opposite Noah's position in the Ark as "Cornerstone." If we multiply Noah = 64 by 2^5 we get 2048/2025 = 1.01135... pretty close. Just a tiny bite for the serpent swallowing his tail. In this case, Noah's Ab consumes Evil's G#.

Noah's special relationship with God within the 45:90 octave, empowered him to function as the scapegoat/savior at the Cornerstone, approximating a comma of 64/45 = 1.42222 between the A♭ and G#. In Figures 62b & c, we see two diagrams describing how four perfect fifths and two major thirds result from adding the distance traveled in each of the two diagrams. The serpent's triple progression wanderings in exile plus the Eagle's quintuple progression ascent toward God. The Pythagorean and Just tuning discrepancies each approximate the diagonal/diameter Axis Mundi length defined by √2. Noah cleansed the Ark of its 13th Evil tone, becoming the first scapegoat/savior to "swallow" sin. Like the High Priest on the Day of Atonement, Noah "pronounced" the Word of God, YHVH, forgiving all sin, and consecrating the Ark for the entire patriarchal lineage: past, present and future.

248 Remember astronomy's *precession of the equinox,* in which the Sun's ecliptic creates a spiral to Heaven never closing the circle made by its orbit.

Figure 62b - Just Tuning Comma: The Eagle as Serpent Holder Ascending to G#

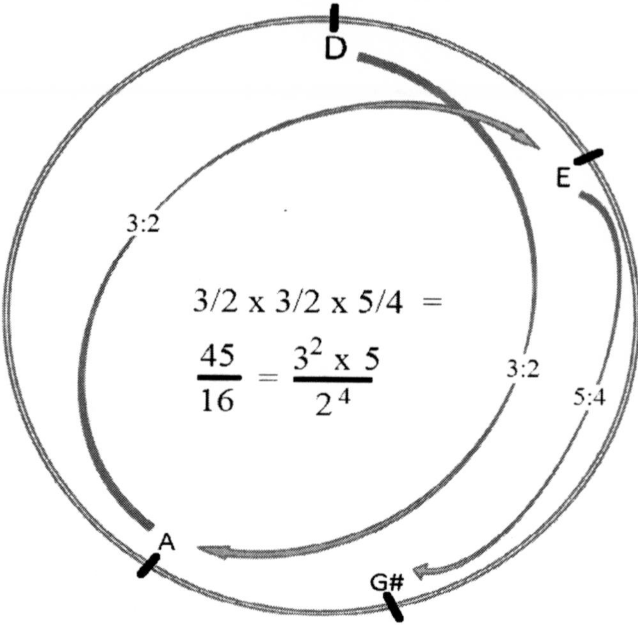

Clockwise 2 Perfect Fifths + Clockwise 1 Major Third

Figure 62c - Just Tuning Comma: The Eagle as Serpent Holder Descending to Ab

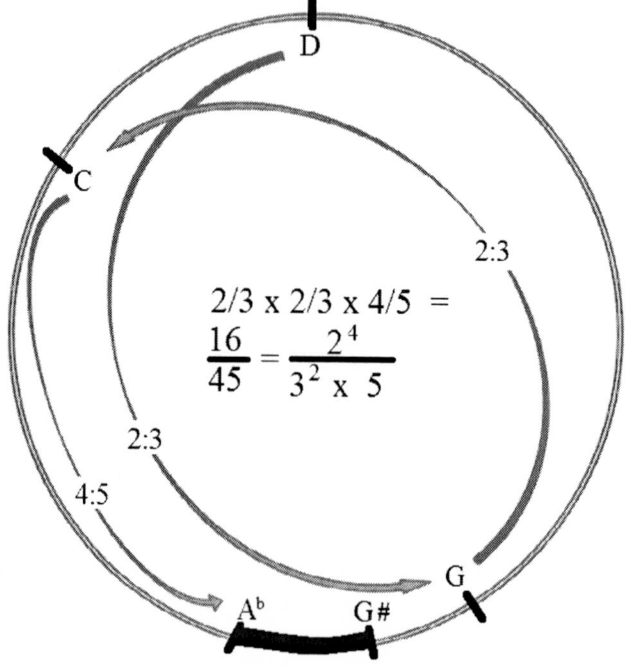

Counterclockwise 2 perfect fifths + counterclockwise 1 major 3rd

Chapter 13: Lot's Salvation from Fire

The Fires of Chaldea

Figure 63 - Lot and Family Saved From Sodom's Destruction

Midrashic Torah commentary relates a story about Abraham's youth. When he was still called Abram, he destroyed his father Terah's stone idols. When Terah complained to Nimrod, he threw Abram into a fiery furnace. The archangel of Fire, Gabriel, saved him from death. When Abram's brother Haran showed support for Abram, Nimrod also threw him into the furnace, but there was no miraculous salvation for Haran. Lot's father, Haran, therefore died by fire. Both Abram and Haran were born in *Ur Kasdim* (literally in Hebrew: the fire of the land of Chaldea). Since that time Abram took responsibility for his brother's son, but Lot and his family settled in Sodom, and both Sodom and Gomorrah had became centers of sexual deviance and unrepentant sinfulness. God was intent on destroying both cities with fire and brimstone. Abraham realized that his nephew lived in Sodom, and he negotiated with God not to destroy any righteous men that might live in either Sodom or Gomorrah. The Lord's two angels found only one righteous man in all of Sodom and none in Gomorrah. That man was Lot. Angels directed Lot and his family to safety, with a warning not to look back while the city was being destroyed (Figure 63). Lot's wife could not resist, and she was turned into a pillar of salt. Lot, however, was saved from the primordial Fires of Heaven by God's angels, but it was Abraham who set the forces of Lot's salvation in motion.

A Fire Among the Parts

Once the backstory was provided in Midrash, Genesis could allude to the miracle of young Abram's salvation from Fire with His statement: "I am YHVH who has brought you out of the fire of the land of Chaldea to give you this land to inherit it." When Abram asked: "Whereby shall I know that I am to inherit it?" God replied by telling him to sacrifice: 3 heifers, 3 goats, 3 rams, a turtle dove and a young dove. "He cut them in the center and placed each piece opposite its counterpart. The birds, however, he did not cut up… There was a smoky furnace and a torch of fire which passed between these pieces." The wings of the dove and turtledove (powers of 5), lifting the inner light of Abram's soul (powers of 2 x 3) according to the mathematical models of Figures 45a, b & c, as well as Figure 64.

A Heavenly Fire harmonized the "Covenant of the Parts." This was Abraham's "burning bush." Within the sacrifice arrangement below, Abram married prime numbers 2, 3, and 5, which enabled him to begin praying like a prophet. On that day YHVH put Abram into a "deep sleep" (Hebrew: *Tardemah*), and his prophetic visions began, revealing the future oppression and exodus of Israel. "Deep sleep" is metaphor for when God induces the hypnagogic state within a prophet. Thus, Torah allegory describes the winged soul of both Lot and Abram cleansed by the Fires of Heaven.

Figure 64 - Abram's Covenant of Fire

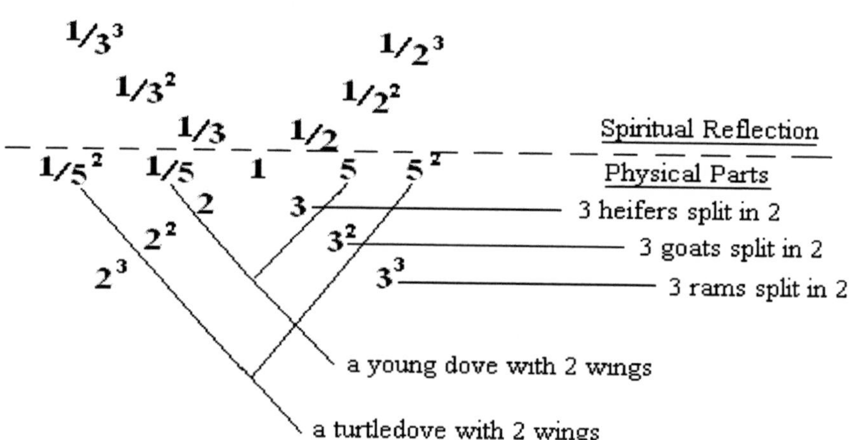

Chapter 14: Abraham's Transformation of Wind

The Great Patriarch

Figure 65 - The Transformation of Abram to Abraham

God waited ten generations from Noah for another righteous man who could move civilization forward. As part of God's Covenant of the Parts, He induced a "deep sleep" in Abram that started his prophetic visions. This was followed by another Covenant between God and Abram, called the "Covenant of the Word." However, this Covenant is better known as the Covenant of Circumcision, since the Hebrew word *milah* translates to both "circumcision" and "word" (i.e., "The Word"; Greek: *Logos*). For example, "His Word (*Milah*) is upon my tongue."[249]

The Hebrew word for foreskin is *orlah,* and its usage in Scripture is "as a barrier standing in the way of a beneficial result."[250] Once Abram was circumcised, there were no barriers to God, and his undistracted energies could be directed upwards. The concept of circumcision as a means to remove those

249 II Samuel 23:2.
250 Genesis 17:13-14 see commentary in Stone Edition.

blockages (*orlah)* effectively truncates the 13th distracting spoke in the Torah's *Navel of Order*. Fulfilling the Covenant of the Word with no distractions would ultimately liberate Abraham's soul. The cleansing of the body and the liberation of the soul, as explained by the mathematics of sin and salvation, provides the framework for Biblical morality that became the centerpiece of Semitic thinking, and the culmination of the Aryan-Semitic collaboration.

The Mathematics of Sin

When the God of Abraham "cross-cut" duple and triple progressions, within so-called, Pythagorean Tuning (Log $2^p 3^q$), He created man's perfect soul as $1/27 \leq 2^p 3^q \leq 27$. Knowledge of the world brought Adam's Heavenly bliss to an abrupt end, extending his soul into imperfection with six additional powers, to embody Good (F#, C# and G#) and Evil (Bb, Eb and Ab) as in Figure 66. Knowledge of Good and Evil brought conflict and dissonance. The gap between the lowest Evil ($3^6 = 729$) and the highest Good ($1/3^6 = 1/729$) does not line up with octave boundaries (powers of 2). Thus, it is associated with a Pythagorean or ditonic comma. In a closed tone circle, these two tones would be the same note, but in a spiral they are different: $729 \neq 1/729$ or Ab ≠ G#. Thus, splitting the Heavenly Firmament tone circle right down the middle, as in Figure 62a, reveals *Sheol* as the "abyss of the serpent."

Figure 66 - Adam's Soul, a Subset of the Tree of Knowledge, was Extended to Include Good & Evil

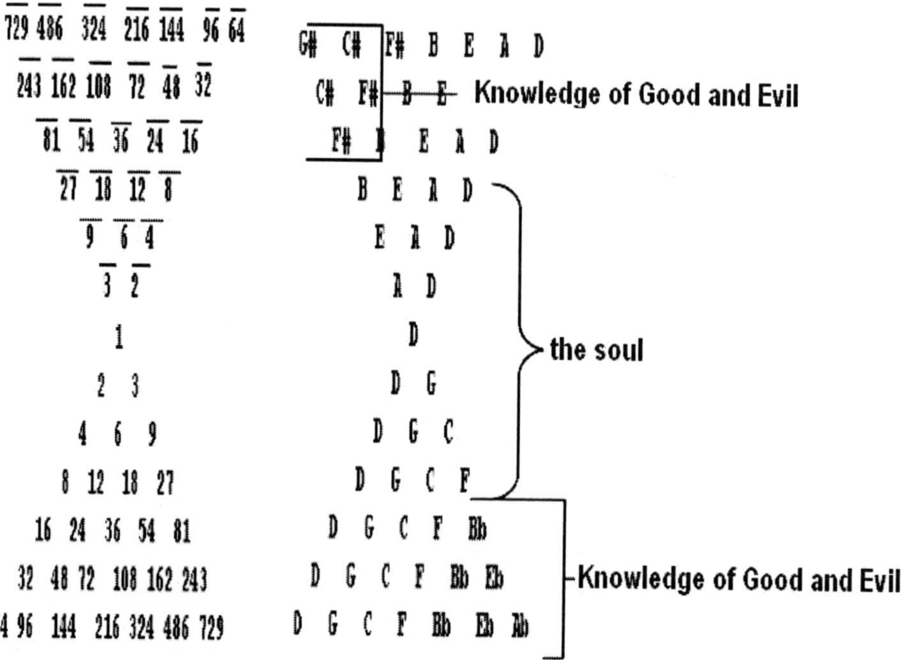

When the God of Abraham "cross-cut" the triple and quintuple progressions within Just Tuning (Log $3^q\ 5^r$), He created all the potentialities within the Tree of Life (Figure 67), both pure and impure, harmonized by the "Breath of God." The soul's triple progression defines a series of musical fifths, while the body's quintuple progression defines a series of musical thirds. The quintuple leg of the tree adds musical thirds together, with six ascending musical thirds, and six descending thirds. It we were to ascend to the B###, ideally it would turn out to be the same pitch as when we descend to the Fbbb. In a perfect world, all three would resonate with God in His Holy Palace = "D", however, B### ≠ D ≠ Fbbb. This tonal gap is a quintuple progression comma called a *minor diesis.* It is a manifestation of the impurities believed to be inherent in man's densely opaque and lustful body. The body's *minor diesis* is analogous to the soul's Pythagorean comma.

Figure 67 - The Tree of Life as Man's Body "Cross-Cut" with His Extended Soul

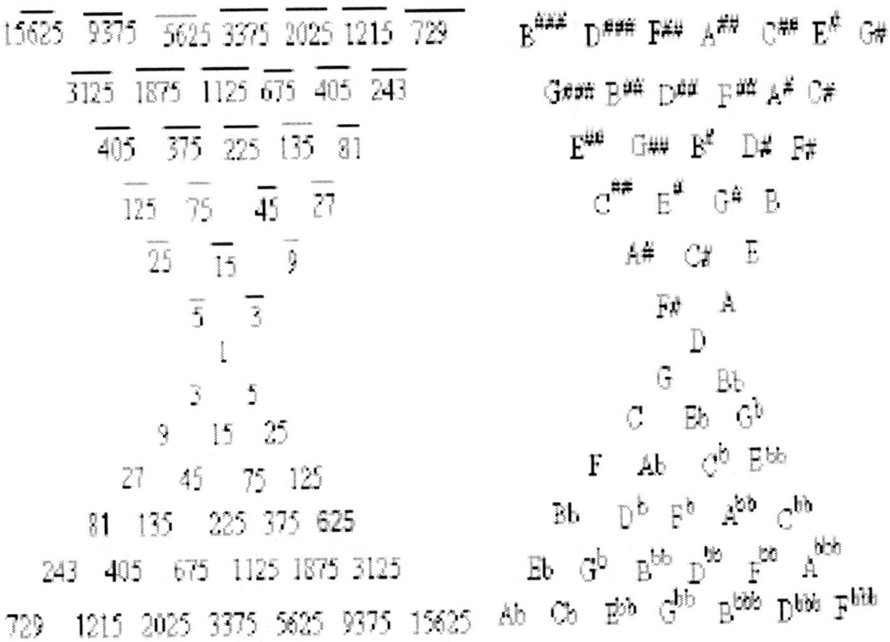

$\overline{15625}\ \overline{9375}\ \overline{5625}\ \overline{3375}\ \overline{2025}\ \overline{1215}\ \overline{729}$ B### D### F## A## C## E# G#

$\overline{3125}\ \overline{1875}\ \overline{1125}\ \overline{675}\ \overline{405}\ \overline{243}$ G### B## D## F## A# C#

$\overline{405}\ \overline{375}\ \overline{225}\ \overline{135}\ \overline{81}$ E## G## B# D# F#

$\overline{125}\ \overline{75}\ \overline{45}\ \overline{27}$ C## E# G# B

$\overline{25}\ \overline{15}\ \overline{9}$ A# C# E

$\overline{5}\ \overline{3}$ F# A

1 D

3 5 G Bb

9 15 25 C Eb Gb

27 45 75 125 F Ab Cb Ebb

81 135 225 375 625 Bb Db Fb Abb Cbb

243 405 675 1125 1875 3125 Eb Gb Bbb Dbb Fbb Abbb

729 1215 2025 3375 5625 9375 15625 Ab Cb Ebb Gbb Bbbb Dbbb Fbbb

The Heavenly Firmament's duple progression that contains all numbers and progressions does not align with the soul's triple progression, nor with the body's quintuple progression. Purification of the body would therefore require a reconciliation between the duple and quintuple progressions. This could be accomplished if we could find a way to split the Heavenly Firmament octave (2:1) into three equivalent musical thirds of ratio (5:4), so that the thirds aligned exactly with octave boundaries (2:1). But, that doesn't happen in nature. To reach perfection mathematically, we would have to trisect the octave with the cube root of 2 or $\sqrt[3]{2}$. The cube root of 2 is 1.2599, a ratio of 126:100. This "supernatural" musical interval is slightly larger than a natural major third of ratio 5:4. For example, if we were to add three natural thirds together, as we do in a quintuple progression of 1:5:25:125, then we would never reach the duple progression's octave boundary, since the octave would always be slightly out of tune with three stacked natural major thirds. To "stack" or add musical intervals we would multiply their ratios together as regular fractions: 5/4 * 5/4 * 5/4 = 125/64. It immediately becomes clear that three thirds 125/64 does not line up with the octave boundary of 128/64 = 2:1. Within the discipline of music theory, the discrepancy between the octave boundary and three consecutive thirds results in ratio 128:125, which has been explained as a *minor diesis*.

The Tree of Life should not be too closely associated with the Torah, as the rabbis tend to do, since it includes all the impurities of the body as well as man's extended, and thus corrupted, soul. What is holy about the Tree of Life is the incorporated Wind element, i.e., the Breath of God, the Holy Spirit, that is associated with the *Heh* = powers of 5 that raises the soul up toward Heaven. The Tree of Life corresponds closely to life, with all its blemishes. Ernest McClain tells us that the $2^p\ 3^q\ 5^r$ are the Three Fates of Greek Mythology, which are described by Plato in great harmonic detail. But, if Fate itself lies in the balance, could man possibly take control of his Fate by harmonizing them? The original authors of the Torah, who knew Abraham's methods best, looked deep into the *Sefer Yetzirah* for answers. Thankfully, Abraham provides us with a "mathematics of salvation" based on powers of 7, as we will soon see.

Before we discuss powers of 7 and mankind's salvation, however, we will take a closer look at the dilemma that nature presents to us. The material impurities of Adam's body, and the inherent sin of Adam's extended soul, caused Adam to be cast out of Heaven. Knowledge of Good and Evil extended the soul's triple progression, and man's extended and knowledgeable soul was slightly "out-of-tune" with the body's quintuple progression.

1 - 3 - 9 - 27 – 81	1 – 5 - 25 - 125
D - A - E - B - F#	D – F# - A# - C##
Triple Progression	*Quintuple Progression*

To clarify what is really going on here, we need to transpose both progressions into the same octave for a closer comparison. Once we do, it will become clear that the tuning for the two F#'s are different. To transpose something into the same octave, we simply multiply or divide by the appropriate power of 2, until we've transposed all tones into the same octave. For example, we would multiply the number 5 in the quintuple progression by $2^4 = 16$ to get an F# four octaves higher (5 * 16 = 80), which is noticeably out of tune with F# = 81 in the Triple progression, by a ratio of 81:80, a *syntonic* comma — not to be confused with the Pythagorean comma or *minor diesis*. 81:80 is the closest superparticular ratio possible with regular numbers as numerator and denominator.[251]

We can think of Figure 68 as a side view of the body's torso, with "D" at the top of the head, and the Pythagorean comma at the base of the spine, at the genitals. This is a side-by-side comparison of tones produced by Pythagorean Tuning juxtaposed against the same notes generated by Just Tuning.[252] The darkened areas correspond to syntonic comma tonal discrepancies between the body's scale tones (that include powers of 5 with lower case names) and the extended soul's powers of 3 (given upper case names).

Figure 68 - Measuring the Dissonance between Body and Soul

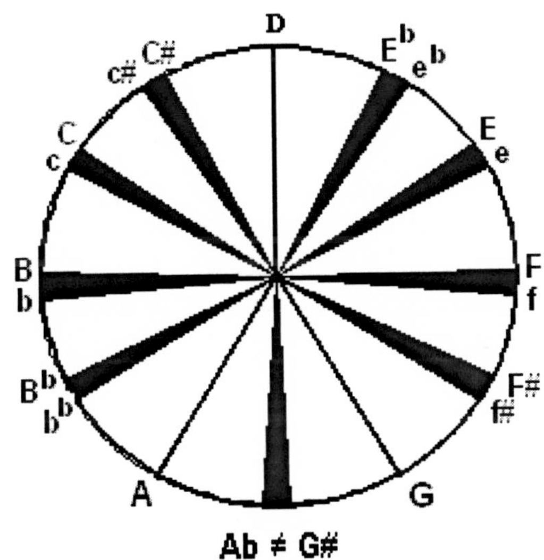

The naturally occurring dissonance that occurs between the only two historically significant integer tuning systems (Pythagorean and Just Tuning), established the mathematical framework of Abraham's theology based on the perceived moral need to somehow bridge the gap between the spiritual and material realms. This underlying mathematical dichotomy shaped Biblical allegory, and inspired man's thinking for thousands of years to come. Chapter 5 has already mentioned Leonardo da Vinci's "Vetruvian Man," which symbolized man's im-

251 A superparticular ratio's numerator is 1 greater than its denominator, and a "regular number" has prime factors of 2, 3, and 5. For Pythagorean tuning, the only possible superparticular ratios are 2:1 (the octave), 3:2 (the perfect fifth), 4:3 (the perfect fourth), and 9:8 (the whole step). For just tuning, six additional superparticular ratios are possible: 5:4, 6:5, 10:9, 16:15, 25:24, and 81:80; See Appendix: A Primer on Music.
252 Ernest McClain, *Children of Abraham*, 2007, unpublished.

perfect material existence as a two dimensional square, measured against his perfect spiritual existence as a circle (Figure 69). Vetruvius is often called Rome's first architect, inspiring Da Vinci, as well as Italian Renaissance architect Andrea Palladio (1508-1580). Palladio found Vetruvius' architectural approach compatible with the theology of St. Thomas Acquinas, who wrote that two worlds existed simultaneously: the divine world of faith and the earthly world of man.

Interest in geometry and human proportion, at least from an architectural perspective, must begin with Bezalel, the chief architect of the Tabernacle in the desert within the Book of Exodus. According to an important Talmudic teaching, Bezalel "knew how to permute the letters with which Heaven and Earth were created."[253] The secret society of Freemasons trace their roots back to the Quadrivium of Bezalel, and to the architects of Solomon's Temple, who, they believe, were once in possession of the "Blueprint" used by God to Create the spiritual and material worlds (which, of course, is the mathematics and acoustics of Yahweh revealed throughout this text). The Freemasons correctly believe that a harmonization of this dichotomy was somehow encrypted within the Holiest Name of God, *Yahweh.* Most Orthodox rabbis and Master Masons believe that the solutions to these great mysteries can be found somewhere within the Zohar. But, the Zohar openly admits that it cannot explain these "hidden paths" to God.[254] The *Sefer Yetzirah* is the only text that explains these paths, but the rabbinate has not understood the necessary music theory since 586 BCE. My first book, *The Lost Word of God*, focuses on deciphering these mysteries within the *Sefer Yetzirah,* while the current effort attempts to chronicle the science of religion that grew out of the perception of separate spiritual and material realms.

Figure 69 - Man's Body as an Imperfect Container of Divine Light

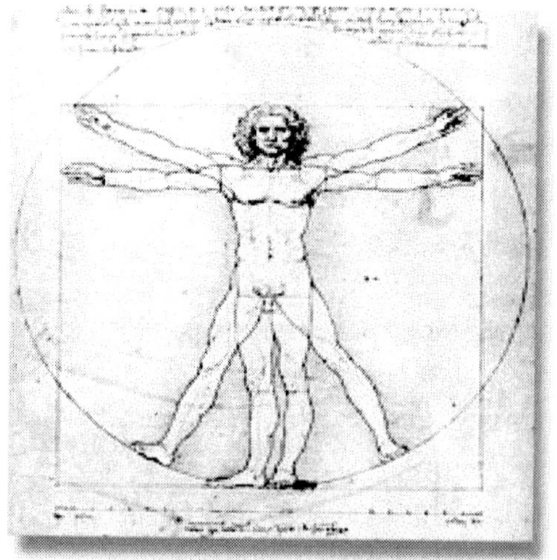

253 Aryeh Kaplan, *Sefer Yetzirah* (York Beach, ME: Samuel Weiser, 1990) 26.
254 Zohar 15b; 30b: "...secret paths which cannot be discovered."

The Mathematics of Salvation

In the transition from polytheism to monotheism, the focus moves from the Gods within the Clock to the God within man. Polytheism describes 7 Gods in the clock astrologically emanating divine light to earth, while monotheism focuses on the same 7 lights emanating from within each individual. These 7 lights are generated by the triple progression, and the triple progression is contained by the etheric body's quintuple progression. Our moral struggle is to an attempt to purge impurities from the soul's triple progression and the etheric body's quintuple progression as a prelude to harmonizing these two aspects of our inner being. The scope of man's moral struggle is embodied by the riddle of "the circle and the square within."[255] A three-term continuous proportion can be established between the circle, the square, and the diagonal of a square, as the mean term, that also functions as the diameter of the circle. In Part I, we have seen how all this has been carved into stone using sexagesimal numbers within the cuneiform tablet YBC 7289. It marks the first use of the Pythagorean Theorem to solve for the length of the diameter/diagonal, the Axis Mundi of man's being that bridges the gap between Heaven and Earth. The solution is also provided on the tablet as the square root of 2, correct to 5 places.

More than a thousand years after YBC 7289 was created in Babylon, Pythagoreans swore an oath of secrecy when they first discovered the imperfect length of the diameter/diagonal in Figures 70a & b. The Greeks finally realized what the Sumerian/Babylonian scribes had inscribed more than 1200 years earlier — how to use the Pythagorean Theorem to define the hypotenuse of a right triangle. The length of YBC 7289's hypotenuse is an irrational number, and, as such, it cannot be measured with precision. What was so significant about this mathematics was its philosophical context. The hypotenuse became the mean term in our struggle to reconcile the spiritual and material realms of the circle and the square.

Since bridging the gap between the material and spiritual realms depended on an irrational number — a number without ratio — the great fear was that man would never be able to adequately reconcile his sinful material existence with his spiritual aspirations. This perceived imperfection appears to have set off the cultural equivalent of a modern day arms race, in which Sumer, Babylon, Egypt, and Israel, all competed to discover the most accurate approximation of $\sqrt{2}$ (see Figure 74). Acquiring that knowledge was thought to hold the key to conquering death, and to harnessing the power of magic, wisdom, healing, prophecy, and eternal life.

255 Zohar 56b; Prologue.

Figure 70a & b - YBC 7289: Bisecting a Circle and a Square

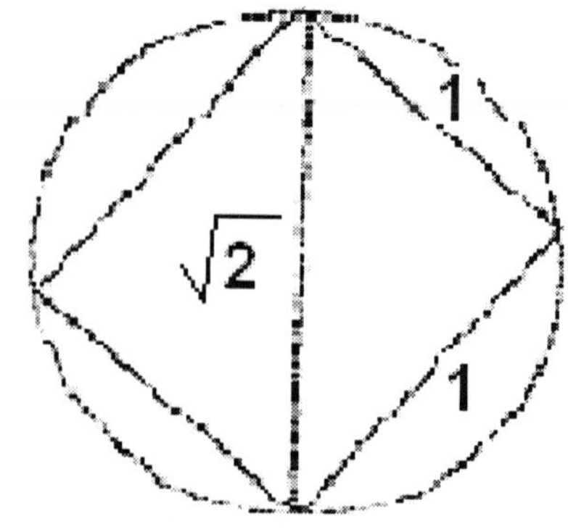

Abraham greatly simplified the existing sexagesimal number system. Within his mixed-base framework, the 7 lights of the soul became the key to the mathematics of salvation. Abraham could approximate the $\sqrt{2}$ using prime number integers less than 10 by simply rewriting the Sabbath ratio 7:5 as a ratio of Fire to Wind, or $7/5 = 1.4$. He reasoned and calculated that an even greater accuracy would be possible with additional powers of 7. The intensity of one's "inner Fires" can purify the body by varying the number of circuits in the sacred practice with additional multiples of 7. The length of the Axis Mundi would then approach the accuracy of YBC 7289, while greatly simplifying sexagesimal numerosity with numbers less than $10^2 = 100$. This cultural war was all about creating the most accurate mathematical context for "lighting the Temple Menorah" in order to strengthen the inner Fires of deep meditation.

In the Torah, the number 1 describes the "Unity" that is God Himself, but the number 7 describes the complexity of vibration that exists within that Unity. The 7th color is a transcendent harmonization of all six colors in the rainbow and the soul, the 7 tones in a musical scale, the 7 days in a week, 7 lights on the Temple Menorah; 7 planets in the universe, 7 seas, 7 firmaments; "Seven is therefore beloved for every desire under Heaven."[256]

Jewish tradition tells us that only 6 laws were given to Adam in Eden, and that he didn't have access to the sacred wisdom of the number 7. Only in the 7th generation from Adam, did the first holy man, Enoch, learn all 7 laws. "My Sabbaths, God said, denotes the circle and the square within."[257] The heart of the Torah is the Sabbath ($= 7^1$), and therefore, the circle and the square within. It occurs every 7 days; the Sabbatical ($7^2 = 49$) occurs every 7 years of Sabbaths; and the Jubilee ($7^3 = 343$) occurs every 7 Sabbaticals of Sabbaths. From the beginning of the 49th year to the Beginning of the 50th year, Leviticus xxv 8-54, and xxvii 16-24, commands us:

---

256 Kaplan, *Sefer Yetzirah*, 264; a paraphrase of Ecclesiastes 3:1.
257 Zohar Prologue 5b -6a.

- To rest the soil;
- Revert landed property to its original owner, who had been driven by poverty to sell it;
- The freeing or manual remission of those Israelites, who, through poverty or otherwise, had become the slaves of their brethren
- Freedom from the exile of sin, and remission of one's soul back to God

The Trees in the Garden of Eden were nourished by Earth, Water, and Wind. As the 6 colors, 6 sounds, and 6 Days of Creation, poured their essence into the 7th color, 7th sound and 7th Day, their function within each given context would be to harmonize the preceding 6 into Unity. Once again, Abraham called it the "Crown" — the Divine Unity of the transcendent God. The Tree of Knowledge defines the soul and its extension into Good and Evil, while the Tree of Life defines the impurities of the body as a container of man's corrupted soul. The two trees of Eden only include three of the four primordial elements: Earth, Water, and Wind as powers of 2, 3, and 5. How does the Bible inform us about the Fires of Heaven that are embodied by powers of 7 within the transcendent Crown? The answer is well hidden within the *Sefer Yetzirah.*

There are two "Trees of Salvation" that are never explicitly mentioned within Biblical allegory, but they exist there implicitly because they explicate the numerology of Scripture, and they do exist within the *Sefer Yetzirah* as the sacred practice of "binding a Crown" to the body and "binding a Crown" to the soul. A "cross-cut" triple and septenary progression purifies the soul (Figure 71a), while a cross-cut quintuple and septenary progression purifies the body (Figure 71b). The intensified Sabbath Fires bind the 6 lights of the soul into a divine Unity within the 7th Heaven (Log 3^p x Log 7^q = Water * Fire). The Fires of Heaven have also purged the impurities within the body's Wind element (Log 5^p x Log 7^q = Wind * Fire).

Knowledge of "Binding the Crown" and the two "Trees of Salvation" were considered too powerful to be revealed to the lay person, because they hold the key to liberation and prophecy. The *Sefer Yetzirah* articulates the mathematics of the two Trees, while the Torah allegorizes this mathematics as the numerology of the sacred priestly practice and the gematria of key patriarch lifespans. The secret of the two hidden Trees of Salvation might be considered the Bible's greatest mystery because it reveals the deepest meaning of God and the Bible. This includes the "rainbow principle" of the Crown, where 1 = 7, in the same manner that 1 = 60 within sexagesimal Babylon. It also includes the parameters of Abraham's sacred practice: the Sabbath (every 7 days), the Sabbatical (7 years of 7 Sabbaths = 49), and the Jubilee (7 Sabbaticals of 7 years of 7 Sabbaths = 343); and the lifespans of Abraham (175), Jacob (147), and even a reference ($7^3 = 343$) to the leading 7's within the gematria of Yahweh Himself as $60^5 = 10^5 6^5 = 777{,}600{,}000$.

Figure 71a & b - The Septenary Fires Purging the Soul (71a) *and Body* (71b)

1/343 1/63 1/147 1/27
1/49 1/21 1/9
1/7 1/3
1
3 7
9 21 49
27 63 147 343

1/343 1/245 1/175 1/125
1/49 1/35 1/25
1/7 1/5
1
5 7
25 35 49
125 175 245 343

On the surface the two Trees of Salvation are simply multiplication tables, but they describe three levels of spirituality that can be attained by articulating the Word of God, YHVH, as the sacred deep meditation practice of High Priests: 7 circuits around the sacred cube. Those three levels include:

1) Purging the extended soul of corruption
2) Purging the body of impurities
3) Liberating the soul from the body

The Torah also states that Abraham died at a hundred years, seventy years, and five years, rather than simply stating 175 years. This might seem to be a negligible detail, however, these three numbers were Abraham's various "birth" numbers:

- When Abraham was 100 years of age, Isaac was born and circumcised, in preparation for receiving the birthright: the sacred practice and the patriarchal lineage of Israel
- When Terah, Abraham's father, was 70 years old, Abram was born but he was not circumcised. Abram sanctified his body with the Covenant of Circumcision at 99 years of age. The ratio of Abram's age at circumcision to the age of his father was 99:70. Historically, among the various ancient cultures, the ratio 99:70 approaches the accuracy of YBC 7289, but with far simpler mathematics. It was a mathematical *tour de force* by the authors of Scripture. With the Covenant of Circumcision, Abram could effectively "swallow sin," by eliminating the 13th "Evil" spoke in the tone circle of the soul's triple progression.

- The Hebrew letter *Heh* (= 5) marks Abram's spiritual birth as Abraham. Jewish tradition equates the *Heh* with *Ruach Hakodesh* (the Holy Spirit or Breath of God). As $3^5 = 243$, Abram's initiation by Melchizedek as Priest of God Most High incorporated the letter *Heh*=5 into his name, making it Abraham (=248). With this added letter *Heh*, Abraham embodied the "Breath of God" within his name and within his being, transforming him into a prophet.

The Trees of Salvation provides the basis for all monotheistic Scripture, including the Tanakh, the New Testament, and the Koran. The key is Abraham's sacred meditation practice, which includes the traditional Jewish practice of "laying Tefillin," by wrapping a leather strap 7 times around the arm, binding God's transcendent Crown to the other six aspects of a man's soul. Abraham's sacred practice of "7 circuits around the sacred cube" is also practiced by Muslims circumambulating the Kabah in Mecca during the *Hajj*. Within Christianity, in the final scene of the New Testament's Book of Revelation, the sacred cube of the New Jerusalem descends from Heaven, heralded by 7 angels blowing trumpets (i.e., 7 tone circles). Although "7 circuits around the sacred cube" is the foundation of the three monotheistic faiths, only Islam links this practice to Abraham. Clergy within the three faiths are still unaware that Abraham's writings contain detailed instructions that describe how to "pray like a prophet" in order to liberate one's soul.

The Meaning and Pronunciation of YHVH

Abraham's sacred practice teaches mankind to "pronounce" the Word, YHVH, in the manner of the ancient High Priests on the Day of Atonement. Of course, this is not a verbal articulation, but rather, it is a deep meditation described as "7 circuits around the sacred cube." Once per year, the High Priest would liberate his soul from his body in a simulation of death, passing through the veil between life and death in order to enter the Holy of Holies. This is where the sacred cube of the Ark of the Covenant held the divine light of the Ten Commandments that was written by the Hand of God on the two stone tablets of Testimony given to Moses. The Priest would then pray from within the Holy of Holies for the Israelites, before returning his soul to his body.

The mystery of God's Name has not been revealed since the last High Priest of Solomon's Temple. I learned from my mentor, Dr. Ernest McClain, that YHVH translates to $10^5 6^5 = 777{,}600{,}000$. McClain also describes a methodology used by Biblical authors for separating large numbers into "heads and tails," i.e., the high and low order digits: 777 and 600,000.[258] My own research identifies these three leading 7's as an articulation of the Sab-

258 Ernest McClain, *The Children of Abraham*, unpublished

bath, Sabbatical, and Jubilee levels of Abraham's sacred practice, written in decimal, but interpreted as Base-7 orders of magnitude (777). The second component corresponds to the 600,000 Israelites that Moses, a personification of 777, led out of Egypt to the Promised Land.

During the sacred meditation practice, our mind "sings" the unique Sabbath scale every Sabbath for 7 years of Sabbaths. This is called a Sabbatical (= 7x7), And, for every 49 years of Sabbaths (7x7x7). This is called a Jubilee. The three leading 7's of YHVH's gematria defines Sabbath introspection, Sabbatical purification, and Jubilee liberation.

After revealing the Ten Commandments to Moses, YHVH revealed them directly to all the Israelites, but only Moses was already accomplished at meditation, and only he could listen at the level of prophecy. God's message has been encrypted for four millennia within the four sacred letters of the Holy Name. The Word *Yahweh* instructs all 600,000 souls of Israel to "sing" the Day 7 scale for 49 years, in order to be shepherded out of the soul's exile within the body and be delivered to the Promised Land. That spiritual high ground is called the *Shechinah*, which is the Divine Presence that hovers above a righteous man. The soul is initially liberated as a *golem,* but after continued exposure to the crucible of the inner Fires, the practitioner's *golem* is "polished" into a *Shechinah* that can "walk with God."

Further corroboration of 777 can be found in the story of Cain. It begins with Abel's offerings at the Foundation Stone on the Temple Mount. His offerings were accepted by God, but Cain's were not. Cain's countenance fell and he rose up to slay Abel. God cursed Cain "more than the earth." He was exiled to wander the earth, but God postponed his vengeance for 7 generations to allow Cain time for redemption. God set "the mark of Cain" upon his forehead so others wouldn't kill him before the time allotted for repentance. Cain procreated, but never repented, and his sinful nature spread across the Earth. Seven generations later, Cain's descendant, Lamech, was hunting with his son, Tubel-cain, who mistook Cain for an animal, leading Lamech to kill him unintentionally. Lamech, although condemning his own sin, declared that if Cain's punishment was delayed for 7 generations, then surely for his unintentional sin he would be given 77 generations to redeem himself. Within the patriarchal lineage of Seth, another Lamech was born. This Lamech became the father of Noah. And, Lamech, the father of Noah, died at precisely 777 years, as if he were a bookend to evil, providing closure to the lineage of Cain, who spread evil throughout the earth. His son Noah would, of course, preside over a purging of the earth's "body of evil." Lamech, Noah's father, was the last generation that Adam would live to see. With Adam's death, God's curse on earth was lifted, and the next 10 generations, beginning with Noah, would start with a clean slate (Figure 81).

The "Salvation of Israel" is encrypted directly within the numerology of *Yahweh's* Holy Mountain as 777,600,000 (Figure 55). The number "777" defines Salvation, while 600,000 (=6 x 10^5) describes the number of souls (*Vav*=6) to be saved. However, "666" has long been associated with sin as the New Testament's "mark of the devil." Unfortunately, "666" is a misreading of the actual number that embodies sin, which is $3^6 = 3*3*3*3*3*3 = 729$ (see Figure 72) — where three 6's have erroneously replaced six 3's. We have already examined the mathematical context for how a square inscribed within a circle generates the "Diabolus in Musica." The resulting ratio of 729:1 bisects the 512:1024 octave double as 512:729:1024. Even if we chose not to transpose the octave ratio 1:2 to 512:1024, we can bisect the 1:2 octave double directly as 1:√2 :2. Bisecting the octave locates both sin and salvation ambiguously as the Portal of Heaven and Abyss of Hell. The line between Good and Evil is blurred by ego. Divine Judgement free of ego enables us to precisely locate the Portal to Heaven, otherwise we fall into the Abyss. Since √2 is an irrational number that can only be approximated, there is a range of frequencies between Ab and G# believed to cloud man's thoughts, desires, and judgement. Transcending the material world to "Walk with God" in the highest spiritual realm first requires mankind to vanquish ego just to begin his spiritual migration. This is only possible through the sacred meditation practice of pronouncing God's Name.

Figure 72 - Bisecting the Heavenly Firmament "Divides the Material Waters from the Spiritual Waters"

Ab	Eb	Bb	F	C	G	D	A	E	B	F#	C#	G#
729	243	81	27	9	3	1	1/3	1/9	1/27	1/81	1/243	1/729

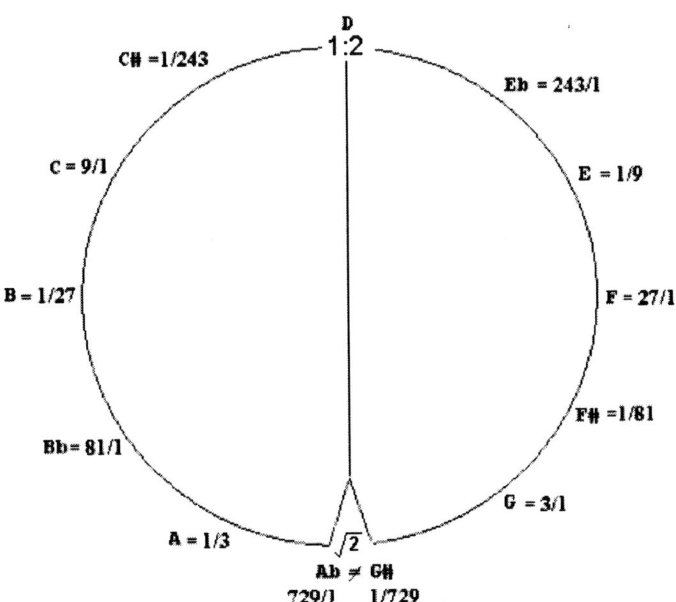

The Sun and the Soul; the Moon and the Body

The triple and quintuple progressions harmonize together to define the Tree of Life. Within the microcosm of body and soul, the harmonics of the soul's triple progression extends into good and evil as the serpent energies of man's alter-ego. This becomes the root-cause of sin that manifests within the body's quintuple progression. In Figure 73a & b, we can see how the Ab ≠ G# gap occurs as an extension of both triple and quintuple progressions. We can see how a musical "cycle of fifths" -- a triple progression -- stacks 12 consecutive perfect fifths (3:2) that do not line up on the octave tone circle (2:1) boundary (Figure 73a). Similarly, within the macrocosm of the Heavens, the Sun's ecliptic never closes the circle in its annual spiral, causing the Sun to overshoot its 360 day solar year by 5 festival days,

Man's inner, triple progression lights are said to be cloaked by his outer, quintuple progression lights. Like a thick burlap coat, the physical body's quintuple progression vibrations exiles man from God, i.e., from experiencing his own soul directly. Its course matter imposes the dullness of materiality that allows sin to manifest, cloaked in ignorance, with respect to the subtleties, joys and power of inner light. Circumcision to remove the tiny foreskin is Biblical metaphor for removing the obstructions of the body that would stand in the way of mankind's ability to experience and realize the soul. Within the macrocosm, the quintuple progression was associated with the orbit of the moon, but its 12 monthly lunations in a 354 day year undershoots the 360 day solar approximation. Similarly, "heavenly music" adds 3 sequential major thirds (5:4) to undershoot the octave (2:1) boundary (Figure 73b).

The science of religion is very concerned with harmonizing the triple and quintuple progressions. By understanding the Vedic ayanamsa, precession's yearly degree component of 50 seconds of arc per year, we gain insight into how Aryan astral theology first described "the circle and the square within" — mathematics describing the sacred practice of deep meditation as an attempt to locate the "portal to Heaven." The various commas and diesis of tuning theory are altered by our approximations of the diameter/diagonal that controls access to this sacred "Gateway."

God's new Covenant with Abram would help man stay focused on God, thus clearing the path to salvation. Jewish ritual circumcision usually takes place 8 days after birth, but Abraham's was the first circumcision to ever take place, and he was already 99 years old. Circumcision was necessary if he was going to receive the Holy Spirit (the "Breath of God" that is transformed from the breath of man). The Breath of God is, of course, embodied in the letter *Heh* (=H), which was then added to Abram's name, making his spiritual name Abraham. This spiritualization process prepared Abraham to father Isaac at 100 years old. One's Age at circumcision would henceforth coincide with the age of a patriarch's father at the time of his birth, however, since Terah's age was 70 when Abram was born, and Abram was 99 when he was circumcised (rather than 8 days old), these two age milestones: 99 and 70, became significant for Abram and for the Torah. The ratio of 99:70 is 1.41428, which described the length of the diameter/diagonal Axis Mundi as √2 accurate to four places, despite using much smaller numbers than any mathematical approximation methods used in Sumer, Babylon, Harappa, or Egypt (Figure 74).

Figure 73a & b- Harmonizing the Solar Triple Progression and Lunar Quintuple Progression

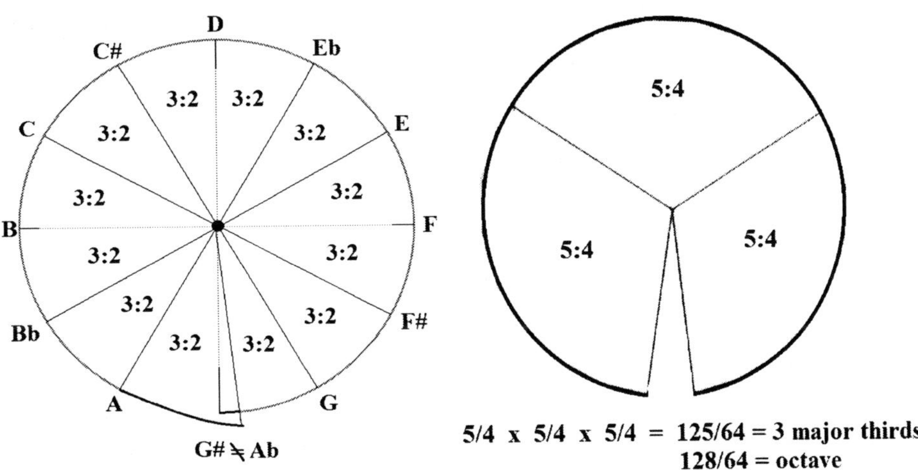

During the solar year, 12 perfect fifths (~1 month each), whirl around Figure 73a until the last perfect fifth forms an Ab ≠ G# gap called the Pythagorean comma when measured against the octave boundary. These 12 solar months exceed the solar year by about 5 festival days. In the lunar calendar (Figure 73b) three major thirds (of four lunar months each) need to be larger to coincide with the solar year.[259]

Figure 74 - Sin and Salvation within the Four Wheels of Ezekiel (Log $2^p\ 3^q\ 5^r\ 7^s$)

$\sqrt{2} = 1.41421356\ldots$ **Modern Calculations**

$1 + 24/60^1 + 51/60^2 + 10/60^3 = 1.41421$ **YBC 7289 (Babylonian Sexagesimal)**

$\frac{99}{70} = 1.41428$ **Abraham's Circumcision**

$\frac{5^{14}}{2^{32}} = \frac{6103515625}{4294967296} = 1.42108$ **the Great Flood** **(Torah's parody of Sumer and Babylon's "Flood" of sexagesimal numbers)**

$\frac{64}{45} = 1.42222$ **Noah as Savior**

$\frac{7}{5} = 1.4$ **Sabbath interval**

259 McClain, *Myth of Invariance*, Op.Cit., 97.

Flood of Numbers

The sexagesimal numerosity of Babylon was parodied within the Bible's portrayal of both the Tower of Babel and the Great Flood. Ernest McClain taught me to appreciate the humor of Jewish authors, as the Torah unveils the greatly reduced numerosity of Abraham's foreskin, as compared to their musical parody of a Great Flood of unnecessary sexagesimal Babylonian numbers that "covered the highest mountains" (see Figure 75a). When the waters rose 15 powers of 5, until "All the high mountains which were under the entire Heavens were covered. Fifteen cubits upwards did the waters strengthen."[260]

The Great Flood and the Tower of Babel, a parody of the Sumerian-Babylonian (and soon to be Indo-Aryan) Yugas, were created within the 4,320,000,000 : 8,640,000,000 octave double (see Figure 75a). Thus, Hinduism's "Immense Being" (*Brahma*) derives from the Mesopotamian mathematics that is parodied in the Torah. It has often been noted that *Brahma* is an anagram of the name Abraham.

In Figure 75a, the highest reaches of the material realm is juxtaposed against the full range of man's spiritual "shadow," i.e., his "ghost" or Soul as corrupted by knowledge of Good and Evil. The mathematics of the Holy Mountain, as well as its spiritual reflection, describes a 3 x 5 multiplication table, with triple and quintuple progression components proceeding from the lower left "Cornerstone." Within Just Tuning, the highest number in the flood extends above the peak of the Holy Mountain within the material realm, while its lowest number reaches the abyss of Hell within its spiritual reflection (the dotted outline in Figure 75a). This comparison juxtaposes the highest Good, the Ab = 5^{14} = 6103515625, at the top of the mountain, against the lowest Evil, the G# = 2^{23} x 3^6 = 8388608 x 729 = 6115295232, to yield a ratio that approaches Unity (6115295232/ 6103515625 = 1.0019...). The Holy Mountain enables us to transpose Good and Evil into a single octave through multiplication by 2^{23} where the triple progression's depths of spiritual Evil (3^6 = 729) is juxtaposed against the quintuple progression's highest material Good (5^{14} = 6103515625). When seen through the eyes of a prophet, the summit of the Holy Mountain transcends time and space until the prophet "Walks with God" in eternal life. When seen through the eyes of ego, man peers into the Abyss of death, suffering and rebirth.

The various mathematical constructions, whether describing God's Holy Mountain, Ziggurats, the Tree of Life, or Circumcision, all derive from the same Aryan-Semitic mathematical tradition, shared among the different civilizations of the Middle East. Within the context of each separate culture, this mathematics profoundly shaped literature, science, theology, and mythology.

260 Genesis 7:20

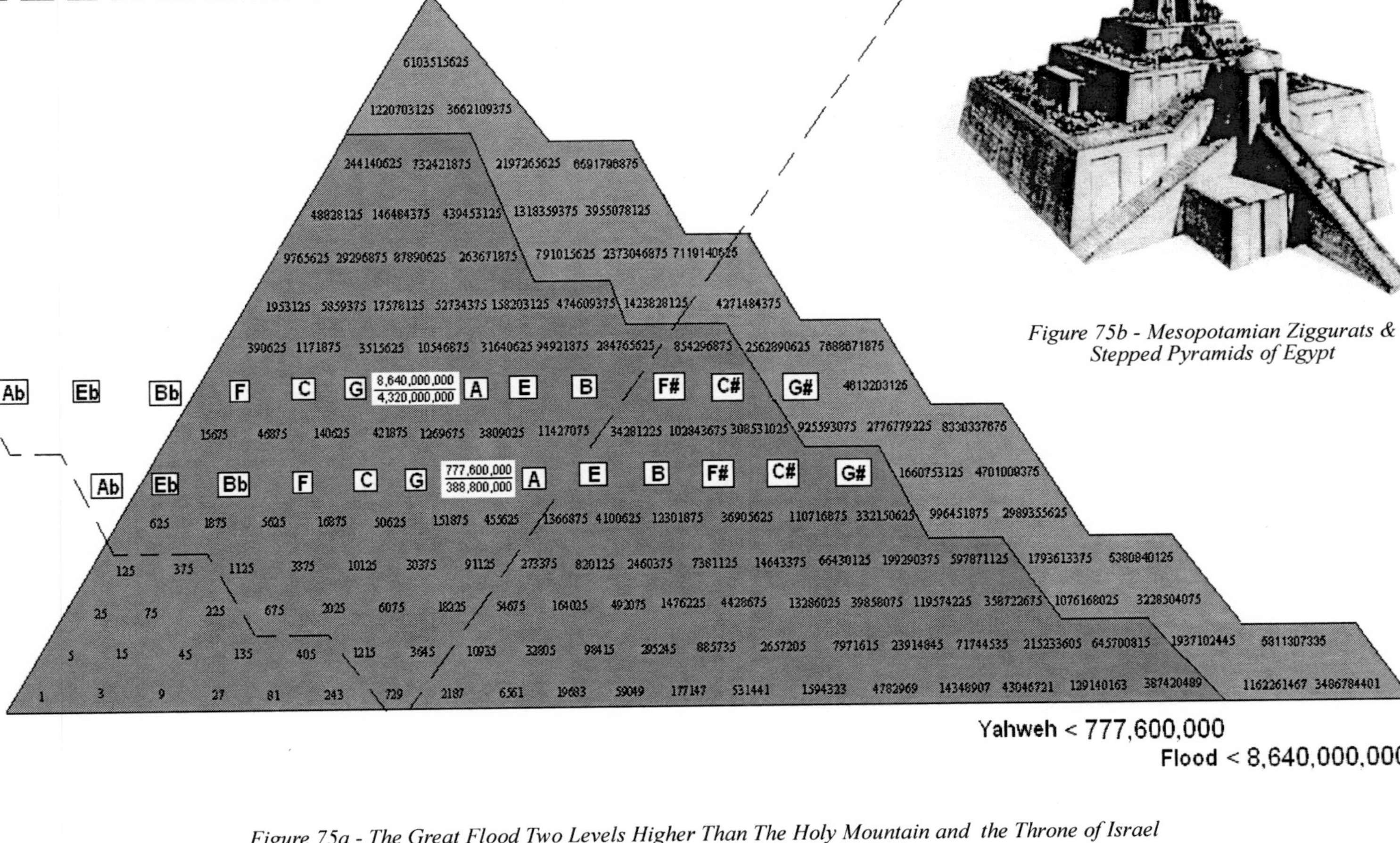

Figure 75b - Mesopotamian Ziggurats & Stepped Pyramids of Egypt

Figure 75a - The Great Flood Two Levels Higher Than The Holy Mountain and the Throne of Israel

The Fires of the Four-Horned Altar

The mathematics of salvation cleanses the body in the Fires of Heaven as all impurities are gradually purged from the body. This process symbolizes what it would have meant for Adam to "partake of the Tree of Life." Adam's ethereal body was created from the vibrations of the Tree of Life (Figure 76a). After 7 generations, Enoch became the first holy man who could "pronounce" *YHVH* by applying the step-by-step procedures outlined in the next few diagrams. They describe the body's purification process in preparation for the soul's liberation.

In Heaven's Tree of Life (Figure 76a), God (=1) is positioned at the center, between the roots and branches (powers of 3 and 5). As the divine vibrations descend into matter, after Adam's Fall, God (=1) becomes the cornerstone of Earth's Holy Mountain (Step 1; Figure 76b). In Step 2, "the Earth quakes" and purges all tones that are > 720, the Navel of Order's upper limit. In Step 3, the Heavenly Firmament defines the octave double 360:720 at the center of the Four-Horned Altar.[261] And, the Heavenly Fires purge away all tones that are not part of the singable, chromatic scale contained within this octave double. Arithmetically, the transition from Step 2 to Step 3 is defined by multiplying step 2's smallest integers by whatever power of 2 is necessary to transpose them into a singable scale that fits, without duplicated tones, within 360:720. Only 11 chromatic pitches remain after the Fires of Heaven have done their work (Figure 76b: Step 4). This method constructs a singable scale that adheres to the symmetry of the ancient Navel of Order: $1/720 \leq 2^p 3^q 5^r \leq 720$. It is the "altar on the mountain" containing the *Ruach Hakodesh* (Winds of Spirit) that transforms a prophet. It describes the inner workings of performing the 365 prohibitive commandments with the proper level of *kavanah* (meditative intent).

Step 4 purges excess tonal material, eliminating the 12th and 13th tones (Ab and G#) from the "outer lights" of the body. The sanctified tones that remain define the vibrations of daily prayer that will gradually purify the body. This is the foundation of the Torah. After Abram was initiated into the practice of High Priests by Melchizedek, he experienced the Covenant (of Fire) Between the Parts (Figure 76a), effectively "singing" this inner vibration to God in deep meditation (Hebrew: *Tardemah*). This four-step process describes only part of the inner workings of Figure 76c. There is still more music theory necessary to understand the Covenant of the Word (i.e., Circumcision), when God changed Abram to Abraham, and the Holy Spirit (the letter *Heh*) became "part of his flesh." The introspection of "singing" the Sabbath scale amplifies the 360:720 daily scale to a scale 7 times its vibration (Figure 77). There are then two Sabbaticals necessary to complete the next spiritual step in the process (Figure 78) in preparation for the soul's final "Jubilee" liberation.

261 Exodus 27:1-2

Figure 76a - Man's Body & Soul is a Subset of the Tree of Life

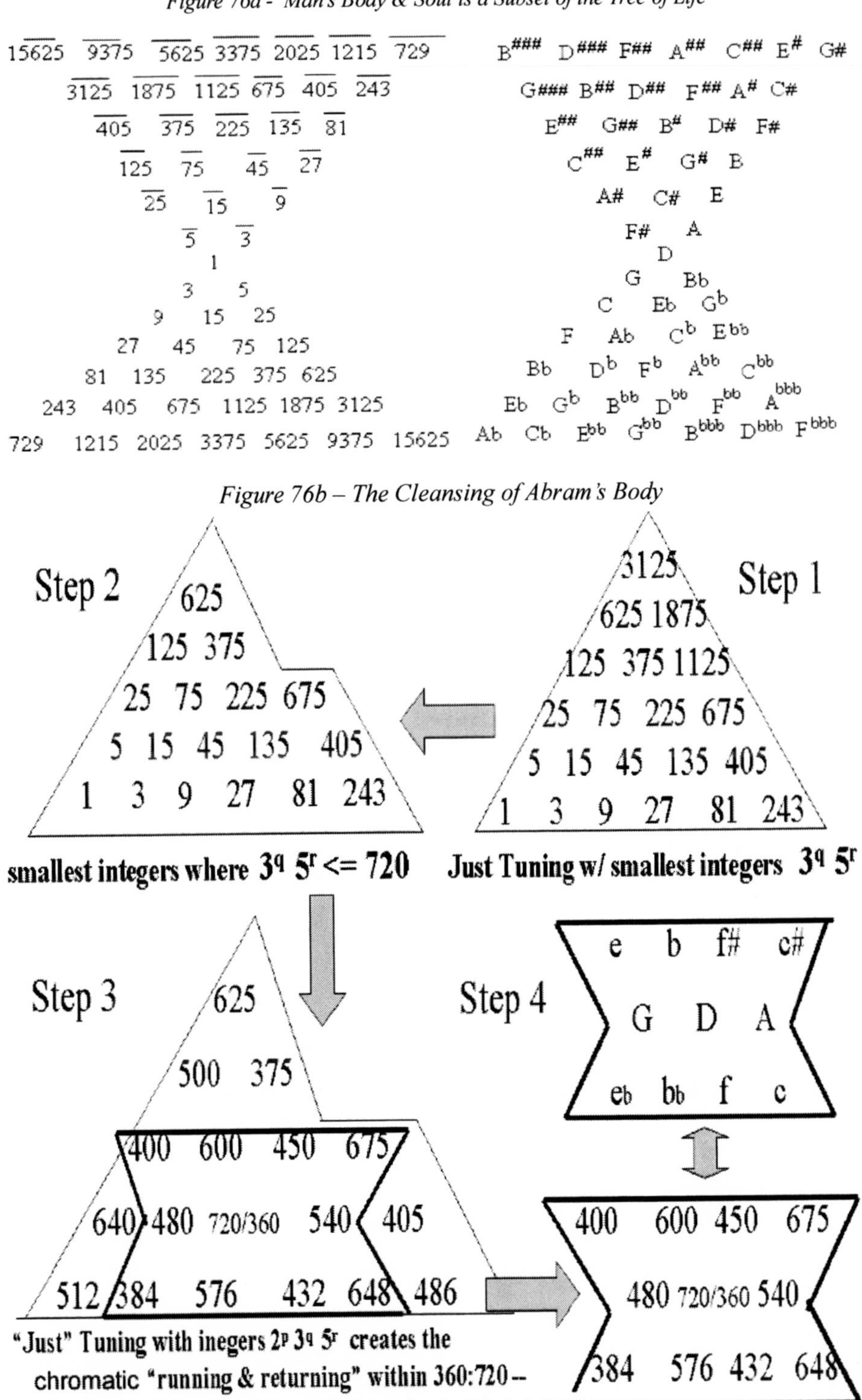

Figure 76b – The Cleansing of Abram's Body

Figure 76c – Partaking of the Tree of Life Will Transform Abram (3^5=243) to Abraham ($3^5 + 5^1$ = 248)

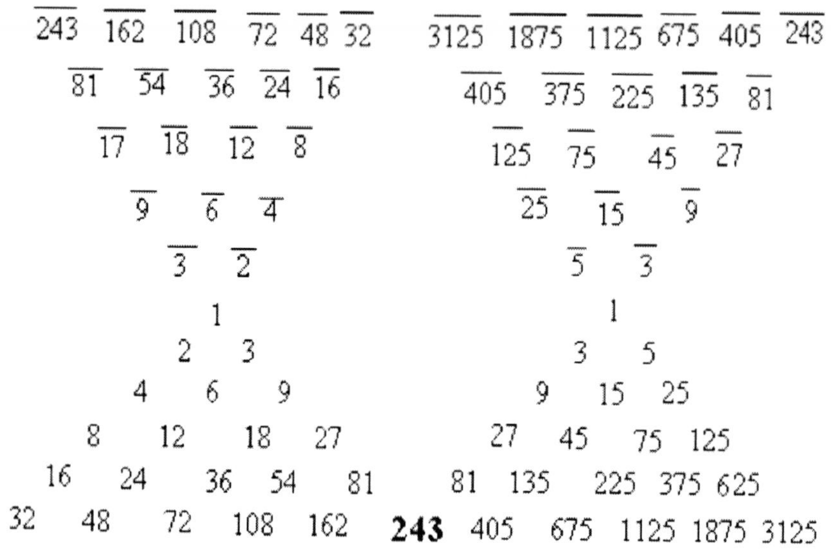

$\overline{243}$ $\overline{162}$ $\overline{108}$ $\overline{72}$ $\overline{48}$ $\overline{32}$ $\overline{3125}$ $\overline{1875}$ $\overline{1125}$ $\overline{675}$ $\overline{405}$ $\overline{243}$

$\overline{81}$ $\overline{54}$ $\overline{36}$ $\overline{24}$ $\overline{16}$ $\overline{405}$ $\overline{375}$ $\overline{225}$ $\overline{135}$ $\overline{81}$

$\overline{17}$ $\overline{18}$ $\overline{12}$ $\overline{8}$ $\overline{125}$ $\overline{75}$ $\overline{45}$ $\overline{27}$

$\overline{9}$ $\overline{6}$ $\overline{4}$ $\overline{25}$ $\overline{15}$ $\overline{9}$

$\overline{3}$ $\overline{2}$ $\overline{5}$ $\overline{3}$

1 1

2 3 3 5

4 6 9 9 15 25

8 12 18 27 27 45 75 125

16 24 36 54 81 81 135 225 375 625

32 48 72 108 162 **243** 405 675 1125 1875 3125

Figure 77 – The Sabbath Scale

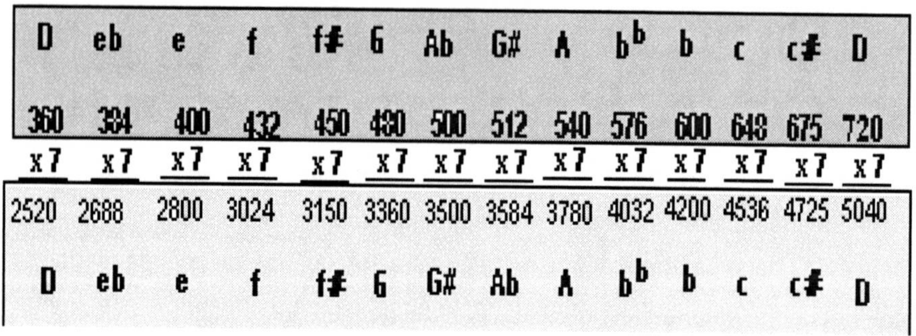

Figure 78 – Opening Up the Central Channel of Liberation

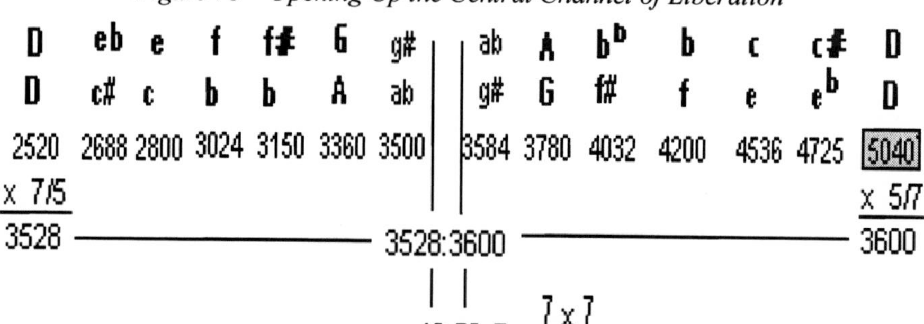

The Sabbath, Sabbatical, and Jubilee

The first "7" of "777" in YHVH defines what it means to keep the Sabbath. The mathematics of circumcision empowers Sabbath prayer to "truncate" one's appetites and transcend the duality of the 12th and 13th tones (Ab ≠ G#). The purification process purges the impurities of both the 12th and 13th tones from the body leaving 11 sanctified tones remaining within the "Four Horned Altar." The cleansed 11 tones of the body then resonate with the extended soul's "singable" chromatic scale (Figures 76b: Step 4).

In Abraham's sacred meditation practice of "7 circuits" the Fires of non-conceptual thought travel 7 circuits around the body (Figures 46a & b). The number 7 does not function as a tone generating ratio, but as an incremental multiplier from 1 to 7. By performing the sacred practice every week day, six days of energy "pour themselves into the Sabbath," the way the six colors of a rainbow pour themselves into white light. Each Day of Creation's sacred scale cumulatively adds its frequencies to the Sabbath mix. Creation week's energy level incrementally increased as the week progressed, all-the-while maintaining equivalent ratios among the scale tones. Each day's energy level adds its frequency and wavelength to that of the day before. So, after 7 days, the energies accumulate as in Figure 77. The inner Fires of the mind's 7 circuits (septimal progression) induces a "divine influx"[262] of heat to purify the Waters (triple progression) and transform the breath of man into the Breath of God (quintuple progression). This influx harmonizes the soul, and enables the "Wings of Metatron" to lift the soul out of the material body (duple progression). It is the Water and Wind prime factor components of the Day 6 scale that are each multiplied by 7 (=7^1), 49 (=7^2), and 343 (=7^3) to define the Sabbath, the Sabbatical, and the Jubilee (see Figures 71a & b).

With 7 years of Sabbaths comes a Sabbatical, describing the second "7" within the Holy Name's trio of 7's. The body's triple + quintuple progression outer lights resonates with the 11 triple progression inner lights of the soul. The soul communicates with the body through the nervous system, with the spinal chord functioning as Axis Mundi. Each circuit of every Sabbath and Sabbatical leverages man's judgement to locate the "Portal to Heaven" at the base of man's spine by approximating the diameter length of the torso's circle. This empowers a practitioner to "clear a path" that direct one's life-force along the spinal chord, ultimately freeing the soul with one's pronunciation of the third "7" in God's Holy Name.

A *tzadek* who has mastered the higher vibrations of Sabbath and Sabbatical prayer has freed all blockages to the resonance between the 11 inner and 11 outer lights. The 7th Sabbatical of the Jubilee year[263] completes the 248 positive com-

262 The divine influx should probably be understood in terms of the electromagnetic spectrum
263 Describing the third "7" within the Holy Name's trio of 7's.

mandments and 365 prohibitive commandments — as codified in the Torah — with the appropriate level of *kavanah,* as specified by Abraham. At this point, the soul's extended subset of vibrations (Figure 66), has filtered back down to the 10 numbers and 7 tones of Adam's innocent soul, where the two Wings of Metatron (2 x 5 = 10) get added to 243 and 360, and empower the soul to ascend. The vibrations of this cleansed body encircles the original 7 aspects of a pure non-dualistic soul —all of which is depicted in the idealized Navel of Order diagram in Figure 79.

Figure 79 – The Fires of the Four-Horned Altar Purges away the Body's Impurities

360	384	400	432	450	480	540	576	600	648	675	720
720	675	648	600	576	540	480	450	432	400	384	360
D	eb	e	f	f#	G	A	bb	b	c	c#	D

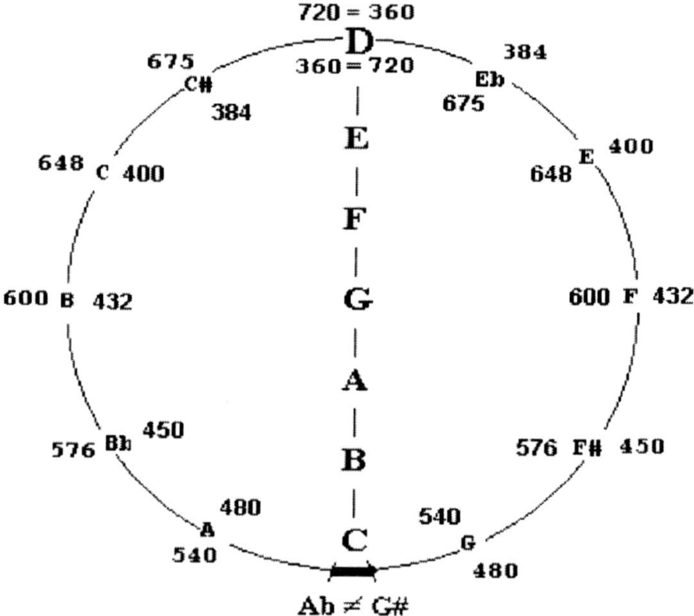

This perfect inverse symmetry is unique in music theory. "… life force flows to the stone … running or returning… waxing or waning… either in direct or reverse order …"

The Zohar explains God's reference to the Sabbath as plural: "My Sabbaths, is a reference to the higher Sabbath and the lower Sabbath which are joined together as One... [which] denotes the circle and the square within, and corresponding to these two the sanctification recital consists of two parts...*Vaikhulu* contains thirty-five words, and the *Kiddush* contains thirty-five words, corresponding to the seventy names of the Holy One, blessed be He, by which the congregation of Israel is crowned."[264] The Zohar admits it has lost the "hidden

264 Zohar Prologue 5b.

musical paths" necessary to explain the Torah, and this specific reference applies to the two Sabbaticals of Sabbath prayer necessary to realize the appropriate level of introspection necessary to become a prophet. Musically, it applies to the application of two reciprocal "ratios of Forgiveness" (5:7 and 7:5) against the Sabbath scale, in the on-going effort to precisely locate the Portal to Heaven and "clear a path" to God. These reciprocal ratios narrow the diesis to 3528:3600, which is reducible to the 49:50 Jubilee ratio (Figures 78 & 80).

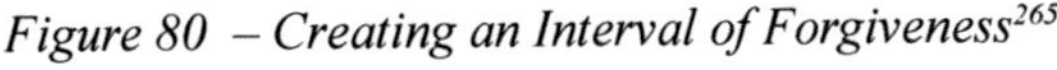
Figure 80 – Creating an Interval of Forgiveness[265]

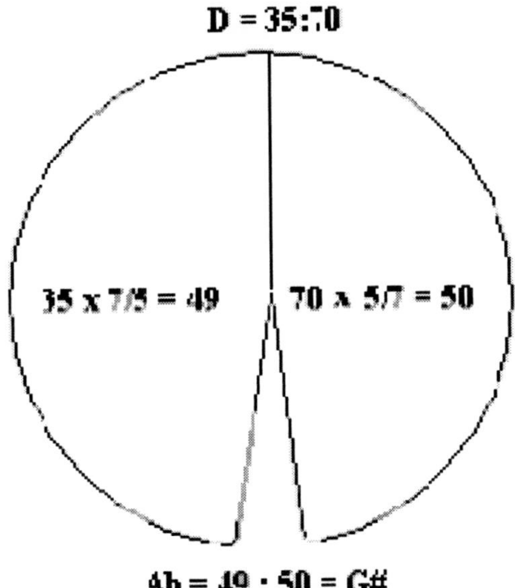

This "clears the path" for the soul's energy to flow in the central channel from the base of the spine to the Crown of the head. However, the energies first converge at the Heart Center in preparation for the final leg of the soul's journey from the Heart to the Crown, which precedes liberation.

Striving for Harmonic Perfection

The Jubilee Year functionally behaves like a calendar's leap year, forgiving a man's debts and sins. On a spiritual level, we "sing" the Sabbath scale every 7th day for a 7-year Sabbatical period, and then continue for 7 Sabbaticals until we achieve the liberation that is associated with the Jubilee Year. This level of attainment requires the practitioner to have cleared a path through the central channel that would allow man's soul to pass through it. According to the Torah's schematic, a harmonized soul would ascend from the lumbar-sacral plexus located at the Navel

265 McClain, *The Myth of Invariance*, 97.

Center, en route to the Heart Center, and finally to the Crown Center before liberating from the body. It would return to the body by entering at the Crown Center, descending back to the Heart, and then proceeding to the Navel Center.

If we were to assume for argument's sake that there were those who could achieve this highly evolved state, without the machinations of Good and Evil pushing and pulling their consciousness this way and that, then those people would be unencumbered as they experience their soul in its original pristine state — in the Unity of God — centered at the Heart. As they proceeded to liberate their soul along the cleared central channel, they would inaudibly "sing" their soul's pure Phrygian mode, and ultimately, they would "walk with God," i.e., resonate with God in the 7th Heaven. The final step in the liberation process would bring the soul up from the Heart Center, through the central channel, until it exits the body as a simulation of death. Since "giving up the ghost" in this manner implies the risk of actual death, Kabbalistic tradition advises the practitioner to take an oath that binds the soul to the body in order to ensure its safe return.

Recreating the mathematics of the dynamic between the *Sefer Yetzirah* and the Torah is still not quite a *fait accompli.* The higher frequencies of Sabbath and Sabbatical scales, as well as the 49:50 "Interval of Forgiveness" within the Jubilee path are necessary to free the soul. But, we would do well to recall that the numbers representing mind, body, and soul, might correspond to an approximation. And, the Semitic tradition is firm in its conviction that approximations are akin to imperfection, which may well be sufficient to prevent the liberation of a soul from the captivity of its body. As a result, the author(s) of the Torah have made a concerted effort to approach numeric perfection.

In their search for a precise mathematics to characterize the liberation process of the Aryan fathers,[266] Torah allegory includes two sets of patriarchal triplets: Noah's triplet sons: Ham, Shem, and Japheth, and Terah's triplet sons: Abram, Nahor, and Haran. These stories span across 10 generations from Noah to Abraham. If we recall our previous discussion of how the body's quintuple progression is slightly out of sync with the Heavenly Firmament's duple progression, we might also recall that the quintuple progression creates musical thirds of ratio 5:4. We can put this into fractional form as: $5/4 = 1.25$. We have already discussed what it would take to reconcile the duple and quintuple progression: three consecutive major thirds with an interval slightly larger than 5/4, such that $\sqrt[3]{2} = 1.26$ or 126/100 and $1.26^3 = 2$. The three consecutive musical thirds would then line up on octave boundaries. The original authors of the Torah understood this, and created a musical allegory that embraced this larger "supernatural" musical third. The story goes like this:

Adam died after 930 years and Noah was born in 1056, exactly 126 years after Adam's death. Noah was the first in the patriarchal line to be born

266 This can also be found in the *Moksha* practise of Hinduism, Buddhism, Jainism, and Taoism, etc.

after Adam's death, when the Earth would no longer be cursed. Noah's father, Lamech, remarks: "This one [Noah] will provide us rest from our work and from the toil of our hands, out of the very soil which the LORD placed under a curse."[267] It is significant that the Earth was no longer cursed from the time Adam died until the birth of Noah — a period of 126 years. The number 126 provides the significant digits for the enlarged musical third that we are looking for, but we would still need to find two more musical thirds to fit together in a sensible way, within the context of this allegory, if we hope to successfully trisect the octave. Here is the rest of that acoustical allegory:

Once Adam died, and the Earth was no longer cursed, we can start enumerating how many years the curse was lifted until the birth of Noah — exactly 126 years. Thus Noah was born in an auspicious year. As we might expect, the two remaining supernatural thirds that we would require in order to trisect the octave, can be measured beginning on the year of Noah's birth. In Figure 81, we can see that they are embedded within Lamech's vibrational essence as (126 x 2) + 343 =595, which is the number of years Lamech lived after Noah was born. Lamech was spared the calamity of the Great Flood by 5 years — i.e., by the Breath of God (= *Heh* = 5). Not coincidently, Lamech completed his Jubilee Year (343 = 7^3), remitting his soul back to God, when he was precisely 777 years old. Coincidence?

We have already discussed the great significance of Lamech's death at 777 years as the Sabbath, Sabbatical, and Jubilee salvation practice embedded directly within God's Holy Name as: YHVH = 10^5 x 6^5 = 777,600,000. We have also discussed how 7 x 7 x 7 = 343 is the upper limit of one of the Trees of Salvation (Figure 71b). If we would like to further corroborate the significance of 343, Noah sent a dove out three times for 7 days each (777), and the final dove didn't return because it found land and was effectively liberated. The following diagram chronicles all of the above. Take special note of the 3 consecutive musical thirds with significant digits of 126. Thus, we have reconciled the duple and quintuple progression with 3 supernatural thirds so that 1:2 became 1: 1.26^3 — and so, the slate was wiped clean, and the world was reborn by dividing the octave into three equal segments — the cube root of 2 or $\sqrt[3]{2}$. This mathematics is encrypted within the death of Adam and the birth of Noah, and reflected in the vibrational essence of Lamech, Noah's father. Thus the first 10 generations from Adam to Noah came to a close with a purging of the Evil of Cain and the cursed Earth of Adam being washed clean in the sacred waters of an anointed Earth. The next 10 generations of patriarchal lineage that began with Noah is brought to fruition with the birth of Abram as part of a set of triplets: Abram, Nahor, and Haran.

267 Genesis 5:29

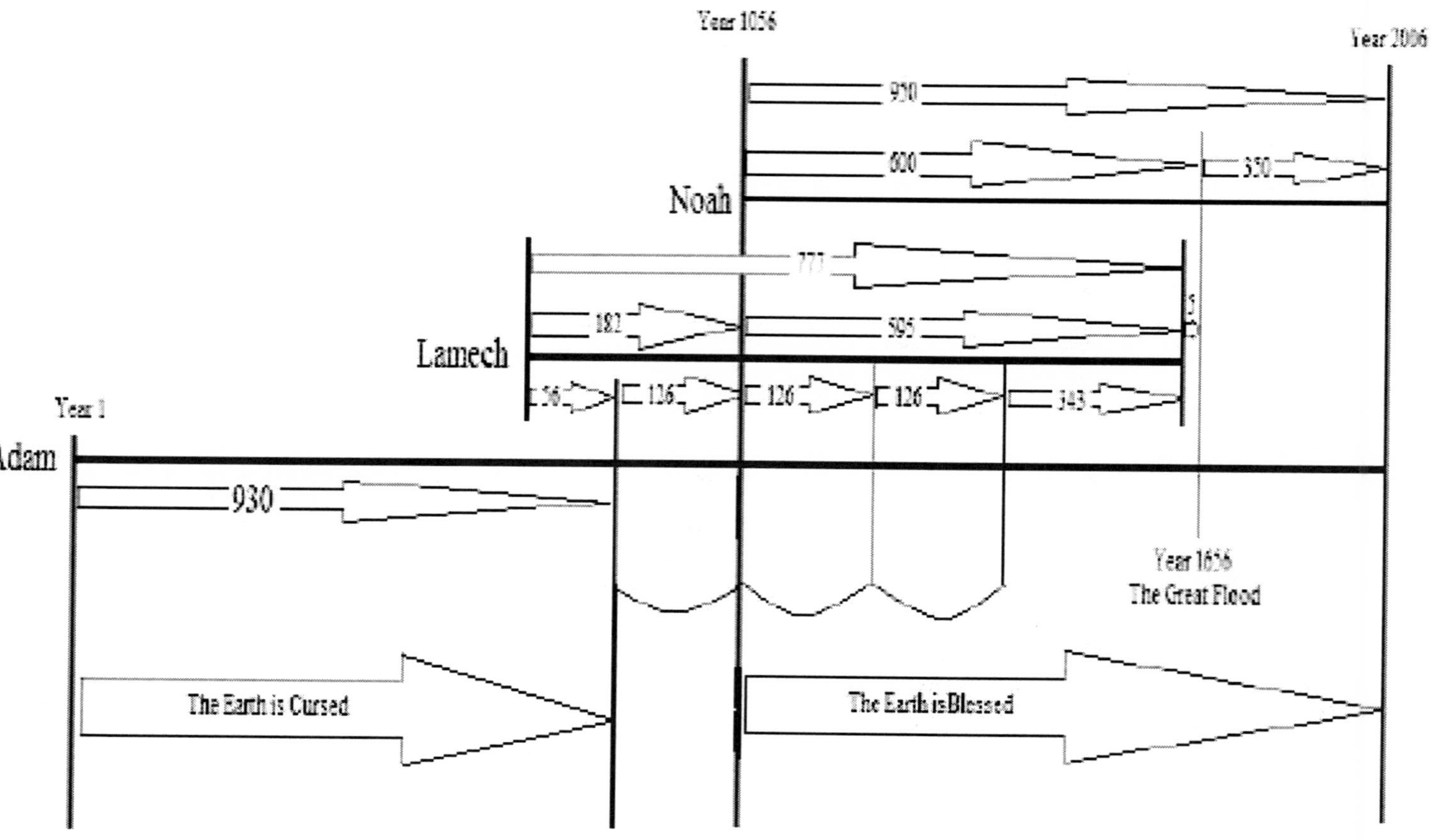

Figure 81 – Numerical Allegory in the Story of Noah

If we still harbor any doubts, the key numerical "coincidences" repeat 10 generations later for Abraham. For example, Shem and Abraham were both 100 years old when their patriarch sons were born. Even the transcendent interval of 1.26 shuttles between the 10 generations from Adam to Noah, and the 10 generations from Noah to Abraham. According to the accepted rabbinical view, Shem reaches across these 10 generations to Abraham as the reincarnation of Melchizedek, who initiates Abram as a Priest of God Most High. It is clear that the Torah's original authors tightly wove this mathematics into Biblical allegory.

Here is how the transcendent musical third of 126/100 makes its way into the story of Abraham, 10 generations after Noah. First, we should recall that Abraham's circumcision at age 99 prepared him for Isaac's "pure" birth one year later. The Torah's authors then share a laugh with Abraham and Sarah, at the thought of a 100 year old man and a 90 year old woman giving birth to a nation of prophets. Abraham and Sarah's laughter at the absurdity of their ages is an aside to the reader, suggesting that their ages should not be interpreted literally, as linear numbers, but rather, harmonically, as logarithmic numbers. McClain brilliantly noticed that the event created two 10:9 musical intervals, one for Abraham and one for Sarah. We can then add these ratios to the 50:49 Jubilee ratio by simply multiplying them together like regular fractions, to get: 10/9 * 10/9 * 50/49 = 5000/3969 = 1.2599 or ~1.26. Since Abraham was born into a set of triplets, we add ~1.26 ratio for each of his brothers (Figure 82). McClain's unpublished diagram provides the mathematics for how the union of Abraham and Sarah "swallows sin" by dividing the octave ("Body of Israel") into 3 equal segments, thus, finding a way to reconcile duple and quintuple progressions through the divine circumstance of triplet births.

Figure 82 -Perfecting the Body

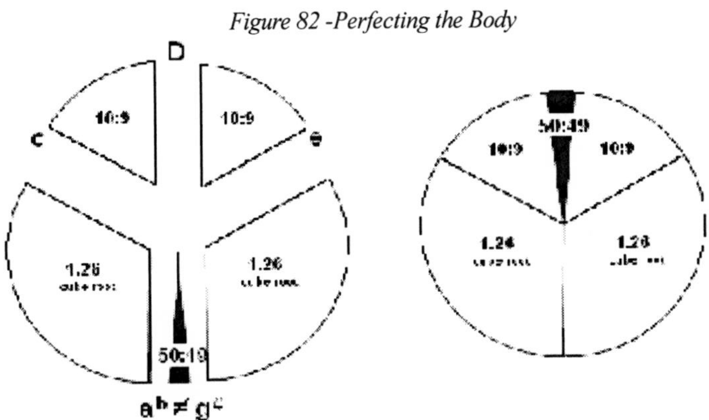

The unique circumstances of a supernatural transcendent third was preparation for the perfect births of "saviors" Noah and Isaac. The mathematics encrypted by these parallel stories provide carefully calculated events in the lives of Adam, Noah, and Noah's father, Lamech, that acknowledges the perfection of Aryan founders, Lamech and Noah; as well as the perfection of Israel's founders, Abraham and Isaac. The 10 generations between Noah and Abraham described a mathematical transition period between Aryan sexagesimal mathematics and Abraham's mixed-base system. This transition explains why the Aryan founders lived so long in the early part of Genesis (Enoch = 365 years and Noah = 950 years), and why God gave Moses a realistic 120 year lifespan, setting the new standard for man's longevity. Within the ancient Aryan numerical system each Sabbatical took 60 years. Within the new Abrahamic system, each Sabbatical took only 7 years.

Abraham's integration of sexagesimal, septimal and decimal mathematics is embodied by YHVH = 60^5 = 777,600,000. The leading "7" reconciles the duple and triple progressions through Sabbath prayer and circumcision, empowering the practitioner to properly judge between Good and Evil. The next spiritual step (the second "7" within "777"), reconciles the duple and quintuple progression to cleanse the body through a process of Sabbatical introspection. In later chapters, we will see that the Torah repeadedly describes two 7-year Sabbaticals as necessary to become a prophet. The third "7" within "777" corresponds to the Jubilee year of liberation and "walking with God," which requires the completion of all 7 Sabbaticals. But, changing the length of a Sabbatical from 60 years to 7 years, would enable a righteous man of 120 years to complete all 7 Sabbaticals.

When a righteous man completes his first Sabbatical, he "climbs the Holy Mountain" ascending through 3½ circuits, and descending through 3½ circuits. This is metaphor for the deep meditation practice that empowers the righteous to "speak with God" at the summit of the mountain. In the East, the Kundalini serpent sleeps within "the Pit" or "Abyss" (Figure 84a & b) between incarnations. After awakening in rebirth, it "uncoils" as time advances and spiritual progress is made.

> Kundalini normally lies asleep in the form of a serpent in three and a half coils … at the base of the spinal column... There is the precedent for supposing that a 'coil' may represent the unit of a year of 360 'days' in which case 3½ would allude secretly to 1,260.[268]

We might recall the 360:720 Navel of Order and how we harmonize the "Wheels of God" (Figure 85), by "cross-cutting" the Navel of Order's duple, triple, and quintuple progressions. We further harmonize the Navel of Order with Abraham's sacred practice by cross-cutting powers of 7 (Figures 71a & b). The act of ascending and descending the Holy Mountain/Ziggurat each require 3½ circuits * 360 = 1260. This mathematical structure also shapes New Testament allegory. For example, in the New Testament's Book of Revelation: " *...a beast rising up out of the sea, "with ten horns and seven heads ....*"[269] The Book of Daniel within the Hebrew Scriptures describes Daniel interpreting the king of Babylon's dream:

268 McClain, *Myth of Invariance*, 122-123.
269 Revelation 13:1

And the ten rays [of light] — from that kingdom, ten kings will arise, and after them another will arise. He will be different from the former ones ...He will speak Words against the Most High, and will harass the holy ones of the Most High ... and they will be delivered into his power for a time, times, and half a time.

It is first important to note that the word "horns" is a mistranslation of the Hebrew phrase *karnu panav* קרנו פניו. The root קרן may be read as either "horn" or "ray," as in "ray of light." "Panav" פניו translates as "his face." Within Exodus, Moses descended Mount Sinai and his face emanated "rays of light" — neither Moses, nor the beast rising from the sea in Revelation, actually had "devil" horns (historically fueling much anti-Semitic sentiment). By now we should easily recognize the original meaning of this symbolism as God's 10 numeric Emanations and the 7 sounds and colors of the soul that result from these "rays." It is also interesting to note how this mistranslation became "devil horns" in Michelangelo's statue of Moses, however, Gustave Dore's depiction of Moses shows two rays of light emanating from Moses' head. Indeed, this mistranslation underscores Christianity's literal interpretation of the mythology of Satan as the serpent, and Christianity's distorted notions of Hell, as previously discussed.

This great beast/dragon pursued the woman who will bring forth Christ to the world, in order to devour the child, but the woman was given "*two wings of the great eagle that she might fly into the wilderness unto her place, where she is nourished for a time and times and a half time, away from the serpent.*"[270] The ensuing battle between the archangel Michael and his angels against the dragon and his angels resulted in "*that great dragon being cast down [to earth], the ancient serpent, he who is called the devil and Satan, who leads astray the whole world.*" McClain explains the woman's time of nourishment by relating a "time" to the 360 day solar calendar, plus "times" meaning 2 x 360, plus "half a time" of 180, for a total of 1260 days.[271] The New Testament itself confirms this arithmetic in Revelations 12:6, "*...where she has a place nourished by God, that there they may nourish her a thousand two hundred and sixty days.*" This arithmetic helps confirm the nourishing vibrations of the first Sabbatical (Figure 84b), as defined by the octave double 1260:2520. Ouroboros swallowing its tail corresponds to 1 complete 360 day cycle in its spiraling ascent around the Axis Mundi. One solar year of 360 days x 3.5 spirals = 1260 days (or 42 lunar months), in which the "beast" was given as time to garner its forces for the final "War in Heaven" (Figures 84a).

Figure 83 - 30 Day Lunar Month

30	32	36	40	42	45	48	54	60
D	e	f#	G	|	A	b	c#	D
D	c	b♭	A	|	G	f	e♭	D
				$\sqrt{2}$				

270 Revelations 13:14-15.
271 McClain, Myth of Invariance, 118.

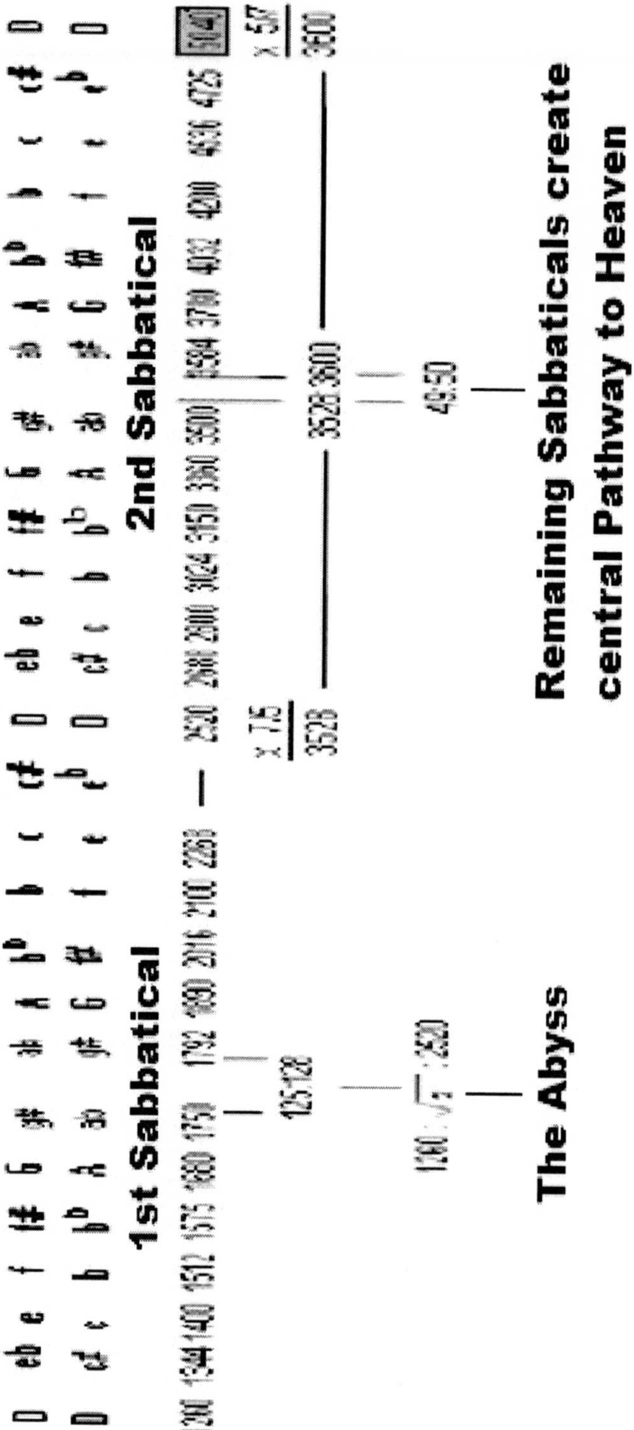

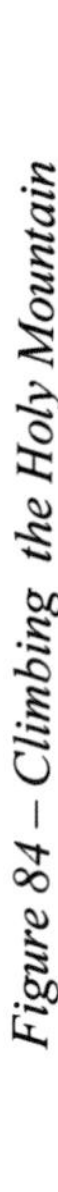

Figure 84 – Climbing the Holy Mountain

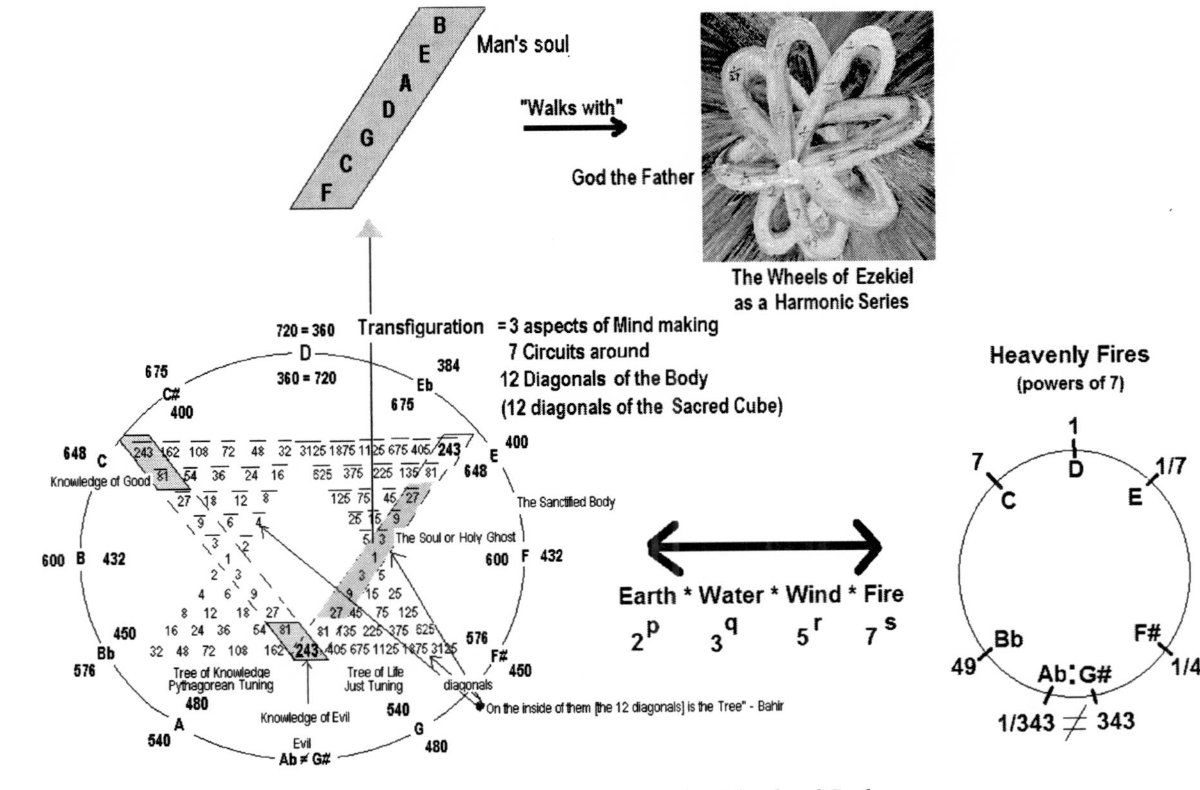

Figure 85 – Harmonizing the Wheels of God

The serpent (or beast) is coiled for 3½ circuits within the abyss of Sheol. It is permitted 42 months (= 1260 days = 3½ circuits) to "speak blasphemies" as we struggle to conquer the "Hell" of the primordial elements that live within us. In Figure 84, we can follow the level of vibration attained during a prophet's 3½ circuit ascent to the summit, as well as his 3½ circuit descent. This process is an inner struggle that attempts to master the powerful elements within. It is therefore associated with the first Sabbatical's "7 lean years" that appears in Biblical allegory. During the first Sabbatical, at the top of the Holy Mountain, the Wind of man's breath is transformed by the Breath of God (Ruach Hakodesh). At the summit, this power of the Holy Spirit transforms the primordial elements within us into their spiritual reflection, and we are transformed as we descend the Holy Mountain for another 3½ circuits, as our Sabbatical draws to a close. We should take note from Figure 84, however, that the musical notes "c#" and "eb" are missing from this first Sabbatical scale.

Spirituality drives the meditator forward toward a second Sabbatical of what should be "7 abundant years" within the octave double 2560:5040. After the second Sabbatical, the prophetic vision and healing capabilities of a true prophet develop. But, completing two Sabbaticals still does not empower the righteous to apply a "ratio of forgiveness" (Figs. 78 & 80) that will clear the central path necessary for the Soul to liberate from the Body and "walk with God." As the prophet completes the 5 remaining Sabbaticals, they ultimately climb through all 7 Heavens until they "Walk with God." Saint Paul claims to have gotten "stuck" within the 3rd Heaven. After Enoch and Noah's Jubilee Year, no further descent (i.e., no reincarnation) was necessary. Remember that Noah sent a dove out 3 times for 7 days each (777 = Sabbath, Sabbatical, Jubilee), but the final dove didn't return because it found land and was effectively liberated.

To establish peace in the world, we must first realize that the War in Heaven is an internal struggle, in which the fighting spirit of archangel Michael does battle with our own "Satanic" self, i.e., to rid ourselves of ego. Man's alter ego, the serpent, follows its appetites and leads man to sin. The "final battle" between Good and Evil is supposed to take place on the battlefield of Armageddon, which is a transliteration from the Hebrew Har-Megiddo, meaning "mountain of Megiddo." Armageddon is not a prophecy for nuclear holocaust or for the end of the world. It must be understood as man's inner struggle on the Holy Mountain. Any ambiguous duality brought about by knowledge of Good and Evil can be resolved with Divine Judgement. And, the Body's material imperfections can be purged in the Fires of the sacred practice's 7 circuits. Figure 85 depicts a summary of this entire "harmonization" process.

Chapter 15: Isaac's Transformation of Fire

Isaac as Sacrificial Lamb

When Isaac was a young man, Abraham walked with him to Mount Moriah, to the place of prophecy, to make a sacrifice. But, as they walked toward the mountain, with no animal in sight, Torah commentary tells us that Isaac understood that he was to become the sacrifice to God. Bravely anticipating his own death in the Fires of the Altar imbued him with *Gevurah* (Strength). This was called *Akeidah Yitzchak* (the Binding of Isaac). At the last moment, an angel of God called to Abraham, and told him not to harm the boy. When Abraham raised his eyes he saw a ram caught in the thicket, which he used for the sacrifice instead of Isaac.

When Isaac was placed on the altar of the *Akeidah,* "he became tantamount to an elevation-offering, a burnt offering that is completely consumed on the Altar."[272] God said to Abraham: "All the nations of the earth shall bless themselves by your offspring, because you have listened to my Voice."[273] God then renamed this location from the city of Salem to *Yireh* (God will see) + *Salem* (peace) = Jerusalem (God will see peace).This name similarly integrates the Hebrew root "*raah*" (shepherd or seer) into Abram's name, as Melchizedek, the High Priest of Salem, initiated Abram into the sacred practice, transfiguring him into Abraham. Isaac's body was purged of sin on the Four-Horned Altar of Sacrifice (Figure 76b), liberating his soul in the Fires of Heaven as if he were actually sacrificed. Christ would later become the sacrificial lamb for Christianity, while Ishmael assumed Isaac's role within Islam.

Within the sacred meditation practice, ascending inner Fires initiate descending Waters. This "anointing" becomes the "wellspring of prophecy" and the spiritual "Waters of wisdom." The Torah compares prophecy to the "hidden waters" of wisdom that must be drawn from a well:

> *...wisdom symbolized by the water below the ground; it is buried and hidden, but it is accessible to those who understand that it is vital to life and worthy of the intense effort needed to bring it to the surface.*[274]

---

272 Genesis 26:2; see commentary in Stone Edition.
273 Genesis 22:18
274 Genesis 29:1-12, see commentary Stone Edition.

The New Testament speaks about a Baptism with Holy Water, but it also speaks about a "true Baptism of the Spirit." As already mentioned, the Holy Waters come in the form of *Soma juice*, *ambrosia*, *tigle* or *drops*, *snow, holy oil, etc.* The "anointing" of a prophet with this "elixir of life" cleanses body and soul with transformational Holy Waters that can only begin to flow once the prophet has breathed the rarefied Air of the Holy Spirit at the summit of the Holy Mountain. The *Akeidah Yitzchak* took place on the holiest of mountains — Mount *Moriah* (Hebrew: "Seeing"), the Temple Mount — which has traditionally been the seat of prophecy.

The idea that each and every prophet must accomplish this same 7-step transformational process is emphasized in the parallel stories of the Covenant between Abimelach and Abraham, and then between Abimelach and Isaac. And, further, these parallel stories describe the prophet's sacred oath of protection as a Covenant of God's Protection, placing a protective shield around each prophet to prevent anyone from doing them harm. Here is that parallel story line:

Aside from the first famine in the days of Abraham, there was also a famine in the days of Isaac. And, just as bad circumstances forced Abraham to the city of Gerar, so too, did Isaac go to Gerar years later. Just as Sarah's beauty would be coveted by the men of Gerar, so too would the fair Rebecca be coveted. So, both Abraham and Isaac, a generation apart, posed as a brother rather than a husband, to avoid trouble from the men of Gerar. Once Abimelach, the king of Gerar's Philistines, realized their dilemma, he offered both father and son the king's protection within their respective time periods, for all the years that they would sojourn in Gerar.

Settling in Gerar, Isaac redug the well that was originally dug by Abraham, who named it *Beer-Sheva.* In Hebrew, *beer* means "well" and Sheva translates to "seven" as well as "oath." Abraham and Isaac had sworn the "oath of seven wells" as a Covenant of Protection with the King, which was symbolic of the Covenant of Protection with the LORD. Abraham commemorated this Covenant with a gift to Abimelach of 7 ewes, symbolizing the divine sparks that could be liberated in 7 burnt offerings within the Fires of the Sacrificial Altar.

The Birth of Israel

All the patriarchs "dwelled in tents," implying that all the prophets secluded themselves in meditation within the miniature ziggurat (or Holy Mountain), described by each prophet's "tent." Within that Holy tent, "praying like a prophet" implied mastering the Elements to form "singable" scales, so that the "cloud of the *Shechinah"* (the Divine Presence; the liberated soul of the prophet) would hover over the tent. The great Tabernacle in the desert was the "Tent of Meeting," where men would gather together to meet God.

The Tent of Meeting was a Ziggurat of number and sound — a miniature Holy Mountain.

Isaac was 40 years old during his next spiritual milestone, when he consummated his marriage to Rebecca "in the tent of Sarah his mother; and thus was Isaac consoled after his mother."[275] Rabbinic commentary explains that Sarah's spirit had returned to her tent, making it apparent to Isaac that Rebecca was a fitting successor to Sarah.[276] Isaac consummated his marriage at 40, but Rebecca was then barren for 20 years, until Isaac reached the holy age of 60, at which point Rebecca gave birth to twins, Jacob and Esau.[277]

We have explained the harmonic and theological significance of each triplet sibling as $\sqrt[3]{2}$. Similarly, a harmonic "twin" plays a role in bisecting the octave, framing opposing sides of $\sqrt{2}$ to reflect the Bible's moral imperative between Good and Evil. Sibling rivalry "within the same tent" began with Cain and Abel, and continued with Isaac and Ishmael, Jacob and Esau, and Joseph and his brothers, etc.. but, this rivalry became mathematically and spiritually more significant with twins.

Esau and Jacob were opposite in nature, but they were both born within a patriarchs (single octave) "tent." Esau became a hunter, and Jacob became a scholar and "dweller in tents." But, their vibrational essence described the reciprocity of harmonic and arithmetic means: 40 and 45, describing "fixed tones" within octave double 30:60 (Figure 87b). YHVH told Rebecca: "Two nations are in your womb [Edomite Rome and Israel] and the elder shall serve the younger." Following the birth of Esau: "his brother emerged with his hand grasping on to the heel of Esau."[278] The rabbis explain that "this embryonic Jacob-Esau struggle represented cosmic forces in Creation (i.e., *pnimiyut*), forces that transcended the normal course of personality development, and that existed even before birth.[279] According to the great commentator Rashi's citation of Midrash, Jacob was spiritually older, implying that Jacob was conceived earlier with the seed of the patriarch, but switched places in the womb. The *pnimiyut* of Jacob was therefore the arithmetic mean: 45 (like Adam). Within the 30:60 octave double, the numbers 40 (Esau) and 45 (Jacob) — the two mathematical means — correspond to the opposing aspects of the mind. Within the *Sefer Yetzirah*, Abraham tells us that "judgement" is born in the harmonic dynamic between the mind's opposites of "advocate" and "accuser."[280]

The middle path of the Holy Spirit requires man's Divine Judgement in order to effect transcendence. This implies purification of the body and soul in the Fires of Heaven as invoked through the sacred meditation practice (i.e., "pronounc-

275 Genesis 24:67
276 Genesis 24:67; see commentary in Stone Edition.
277 Genesis 25: 26
278 Genesis 25:26
279 Genesis 25:22 see commentary in Stone Edition.
280 *Sefer Yetzirah* 6:5

ing" the Holy Name). In keeping with the reciprocal relationship defined by harmonic and arithmetic means, Biblical allegory describes their competitive spirit: Jacob bought the birthright from his brother. And, nearing the end of Isaac's life, Rebecca advised Jacob how to trick the aging and blind Isaac into giving him his final blessing instead of Esau.[281] Hebrew law specifies that the first born inherits, but Rebecca knew God's prophecy that "the elder son shall serve the younger," and that Jacob would be renamed Israel, as the most spiritual of their two sons.

From a prophetic perspective the birth of Israel melds into all the generations of Adam.[282] The "descent of the Divine Sparks degree by degree" through matter and time, is very much a part of the continuing Kabbalistic tradition. The ability of *Chayot* to both ascend and descend Jacob's Ladder underscores the symmetry of musical paths that transcend the constraints of time. These "hidden paths" unfold as Adam's *pnimiyut* comes into full view, spanning all the generations from 1440 to 45 and back again (Figures 61b, 86a & b). [283] The *pnimiyut* of Enoch at the end of his sojourn describes how Enoch's embodiment of the Aryan Navel of Order (360:720) enabled him to "walk with God."

Figure 86a – Adam Before His Fall from Grace

720	768	800	864	900	960	1080	1152	1200	1296	1350	1440
1440	1350	1296	1200	1152	1080	960	900	864	800	768	720
D	eb	e	f	f#	G	A	bb	b	c	c#	D

Figure 86b – The Generations from Adam to Enoch[284]

D	eb	e	f	f#	G	A	bb	b	c	c#	D	eb	e	f	f#	G	A	bb	b	c	c#	D
360	384	400	432	450	480	540	576	600	648	675	**720**	760	800	864	900	960	1080	1152	1200	1296	1350	1440

The descent of the Divine Sparks, as well as their ascent along the same hidden musical paths, continued from Enoch to Isaac. They both embodied the soul's attribute of *Gevurah* (strength = 360 +5). Isaac died at 180 years old, thus we have Isaac's 180:360 octave double (Figure 87e). Sarah was 90 when Isaac was conceived, and since Isaac's marriage was "consummated in the tent of Sarah," the birth of Israel (i.e., Jacob) effectively occurred within the "tent" (womb) of Sarah (Figures 87c & d). The Birth of Israel continues the descent of the "Divine Sparks" from Adam to Enoch to Isaac to Sarah to Jacob as 1440:720:360:180:90:45. The ascent of Israel's 12 tribes culminates in the Book of Exodus, where Moses, embodying the sacred practice of 777, leads 600,000 Israelites to the Promised Land (Figures 87f & 90).[285]

---

281 Rambam, Hil. Melachim 10:7
282 *Tanya* Igeret Hakodesh 7: "For all the souls in the world were contained in Adam."
283 Adam's name is equivalent to (*Alef* = 1)+ (*Dalet* = 4)+(*Mem* = 40) = 45 but, if read as place holder values, 1-4-40 becomes 1440 (Figures 86a & b).
284 McClain, *The Myth of Invariance, 126.*
285 *YHVH* = $10^5 6^5 = 60^5$ = 777,600,000.

Figure 87a & b - The Pure Births of Enoch & Isaac; The Birth of Twins Esau & Jacob

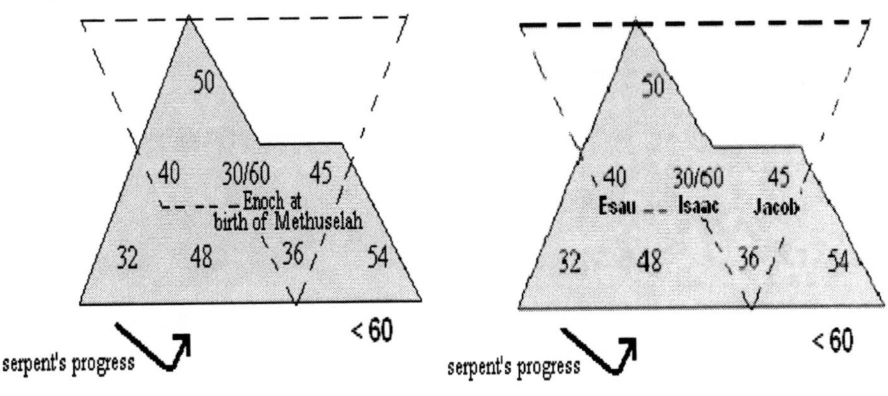

Figure 87c & d - The Birth of Jacob and Death of Isaac within the Tent of Sarah

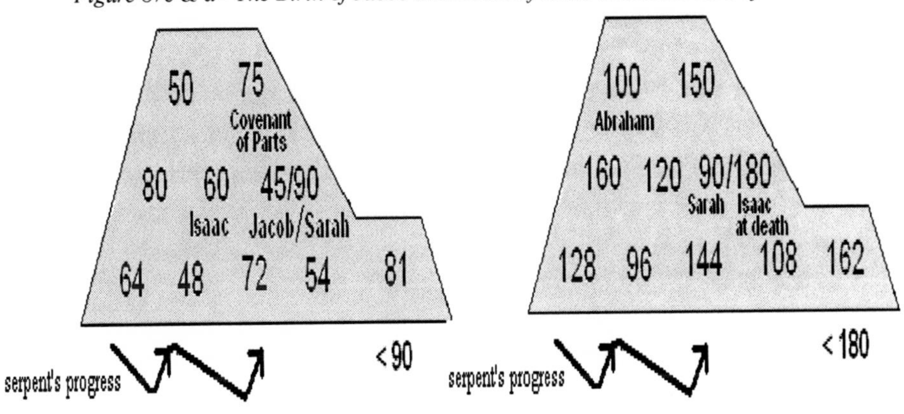

Figure 87e - Isaac Died Embodying Gevurah (360 +5) *Figure 87f - Israel as the "Navel of Order"*

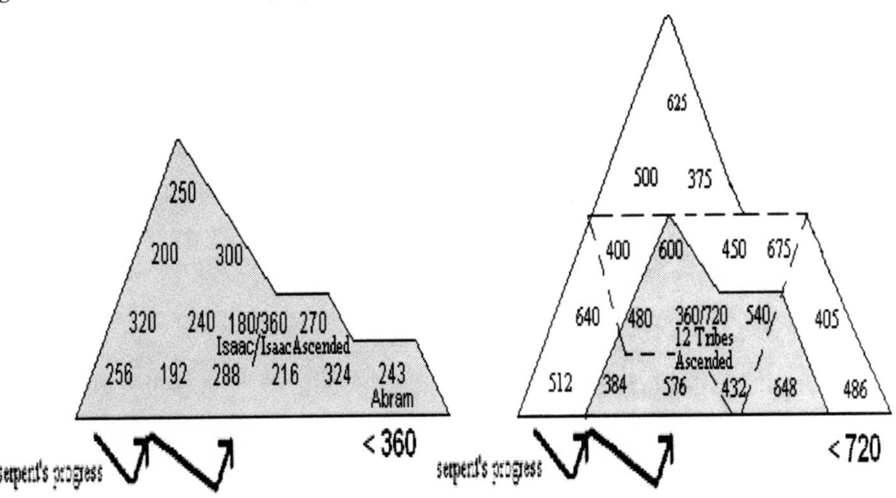

Chapter 16: Jacob's Transformation of Water

Jacob's Ladder

After Jacob left Beer-sheva, the home of his parents, he came to Mount Moriah, to the spot where Abraham bound his father, Isaac as a sacrifice. This spot is the *Axis Mundi* — the seat of prophecy. It would also become the precise location of the Holy of Holies within Solomon's Temple. After Jacob arranged 12 stones around his head, they miraculously fused into one,[286] he lay down and dreamt a vision of angels ascending and descending a ladder that connected Earth to Heaven. He then built an altar from this miraculous pillar and anointed it with oil. He called the altar Beth-el. Beth-el marks the location of the *Axis Mundi*, drawing on the sexagesimal tradition of the Aryan Clock of Heaven and the Precession of the Equinox annual spiral that became Jacob's Ladder. The God of Abraham "engraved" Creation using the sexagesimal "stones" of pebble arithmetic:

Two stones build 2 houses
Three build 6 houses
Four stones build 24 houses
Five stones build 120 houses
Six stones build 720 houses
Seven stones build 5040 houses
From here on go out and calculate that which
the mouth cannot speak and the ear cannot hear.

When we did "go out and calculate," the reader may recall that what we constructed was a harmonized musical spiral of tones generated from duple, triple, quintuple, and septenary progressions. The ascending and descending twin serpents described the reciprocal paths of ascending angels (Hebrew: *Chayot*) of Fire and the descending *Chayot* of Water. The *Chayot* were angels that traveled along circular "whirlwinds" or "spirals" (angels called *Ophanim*). They created 7 aspects of the soul through a triple progression, and 12 aspects of the body by "cross-cutting" a quintuple progression. Then by utilizing the sacred deep meditation practice, man

286 Genesis 28:11; This passage describes how Jacob took stones (in plural form) to put under his head as a pillow, but Verse 28:18 refers only to one stone, leading the rabbis to conclude that they miraculously fused into one. The Aryan predecessor to this allegory involves the sexual rites of the Sumerian goddess Inanna, in which the 12 Ages of Man were similarly "integrated" into the Unity of the Clock of Heaven.

binds the body (powers of 5) and soul (powers of 3) to the Crown (powers of 7) until we hear a dripping and feel a sensation of being anointed. This "anointing" is a by-product of the patriarch's birthright: the sacred meditation practice.

Two Levels of Prophecy

Jacob finds his wife, Rachael, at a well among her 7 sisters, but he had to work for 7 years to win the right to marry her; just as Moses met his wife at a well, also among her 7 sisters. We should be well aware of the significance of 7 with respect to the core wisdom practice. We have already mentioned the significance of the "oath of the 7 wells" as the "wellspring of prophecy." We have also discussed an expanded perspective on the *gematria* of *Yahweh* as 777,600,000, in which the leading 7's define the Sabbath, the Sabbatical and the Jubilee Year, respectively.

We court wisdom and prophecy with our sacred practice each Sabbath; each Sabbatical (7 years of Sabbaths); and each Jubilee (7 Sabbaticals). From this mathematical perspective, pronouncing the Holy Name declares the solution to the ancient mystery of inscribing a square within a circle. So, we witness Jacob's first 7 years, spent working as a shepherd for Leban to win the right to marry Rachael. He was tricked on his wedding night into marrying Leah. After these 7 years of struggle, Jacob was rewarded with a Sabbatical "bride," but since it was not the bride he hoped for, he was inspired to begin a second Sabbatical in order to win the hand of his heart's desire, his second Sabbatical "bride,"Rachael.

Genesis allegories tell us that we must meditate for at least two Sabbaticals (14 years) to partially clear the central channel (Figure 78) and become a prophet, whereas liberating the soul to "Walk with God" would require a Jubilee of 7 Sabbaticals.[287] We have already discussed the difference between the Sumerian Clock of Heaven and the Clock of Earth. Within the Torah, this also manifests as the difference between linear numerical measurements and logarithmic ratios. After the time of Moses, Sabbaticals were no longer measured with a sexagesimal metric. But, within the sexagesimal system that Abraham inherited from Sumer and Babylon, the numbers 60, 600, and 3600 bear the names, *soss*, *ner*, and *iar*. Enoch's first Sabbatical took 1 *soss* or 60 years, the basic unit in sexagesimal Mesopotamia. Figure 58b describes Enoch's sacred practice, ascending and descending a 7-tone diatonic scale in preparation for the auspicious birth of his son Methuselah. This defined Enoch's first Sabbatical as 7 scale-tones that he "sang" to God. From that point forward, the Breath of God (*Heh* = *5*) was incorporated into his being, as with Abram's transformation into Abraham. Thus, Methuselah was born when Enoch was 65 years old. Enoch's Jubilee year took 1 *soss* x 6 = 360 Earth years to acquire the second *Heh* in God's Name. This is what it took for Enoch to earn both his

287 Buddhists call this attaining the Sambhogakaya, followed by attaining the Dharmakaya (Buddha body). Kabbalist tradition calls them the *golem* and *Shechinah* (Divine Presence).

"Wings." At 365 years of age, the Torah does not say that Enoch died, but that "God took him" and he "walked with God" in the 7th Heaven. Since the time of Moses, man lives a maximum of 120 years, and does not have the time to complete a lifespan of 6 *soss* in order to earn both Wings to walk with God, like Enoch's 365 years and Noah's 950 years. After Moses lived 120 years, God limited man's lifespan. Moses witnessed the promise of liberation from Mt Nebo, but he was forbidden from "crossing over the Jordan" to "walk with God" in the Promised Land. According to the sexagesimal metric used during the time of Enoch and Noah, 120 years (2 *soss*) is just enough time to complete 2 Sabbaticals in a single lifetime.

In terms of light or sound, the Hand of God, unites its 6 components into a transcendent 7th level of unification that Abraham explained in terms of a harmonic series. Today, we understand the harmonic series to be an empirical fact. Therefore, the Living God of Abraham has an empirical foundation. From there, Abraham uses the "substance" of the harmonic series to speculate about the nature of its harmonic components to define the mathematical structure of the four primordial elements: Earth, Water, Wind, and Fire. He also uses mathematics to explain how to liberate the soul from the body. His solution to harmonizing the triple and quintuple progressions was to devise a practical way to work around the "weakness of the flesh" by truncating the 12th spoke of the Navel of Order through circumcision — symbolic of the *Gevurah* (Strength) necessary to "truncate" our distractions from God, so the body can be purified and the soul can be liberated.

The Children of Israel

Like Abraham and Isaac before him, Jacob spiritually prepared himself to continue the lineage of patriarchs. Once God gave Jacob his spiritual name, Israel, Jacob's seed was effectively transformed into the spiritual body of Israel. In order to emphasize the significance of the four primordial elements, Jacob's 12 sons were born to 4 wives — Leah, Rachael, Bilhah and Zilpah. This transformation purged the impurities in Jacob's "tent" leaving a "singable" musical scale within the Four-Horned Altar of Figure 76b, thus sanctifying the seminal waters that fathered each of Jacob's 12 sons. We can assign each of Jacob's 12 sons, in the order they were born, to the next number value of Jacob's "tent" as Israel is transformed into a microcosm of God's Holy Mountain (Figure 89a).

Each of Jacob's children stood to inherit their share of Abraham, Isaac, and Jacob's legacy, which included material wealth and the land of Israel. But, geography is just metaphor for the true birthright, which has nothing to do with material wealth and land and everything to do with "7 circuits around the sacred cube" — Abraham's sacred meditation practice. Learning to pray like the prophets by pronouncing God's Name purges impurities from the Divine Sparks of the body, leaving a chromatic scale within the Four-Horned Altar. Even the subtle nuances of this story are driven by the mathematics of Figure 76b. This may be the most significant example of how ancient music theory shapes Biblical allegory, and how understanding the relationship between spirituality and materiality is the main message of the Torah. Unfortunately, this message was lost about 2500 years ago, and the world has remained obsessed over land and money ever since.

Jacob and Leah had a daughter named Dinah — potentially a 13th tribe in the body of Israel. However, since Dinah is a woman and could not inherit the birthright by Hebrew law, she was the first to be removed from the inheritance of the spiritual Israel. This piece of the story line relates to the 13th constellation of the zodiac, and the musical "comma" that exists between the 12th and 13th tones. Thus, the 13th tone was eliminated in order to transcend the duality of Good and Evil.

In Figure 76b we see the Fires of the "Four-Horned Altar" purge away those who do not stand to "inherit in the Promised Land." This is metaphor for the deep meditation crucible that liberates the divine sparks in the Fires of sacrifice. Within this crucible, we look to the first born, Reuben. According to Hebrew law, the first born is the son who inherits the birthright. In this case, however, when Reuben grew into adulthood he lay with Jacob's concubine Bilhah, the mother of Dan and Naphtali. When Jacob heard of this, Reuben forfeited his birthright; and so, Reuben's *pnimiyut* are not included within the 11 tones of the Four-Horned Altar (Figure 76b; Reuben = 512). In keeping with our theory of mathematically driven textual nuances, Torah commentary states: "Although the birthright was later transferred from Reuben to Joseph (see I Chronicles 5:1), our verse calls Reuben the firstborn, to indicate that he would continue to have certain privileges of his status."[288] Thus, Reuben was not taught to pronounce YHVH — which was his birthright — but, he would still be allowed to lead one of the 12 tribes. Since there are only 11 sanctified tones within the Four-Horned Altar, this describes the extenuating circumstances of leadership for the "Cornerstone" Reuben, the 1st of the 12 brothers in Figure 89a.

The stepped shape of a Ziggurat is formed from the mathematics of filtering tones < 720. Since Benjamin was actually the 12th and final son to be born to Jacob, the mathematical shape of the Ziggurat requires some creativity in the story line, i.e., how to include Jacob's grandchildren to complete the ziggurat, as if they were his own sons, which explains why Jacob told Joseph the following:

> *And now, your two sons who were born to you in the land of Egypt before my coming to you in Egypt shall be mine; Ephraim and Manasseh shall be mine like Reuben and Simeon. But, progeny born to you after them shall be yours: they will be included under the name of their brothers with regard to their inheritance.*

288 Genesis 35:23 (see commentary Stone Edition).

Joseph would have a double share in the land of Israel through his two sons, Manasseh and Ephraim, but he himself would be omitted from the divine sparks of the Four-Horned Altar — just as the mathematics prescribes (Compare Figures 76b and 89a, and note that Joseph = 125). Joseph, who was given the rights of the first born, was therefore given a double portion in the inheritance, through his two sons, in order to properly complete the Four-Horned Altar construction.

With Reuben and Joseph now excluded from the inheritance of the 12 tribes, there were 10 sons left. Jacob could now pay his 10% tithe to the priesthood by offering his son Levi to be the servant of God. The great Kabbalist Isaac Luria is quoted in the Tanya, stating the following about the priests, the Levites:

> *The service of the Levites was to raise the voice of melody and thanksgiving, with song and music, with tunefulness and harmony, in a manner of 'advance and retreat'...*"[289]

As such, Levi's tribe was not given a portion of Israel to inherit, and were also excluded from the *pnimiyut* of the Four-Horned Altar (Levi = 640 in Figure 89a). Here is a brief summary of this allegory as shaped by the mathematics:

- Dinah was excluded because she was a woman (powers of 2 were relegated to the role of musical transposition)
- Reuben forfeited his birthright to Joseph
- Joseph would be excluded from his own place in the Four-Horned Altar containing the purified soul of Israel, but he would have a double share of the inheritance within the next generation through his two sons Manasseh and Ephraim.
- Levi was Jacob's 10% tithe to the priesthood. The tribe of Levi would have no direct share in the Promised Land, but would become the priestly "musicians" attending the Throne of Glory.

In the chronology of Genesis, the birth of Israel (Jacob) completes the transition from the Aryan Base-60 to Abraham's mixed-Base system (Base-6, Base-7, Base 10, and Base 60). We know that Jacob died at 147. That arithmetic exists within the Sabbath Tree (Figure 71a). We therefore know that Jacob's soul was remitted back to God in his third Jubilee Year (3 * 49 = 147). After the time of Noah, no prophet lived long enough to "walk with God." Enoch and Noah were part of the Aryan tradition, and the Torah stopped using sexagesimal *soss* to explain the length of Sabbaticals.

289 Tanya, Likutei Amarim 50; Talmud, Chagigah 13b; The term "advance and retreat" is taken from Ezekiel 1:14 as a direct reference to the perfect inverse symmetry of the *Chayot* (angelic flames of sound and light) within the soul's Phrygian mode and the body's Chromatic scale — based on the Aryan Navel of Order (360:720) — Jacob's Ladder of ascending and descending *Chayot.*

Chapter 17: Joseph's Transformation of Earth

A Master of Dreams

Jacob passed on knowledge of the Word — along with his blessing for the first born — to Joseph, as his birthright. Joseph therefore became the "Anointed One" and prophet of his generation. In the context of this allegory, Joseph was sold into slavery in Egypt by his brothers for 20 pieces of silver. He found his way to the Pharaoh's palace, where he successfully interpreted the Pharaoh's dream of 7 beautiful cows emerging out of the river, followed by 7 ugly and gaunt cows. Like Vishnu dreaming the world dream, Joseph's birthright made him a master of the unconscious mind. That was the intended meaning of the Torah's authors. Because he understood the nature of Sabbatical, Joseph could interpret 7 abundant years followed by 7 years of famine. This was acceptable to the Pharaoh, and Joseph was appointed vice-roy of Egypt, in charge of implementing a plan for national salvation. When a famine hit all the surrounding countries, Joseph had already stockpiled abundant provisions, and the world came to Joseph to buy provisions, including his own family who had forsaken him for 20 pieces of silver.

In an important way, Joseph's dream reflects the story of Jacob. Jacob spent his first Sabbatical laboring for the hand of Rachael, but, his countenance fell when he was given the hand of Leah instead. This inspired a second Sabbatical to win his heart's desire, Rachael, which, of course, lifted his countenance. The first Sabbatical both ascended and descended the Sabbath scale, bringing Jacob to the summit of his material existence. The second Sabbatical also ascended and descended the Sabbath scale, but ultimately, rewarded Jacob's highest aspirations — to win the hand of Rachael. The normal order of Sabbaticals is to journey through the 7 aspects of Hell before clearing a path through the 7 aspects of Heaven. And, it might seem as though Joseph's 14 years of Sabbatical were marked first by abundance and then by famine, but, if we examine the circumstances more closely, Jospeh was the catalyst to transform the Hell of a squandered material abundance into the Heaven of material and spiritual fulfillment. By storing Egypt's grain over the first 7 years, Joseph became a "master of Earth," as well as the savior of Egypt and all the surrounding countries. The sons of Israel came to Joseph, with head bowed, for salvation. As the Anointed One of his generation, Joseph's good judgement during the abundance of his first Sabbatical prepared him to nourish the spiritual and physical hunger of the people during his second Sabbatical. His spiritual, physical, and political transformation, empowered him to become the savior of Egypt, and, during his second Sabbatical, he sanctified the 12 aspects of the body of Israel (i.e., his 12 siblings) by "ruling over them" with justice and mercy, as if he were the first King of an exiled Israel.

The Transformation of Israel

As metaphor for the sacred practice, the 12 aspects of the body of Israel had been transposed into an 11-note singable scale, cleansed within the crucible of the Four-Horned Altar. However, Israel would have to wait for the 12 tribes of Israel to increase in number and power before it's collective "Soul" could emerge from the "Body" of Egypt as the Kingdom of Israel. This came to pass after the death of Joseph. Exodus 1:7-8, states: "The children of Israel were fruitful, teemed, increased and became strong – very, very much so; and the land became filled with them. Eventually, a new king arose in Egypt, who did not know of Joseph. He said to his people, "Behold! The people, the Children of Israel, are more numerous and stronger than we. Come, let us outsmart it lest it become numerous and it may be that if a war will occur, it, too, may join our enemies, and wage war against us and go up from the land." Israel had grown in power to the point of being "more numerous and stronger" than the Egyptians. During the next three generations of oppression, knowledge of the Word of God had been lost. It therefore had to be revealed to mankind once more; this time through a new shepherd and seer, Moses, who would lead Israel out of Egypt during the Exodus, and who would receive the Word of God atop Mount Sinai. Thus, allegories about the 7 Shepherds of Genesis comes to a close, and a new cycle of exile and salvation begins within the Book of Exodus.

If we attempt to reconcile the Torah's perspective with the archeological record, Semitic Canaanites are often identified with the Hyksos migration that rose to power in lower Egypt. The Hyksos tribes ultimately took control and reigned in the delta region, called lower Egypt, during the 15th and 16th Dynasties, from 1800 - 1550 BCE.[290] "By the mid-seventeenth century, the Semitic population in the delta had managed to gain political control of much of northern Egypt. During the next century (1650-1550) their domination widened, encompassing most of Lower and Middle Egypt."[291] Unfortunately, a lack of Egyptian records during this period makes it difficult to confirm the suspicions of historians Manetho and Josephus in identifying the Israelite Exodus with the Hyksos "shepherds" who left Egypt for Jerusalem.

290 Oxford History of the Bible, Op.Cit., 74
291 Ibid., 42.

After the Exodus, upper and lower Egypt was reunited in the period known as the New Kingdom. History suggests that Egypt had a profound impact on Israel. We know that Abraham was greatly influenced by the Egyptian decimal mathematics that became so important to his "mixed-base" system. Long before Israel's exile in Egypt, the temple at Karnak was built around a "Holy of Holies" — like Solomon's Temple — with the innermost sanctuary holding Amun's statue, within a ceder wood shrine, which was considered capable of receiving the divine spirit of Amun. The Divine Presence as the wellspring of prophecy is similarly said to hover above the Ark of the Covenant within the Holy of Holies. Amun represented the hidden life-force of the universe, and ultimately, all of Egypt's gods came to be seen as aspects of Amun. He was alternately referred to as: "the supreme mystery"; the "divine creative force of the universe"; and, as "the Unknowable." He thus appears to have been *Yahweh's* immediate predecessor.

Soon after the Exodus, history suggests that Israel also had a profound effect on Egypt. This occurred during the reigns of Amenhotep III (ca.1390 – 1352) and his son Amenhotep IV, also known as Akhenaten (ca 1353-1336 BCE). Political power in Egypt began to shift away from the clergy of their main God, Amun. Akhenaten is especially noted for mandating that the Egyptian population abruptly change their polytheistic ways in order to worship one god, Aten. Akhenaten declared that Aten was not merely the supreme god, but the only god, and that he, Akhenaten — adopting a very Christ-like role — was the sole intermediary between Aten and his Kingdom.

Akhenaten's chief wife was Nefertiti. The royal couple ordered the defacing of Amun's temples throughout Egypt, and in a number of instances inscriptions of the plural 'gods' were also removed. He forbade the worship of other gods, including a ban on idols, with the exception of a rayed solar disc, in which human hands emanate from the rays. This represents the unseen spirit of Aten, who, by then, was not merely a sun god, but rather, a universal deity. Monotheism completely destabilized Egypt politically, and all the temples were ultimately reopened once Akhenaten left power. Egyptians were once again free to worship their many gods. The names of Akhenaten and Nefertiti were soon stricken from all monuments and official records by his successors.

According to I Kings 6, it took 480 years after the Israelites left the land of Egypt for Solomon to begin building the House of the Lord. Not surprisingly, the Temple was 60 cubits long, 20 cubits wide, and 30 cubits high; which can all be factored into powers of 2, 3 and 5. Mathematically, this is known as "5-smooth." The Holy of Holies that would hold the Ark of the Covenant was to be built atop the Foundation Stone, which King David bought from Arunah the Jebusite for fifty shekels of silver, and "YHVH endowed Solomon with wisdom and discernment, with understanding as vast as the sands on the seashore... He was the wisest of all men."

Finally, there would be a Temple built for the Name of God. Once the House of Yahweh was completed and consecrated, the Divine Presence, as the "wellspring of prophecy," would hover over the Ark of the Covenant, and the Word of the LORD would come to Solomon. The Divine Presence that hovered over the early patriarchal "Tent of Meeting" took up a more permanent residence within the Holy of Holies, filling the House of the Lord, and establishing Israel as the Kingdom of Heaven on Earth. The Kingdom of Israel would then introduce a new tuning system to the world — Equal Temperament — as the pnimiyut of Democracy — introduced with the promise of bringing inner and outer peace to mankind. But, history has not been kind. Israel was defeated, and Solomon's Temple was destroyed. Nevertheless, the monotheistic world still anxiously awaits a Messiah to reestablish God's Kingdom on Earth.

All three of today's monotheistic faiths concur that the days of prophecy are over, so how is it possible for another prophet to lead the way? Who would believe him? The Jewish elders of Sanhedrin did not believe in Christ, and the Jewish elders of Yathrib (later called Medina) did not believe in Mohammed. Why? Because, as far as the rabbis knew, prophecy died with the last High Priest of Solomon's Temple. The world seems to be waiting for a Messiah cast in their own image. American Christians are waiting for a blond, blue-eyed Caucasian; "Twelver" Shia Muslims are waiting for a 12th Imam. And, Orthodox rabbis are expecting the Messiah to be a learned Chasidic rabbi, complete with black coat and fur hat. Once again, we are faced with a paradox. How could the God of Abraham, or any true Messiah, take sides? Which child of Abraham is more worthy than the other?

The current effort has attempted to bring to light a preponderance of evidence suggesting that Abraham's writings are both authentic and authoritative, and only by understanding his text can mankind hope to find spiritual salvation. Only in the *Sefer Yetzirah* can the "Children of Abraham" learn the meaning and pronunciation of the Word of God, *Yahweh.* The *Sefer Yetzirah* is a mathematical and scientific treatise that encrypts a detailed set of instructions on how to access and harness the power of God within. Each man's inner struggle to liberate the soul is said to bring the gifts of healing and prophecy, and even conquer death, suggesting a nation of "Anointed Ones." Abraham understood that God's Law applied to all men, and not to any one man.

Chapter 18: A Framework for Peace

Holy War

The concept of Holy War is deeply troubling, and tragically misunderstood. Throughout history, so-called Holy Wars have been fueled by religious strife, bigotry, and hatred, all in the Name of God. Among the most well known Holy Wars in history were the Crusades. There were eight different Roman Catholic military campaigns that lasted about 200 years (1095 - 1291 CE). After taking a solemn vow, each warrior was given a cross by the Pope and sent into battle in order to recapture the Holy Land from the Muslims. The Crusades were largely a reaction to the Arab conquests, which began after the death of Mohammed. The four "right-guided" caliphs[292] had extended the Islamic empire from the Arabian peninsula to the Holy Land, defeating the Persian Empire, and much of the Byzantine Empire. Additional Crusades, lasting through the end of the 17th century, made it no secret that Rome wanted to spread its power and influence, just as Muslims did. No matter who the "adversaries" are: Protestants vs. Catholics, Sunnis vs. Shiites, Jews vs. Muslims, Conquistadors vs. Aztecs, etc.. Religious fundamentalists attempt to take ownership of the religious highground and then bludgeon their enemy with righteousness. However, without a deep understanding of the science of religion and the sacred practice, which lay at the heart of all the various historical religions, militaristic fundamentalists will never set foot on the "spiritual high ground." The science of religion will also enable us to silence the recent crop of scientifically-minded atheists who are convinced that religion is just superstition and delusion.

A new type of Holy War requires new types of weapons: science, meditation, knowledge, wisdom, common sense, open-mindedness, compassion, and truth. Truth is the most powerful weapon on the battlefield of hearts and minds. Religion and science seem to have become mutually exclusive in today's society. They are not. Each of the world's religions can and must keep pace with modern science if it hopes to be viable in the 21st century — and —if it actually hopes to contribute to a lasting world peace. This text provides substantial evidence that Holy War in the Bible was originally intended as an allegorical description of man's inner struggle to master the elements, time, and his own material nature, in order to liberate his soul. But, whether or not we actually believe in the liberation of the soul is not at issue here. All we need to do in order to begin the healing process among the world's major religions is to stress their common scientific frame-

292 Called the *Rashidun* Caliphate.

work. The science of religion provides a profound common ground for interfaith discussion, understanding, and reconciliation.

In his book, *Nahum*, Duane Christensen suggests that "Nahum is to be read in conjunction with other oracles against foreign nations, particularly those of Isaiah 13-23..." He describes studies that "placed the Book of Nahum in the sphere of international politics in premonarchic Israel, as reflected in the larger tradition of oracles against foreign nations."[293] Christensen discusses Nahum in relation to Holy War in ancient Israel, but he consciously makes a distinction...

> ...between holy war as a military institution and the 'wars of YHVH,' which reflect symbolic speech in reference to cultic events in the worship experience of ancient Israel.[294]

The pioneering efforts of Christensen and McClain stress the hermeneutical role of music theory in distinguishing between the transcendent and the mundane. I have presented a great deal of material that should identify Christensen's reference to "cultic events in the worship experience" as Abraham's sacred practice of "7 circuits around the sacred cube." Christensen's insight here comes as a result of his work with Dr. McClain. And, it represents a major breakthrough. Hopefully, my own insights will help clarify the deepest meaning of Holy War as the inner struggle of Abraham's sacred priestly practice. Pronouncing the Word of God, *YHVH*, enabled the ancient High Priests of Solomon's Temple to harmonize the "12 who stand in war" within their body, which empowers them to liberate their soul. History has distorted the meaning of the Bible. A literal interpretation of the Bible does no justice to the brilliance of its authors. The Book of Revelation's "Armageddon" reduces to a deeply personal inner struggle, not a world-wide nuclear holocaust.

Biblical allegories of sibling rivalries and military conflicts were just literary devices that were meant to communicate Abraham's science and sacred practice. For example, just as Israel (symbolic of the *Shechinah* or soul) was freed from Egypt's oppression and bondage (symbolic of the body), leading Israel to the Promised Land (symbolic of the soul's liberation) — Nineveh too, must be considered a "wicked city" — equal to Egypt in its wicked oppression of Israel's soul. Nineveh was the capital of Assyria, the empire that destroyed Israel's Northern Kingdom by capturing and oppressing Israel's 10 tribes. Just as the 10 Plagues ravaged Egypt, Nahum prophesied that the "body" of Nineveh would be destroyed and transformed in order to bring forth the rebirth of the remaining two tribes: Judah's soul. The pseudo-historical nature of Egypt and Nineveh's destruction is not the point, and it should not be taken literally. All lessons learned must be understood metaphorically, as a simulation of death through deep meditation in order to liberate the soul.

293 Christensen, *Nahum*, Op.Cit., 22-23.
294 Ibid., 22.

The Ancient Origins of Ethos

Semitic tribes (circa 4000 BCE) invaded the Aryan pre-Sumerian founders of Sumer (5400 - 4000 BCE) and learned the science of religion from their Aryan/Iranian hosts. The Sumerian King List is currently the earliest written record of the science of religion that provides hard evidence describing the structure of the Clock of Heaven as a harmonic series. It is the harmonic series that links the macrocosm of the Clock of Heaven and the Precession of the Equinox to the microcosm of the Clock of Earth. It was never the clock itself, but rather, the harmonic series that guides man's immortal spiritual self within Heaven's macrocosm, as well as the mundane activities of man's mortal and material self within our Earthly microcosm.

The Bible's strategy for creating inner peace and peace in the world depends on the sacred meditation practice of priests and prophets, which "tunes in" to the harmonic series that lives within us, and governs what the ancient Greeks called "Ethos." Ethos describes how musical vibration directly effects the human soul, man's character, the political climate, the nation, and the world. Although there are no examples of ancient musical practice except for what we can surmise from theoretical treatises and literary descriptions, music historian Donald Grout tells us:

> Greek mythology ascribed to music a divine origin and named its inventors and earliest practitioners gods and demigods, such as Apollo, Amphion, and Orpheus. In this dim prehistoric world, music had magical powers: people thought it could heal sickness, purify the body and mind, and work miracles in the realm of nature. Similar powers are attributed to music in the Old Testament...[295]

Greece, Pythagoras, Plato and Aristotle were all in agreement about laws to regulate what was musically permissible:

- **<u>Ethos of character:</u>** If one listens to the wrong kind of music he will become the wrong kind of person; but, conversely, if he listens to the right kind of music he will tend to become the right kind of person. Aristotle, Politics, 8, 1340a,b
- **<u>For the soul:</u>** (The just man) will always be seen adjusting the body's harmony for the sake of the accord in the soul. Plato, Republic 591d
- **<u>For the city:</u>** The city's guardians must "build their guardhouse" in music and permit "no innovations, for never are the ways of music moved without the greatest political laws being moved." Plato, Republic 424c, d

295 Grout, Donald Jay, *A History of Western Music* (New York: W.W. Norton, 1973) 3.

- **For society:** The foundations of music, once established must not be changed, for lawlessness in art and education inevitably leads to license in manners and anarchy in society. – Plato, Republic, IV, 424; also Laws, III, 700C

It is the *Ethos* of man's harmonic mind, body and soul that describe the first principles of monotheism's Divine Law. Abraham didn't have access to the sophisticated tools used in a new branch of biophysics called electro-physiology, which studies the effects of the sound, electricity, and light on living creatures. Of course, sound, electricity, and light, are all forms of wave energy structured by the harmonic series. Abraham had to resort to studying the harmonic series (i.e., studying God Himself) from the perspective of its harmonic components: Earth (duple), Water (triple), Wind (quintuple) and Fire (septimal). He speculated about how these components combined with one another in order to create the objects and beings of Creation. He attempted to reconcile the duple and triple progressions with the attribute of Divine Judgement," which he believed could harmonize ambiguous tunings between the *pnimiyut* of Good and Evil that manifested in the soul.

Following man's spiritual compass, therefore, implied reconciling the natural dissonance between the duple and triple progressions of our soul through meditation, i.e., through the Fires of Heaven's septimal progression. Sabbath prayer theoretically enables us to introspectively pinpoint and forgive sin. From Abraham's monotheistic perspective, it is musical mathematics that enables us to better approximate the $\sqrt{2}$ that bisects our soul's octave tone circle (duple progression); just as the Torah describes *Yahweh* "splitting the Great Serpent" (triple progression) to eliminate the duality of Ab $\neq$ G#. Splitting the serpent approximates a 12th spoke on the Pythagorean Tuning tone circle (Log $2^p 3^q$) that would effectively eliminate the 13th spoke. Within the Abrahamic faiths, one's ability to clearly discern between Good and Evil enables us to see the truth more clearly so we can judge ourselves and others more wisely.

Bisecting the soul's duple and triple progressions at the $\sqrt{2}$ with Sabbath prayer gives us the wisdom to judge between Good and Evil. The Torah describes how the sacred Fires of Sabbatical prayer theoretically (albeit unrealistically) enables us to trisect the quintuple progressions at the $\sqrt[3]{2}$ in order to achieve perfection by "swallowing sin"; completely absorbing sin into our perfected body (see Figure 82). But, like Moses, man can no longer be expected to "cross over" to the Promised Land and "walk with God" in the manner of Enoch and Noah. What is within the realistic expectations of Torah prophecy, is for the entire nation of Israel to at least accomplish two Sabbaticals — empowering them to become a true prophets in the Biblical tradition — clearing a path for the divine energy to travel within the central channel up to the Heart Center, and, at least partially, to the Crown Center.

Good judgement helps us discern between Good and Evil during our moral dilemmas, while bad judgement manifests sinful choices directly within our body, which often surfaces as health issues. Sickness then further skews our thoughts, emotions, and actions in a self-perpetuating cycle. Abraham describes "12 Directors of the Soul" that connects our body's organ systems to our soul. But, the 12 typically "stand in War." According to Abrahamic teachings, they remain "at War" until Sabbath and Sabbatical prayer harmonizes the body and soul's Wind, Water, and Earth elements with the Fires of the sacred practice, which ultimately "anoints our head with oil" and purges away our sickness and sins. Once the "12 Directors of the Soul" no longer "stand in War," we will have successfully transcended the duality of our loves and hates through the sacred meditation practice of High Priests and prophets.

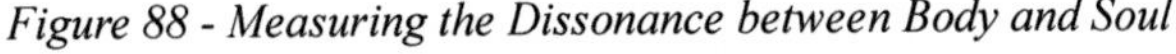

Figure 88 - Measuring the Dissonance between Body and Soul

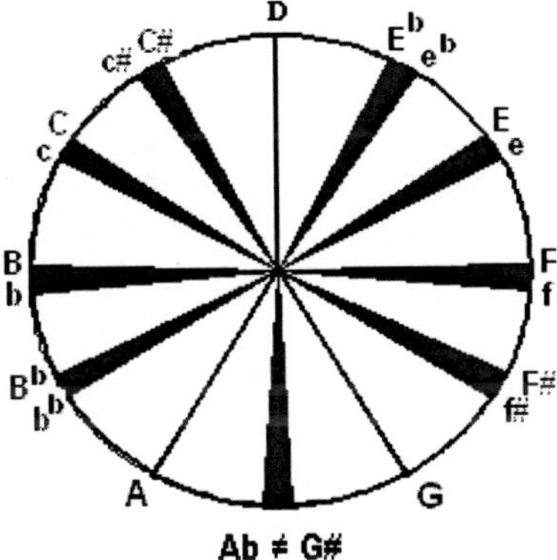

We have mentioned the gap of ratio 80:81 (which Ptolemy called the *syntonic* comma) that exists between the soul's Pythagorean Tuning and the body's Just Tuning. Figure 88 graphically illustrates this gap, demonstrating how the soul's triple progression tone circle is "out of tune" with the body's quintuple progression tone circle. This same divine template reflects how the orbits of the Sun and the Moon are also "out of sync" with one another. The 12 sons of Israel that form the 12 tribes are well known, but there were also 12 sons of Ishmael.

> "But as for Ishmael, I have heard thee: behold I have blessed him, and will make him fruitful, and will multiply him exceedingly; twelve princes shall he beget, and I will make him a great nation." Genesis 17:20

Like all the Biblical allegories of sibling rivalry (Cain and Abel, Jacob and Esau, Joseph and his brothers), the 24 princes born within the "tent" of Abraham" (Figures 89a & b) are intentionally set against one another. Why? Here is the theological underpinning for all the hatred that currently exists in the Middle East.

Abraham's Legacy of Peace

The sibling rivalry between Isaac and Ishmael to inherit the birthright of Abraham, translates into a Biblical tuning allegory between the 12 princes of Arabia born to Ishmael, and the 12 princes of Israel born to Isaac's son Jacob. This inner struggle between the body and soul has been graphed in the harmonics of the tone circle in Figure 88. The tent of Abraham includes the 12 princes of Israel and the 12 princes of Arabia (Figure 89a). To harmonize the body and soul is to harmonize all 24 princes who "stand in War." In Figure 89b, the "fixed tones" "G", "D", "A" are the three aspects of mind that define common harmonic ground between Pythagorean and Just Tuning, and between the Princes of both Arabia and Israel. The true birthright of Abraham is the sacred meditation practice that was shared among all 24 princes. It enhances the Fires of Divine Judgement necessary for all the Children of Abraham to ascend toward the Throne of Glory (Figure 90). This occurs in generational steps beginning with the *gematria* of Abram himself, which is well-known within the Jewish Kabbalistic tradition. Its arithmetic proceeds as follows:

Alef (א) 1 + Bet (ב) 2 + Resh (ר) 200 + Mem (מ) 40 = ABRM = 243

After Abram was initiated by Melchizedek into the practice of High Priests, the *gematria* of Abram (=243) was transformed into Abraham (248), with the "Breath of God" (Heh = ה = 5) added. However, this is not simple addition, it indexes the entire transformation process of the sacred practice. Perhaps this is why the Zohar[296] asks and answers the question: "*When did that key open the gates and make the world fruitful? It was when Abraham appeared...as soon as the name Abraham was completed the Sacred Name was completed along with it.*"[297] Thus, to "complete" the Holy Name *Yahweh*, we first complete the mathematical transformation from Abram to Abraham: In Figure 90, we see Abram ascend as 3^5 (=243) raised through five powers of five ($5^5 = 3125$), which is equal to 759,375. But, since God transcends the Throne of Glory, even 759,375 must be transposed to a higher octave, multiplying by 2^{10} so that 759,375 x 2^{10} = 777,600,000, Yahweh's *gematria*.

Thus, we have finally completed the name of Abraham within the precise location of the Throne of Glory, YHVH's octave double 777,600,000/388,800,000 which contains the sanctified tones within the Four-Horned Altar (pictured as a Star of David) in Figure 90. At this point, it should be clear that the Bible, at its deepest layer of interpretation, is really a book of music theory describing the inner vibrational essence of Time, the Soul, and the Universe, with detailed instructions on how to ascend through the Heavens on Jacob's Ladder.

296 Generally considered the most authoritative Kabbalistic text after the *Sefer Yetzirah*
297 Zohar, 3b-4a.

Figure 89a - The Legacy of Abraham: 12 Princes of Israel & 12 Princes of Arabia

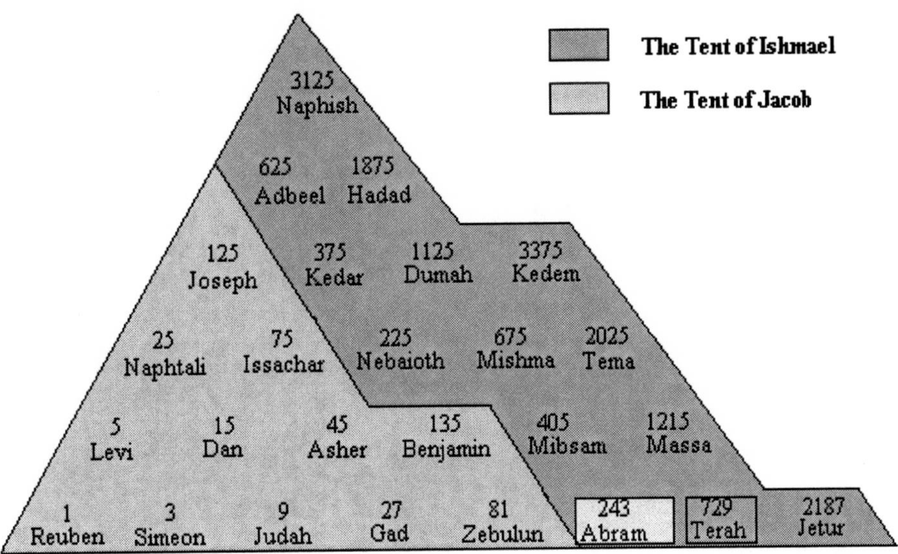

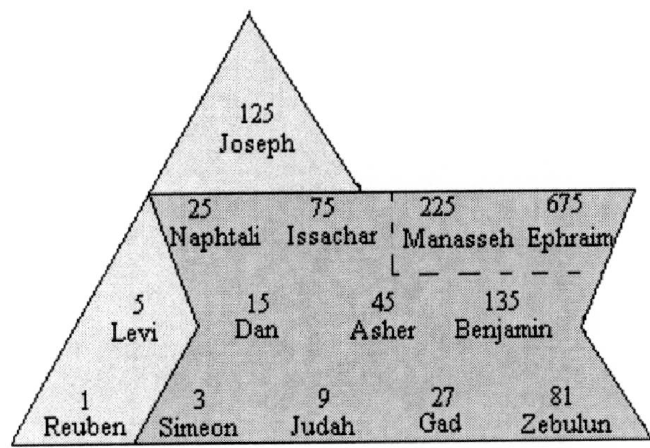

Figure 89b - The 12 Princes of Ishmael share the "Three aspects of Mind" (G,D,A) with the 12 Princes of Israel[298]

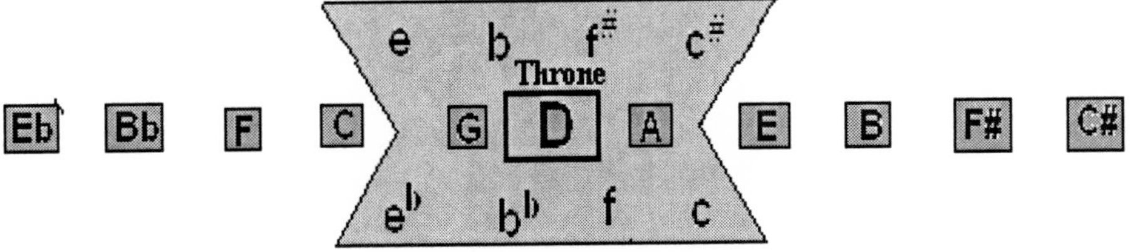

298 Ernest McClain, *The children of Abraham*, unpublished.

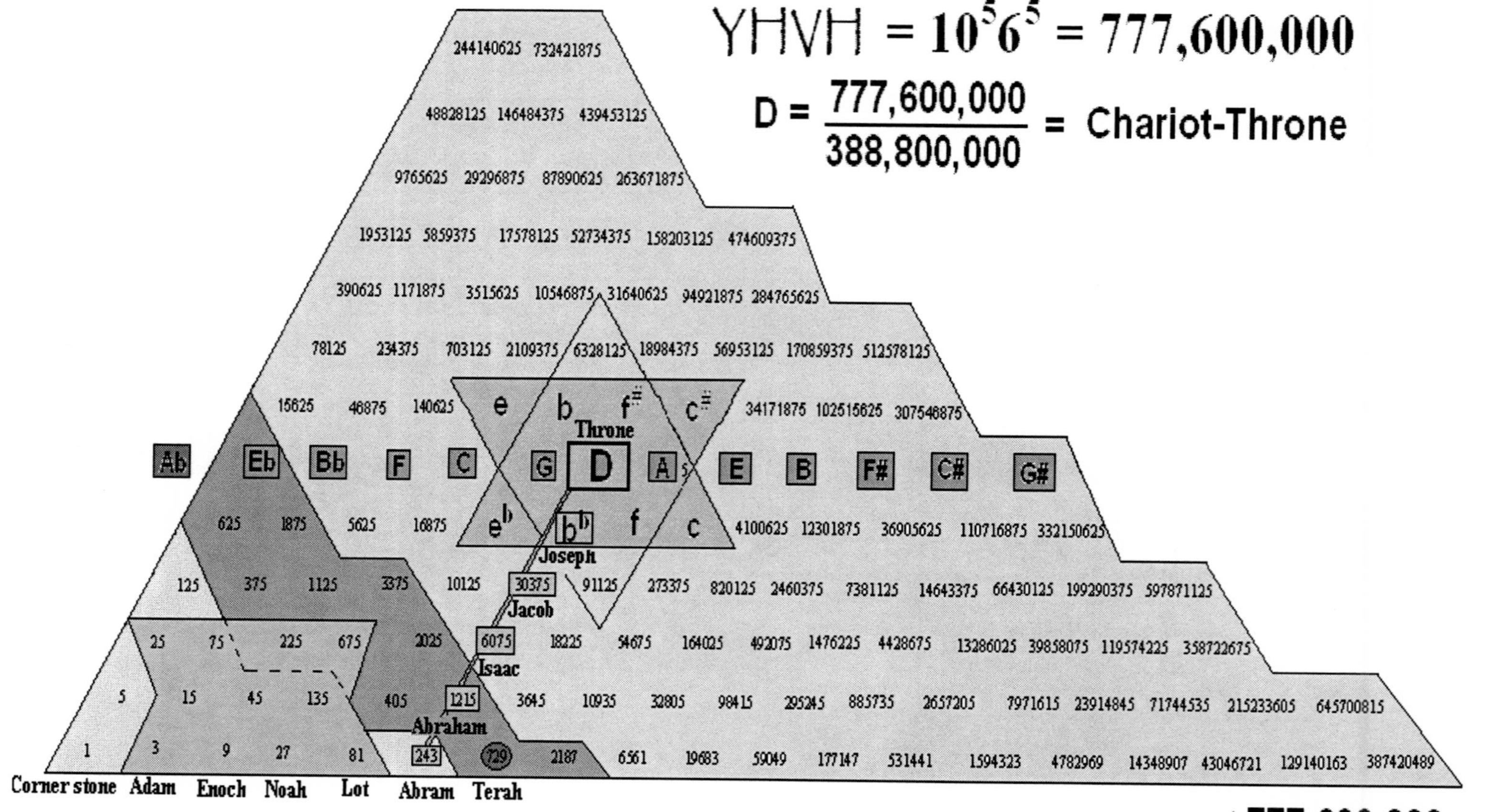

Figure 90 – The Children of Abraham Ascending to Israel's Throne of Glory

Within the Jewish tradition, the writings of the great Kabbalist Isaac Luria, the "Ari" (1534-1572), have come closest to realizing the Torah's ancient music theory. Unfortunately, Lurian doctrine also falls short of providing any of the mathematical details provided in this text; details that were once well-known, but have been lost to Judaism since the destruction of Solomon's Temple in 586 BCE. "His doctrine of *Tzimtzum* [contraction] refers to a refraction and concealment of the radiating emanation from the G-dhead, in a number of stages and in a progressive development of degrees, until finite and physical substances become possible."[299] "This is the concept of the *Hishtalshelut* (downward gradation) of the worlds and their descent, degree by degree, through a multitude of 'garments,' which screen light and life that emanate from Him, until there is this material and gross world, the lowest in degree..."[300] "...by means of cause and effect..."[301] In Chapter 15, we mentioned the descent of the Divine Sparks degree by degree through matter and time within all the generations of Adam. We described how the *pnimiyut* of past, present, and future prophets were also saved in Noah's Ark, spanning all the generations of Adam, i.e., 1440:720:360:180:90:45. The doctrine of *Hishtalshelut* states that the time of Creation was much closer to God and it carried with it a greater number of Divine Sparks (i.e., a higher frequency of vibration). A modern scientific approach would interpret this as the expansion of the universe from the days of the Big Bang.

Therefore, it is not that prophecy is dead, as the rabbis proclaim, but perhaps modern man's failed efforts to "walk with God" in the manner of Noah and Enoch, suggest a lost Aryan meditation expertise. In documenting the transition from sexagesmal to a mixed-base system, the Torah describes the legend of the "sons of God" and their *Nephilim* offspring ("men of renown"). In the tradition of unrealistic reigns within the Sumerian king List, the Torah bows to the Aryan legend by chronicling the early patriarchs with similarly unrealistic lifespans. They simply lived longer than the 120 year standard age that began with Moses. The larger sexagesimal numbers in the Aryan tradition informs us that it took 60 years to complete each Sabbatical, rather than 7 years. With the transition to the new numeral system each Jubilee Year would take 7 Sabbaticals of 49 years rather 6 *soss* of 360 years. If each 360 day year on Earth took 1 second in Heaven, and each Heavenly minute took 72 Earth years, then perfecting one Sabbatical in 60 years implied 360 days * 60 years = 21,600 days. The 21,600 unit length of Sumerian king Enmender-Anna's reign should probably be interpreted as one 60 year Sabbatical lasting 1 Sumerian *soss*.

Completing a Jubilee Year (whether sexagesimal or mixed-base) implies an inner struggle for harmonic perfection in which the 11 sanctified chromatic tones of the body resonates with the 11 sanctified chromatic tones of the soul. If we refer

299 Zalman, 819.
300 Zalman, 163.
301 Zalman, 23.

to Figure 88, we can see that harmonizing the spiritual and material realms in this diagram seems to call for a harmonic "middle-ground." Finding that middle ground evolved into the earliest prototype for our modern-day Equal Temperament system.

Scripture reconciled the duple and triple progressions of the soul by articulating "the circle and the square within." This solution required more than simple integers, because bisecting the octave generated an irrational number: $\sqrt{2}$. Furthermore, harmonic perfection within the body required allegories of sibling triplets who could reconcile the duple and quintuple progressions by trisecting the body's octave as $\sqrt[3]{2}$. Figure 88 describes a Holy War. It is the inner conflict between 12 triple progression lights (the circle) and 12 quintuple progression material lights (the square). Within Biblical allegory, this question was framed as follows: How do 12 Arab princes and 12 princes of Israel live in peace? Scripture suggests that peace can be realized in the logic of bisecting the octave ($\sqrt{2}$) with sibling twins, trisecting the octave ($\sqrt[3]{2}$) with sibling triplets, and ultimately, splitting the octave into 12 equal portions $\sqrt[12]{2}$ — which is the interval that defines Equal Temperament within modern music theory. Modern piano tuners Equally Temper pianos by using their judgement to master the art of tonal compromise. Finding the "mean" between the spirituality of the circle and materiality of the square was allegorized by the "wisdom of Solomon" as the ideal of divine judgement to "split the baby,"[302] i.e., to "temper" the syntonic comma that exists between the sanctified 11-tone chromatic scale of the body and the 11-tone chromatic scale of the soul.

Israel reaches its historical and philosophical peek with the democratic egalitarianism of King Solomon's Israel, and on display is the legendary wisdom of Solomon to "split the baby."[303] It is metaphor for tempering the diesis of 22 logarithmic "cents" that exists between the 24 Princes "who stand at War" (Figure 88). Equal Temperament can be embraced somewhere between them.[304] Just as it was the ideal for Biblical Israel, Plato became an exponent of Equal Temperament, as was Zarlino during the Renaissance, and Rameau during the Enlightenment. In allegory, Plato equated tones with the fine citizens of Athens, in which each citizen did not demand "exactly what he was owed," but rather, moderated their demands, and remained "temperate" in the interests of "what is best for the city."[305] Being "temperate" and living in moderation was the Greek philosophical ideal. Greek moderation certainly sounds like a more reasonable and moderate way of life than the extremes of an Essene ascetic or a Himalayan monk. The Bible idealizes Equal Temperament as mankind's salvation, as did Plato, Zarlino, and Rameau. From the ancient Greek perspective on *Ethos*, could Equal Temperament actually bring peace to the world as the Bible and Plato both suggest?

302 I Kings 3:16-28.
303 I Kings 3:16-28.
304 A system devised by Alexander J. Ellis (d. 1890) describing 1 cent as 1/100th of a semitone, thus 100 cents = 1 semitone and 1200 cents = 1 octave.
305 McClain, *The Pythagorean Plato*, 5.

Modern scientific instrumentation can measure even the smallest change in pitch. The existence of the *syntonic* comma underscores the theoretical gap between materiality and spirituality, between the "circle and the square within"; the gap between body and soul, and, the gap between the 12 princes of Israel and the 12 princes of Arabia. Within the context Greek *Ethos,* could the Biblical ideal of Equal Temperament really find peace in compromise?

To answer that question, we must first realize that Equal Temperament is not a natural tuning system like Pythagorean Tuning or Just Tuning, because it is not based on simple integer ratios. Remember that an irrational number is called "irrational" not because it is "without reason" but because it is "without ratio." We must first acknowledge that Equal Temperament artificially "tempers" musical intervals and does not tune them according to nature's integers. Equal temperament has long been understood by music theorists as the most efficient way to spread the diesis evenly across the octave until the differences become imperceptible. From a theological perspective, this process would appear to simply hide sin without confronting it. Our ears can certainly be fooled by compromise, but can our souls?

The modern world has already been living this bold religious experiment for the last 300 years. Equal Temperament has made the last 300 years of beautiful music possible, creating what is called "the common harmonic practice period." But, does 300 years of beautiful music necessarily mean that Equal Temperament is a good thing? Many would say that just the existence of a Mozart Symphony or Bach Cantata proves it is good. It has certainly provided the harmonic freedom to transpose from one key to another with impunity. Its predecessor, "Well Temperament," was born within Bach's *Well-Tempered Clavier*, and today, Equal Temperament is still the most prominent theoretical basis of modern music. It has been the lingua franca of music since the time of Bach. But, does that really prove that it is right for civilization? Modern technology does not mistake the natural tuning of a harmonic series for Equal Temperament, even if man's hearing cannot always discern the difference. If we are to follow "wherever the truth leads" then perhaps the appearance of sonic perfection does not equate to perfection. So, are we really back to where we started? Does the science of religion offer us any clear path forward?

If there is truth to the concept of Ethos; and, if Biblical allegory proposes the compromise of temperament as its model of democracy and wisdom; if it is also the model of Plato's "wise men of Athens"; then, why hasn't civilization been healed during its ubiquitous use over the past 300 years? The Greek notion of *Ethos* explains why King David's 10-stringed lyre soothed the troubled soul of King Saul. Theoretically, the music that man listens to on a daily basis would impact the peacefulness and health of a man's soul, his character, his nation, and the world as a whole. Judging by the world's chaos, Equal Temperament is not as effective as David's 10-stringed lyre. Could the Bible and Plato both have gotten it wrong?

The Way Forward

We may recall that this book's thesis is largely based on the premise that the stillness and solitude of Ice Age cave life imposed meditation on the Aryan fathers. And, that sacred practice forced them to listen to the sound of their own soul. Perhaps, if today's music reinforced the sound of a person's soul (Sanskrit: *mantra*), it could, theoretically, function as a catalyst for meditation, health, and peace. This thesis implies that the world is chaotic precisely because man's physiology and psyche have not been resonating to the sound of God (or gods) that the founding fathers of both polytheism and monotheism have equated with the harmonic series.

We know that the harmonic series structures sound itself; and further, that the amplitude (i.e., loudness) of each harmonic within a person's soul varies uniquely with each individual. In other words, the timbre (overall sound quality) of each man's soul is like the unique timbre of his voiceprint. Timbre differentiates a violin from a clarinet, for example. Perhaps illness or "sin" impacts the natural resonances of the mind, body, and soul. If we assume for the moment that the principle of *Ethos* is correct, it would imply that each man's state of health critically depends on the harmonic series (i.e., God) that is anchored to our physiology within the nervous system. Joseph Fourier (1768–1830) introduced the Fourier series, which applies the study of harmonics to many fields, including optics, acoustics, electrical engineering, and electrophysiology, a branch of Biophysics, that promises to provide a better understanding of the body's electrical and tonal landscape.

Until our science advances to the point that we can prescribe a musical antidote for the organ and endocrine secretions that fuel anger and hatred, peace between Arabs and Jews must depend on knowledge and wisdom, two items in very short supply today. There is hope in our observations of renowned meditators, like the Dalai Lama, who appears to have surrendered all ego and agenda, and does not cling to the trappings of material existence. He is a man of peace, and the Tibetans often appear to be the most peaceful people on the planet — as if they inherited a genetic makeup that predisposes them toward a meditative posture.

World peace must begin with the inner peace of each individual. Harmonizing opposing religious and political positions tainted by ego is like penetrating the "Walls of Jericho." Prophecy that Israel will become a nation of prophets implies that each citizen will surrender their ego before they can purify their body and liberate their soul. The spiritualization of a nation takes time to "bubble up" sufficiently to impact its political identity. A spiritual Israel can only be born if it matures in the fertile soil of Abraham's legacy — one person at a time — for all the Children of Abraham, not just for the Jewish people. Education can occur swiftly in a "global village," and if the entire global "Ummah" can be educated on how to pray like the prophets, then perhaps Abraham's sacred deep meditation practice will resonate with the chord of nature that lives within each of us.

The writings of Abraham never suggested Equal Temperament as the road to peace or wisdom, although the Bible's evolving mathematical/musical allegories gradually builds to that conclusion.[306] Equal Temperament is presented as an intellectual theory of peace through compromise. It was taken up by Plato and others. However, the chaos and desperation of modern society makes a good case to suggest that Equal Temperament is not an effective way to heal our body, mind and soul. My own tentative conclusions about this outcome lacks empirical data as to how tone affects human physiology — a branch of electrophysiology that I take great interest in.

It must be stressed that Equal Temperament is not Abraham's truth! What I can be sure of, is the truth that history has reinforced across thousands of years: the truth of *Yahweh* as 777,600,000, i.e., Moses, as enlightened prophet (777), leading 600,000 Israelites to liberation. Peace becomes possible when all men can share in the knowledge of how meditation harmonizes the body and soul into a unity of Divine Light in which the whole becomes more than just the sum of its parts. It is from this perspective that the *Shema*, Judaism's oldest prayer derives its meaning:

Hear, O'Israel the LORD our God, the LORD is One

The way forward is for each of us to meditate religiously if we ever hope to recapture the peaceful spirituality and superior capabilities of the Biblical prophets and the Aryan founders of civilization. Even if we were to question the legend of the Aryan fathers, modern science is clearly telling us that meditation is a very good thing. It strengthens our limbic system, and it offers us a level of control over our endocrine and autonomic nervous systems. It also provides us with access to what Jung called the collective unconscious mind. Meditation creates new circuits that integrate our knowledge at a deep level, and taps into our wellspring of creative solutions. Strengthening our limbic system through meditation empowers us to "see the truth" — to tap into resources that cut through to the root of all problems and stressful situations. Finding inner peace is a direct result of "staying in the light" of the hypnagogic state. Our worldly problems can be resolved spontaneously. The history of religion calls this Enlightenment or Wisdom.

As suggested in my Introduction, society's disproportionate focus on the logic of the brain's frontal lobes may not be helping the evolution of our species. Ideally, we will rediscover the Renaissance ideal of knowledge and the ancient "wisdom practice" of the Aryan fathers. Learning how to reach the hypnagogic state for extended periods of time is a precious skill that may be mankind's best

306 The Documentary Hypothesis suggests that the Hebrew Scriptures had more than a single author.

chance for survival. It implies that our mind, body, and soul will resonate with the harmonic series that lives within us. The Torah's main purpose was to preserve Abraham's legacy as the patriarchal birthright of "7 circuits around the sacred cube." This is the one practice still shared to this day between the 12 princes of Arabia (circumambulating the Kabah) and the 12 princes of Israel (laying Tefillin). Abraham's true legacy was never about the geographical Israel. It was always about the spiritual "High Ground" of Israel and the sacred practice that empowers man to make peace within his own mind, body, and soul, and then empowers him to securely and compassionately reach out in peace to his fellow man.

Judaism's Pursuit of Peace

A good deal of today's religious strife can be traced back to the Jewish belief that prophecy died along with the last High Priest of Solomon's Temple in 586 BCE, when the Temple was destroyed by Nebuchadnezzar. At that point, any knowledge of the transcendental meaning of YHVH as the encrypted instruction set to explicate the Torah was lost — right along with the "pronunciation" of YHVH. I leave it to the reader to determine if I have rediscovered the lost meaning and "pronunciation" of *Yahweh* as the scientific context for Abraham's deep meditation practice to purify the body and liberate the soul. This was the practice of the *Kohan Gadol* (literally: Great Priest) on the Day of Atonement. It is the deepest meaning of the "7 Noahide Laws" that became Abraham's "7 circuits around the sacred cube." Only by understanding the meaning and learning the "pronunciation" of the Holy Tetragrammaton can the rabbinate restore knowledge of the *Merkavah* (the Chariot); a step that is necessary to perform each *mitzvoth* with the appropriate level of *kavanah* (meditative intent).

"Build a fence around the Torah" is the Jewish battle cry against persecution from the outside world. Jewish exclusivity is the defensive posture for Jews who have waited over 2500 years to understand the meaning and pronunciation of YHVH. This defensive posture is intended to perpetuate Judaism despite centuries of intermarriage and assimilation. In light of our new understanding of Abraham's writings, an enlightened rabbinical establishment would be obliged to consider the possibility that Christ and Mohammed's prophecy were completely consistent with Abraham's writings and theology. Understanding the Torah through the eyes of Abraham should bring a new spirit of openness to Judaism that is capable of nurturing a much deeper appreciation and understanding in the rabbinate for all the Children of Abraham.

There might also be a new appreciation within the rabbinate for the Aryan "sons of God" and their *Nephilim* offspring, who were "men of renown." An expanded historical perspective suggests that the "sons of Seth" may well have been

Aryans, with no implication of Evil. The *Nephilim* may have been true giants in both physical and spiritual stature, but the legend of evil giants and the distortions of the Book of Enoch must be purged from the Jewish psyche.

Christianity's Pursuit of Peace

According to the New Testament, the Jewish authorities of Sanhedrin charged Jesus with blasphemy and sought his execution.[307] Although the rabbis take issue with this extreme perspective, there is a general consensus that the Sanhedrin elders would not have vouched for Christ in any favorable way. They rejected him as a prophet in the Biblical tradition because they sincerely believed that prophecy died with the last High Priest of Solomon's Temple. In light of this fact, how could the Sanhedrin elders, or the Jewish people, be held accountable. Nevertheless, charges of deicide account for an anti-semitism that has lingered for almost 2000 years. Christianity's response to the Jewish rejection of Christ was to profess Christ's superiority to all the Biblical prophets. Since the first Ecumenical Council, Christianity has strayed most from the monotheistic theology of Abraham because of a concerted effort to impose Christ's superiority over all other prophets and faiths. Adding to that incongruity, the King James version of the Bible may have translated YHVH to *Jehovah*, but today, Christian popular tradition commonly uses the Septuagint's translation of the Hebrew *Adonai* ("My LORD") as *Kyrios* ("LORD"). Due to the ambiguities of the Holy Trinity, Christ has become personified as the LORD Himself. Since only Abraham's writings explain the exact nature of how the Holy Trinity differentiates within One Substance (Greek: *homoousian*), the conclusions of the First Ecumenical Council must be reexamined in light of this revelation. Failing to properly understand the Holy Trinity through the eyes of Abraham poses a difficult challenge for anyone who would seek peace and truth.

Theologian Elaine Pagels describes the 1945 discovery of numerous "Gnostic Gospels" in Nag Hammadi, Egypt. The gnostic beliefs that Pagels describes within these important texts reveals that Christian gnosticism is, in many ways, consistent with Abrahamic gnosticism. Pagels also describes how Christianity ultimately turned away from any gnostic notions of a liberated soul, and insisted on the implausible notion that Christ's physical body rose from the grave to reconstitute itself:

> If the New Testament accounts could support a range of interpretations, why did orthodox Christians in the second century insist on a literal view of resurrection [i.e., bodily resurrection "of the flesh"] and reject all others as heretical... We can see, paradoxically, that the doctrine

307 Mark 14:53–65, Matthew 26:57–68, Luke 22:63–71, and John 18:12–24.

> of bodily resurrection also serves an essential political function: it legitimizes the authority of certain men who claim to exercise exclusive leadership over the churches as the successors of the apostle Peter...Gnostic Christians who interpret resurrection in others ways have a lesser claim to authority: when they claim authority over the orthodox, they are denounced as heretics.[308]

The Church's orthodox position was solidified during the First Ecumenical Council (ca. 325 CE), when Bishop Athanasius (ca. 293-373) espoused that Christ, as the Word of God Incarnate, belongs to the Divine realm. Karen Armstrong[309] believes there would be serious consequences for mankind: "If Jesus had not been a human being, there would be no hope for us... nothing for us to imitate."[310]

In the opposite camp to Athanasius was the deacon Arius, who's concept of salvation required an exemplary life of good works. This was close to the thinking of Plato and other Greek philosophers: "The Stoics, for example, had always taught that it was possible for a virtuous human being to become divine through *theoria* [meditation]"[311] However, the First Ecumenical Council declared that Arius' practice was heresy, calling it the "Arian heresy."

At that same Ecumenical Council, another decree included the categorization of any and all "special knowledge of God" as heretical. As we have attempted to establish, Abraham's writings comprise the seminal mathematical and scientific treatise on monotheism, providing the scientific framework of the Hebrew Scriptures. However, according to the rulings of the First Ecumenical Council, Abraham's writings, and thus the Torah itself, would therefore be considered heresy — a "gnostic heresy." This was the start of a misguided and troubled relationship between Christianity and science. The Vatican has recently made an effort to help repair its relationship with science by apologizing for its treatment of Galileo. Clearly, there is much more that the church would need to do in this direction, especially if the public comes to understand the tight coupling of science and religion. Common sense dictates that if the Church hopes to survive it must attract more parishioners and clergy, but it can only do that if it can come to terms with science. The Church must reconsider its position with respect to the gnostic heresy in light of our new scientific understanding of the Hebrew *Logos*: *Yahweh*, as explained by Abraham.

The Church's Orthodox position declares that Jesus Christ was the only Son of God, and, as such, he was both "true God and true man." Christ would be the only one capable of liberating his soul, as he did in "The Transfiguration" on Mount Tabor. Of course, Abraham would say that all men were both "true God and true man," and

308 Pagels, Op.Cit., 6-7.
309 Karen Armstrong, a renowned theologian; as a nun for 7 years, Armstrong provides perspective on this issue.
310 Armstrong, *A History of God*, 110.
311 Ibid, 109.

further, that all men were capable of both transfiguration and resurrection. Perhaps the most challenging problem for the rest of the monotheistic world is the Christian notion that Christ is superior to both Moses and Mohammed. It can be argued that Christ's alleged superiority, as described in the Nicene Creed of the First Ecumenical Council, has been the root cause of much religious strife throughout history.

Without any understanding of Abraham's text, there was no way for Church Fathers to understand the Greek terms *ousi*a and *homoousion* as the inner vibrational essence of God's Light (Hebrew: *orot*). God's essence (Greek: *ousia;* Hebrew*: pnimiyut*) was, and still is, widely considered as unknowable — thus, God is considered unknowable. Hopefully, this text has been successful in bringing Abraham's writings to light, enabling us to know the *Living God*, first described by the great patriarch of monotheism.

The ancient Greeks believed that they could only know God through three expressions (*hypostasis*): the Father, Son, and Holy Ghost. Saint Jerome, and many others, thought that *ousia* and *hypostasis* were roughly equivalent, concluding that the Greeks, therefore, believed in three divine essences.[312] Abraham's writings explain *ousi*a and *homoousion*, and originally defined the theology of the Holy Trinity as the trinity of Hebrew letters within God's Holiest Name, with all its scientific and theological implications. He did this about 1500 years before Aristotle ever used the term *hypostasis*.

There is a long tradition of conflating the Father and the Son, based on the Western Church's oversimplification of the Holy Trinity. Making God too understandable was not the intention of Augustine, nor of the ancient Greek philosophers. The Greeks started with the *hypostasis*, but struggled to fathom God's Unity. The Western Church starts with God's unity, but conflates three "divine persons" into one God,[313] while dismissing the details as an unknowable "Sacred Mystery."

This difference of approach in Christianity's attempt to know God was the underlying reason for the split between the Eastern and Western Church. What precipitated the split, however, was a new controversial clause that was added to the Nicene Creed in 796 called the *filioque* (and the Son). The East felt that the clause made the Trinity too simple and rational.[314] The Greeks, and the Eastern Church, preferred to contemplate the nature of their God, but the *filioque* implied that there was no need for such contemplation. French philosopher, Peter Abelard (1079-1147), later tried to steer Christians away from any confusion by stressing Unity at the expense of the Three Persons.[315] The Christian theological position of superiority has fostered a war of dogmas among the three Abrahamic faiths that has contributed significantly toward dragging monotheism into a militaristic approach to

---

312 Ibid., 116.
313 Ibid, 200-201.
314 Ibid, 200.
315 Armstrong, *A History of God*, 203.

the "Wars of Yahweh." It can be argued that believing Christ is God, without regard for the nuances of etymology and translation, is a very real impediment to peace.

One case in point is the on-going controversy involving the translation of the Hebrew Scriptures into the Greek *Septuagint*. The Hebrew term *almah,* as used in Isaiah 7:14, translates to "young woman." In Israel, at that time, a young woman might also be a virgin, but there is a distinct Hebrew word for "virgin," which is *betulah*. In the *Septuagint*, the Greek word *parthenos* is a more general word, taking on the meaning of either a young woman or a virgin. We know that the early Church fathers decided to translate this word as "virgin," which, of course, had an enormous impact on Christian theology, and thus, on the rest of the world. To further complicate the issue, the Hebrew Scriptures used the present tense for this passage in Isaiah:

Hebrew Scriptures:

> *Behold, the young woman (almah) is with child, and she will bear a son and she shall call his name Immanuel.*

Greek Septuagint:

> *Behold, a virgin shall be (parthenos) with child, and shall bear a son, and they shall call his name Immanuel.*

The *Septuagint,* however, used the future tense, effectively turning an innocent event into a miraculous prophecy. Within Roman Catholic dogma, the miraculous birth of Christ substantiates the idea that Christ is superior in his divinity to Moses and Mohammed, and to Eastern prophets, like the Buddha, etc. Translating this as a virgin birth describes the "miracle" that God is Christ's biological father ("*begotten not made*"). And so, Christ is literally thought of as the only "Son of God." Thus, any theological discussion or interaction between a Christian and a non-Christian could no longer take place on a level playing field.

Once Christ was espoused as superior, other faiths took a defensive posture, and monotheistic dogma fractured into exclusive and often militaristic camps. The impact of so subtle a nuance in translation might be likened to the "butterfly effect" of mathematical chaos theory, which, in simplistic terms, tells us that a butterfly flapping its wings in China could potentially change the course of history around the world. Certainly, this nuance of translation has altered the course of history, rendering interfaith reconciliation impossible and theological discussion contentious.

In order to compete with Christian claims of superiority, Muslims focus on the Koranic idea of the "Seal of the Prophets," which implies that Mohammed is the most important prophet to heed, because he was the last prophet in the Biblical tradition. The defensive posture of Jewish theologians is to ignore and reject

Christ and Mohammed as prophets, because prophecy is still thought to be dead ever since the last High Priest of Solomon's Temple died protecting its secrets.

There would be no argument from Abraham that Christianity is based on the life and teachings of a true prophet. There is little doubt that Christ himself would consider any notion that he alone embodied either YHVH or Adonoi as completely blasphemous. Becoming One with the LORD (YHVH) is not the same thing as being YHVH. Abraham teaches us that we are all the Word of God Incarnate in man. His writings reveal that we are all capable of following in the footsteps of Moses, Christ and Mohammed, to become prophets and healers.

Thomas Jefferson redacted the Bible in order to "level the playing field" among the world's religions. He felt the need to edit out all of the Bible's miracles, such as Christ's transfiguration, resurrection, and virgin birth — until what remained was what he believed to be the core of Christianity — the compassion of Christ as espoused in the gospels. For Jefferson, Christ's model of compassion was Christianity's main contribution to mankind. By editing out all the miracles, his attempt to level the playing field inadvertently discarded the entire science of religion, all prophecy, all healing, and any need for meditation as religion's foundation practice.

For many years, Jefferson's Bible was given to incoming members of Congress as a rite of passage, intended to bring ecumenical thinking to the reins of government. Unfortunately, Jefferson was unknowingly rejecting the notion of "divine gifts" that derives from Abraham's sacred practice, including: Enoch and Noah "walking with God"; Christ's transfiguration and resurrection; the liberation of a man's soul, and its subsequent return to his body; Mohammed's "Night Journey," etc.. Jefferson, of course, had no way of knowing that all the "miracles" he redacted from the Bible were completely consistent with Abraham's writings. He probably knew little or nothing about the *Sefer Yetzirah*.

In light of our new understanding of monotheism's authoritative founding document, it behooves the Church fathers to reexamine the rulings of the First Ecumenical Council, and to push for reform that considers the Abrahamic notion that all men should be considered both true God and true man — not just Christ. Serious Christian scholars should also examine the Gnostic Gospels discovered in 1945 against the backdrop of Abraham's seminal work on gnosticism. Elaine Pagels stresses equanimity, summarizing the impact of the Christian Gnostic Gospels as follows:

> The "living Jesus" of these texts speaks of illusion and enlightenment, not of sin and repentance, like the Jesus of the New Testament. Instead of coming to save us from sin, he comes as a guide who opens access to spiritual understanding. But when the disciple attains enlightenment,

Jesus no longer serves as his spiritual master: the two have become equal — even identical.[316]

Serious church reform would also reconsider their edict that a sacred meditation practice is heretical, especially if it was described in great detail by the father of the faith, Abraham. Since Abraham's gnostic writings provide the scientific framework of the Torah, the Tanakh, and the New Testament's Book of Revelation, Christian Orthodoxy should feel compelled to reconsider its notions of heresy as articulated by Tertullian, the so-called "father of Latin Christianity." Tertullian was the main advocate of bodily resurrection, espousing that any other position was heretical. Elaine Pagels writes:

> Attempting to prove that gnosticism was essentially non-Christian, they [Tertullian's orthodox contemporaries] traced its origin to Greek philosophy, astrology, mystery religions, magic, and even Indian sources ... Tertullian ridiculed the gnostics for creating cosmologies, with multi-storied heavens like apartment houses, 'with room pile on room, and assigned to each a god by just as many stairways as there were heresies: The universe has been turned into rooms for rent!'[317]

The sources of gnosticism were traced to many places, but not to Abraham and the Torah, as we have done here, rendering Orthodox Christian criticism moot. If Tertullian's contemporary, Origen of Alexandria, was the one to articulate Catholic doctrine, it would have embraced an interpretation of Scripture that describes a soul passing through successive stages of incarnation before eventually reaching God.[318] Origen was a respected Christian scholar and theologian who has been said to support reincarnation and the gnostic idea of a separation between body and soul.[319] However, the Emperor Justinian and the Empress Theodora supported the *Miaphysitism* position which maintains that Divinity and Humanity are united in "one nature" ("physis"), without separation, without confusion, and without alteration.[320] In the Fifth Ecumenical Council, Justinian forced the ruling cardinals to draft a decree punishing with death anyone who believes that the soul of man comes from God and returns to God.[321]

From Abraham's perspective, a complex rich harmony describes a person's soul. The *ousia/pnimiyut* of man resonates as a microcosm of the *ousia/pnimiyut* of

316 Pagels, Op.Cit., xx.
317 Ibid., xxix.
318 Will Durant, The Story of Civilization: Caesar and Christ (New York: MJF Books, 1994).
319 *Tanya*, Igeret Hakodesh 7; T: "Every soul of Israel needs to be reincarnated in order to fulfill all the 613 commandments..."
320 Ken Parry, ed.,The Blackwell Companion to Eastern Christianity (Malden, MA: Blackwell Pub., 2007) 88.
321 In the Anathemas against Origen, this was attached to the decrees of the Fifth Ecumenical Council, A.D. 545, in Nicene and Post-Nicene Fathers, 2d ser., 14:318.

God. The sameness and difference among the members of the Holy Trinity can only be explained by Abraham's mathematical and musical descriptions. Understanding the essence of God as the transcendent "Blueprint" that is the harmonic series (i.e., God the Father), must be differentiated from God the Son,[322] which gets its name from Christ's ability to liberate his soul into a "Heavenly Body" that "walked on water" and liberated on Mount Tabor during the Transfiguration. The Holy Ghost needs to be differentiated from the Holy Spirit. The first term describes the un-liberated soul still contained within the body as an instantiation of the Divine Blueprint. Within that context, "giving up the ghost" refers either to death, or to a liberation of the soul through the sacred practice, thus manifesting the principle that defines a "Son of God." Each man must experience the Biblical "End of Days" for himself, by liberating the soul and transcending the constraints of time and space that define the body as container, thereby helping to fulfill the Bible's prophecy for all "Children of Abraham" to become prophets. The Holy Spirit, on the other hand, refers to the transformative Breath of God, or Divine Influx, that visits the pilgrim at the top of the Holy Mountain. It is symbolized by the Hebrew letter *Heh* that was added to Abram's name making it Abraham. This indicated that the Holy Spirit took up residence within him as part of his being.

Islam's Pursuit of Peace

It is important to note that Mohammed began his career as a man of peace. He called Jews and Christians "People of the Book," and he always respected their shared Abrahamic origins. *Hanīfiyyah* is the law of Abraham that existed before the advent of Judaism, Christianity, and Islam. Mohammed considered himself a *Hanif* during the *jahalia* ("Days of Ignorance" that existed before he wrote the Koran). During this period, Mohammed, and other spiritually minded men, sought the "true religion of Abraham."

When Mohammed was still in Mecca, he was asked to come to *Yathrib* (later renamed Medina) to manage the peace within an *Ummah* (community) consisting of pagans, Jews, Christians, and Muslims. They wanted freedom from inter-tribal warfare and heard about Mohammed's diplomatic skills. After writing a document called the Charter of Medina, Mohammed successfully managed the *Ummah* as its head magistrate, brokering the peace and settling disputes. His document is widely considered the constitution for the first Islamic state.

After this positive experience he anticipated acceptance from the three Jewish tribes in Medina as a prophet, but what he got instead was unabashed rejection. He could not fathom the rabbinic notion that prophecy died with the destruction of Solomon's Temple. Mohammed knew he was a prophet in the lineage of Ishmael,

322 As in the Nicene Creed: "...Light from Light; True God from True God..."

and in the tradition of Abraham, but he remained baffled and greatly saddened by Jewish intransigence. He recognized Abraham's "7 circuits around the Kabah" as one of the 5 pillars of Islam, and he had a cave meditation practice for much of his life. When Jews in Medina eventually plotted against him alongside Meccan merchants who feared him, he became particularly violent, and over time, wiped out all three Jewish tribes.

Those who seek Holy War today use the term "*jihad.*" It is the battle cry of Muslims who seek freedom from perceived oppression. *Jihad* has special meaning when used militaristically against the "People of the Book." It is not the Jewish or Christian religion that Muslims fear. Muslims sense a wave of Western oppression in the form of encroaching materialism, science, technology, secularism, and atheism. Literally, the word *jihad* refers to a struggle in the ways of Allah. What needs greater clarification in the minds of militaristic *jihadists* is a basic understanding of the Koran as a reflection of the writings of Abraham.

As all Muslims know, the word *Islam* means surrender. Muslims prostrate themselves before God five times each day. Karen Armstrong describes the significance of these prostrations for the first Muslims living within a thriving mercantile and pagan Mecca:

> The prostrations were designed to counter the hard arrogance and self-sufficiency that was growing apace in Mecca. The postures of their bodies would re-educate the Muslims, teaching them to lay aside their pride and selfishness, and recall that before God they were nothing.[323]

Muslim Fundamentalists, however, demonstrate that they do not understand *Islam* when they misinterpret the following Koranic passage:

> *Whoever leaves home in God's cause will find on earth frequent and ample place of refuge. If death should overtake the one who leaves home and migrates to God and His Messenger [Mohammed], God is certain to reward that person.*[324]

The Imam Ruhallah Khumayni interprets this passage as follows:

> If a person departs from the home of egohood and migrates toward God and His Messenger, and then reaches a state where he is "overtaken by death," where nothing remains of his self and he sees all things as coming from God — if he engages in such a migration, then it is incumbent upon God to reward him… there is a class of people who

323 Karen Armstrong, Islam: A Short History (New York: Random House, 2000) 6..
324 Koran, *Women* 4:100; Renard, 53.

> have accomplished this… there are others who have migrated but not yet reached the goal of being "overtaken by death." And there is still another group—to which you and I belong—that has not even begun to migrate. We are still caught up in the darkness; we are captives in the pit of attachment to the world, to nature, and worst of all to our own egos. We are enclosed in our home of selfhood, and all that exists is ourselves … As time goes on we become more and more distant from the point of origin, that place toward which we are supposed to migrate.[325]

According to the Imam, being "overtaken by death" does not imply surrendering one's life to kill others in order to vanquish perceived oppression. The true meaning of Islam requires the death or surrender of one's own ego. This Koranic passage describes the internal struggle within each of us in which the enemy to be vanquished is one's own ego. Before one can begin "migrating to God" one must "leave home," i.e., vanquish the ego. From Abraham's perspective, the soul will only ascend after "tuning" the body and soul through the sacred practice of the *greater jihad,* otherwise the soul wanders like Adam and Eve in exile from God and Paradise.

According to the *Sefer Yetzirah*, the true religion of Abraham describes the need to transcend the anger and hatred of the *lesser jihad* by subduing the lower self (*jihad al-nafs*). We have already studied the mathematical/musical details of how the twelve body organs "stand in war." This manifests in the dualistic biological imperatives of love and hate, that lead man to procreate and kill. Only after we have learned to subdue the lower self and surrender our ego, can we begin to migrate toward God. Abraham characterizes man's inner struggle in the following stanza:

6.5 *Twelve stand in war:*
Three love,
three hate,
three give life
and three kill
Three love: the heart and the ears.
Three hate: the liver, the gall, and the tongue.
Three give life: the two nostrils and the spleen.
Three kill: the two orifices and the mouth.

To follow in the footsteps of the prophet Mohammed, implies liberating one's soul and transcending the mundane. The *Sakinah* (Hebrew: *Shechinah;* English: *inner tranquility of a liberated soul*) can only be experienced through Abraham's meditation practice. It is well known that Mohammed had a meditation

325 Renard, 53-54.

practice for much of his adult life. God's tranquility *(Sakinah)* descended on Mohammed as he meditated in the cave.[326] Muslim tradition also tells us that his soul was liberated in his "Night Journey" at the Temple Mount in Jerusalem.

For Mohammed, leading the pagan world "toward the light of the Kabah" required a vision that could only have been a divine gift born out of his sacred practice. Theologian Karen Armstrong acknowledges that Mohammed's divine guidance resulted from his meditation practice:

> When faced with a crisis or dilemma, Mohammed had entered deeply into himself and heard a divinely inspired solution. His life had thus represented a constant dialogue between transcendent reality and the violent, puzzling and disturbing happenings of the mundane world. The Quran followed public and current events, bringing divine guidance and illumination to politics. Mohammed's successors, however, were not prophets, but would have to rely on their own human insights.[327]

Mohammed himself differentiates between a greater and lesser *jihad*. His own words are recorded in the *Hadith*:[328]

> We have come home from the lesser sacred struggle (*al-jihad al asghar*).
> We are returning to the greater sacred struggle (*al-jihad al-akbar*).

Abraham's writings reveal that the *Hajj* is the sacred practice of the *greater jihad*, where all Muslims are compelled to surrender to God. The *Hajj* is one of the five "Pillars of Islam." It is the annual pilgrimage to Mecca to perform Abraham's sacred deep meditation practice of "7 circuits around the sacred cube." Before Mohammed's Koranic revelations, he sought the *Hanīfiyyah* (the true religion of Abraham). Without the esoteric meaning of Abraham's *Sefer Yetzirah* to shed light on how to pray like the Biblical prophets, Muslims, like their Jewish and Christian counterparts, can not even begin "migrating to God." Mohammed's lesser jihad was to secure the Kabah for Islam — for all time — so that Muslims could devote their lives to the greater jihad. This is what the prophet means when he states: *We have come home from the lesser sacred struggle*. *Al-jihad al asghar* was eminently accomplished in Mohammed's own lifetime, and Mohammed died soon after achieving that goal. It behooves all Muslims to realize that they are finally *home from the lesser jihad,* and they should now devote their lives *to the greater jihad.*

From Abraham's perspective, fundamentalist *jihad* has an ill-conceived, self-aggrandizing, and short-sighted goal of martyring themselves to kill others,

326 *Koran*, Repentance 9:40.
327 Armstrong, *Islam: A Short History*, 24.
328 The Hadith is a collection of sayings and actions of the Prophet Mohammed. After the Koran, it is the most important source of Islamic law.

vainly and ignorantly believing that they are on a divine mission that will fulfill their prerequisite for divine reward. The Imam Ruhallah Khumayni wisely tells us that the true meaning of Islam requires the death or surrender of one's own ego. It does not imply surrendering one's life to kill others in order to vanquish perceived oppression. The Imam's commentary must also be applied to Westerners guilty of imperialism, materialism, and atheism. They too, are caught up in the "pit" of ego, sin, and worldly attachments, and they too, regularly speak God's Name in vain.

Toward a New Jerusalem

Abraham's writings authoritatively inform us that no man could have become a prophet without the meditation process that binds man's body and soul to God with "7 circuits." Mohammed's revelations and wisdom resulted from his well-documented cave practice — a mental articulation of 7 circuits around the sacred cube — incorporating the Hajj into his very being through his meditation practice. We can assume this to be true of Christ as well, as recent historical speculation regarding the Essenes and the Qumran community seems to suggest.

Both the Muslim *Hajj* and the Jewish practice of "laying *Tefillin*" require "7 circuits around the sacred cube." Both practices, however, must be recognized as merely symbolic of Abraham's meditation practice. One does not automatically enter the hypnagogic state by performing religious rituals, although the rituals might be conducive to achieving the desired meditative state. Ceremonial practices have provided Jews and Muslims with important symbols of Abraham's practice. By understanding the science of religion, Abraham's *Sefer Yetzirah* reveals what this symbolism means in terms of a sacred meditation practice — a practise capable of transforming men into prophets that would be fit to inhabit a *New Jerusalem.*

All children of Abraham are compelled to realize the spiritual Israel (*Shechinah/Sakinah*) through this practice, and not become sidetracked by violence in the name of securing the illusory birthright of a geographical Israel. The proposed "two state solution" for Jews and Palestinians acknowledges a duality that retains barriers between them. The existence of a theocratic Jewish state, a theocratic Muslim state, or even a two-state political solution, is not really relevant to Abrahamic thought.

If a joint committee of monotheistic clerics that includes Jews, Muslims, and Christians can learn to read Scripture from Abraham's perspective, and devoutly follow his practise, perhaps they would come to realize the importance of the "New Jerusalem," not as an abstract Biblical concept, but as an *Ummah* (community) for the three faiths. In light of Abraham's writings, perhaps the Charter of Medina, written by Mohammed himself, is a good starting template that should be acceptable to all parties, as it once was during Mohammed's early years. "Brotherhood laws" could be strictly enforced, and any violators of the peace would be immediately expelled from the privilege of living in the Holy City. As spirituality evolves among its inhabitants, peace, and a new way to live, will hopefully evolve along with it.

The Middle East crisis can only be solved when men learn the wisdom of choosing Oneness with God over squabbles about land, material possessions, and "sibling rivalry," as depicted in Biblical allegory. The three Abrahamic faiths often behave like quarreling children — as do many ego-driven nations of the world. It cannot be restated often enough that the land of Israel and Abraham's material possessions might belong to Isaac and his descendants, but Abraham's true birthright of 7 circuits around the sacred cube was equally shared between Isaac and Ishmael. Imams and rabbis must come to recognize "7 circuits" as the true religion of Abraham that is the foundation of all three monotheistic faiths. The actual existence of the Kabah and its tradition proves that Isaac and Ishmael shared the true birthright, despite competing stories in the Torah and Koran. This implies that the *Sefer Yetzirah* rightfully belongs to Muslims as well as to Jews. But, Abraham was also the model of Christian faith. The sacred cube of the New Jerusalem that descends from Heaven is also the climax of the New Testament. It was heralded by 7 angels blowing 7 tone circles. In other words, "7 circuits around the sacred cube" is the linchpin of "community" and the main prerequisite for peace (see p.299, The New Jerusalem by Charles Bentz.). Members of the three faiths should feel compelled to learn more about the depths of this foundation of their faith, and they should feel compelled to learn how to "pronounce" the Holy Name in the manner that was originally intended.

In summarizing Part II, we have considered sufficient evidence to establish that the Torah was written in order to expound on Abraham's important scientific discoveries. Part III elaborates on the notion that Abraham's calculations, based on his observation of sound and light, marked the beginnings of modern science. Abraham's concept of the Living God was the first "Theory of Everything." The *Sefer Yetzirah* reveals that its author had an extensive knowledge of the most sophisticated mathematical and scientific tools of his day, circa 1800 BCE; which is exactly what we might expect from a mathematical and scientific genius born in the Babylonian city of Ur at the highpoint of Old Babylonian mathematics and science. Meditation enabled him to explore the inner esoteric world of the unconscious mind, while his calculations and observations enabled him to probe the physical exoteric world of light and sound. For Abraham, music theory figured prominently in his mathematical toolkit, as both his microscope and telescope. He discovered how to "tune" the mind, body and soul as if they were musical instruments. Abraham teaches us to cultivate them through meditation and self-realization, all within the acoustical framework of the "theory of everything" that he called the Living God. It has often been said that Albert Einstein came the closest to understanding God because of his vast scientific knowledge, but, Abraham actually defined God in terms of mathematics and science.

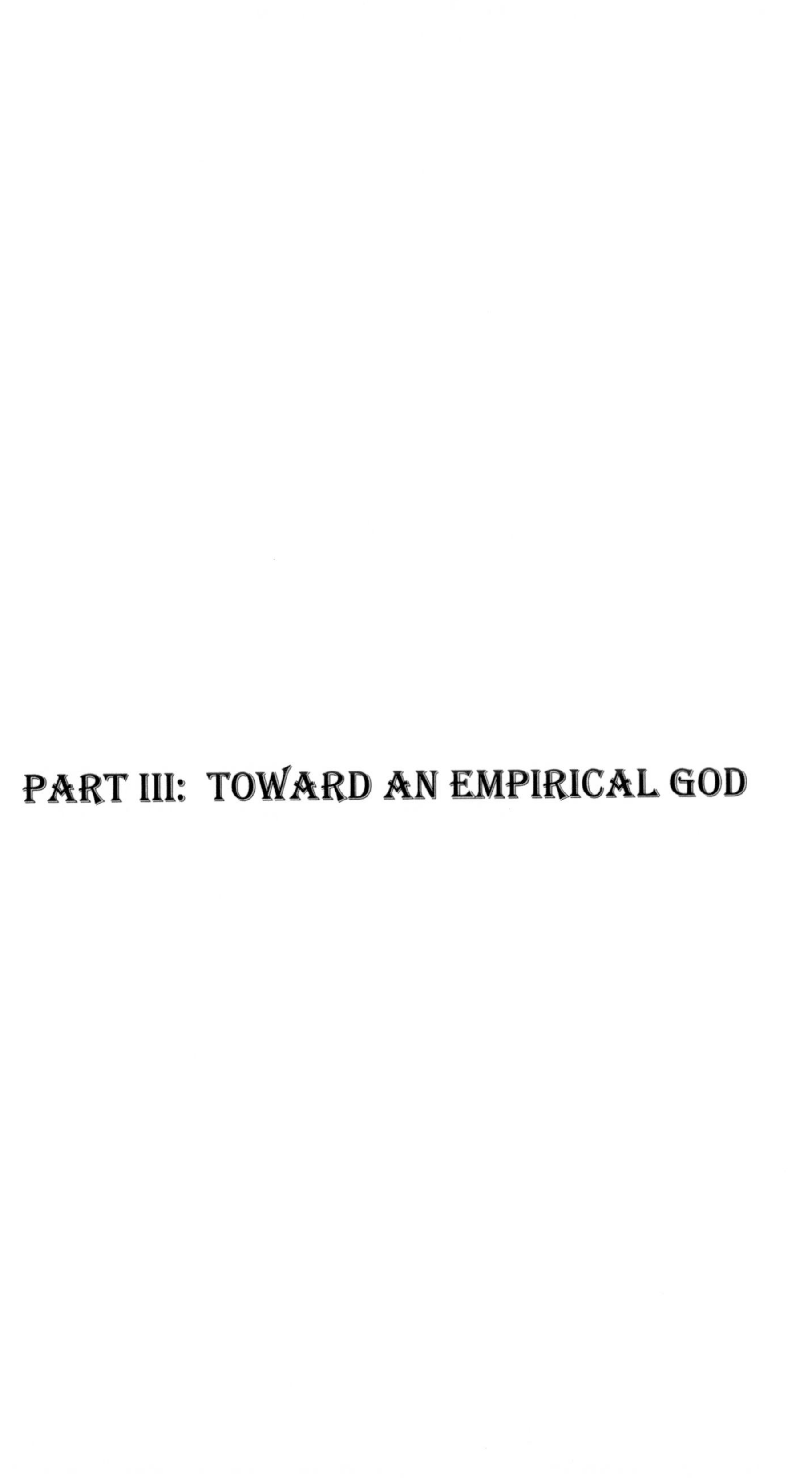

PART III: TOWARD AN EMPIRICAL GOD

Chapter 19: The Modern Quadrivium

Searching for a Common Vocabulary

Before we can speak realistically about reconciling science and religion, we find a vocabulary that both clerics and scientists are comfortable with. This is not easy, since science and religion have largely been mutually exclusive for much of the last 2500 years. The concept of faith-based religion is not familiar to scientists anymore than an empirical proof of God's existence would be familiar to clergy. It is as if these two camps spoke completely different languages. A new type of discussion about God and Creation in the universal terms of music and mathematics requires an interdisciplinary approach with a basic lexicon of related terms. The following equivalencies should make sense to anyone who has read this text:

SCIENCE	RELIGION
Big Bang	"Let There Be Light"
cooling after Big Bang	*Tikun* (Reordering)
4 phases of matter	4 Wheels of Ezekiel; 4 Rivers of Eden
4 phases of matter	4 primordial elements
frequency and wavelength	running and returning
$E=mc^2$	*YHVH*
rainbow principle	The Living God
spectrum	Holy Ghost
harmonic series	Blueprint of Creation
harmonic series	Clock of Heaven; Ten Sefirot of Nothingness
Superstrings	*ousia; pnimiyut;spanda*
Quadrivium	Divine Law
light and sound	Hand of God
symmetry	duality
unconscious mind	soul
hypnagogic state	*Tardemah* (deep meditation)
hypnagogic state	Praying like the Prophets
hypnagogic state	7 circuits around the sacred cube
time dilation (time travel)	*Moksha* (liberation)
evolution	reincarnation
Precession of the Equinox	Path to Heaven: Jacob's Ladder
musical diesis or comma	the Gates of Heaven & Hell

In an effort to construct a language of inclusion for anyone with an interest in either science or religion, this is a lexicon of significant terms, one or the other of which should hold meaning for scientists, monotheists, polytheists, agnostics, atheists, etc.. After our struggle with words, the next step would be to attempt a narrative that utilizes this vocabulary without abandoning the basic tenets of science as empirical, nor religion as theological. We proceed on the assumption that there has been a parallel development of terminology within both fields that can be mapped into an interdisciplinary approach. The ambiguity of language and the existence of cultural taboos and religious norms are like land mines that threaten to disrupt communication at every turn — so — if clergy is willing to look to mathematics and music to resolve any ambiguities, they should find theological solutions within religion's structural framework. Putting a rabbi, a priest, an imam, and a scientist together on a street corner might be a good setting for a joke, but it is doubtful that there would ever be any meeting of the minds. To earn a seat at the peace table between science and interfaith religion, a non-dogmatic open mind with mutual respect for opposing perspectives is a prerequisite.

To suggest that one religious doctrine might be closer to the truth than another can be very unproductive. If the *Sefer Yetzirah* was actually written by the man that we have come to know as Abraham — and, if I am correct in my interpretation of this ancient and holy text as the scientific framework of religion — then the details should easily stand up to the scrutiny of the best and most learned Jewish, Christian, Islamic, and scientific minds. The real enemies here are ignorance and the tendency to cling to nonscientific dogma. Only Abraham's science of religion is qualified to be the arbiter of which dogma passes science's litmus test. Abraham's writings can do the heavy lifting of bringing the world together in peace, but we must allow its meaning to resonate throughout the world. Each of us must be prepared to adjust long held positions for the sake of truth and peace. The Bible has never fulfilled its promise of peace. Perhaps, the Bible's instruction manual — the *Sefer Yetzirah* — will help civilization bring that promise to fruition.

Developing an Interdisciplinary Narrative

The Divine Light of the Monad can be defined by the primordial superstring that existed before time and space, as what Aristotle called "the Unmoved Mover." Once the Divine Light extended into "Ten Utterances" during the Big Bang, time and space were created, and the vibratory "substance of God" (Hebrew: *pnimiyut;* Greek: *ousia*) gradually acquired matter as a result of the cooling and reordering (*Tikun*) of matter and energy that occurred after the Big Bang. Modern science has hypothesized the details of the Creation time line (see Figure 95).

As the Ice Age came to a close, early modern humans emerged from their caves, and constructed archeoastronomical devices. Aryan astronomers became the first to peer into the heavens, where they noticed cyclical patterns among the sun, moon, planets, and stars. They used these periodic cycles to tell time even before the Neolithic Period began. The Aryan pre-Sumerian culture had been studying the heavens for thousands of years, and they passed their abundant knowledge of time, astronomy, and mathematics to the Sumerians and Babylonians. This knowledge culminated in the discovery of the clock as a harmonic series of integers 1 to 12, linking the microcosm of the daily clock to the macrocosm of the heavenly clock through careful observation of the Precession of the Equinox. We might say that this scientific observation marked the birth of religion.

The theory of vibrating strings, as part of the ancient Quadrivium, was well known in ancient Sumer, Babylon, and Egypt. However, the man that we have come to call Abraham, recognized an organizing "rainbow principle" that integrated sound and color into a Unity that he labeled the *Living God.* Based on the *Sefer Yetzirah*'s mathematics, one can conclude that Abraham saw the perfection of a rainbow through the prism of a raindrop, or perhaps in the mist after a storm. He observed that a single complex light source created a rich diversity of colors. Guided by his observations of light, Abraham's recognition of a transcendent mathematical "Blueprint of Creation" could be directly calculated from experiments on a single stringed instrument known as a monochord. A monochord is like a violin or cello, but with only one string. Underneath that string is a ruler that can measure string length precisely. This enabled Abraham to measure the integer ratios that produced different musical tones.

Abraham's experimentation and observations revealed that the complex "rainbow of light" that he called the *Living God,* also described the inner structure of sound, in a similarly complex "rainbow of sound." His realization that this "rainbow principle"of sound and light was the "Hand of God" — the manifestation of a transcendent *God* that could be described by a simple mathematical structure: counting. Abraham's conclusions could only have been reached through experimentation and through observations of natural phenomena. But, because light was difficult to measure with precision, he became more of a musician than an astronomer.

Abraham integrated the 6 numbered lights and sounds into a 7th, all-inclusive "White Light of God." The Bible presents us with allegory that encrypts Abraham's "science of the Living God" as the chiastic structure of the "7 lights on the Temple Menorah," and with this template shapes all Biblical allegory. In Part II, we discussed how "Lighting the Temple Menorah" can be understood as metaphor for a High Priest's pronunciation of the Word of God, *Yahweh.* And, how this pronunciation is not verbal one, but rather, a mental articulation intended to master the primordial elements within us.

Philo states that Plato got his metaphysics from the Torah. This can be corroborated by the fact that Plato's construction of the World Soul in the Timaeus is mathematically identical to Abraham's construction of the soul within the *Sefer Yetzirah*.[329] Abraham's tonecircle version of this construction also became the mathematical model for Isaac Newton, who correlated colors and planets with the Phrygian mode (Figures 91a & b) as derived from Pythagorean Tuning (Log $2^p 3^q$). However, indigo is often considered a shade of violet, since it overlaps indigo's wavelength, and it is often omitted from modern versions of Newton's ROY G. BIV schematic.[330] Abraham's 7th color was white, the color of transcendent unification.

Figure 91a & b - Isaac Newton's Color Wheel

Color	Nanometers
red	620-750 nm
orange	590-620 nm
yellow	570-590 nm
green	495-570 nm
blue	450-495 nm
violet	380–450 nm
indigo	420-450 nm

Abraham unified the duality of spiritual and material Creation by defining 4 primordial elements within the 10 dimensions and 7 Lights of God. Einstein's famous equation unified the duality of matter and energy, while Superstring theory unified the following four forces of nature within 10 dimensions:

- Gravitational Force - The "m" in $E=mc^2$ stands for mass, which is commonly understood as weight. Gravity is the attractive force between material objects with mass.
- Electromagnetic Force - Defines the structure of light and sound as part of a larger spectrum of wave energy that interlocks an electrical oscillating wave with a magnetic oscillating wave, binding electrons to an atom's nucleus.
- Strong Force - The "glue" that holds the nucleus of an atom together
- Weak Force - The heaviest elements on earth decompose by radioactive decay into lighter more stable elements.

329 For a side-by-side comparison of these two mathematical constructions refer to: Schatz, *The Lost Word of God*, 156 -161.
330 ROY G. BIV is a well known acronym for Newton's spectrum: red, orange, yellow, green, blue, indigo, and violet.

Einstein worked unsuccesfully on the unified field theory for the last 35 years of his life. A comprehensive framework for the four forces of nature was finally discovered in 1984 by John Schwarz and Michael Green, 29 years after Einstein's death. These four forces were "tied together" by a string — Abraham's vibrating harmonic string — the unseen vibrating essence of every atom on the Periodic Table of Elements. Modern "Superstring Theory" describes the deep structure for all matter and energy in the universe. Whether light, sound, electricity, the gravitational pull of material objects, the "glue" that binds an atomic nucleus together,... each of these forces is analogous to different wave-particles vibrating as different quantum number "harmonics" within a vibrating superstring.

When a man's vocal chords vibrate according to the principles of string theory, and two people sing the same note, we can still differentiate between their voices, because the relative loudness (amplitude) of each harmonic is different for each person. Some people have long vocal chords, fat vocal chords, a thicker neck, etc. Each factor contributes to the overall sound quality. When someone sings, they are singing the "white light" of a complex natural sound. If that complex tone is then put through a harmonic analyzer, a unique voice print would be capable of identifying an individual, just as a fingerprint would.

The harmonic series also structures the vibrations of the spinal chord within the medium of electricity. Like the uniqueness of a man's voice, the unique "Temple Menorah" of a man's soul is rooted within the electrophysiology of the spine and nervous system. Once we leave the more human scale of electromagnetic vibrations and enter the tiny but powerful vibrations of the quantum world, every atom on the periodic table of elements could be considered a miniature, but perfectly complete, "White Light of God." Within the framework of superstring theory, every sub-atomic particle, whether electrons, neutrons, protons, gravitons,... looks like a particle up close, but from a distance, it looks like a wave. This wave-particle duality of an atom is organized by spherical harmonics. Differences between the elements can be defined by its unique spectral signature, which is analogous to a voice print.

The harmonic series provides a comprehensive framework for a theory of everything within Abraham's time and within modern times. The harmonic series defines the objective, empirical truth that defines the God of Abraham. Leading Superstring physicists suggest that we are on the cusp of empirically proving that Superstring Theory describes the theory of everything. Abraham began with the objective truth of a harmonic series as the lynchpin of Divine Law. He borrowed these ideas from the sexagesimal clock of his polytheistic ancestors. But, Abraham authoritatively tied the harmonic series to nature, observing that the rainbow structure of sound and light was based on the mathematics of simple counting.

The "Voice" of God's "Ten Utterances" that emanated Divine Light in the first step of Creation was an empirical phenomenon known as the harmonic series. However, during the second step of Creation (*Tikun* or reordering), Abraham's mathematical speculation might appear simplistic from a modern scientific perspective. Abraham's "2nd Step" theology is based on functional subsets of the harmonic series that Abraham ascribes to God's construction of the Soul; another was used to construct the Body; and a third subset construct describes the mathematical model for the Soul's liberation from the Body. Powers of 2 formed the primordial element Earth used to construct the Body that contained man's Soul; Powers of 3 formed the element Water to begin construction of the Soul that was contained by the Body; Powers of 5 formed Wind, that would empower man to "rise up on wings" and liberate one's Soul from the Body. Powers of 7 formed the element Fire, which was used to purge the Body of any impurities, and sanctify our extended Soul's knowledge of Good and Evil, by raising man's vibration to the level of "Holy Ground" or "Walking with God."

Abraham's concept of a monotheistic God was based on the number 1, i.e., the "Big One," an all-inclusive Monad that contains the harmonic series within Base-10. Music theory dictates that it takes a new prime number to generate a new musical tone, thus Abraham realized the power of the first four prime numbers: 2, 3, 5 and 7 within Base-10. He harmonized powers of 2 and 3 (Earth and Water) to create the Soul. He harmonized powers of 2, 3 and 5 to construct man's Body from Earth, Water, and Wind. And finally, he harmonized powers of 2, 3, 5 and 7 (Earth, Water, Wind, and Fire) to explain how a man's Soul can be liberated from the Body in the manner of the Aryan fathers. Abraham's simple integer constructions subsequently shaped all Biblical allegory.

Science or Superstition?

In the second step of Creation, Abraham "reordered" the harmonic series into the primordial elements of the body and soul, and mathematically explained how to extract the soul from the body. We should not be too quick to denigrate his approach as primitive. We should not forget that he was 4000 years ahead of his time with respect to recognizing the harmonic series as the theory of everything. In addition, he thought of the universe in terms of 10 dimensions, rather than the four dimensions of length, width, depth, and time that we are generally familiar with today. And,... it turns out that the mathematics of Superstring Theory — and a later derivative called M-Theory — only seems to work in 10 or 11 dimensions, rather than the four we just mentioned. Modern science is hard at work trying to understand these hidden dimensions. Abraham too, spent much time on explaining these esoteric dimensions. I have faith that whatever modern science discovers regarding these hidden mathematically abstract dimensions, will not conflict in any way with Abrahamic thought.

About 1,400 years after the time of Abraham, Plato describes identical acoustical constructions that have often been associated with Pythagoras.[331] These constructions defined a "Music of the Spheres" that linked vibrations within the "7 spheres" of the soul to the macrocosm of the seven planets and the twelve constellations. Unfortunately, academic texts describing the Music of the Spheres omit most, if not all, of the mathematical detail. In addition, Christianity has struggled mightily in the name of fighting heresy to detach the Bible from any Greek philosophical or mathematical concepts. By demonstrating exactly how Abraham and Plato defined the soul using an identical mathematical construction, the Christian point becomes moot.[332]

About 3500 years after Abraham, and some 2000 years after Pythagoras, the first corroboration came from the modern scientific community, when Johannes Kepler (1571-1630) "discovered his famous laws of planetary motion, in which integer ratios held between the length of each planet's year and its distance from the sun."[333] Since the time of Kepler, however, astrology and astronomy have gone their separate ways. Modern astronomy is no longer governed by the stars, and the importance of integer ratios had largely lost its appeal, that is, until the 1950's, when it was shown that "the hadrons, strongly interacting particles, are also quantum manifestations of this Pythagorean [or rather, Abrahamic] ideal."[334]

Finally, in 1984, unit multiples deriving harmonic waves, emerged within the scientific community as the "deep structure" of nature's framework, and the organizing design principle of Creation. This discovery suggests that the century old debate about Intelligent Design needs to be revisited. Abraham's text clarifies the debate between Creationists and Evolutionists, because it defines Intelligent Design as a mathematical formula — the harmonic series defines the substance of God and the essence of Creation — while evolution takes care of the rest. They are not in conflict because they are two sides of the same coin. The 6000 year "age of the universe" also enters into this debate. The number originally comes from Abraham's text, where it is explained as Creation's upper limit to the 231 Gates of Heaven. But, it was defined as a logarithmic number, not a linear number. (See Figure 98a - bottom right; the upper limit of 231 Gates).

331 McClain, Op. Cit., *The Pythagorean Plato*, 3.
332 Schatz, Op. Cit., 156 - 161; Plato's *Timaeus* defines the World Soul, and Abraham's *Sefer Yetzirah* defines Supernal Man by "cross-cutting" powers of 2 and 3 with means inserted (see Figure 42b) .
333 F. David Peat, *Superstrings and the Search for the Theory of Everything* (Chicago: Contemporary Books, 1988), 53.
334 Peat, 53.

The Grand Design

To explain God's light in scientific terms, it is best to begin with the nature of light itself. In 1666, Newton refracted sunlight through a triangular glass prism onto a white screen and he did not get the single spot of light that he had expected. Instead, the light was spread out in a band of colors: red, orange, yellow, green, blue and violet. It is interesting that this hidden band of inner components received the name "spectrum," which derives from the Latin term for "ghost." Newton's discovery provides an interesting perspective to the Biblical story that a rainbow is God's signature on His Covenant with Noah. Abraham's mathematical observations of sound, light, and cosmology, would finally be reflected (thousands of years later) in the work of Nicole Oresme, a 14th century Frenchman; and Joseph Saveur, a 17th century Frenchman.

In the twentieth century, the physics of the very large (relativity) and the physics of the very small (quantum mechanics) could never be reconciled. In the last 30 years of his life, Einstein set out to define a "unified field theory" that would describe a comprehensive mathematics tying together all four forces of nature: gravity, electromagnetism, and the strong and weak forces of the atom. He intuitively believed in a set of natural global laws that were capable of reconciling these bookends of twentieth century physics, but after 30 years of trying, he was unsuccessful.

Abraham was correct in his belief that the most universal of all mathematical and physical laws could be explored by using sound. Within Abraham's cosmology and cosmogony, God's Utterances were reorganized into musical tones, progressions of musical intervals, and finally, into musical scales that defined Creation. The sound of God's "Voice" was a harmonic series. Each of the prime number "Utterances" less than 10 described a series of musical intervals that became Abraham's "building blocks" of Creation, namely: Earth: a musical octave, Water: a musical fifth, Wind: a musical third, and Fire: a musical seventh.

These four elements were then combined into increasingly complex musical scales that became the vibrational essence of different classes of objects and beings in Creation. The more etherial elements were closer to God, while Earth, the most dense of the four elements, would be the furthest away from God. Earth obscured divine light and weighed down the spirit with ignorance and dullness. Fire rises up toward God like prayer, forming the Heavens; while water flows downward and forward, like time and God's blessings. Wind was the Breath of God that arbitrates between Fire and Water, transforming a mundane creature into its immortal essence. Of course, this sounds like primitive science by today's standards, but we must keep in mind that the concept of matter's vibrational essence was not successfully described in mathematical terms until 1984. In 1984, John Schwarz, from the California Institute of Technology, and Michael Green from Queen Mary College at the University of London finally figured out the mathematics that "ties it all together." The result of their efforts, called superstring theory, has emerged over the last 28 years as the most viable candidate for a "theory of everything" (TOE). As it turns out, the key to Green and Schwarz's mathematics is the same theory of vibrating strings recognized by Abraham: the harmonic series.

Particles & Fields

> *A new concept appears in physics, the most important invention since Newton's time: the field. It needed great scientific imagination to realize that it is not the charges or the particles but the field in space between the charges and the particles which is essential for the description of physical phenomena. - Einstein*[335]

Newton's concept of light as particles, which he called "corpuscles," did not account for why the bands of light within the spectrum didn't collide, nor why each color refracted differently. A few years later, a Dutch physicist named Christian Huygens was able to explain the refraction phenomenon by proposing that light was made of little waves rather than corpuscles, with each different-color wave having a different wavelength.[336] For hundreds of years Newton's "mechanical" view dominated physics; however, it eventually became clear that Newton's "particles" did not sufficiently explain new insights into electrical and optical phenomena, and Newton's view needed to be revised.

This revision marked the birth of modern physics.[337] It began in the 1860s, when Michael Faraday worked out the lines of force around a magnet. James Clerk Maxwell then "evolved a set of four simple equations that, among them, described almost all phenomena involving electricity and magnetism. These equations, advanced in 1864, not only described the interrelationship of the phenomena of electricity and magnetism, but showed that the two could not be separated."[338] Magnetism was inseparably intertwined with electricity as two waveforms that continually radiated outward at 90° to one another, and that this outward radiation defined a single electromagnetic field. He also determined that visible light was an electromagnetic radiation, and that there were different types of electromagnetic radiations with either

335 Albert Einstein and Leopold Infeld, *The Evolution of Physics* (New York: Simon & Schuster, 1938), 244.
336 Isaac Asimov, *Asimov's Guide to Science*, (New York: Basic Books, 1972), 340.
337 Einstein and Infield, 125.
338 Asimov, 346-7.

shorter or longer wavelengths. "The formulation of these equations is the most important event in physics since Newton's time… because they form a pattern for a new type of law…laws representing the structure of the field."[339]

The particle view, however, was certainly not dead. It took a major step forward in 1871, when Dmitri Mendeleev was able to recognize different patterns within the chemical elements. This allowed him to organize the elements into different groupings and he is credited with creating the Periodic Table of Elements. Mendeleev didn't understand the underlying reason for these patterns, but his table proved accurate. The periodic table had gaps that were later filled by newly discovered elements toward the end of the century, underscoring the accuracy of his groupings. In is interesting to note that the periodic table's grouping into metals reflects the ancient element of earth (solids), while its other main grouping, gases, reflect different states of the other three ancient elements: requiring the element of fire (plasma) to heat water (liquid) to get air (gas); indicating that the ancient designations may have been primitive, but they were accurate reflections of the physical world.

In 1900, Max Planck may have been the first to formulate a synthesis between particle theory and field theory. He continued Maxwell's exploration of light's inner structure by describing light "particles" as electromagnetic, massless, discrete packets of energy, called photons, which are released or absorbed by electrons. Each packet of energy contained a discrete quantity of energy, and quantum theory was born. "Plank argued that radiation could be absorbed only in whole numbers of quanta."[340] Could it be that the "integer multiples" that characterize the harmonic series manifests once again as a phenomenon of nature even at the sub-atomic level? It appears so, since Planck goes on to describe light as electromagnetic waves, despite their particle-like characteristics. His theory describes wave-like properties that make particles look more like vibrations than well-defined points in space. "Planck and Einstein had related energy to the frequency of waves."[341]

The differences between particles and waves were irrevocably blurred by Einstein's famous equation: $E = mc^2$. In 1905, Einstein hypothesized the basic interchangeability between matter and energy. A very tiny amount of matter could be transformed into enormously high energies and back again. This implied that particles could be described in terms of the wave, i.e., the field, or vice versa.

"Mendeleev's 'periodic table' (so-called because it showed the periodic recurrence of similar chemical properties)…", could not explain how increasing atomic weights resulted in recurring patterns of chemical properties because those were determined by the varying number of electrons in the element's outer

339 Einstein and Infield, 143.
340 Asimov, 352.
341 Brian Greene, The Elegant universe (New York: Random House, 1999), 104.

orbit.[342] But this underlying reason for Mendeleev's groupings "came some half a century later [in 1913] as the structure of atoms was untangled. Niels Bohr discovered that in going from atom to atom – starting with hydrogen, which has one electron around the central nucleus, and building up the various elements by adding electrons – a repeating pattern was formed."[343] From that pattern he developed a progressive model of atomic structure that depicted electrons orbiting its nucleus in different "shells" or orbits. Electrons appeared to move between "inner" or "outer" orbits, depending on whether specific wavelengths of radiation were absorbed or emitted.[344]

In 1923, Louis de Broglie "suggested that the wave-particle duality applied not only to light but to matter as well."[345] He predicted that an electron's wavelength would be inversely proportional to its momentum (mass * velocity). De Broglie's prediction would give electrons of moderate speed (i.e., frequency) a wavelength in the range of x-rays.[346] He was proven right in 1927. When de Broglie incorporated the concept of mass into the acoustical reciprocity of wavelength and frequency, he was essentially explaining the mechanism of how God's harmonic Utterances "descended into matter." Today's search for the God particle, the Higgs boson, is a search for the "background realm" where all matter acquires mass, and within which, all beings and things manifest. Within Abrahamic thought, this is analogous to the 2:1 octave double allegorized as the Torah's Heavenly Firmament.

In 1926, Erwin Schrödinger developed a mathematical description of the atom called either wave or quantum mechanics. He started by investigating the behavior of electrons as the standing waves so familiar to acousticians. He then expanded on quantum theory, by working out a mathematical system in which very small particles and forces interacted. "Schrödinger's wave equation, for example, is a differential equation, relating what is happening at one point to what happens at another point an infinitesimally short distance away."[347] The solution to Schrödinger's differential equation describing this phenomenon is called the wave function, which defines the wave at each infinitesimal point in space and instant of time. This quantified wave perspective replaced Niels Bohr's particle view of electrons orbiting like a planet around the sun. Schrodinger's electron wave was a "smeared out" orbital path around the nucleus (Figure 93b), in which "part of it is here, and part of it is there."[348] Within this extended wave, it would prove to be impossible to take a snapshot of the electron's particle-like location.

"Werner Heisenberg had presented his own model of the atom. He had abandoned all attempts to picture the atom as composed either of particles or

342 Asimov, 231.
343 Peat, 80.
344 Peat, 80.
345 Greene, 103.
346 Asimov, 370.
347 Peat, 21.
348 Greene, 105.

waves."[349] His method of "matrix mechanics" described the various energy levels of different electron orbits. In an effort to pinpoint the location of electrons, he developed his uncertainty principle. Heisenberg showed that there was no way of determining both the position of a subatomic particle and its motion at the same time. He won the Nobel Prize in 1932 for his efforts.[350]

Some believe that the uncertainty principle has shaken man's sure-footedness with respect to cause and effect, impacting his natural inclination to locate and touch what he believes to be an object. At first, the electron appears to us to be a point particle when viewed from a great distance (which is equivalent to viewing it at low energies), but it proves to be elusive when viewed up close (at high energies), when it turns into an extended object, i.e., a wave.[351] In a very literal way, the Heisenberg principle acknowledges modern man's difficulty in relating to God as an object that can't be touched or seen, but exists nonetheless.

Our ability to peer inside the atom to actually see a vibrating Superstring that is the source of all energy and matter is analogous to seeing God. To make any headway at all requires linear accelerators, cyclotrons, synchrotrons, colliders, and supercolliders, etc. These devices accelerate subatomic particles to higher and higher energies. An increase in energy translates to an increase in speed or frequency. Since we know that any increase in frequency implies a corresponding decrease in wavelength, we can expect that smaller and smaller wavelengths will require proportionally higher energies to probe smaller and smaller structures. This is because we need tiny wavelengths to explore all the nooks and crannies of a particle.[352]

When two high-energy particles are accelerated in opposite directions and then collide, a distribution of energy spectra is produced that enables us to identify the exact nature of the particles we are dealing with. Each subatomic wave-particle is analogous to a single color that gets added to the rainbow of "wave-particles" that define each particular element. In other words, each element's spectral signature is a unique combination of wave-particles that coalesce, like the colors of the rainbow, into a complex entity called the atom. The atom is therefore a prime example of unity from diversity, and each atom is like a little ball of white light or complex sound. The fact that each element's blend of "colors" is slightly different than the next, identifies and differentiates the elements from one another. By 1950, more than 200 subatomic particles had been discovered as short-lived resonances using these high-energy techniques.

If we can't locate an electron's position, perhaps we can approximate where it might be. In 1937, John Wheeler introduced a scattering matrix, or s-matrix, and his student Richard Feynman later refined his mentor's approach by introducing simple diagrams that, when taken together, add up to the total

349 Asimov, 378.
350 Asimov, 378.
351 Peat, 63.
352 Greene, 215.

interaction between particles. This series of complex approximations is called perturbation theory.[353] It is a statistical method that has proven very accurate and practical for approximating the infinite solutions to Schrödinger's wave functions and Heisenberg's matrix. An advance in field theory came two years after Schrödinger and Heisenberg developed quantum theory:

> Quantum field theory was generally the work of P. A. M. Dirac, who in 1927,... showed how the new quantum concepts could be extended from atoms to the electromagnetic field. This field was treated as an 'orchestra of oscillators.' Where conventional quantum theory produces a wave function corresponding to each particular oscillation, the field theory creates a sort of super wave function composed out of all possible oscillator wave functions.[354]

In other words, a quantum field is a harmonization of all discrete wave function equations, which is mathematically analogous to a harmonic series. Einstein was never able to foresee the comprehensive synthesis of superstrings over all matter and energy, but he did understand the key role of harmonics and classical string theory as it related to the inner workings of quantum mechanics, at least as early as 1938, when he teamed up with Leopold Infeld to write this passage from *The Evolution of Physics*:

> The atoms of every element are composed of elementary particles, the heavier constituting the nucleus, and the lighter the electrons. Such a system of particles behaves like a small acoustical instrument in which standing waves are produced.[355]

Global Laws of Quantization & Symmetry

Abraham's mathematics was the first to teach us that Divine Law was defined by quantization and symmetry. Abraham's concept of quantization taught us to count in unit multiples of a fundamental value by describing God's Ten Utterances as *Sefirot* (Hebrew: Counting). The second principle of Divine Law is its symmetry. Abraham "engraves" Creation from the reciprocity of frequency and wavelength within the ancient Quadrivium. In the earlier days of quantum theory, P.A.M. Dirac "had hypothesized on purely theoretical grounds that every particle has its corresponding antiparticle, with mirror-image properties..."[356] Today, we know this to be true. "Particle and

353 Peat, 38-39.
354 Peat, 304.
355 Einstein and Infield, 276.
356 Peat, 75.

antiparticle is a fundamental symmetry of physics."[357] These two principles — quantization and symmetry — are global laws of the harmonic series that define Creation and link the microcosm to the macrocosm.

We also know that when electrons move to higher or lower orbits within the atom, they absorb or emit discrete packets of radiation, which Max Planck first described as "particles," or "quanta" of light waves known as photons. It is these unit quanta of light that give quantum theory its name. Schrödinger's probabilistic solutions to locate the electron within higher or lower orbits occurs within the atom's grid of spherical harmonics. "The electron cannot have an arbitrary distribution in space when bound to the proton. If the distribution is to be stationary... the wave pattern must be a standing wave. This obliges the phase pattern of the electron to behave in a strictly ordered quantized fashion: the zones are separated by a whole number of meridians and parallels which form the nodes of a phase pattern... The resulting partitions of space are called spherical harmonics."[358] Quantization determines the whole-number multiples of meridians and parallels representing the possibilities of electron distribution across an atom's spherical surface.

"The spherical harmonics of an electron's orbit around its nucleus is analogous to the earth's orbit around the sun, i.e., its orbital spin.[359] There is also rotational spin around its axis, which, in the quantum world, can never be disentangled from its orbital spin.[360] Rotational spin in the quantum world, however, is not completely analogous to the earth spinning around its central axis. When a sub-atomic particle is viewed at low energies to make it appear like a point particle, there would be no other points next to it that could spin around a central axis.[361] That being said, "each particle is endowed with a property, called spin, which behaves like a rotation."[362]

When considering a particle's spin, there is exactly one other symmetry that many modern physicists believe exists — supersymmetry. Those particles with whole number spins are called *bosons,* corresponding to the forces of nature, such as; photons, gluons, gravitons, etc.. These spin at the integer multiples near and dear to Abraham's heart; 1, 2, 3, etc.. Although spin occurs in our space, supersymmetric spin occurs in an abstract mathematical dimension called isospin space. Here, another family of particles called fermions define all matter in the universe (electrons, protons, neutrons, mesons, etc.). Staying true to the global law of quantization, fermions also spin at unit multiples of a quantized value."The spin of a fermion is half an odd integer; ½, 3/2, 5/2,..."[363]

357 Peat,75.
358 Vincent Icke, The Force of Symmetry (Cambridge: Cambridge University Press, 1995), 151-2.
359 Greene, 170.
360 Icke, 136.
361 Greene, 170.
362 Icke, 137.
363 Icke, 145.

Supersymmetry is counter-intuitive partly because a boson in four dimensional space must rotate 360° to complete a full rotation, however, "a fermion does not produce an exact replica of itself after rotating 360°. Instead, it requires two full turns, 720°, to make a fermion identical to what it was before the rotation."[364]

It is an interesting coincidence to note that bosons and fermions, defining the forces of nature and matter, are defined by the parameters of spin (360°) and isospin (720°), respectively. In a manner of speaking, The Sumerians and Abraham both defined the physical world by spinning around an octave tone circle ratio of 360:720.[365] We may also recall that "Heaven and Hell" were created at Fire's higher energy level by the ratios within the octave double (360*7): (720*7) = 2520:5040.

Fermions, responsible for all matter in the universe, break down into quarks and leptons, while the known bosons, responsible for the four forces of nature, include: gravitons (accounting for gravity), photons (electromagnetism), gluons (strong force), and the Z^0, W^+, and W^- intermediate vector bosons (weak force). Supersymmetry states that "fermions and bosons could be transformed one into the other [as mirror images] and all particles could be gathered into a single great family."[366]

The Doctrine of Opposites and the Mean

Within Abraham and Plato's construction of the soul, we might recall that means were inserted between opposing powers of 2 and powers of 3. Similarly, when the body was constructed, powers of 3 and powers of 5 were also harmonized by inserting means. What would we be left with if we eliminated the mean between two opposing forces? Presumably, just the two opposing forces, with no way to reconcile them. However, what nature exhibits instead, is that the duality of opposing forces could be completely eliminated if we were somehow able to raise the energy level to recreate the conditions that existed immediately before and immediately after the Big Bang. For example, in both spin and isospin space, there is a basic two-valuedness of "up" or "down." The electron can be thought of as having a special spin in either one of these two directions. "Spin up would signify a proton and spin down a neutron."[367] "Heisenberg guessed that if the electromagnetic field could be mathematically switched off [which happens at high energies], then the proton could not be distinguished from the neutron."[368] At high energies, this type of nongender particle would be called a *nucleon* (neutron + proton), and mathematically expressed as "rota-

364 Icke, 141.

365 There are 360° in an octave tone circle of ratio 1:2 (in this case 360:720), and Abraham's divisions of the octave are described as integer ratios of frequency and wavelengths. But, we should keep in mind that his music theory derives from Sumerian and Babylonian geometry and astronomy.

366 Peat, 92-3.

367 Peat, 76-7; Of course, in isospin space "up" and "down" don't mean the same thing as in our space.

368 Peat, 76.

tionally symmetric," i.e., all spin directions would be equivalent.[369] Switching the electromagnetic field back on (which happens at low energies) clearly differentiates the proton from the neutron. In other words, the way to unite two apparently opposite wave particles, is to raise its energy level. Analogously, man raises his energy level in a very real way as he learns to transcend the world's dualities during the meditation process by uniting his internal energies.

Electromagnetism is now seen as a gauge field between two opposing electron properties (electricity and magnetism). Could it be that what is true for electromagnetism is also true for the strong and weak nuclear force, and even for the gravitational force? Are the four forces of nature simply on-off switches for local particle symmetries? "Whenever nature exhibits some form of global symmetry,... it is probably the result of a powerful local symmetry plus a gauge field."[370] Within the parlance of string theory, a gauge field effectively "harmonizes" wave-particles.

Einstein believed that underneath it all there was a unity to nature, and that different local symmetries could all be resolved by underlying global laws that would ultimately unify all force fields and particles. For example, without gravity tugging particles downward, who is to say which way is up? Similarly, without electromagnetism the particles become uniform; who could then tell which particle has a positive charge and which a negative? If the various gauge theories, such as gravity, the strong force, the weak force, and electromagnetism could be "turned off" and then "turned back on," like a mathematical light switch, then the unity of that symmetry group would be broken and we would suddenly know up from down, a positive charge from a negative charge, etc.

If we turn from the physics of the very small to the physics of the very large, Einstein's general theory of relativity shifts the study of electromagnetic and quantum waves to a larger scale, where large amounts of energy correspond to large masses, curving space-time itself. This curvature of space-time caused by the gravitational field around planets is analogous to the way a magnetic field can be delineated around magnets. Einstein and Infeld state, "Maxwell's equations are laws representing the structure of the field." When formulating his "general theory of relativity" Einstein was only generalizing Maxwell's field equations to include gravity. Einstein's gravitational field theory and Dirac's quantum field theory could both be considered logical extensions of Maxwell's original electromagnetic field theory equations.

Einstein's "special theory of relativity" implies that if an event (like an orbiting, spinning planet) and the event's observer are moving at different speeds, then as their speeds approach the speed of light, strange things happen as everything converges. The space coordinates can get mixed up with the time coordinates. Because of this confusion, it would be important to give space and time coordinates together, as a space-time continuum, when translating between the two different coordinate systems. Each coordinate system is

369 Icke, 192.
370 Peat, 85.

relative to its viewing perspective, and all local symmetries must be translated to global terms in an effort to find the invariant underlying global laws.[371]

Each side of the equation $E = mc^2$ creates a bookend that relates the distortion of the space-time fabric by objects approaching the speed of light (special relativity) — to the warping of the space-time fabric by large masses (general relativity). Like the ripples caused by a pebble thrown into a lake, Einstein's large-scale perspective enables scientists to follow the universe's acoustical trail backward in time, to about 13.7 billion years ago, by analyzing the faint background harmonics of the Big Bang. We converge on a point that could be called the primordial superstring of God's harmonic Utterances. All guage theories were switched off and all local symmetries were melded together in an intense caldron of heat and compression — the unrealized potential of Creation — an ultimate unification within the harmonic source of everything that Abraham called the unity of the Living God.

The Breaking of Symmetries

Scientists speculate that before the Big Bang, a state of supersymmetry existed, with no differentiation between bosons and fermions. Abraham's mathematical definition of God existed *ex nihilo* (Latin: out of nothing) before the Creation event took place. This is comparable to the state of undifferentiated symmetry that existed prior to the Big Bang. Abraham's account of Creation begins with his mathematical representation of God as the undifferentiated "One" or Monad. Abraham proceeds to describe Creation in terms of five acoustical events. The first of these events, on Day 1 of Creation, "Let there be Light" reveals the harmonic series that provides the "deep structure" of God and Creation. It "descends into matter" through a reciprocal arithmetic progression (see Figure 36). It should be easy to see that the initial expansion of Divine Light described in Figure 36 is essentially identical to what modern scientists call the "Big Bang." God's Ten Sefirot of Nothingness, like the Big Bang, emanated outward to fill and overflow all sacred cube containers, effectively "breaking each vessel" in turn,[372] until this expansion of Light reached the final sacred cube, at the hypothetical boundaries of the universe. After the high energies of Creation's Big Bang, expansion and cooling lowered energy levels, differentiating the various mathematical symmetries. One level after another, the cooling of these energies revealed the duality of matter at each successive layer, until the universe unfolded to its current state.

In four subsequent acoustical events, God's light descends into matter to define four distinct "worlds." Kabbalistic tradition calls this the "Breaking of the Vessels."

371 Peat, 105.

372 The Kabbalah of Isaac Luria ("The Ari") describes *Shevirat HaKelim* (Breaking of the Vessels) as loosely explained here. The Ari had somehow pieced together the meaning of Abraham's text, stripped of most mathematical detail, as *Tzimtzum* (contraction) of Divine Sparks, degree by degree.

Science calls it the breaking of symmetries — slightly different terms to define what is essentially the same process: the initial Big Bang expansion of a highly compactified primordial superstring within ten (or eleven) dimensions, followed by the breaking of four additional symmetries as a result of cooling after the initial expansion.

Abraham's mathematical description of the Heavenly Firmament (octave tone circle = 2:1) as the womb of Creation, has a modern analog in Schwarz and Green's mathematical description of the SO(32) symmetry, within the language of superstring theory:[373] God's unity gives way to the duality of local symmetries. Physicist David Peat gives us some sense of their breakthrough moment in overcoming the many scientific and mathematical hurdles:

> It became possible to create a superstring theory that had all the features physicists had been dreaming of. It was chiral, supersymmetric, and free of ghosts, tachyons, infinities, and anomalies. It accounted for the forces of nature and the symmetry patterns of the elementary particles. The theory of everything had been born.[374]

Supersymmetry was broken by cooling and expansion immediately after the Big Bang, exposing gravitons, bosons and fermions. In other words, fermions (all matter in the universe) and bosons (the four forces of the universe), can be considered opposing modes of vibration that exist on the same ten-dimensional superstring. Supersymmetry's gauge field is the gravitational field of the graviton (a massless, spin 2 vector boson). When cooling and expansion lowered the universe's energy level, supersymmetry's light switch turned on this gauge field — supergravity — exposing fermions and bosons as the basic duality of nature. This is how Abraham's metaphysical doctrine of "opposites and the mean" manifests as global law within the physical universe. After SO(32) was broken by further expansion and cooling, the next symmetry occurred at grand unification energies, SU(3) * SU(2) * U(1). Before hypothesizing superstrings, particle physicists touted the grand unified theory:

> The grand unified theory was supposed to be the great success of contemporary theoretical physics, the Holy Grail that would finally be grasped after decades of searching.[375]

Cooling and expansion of the universe lowers its energy level and turns on the local symmetry: the gauge field for grand unification — SU(3) * SU(2) * U(1) — and suddenly everything differentiates; the strong force that bind hadrons together

373 These different symmetries get their name from scientists who group elementary particles into various patterns of 3, 8, 10, etc. Each grouping of particles is characterized by mirror reflections within various types of space, such as three-dimensional space, space-time, isospin space, strangeness space, etc.
374 Peat, 119.
375 Peat, 97.

SU(3) as well as the opposing forces that characterize lepton interactions SU(2) * U(1). The various types of hadrons (like the proton and neutron) are bound together in the nucleus by a gauge field called the strong force SU(3), which is carried by gluons. Very high energy collisions of hadrons helped us to peer into their inner structure, suggesting a sort of internal "graininess" in which tiny internal gritty pieces were considered evidence of the elemental building block of hadrons, known as the quark.[376] Physicists developed the "standard model" of all matter in the universe as a view of grand unification energies with the local symmetries of quarks and leptons linked by the gauge fields: SU(3) * SU(2) * U(1).[377] Now that we understand grand unification in terms of its most elemental components: quarks and leptons, we also know that quarks and leptons are exposed as opposites once grand unification energy is turned on. Of course, this would have occurred before the formation of atoms and molecules. This is analogous to Day 3 of Creation.

With the advent of bigger accelerators in the 1960s, additional abstract mathematical symmetries helped organize the zoo of particles that had been discovered since the 1950s. This required more mathematical symmetry mirrors to be erected in abstract space. Principles of symmetry reveal properties that describe the structure of the underlying forces within these new particles. Additional symmetries enable particle theorists to organize particles into various families. For example, a threefold pattern of quark organization became known as color. The color symmetries were named *red, green*, or *blue.*[378] A six-quark symmetry was then developed called flavor: *up, down, top, bottom, strange* and *charmed.* Each of three colors of quark could come in six flavors creating the possibility of 18 different types of quark.

One second after the Big Bang (see Figure 95), the constant exchange of gluon particles bound the different types of quark together into more complex structures called *hadrons*. Meson hadron patterns are two-quark composites, while baryon hadron patterns are three-quark composites. Protons and neutrons, for example, are three-quark composites called baryons. A proton is usually composed of two up and one down quark, but other combinations are possible. A neutron can be composed of two down and one up quark. Based on quantum numbers, the permutations of combining three quarks enable creation of eightfold and tenfold patterns (Figure 92b) of resonances called *symmetry relationships*, which are then collected together to form the SU(3) symmetry group. After Supersymmetry and grand unification comes the strong force of SU(3), which is like Day 4 of Creation. Once it is turned on, the opposing quark characteristics are differentiated.

The eightfold pattern of hadron resonances is based on three types of quark with roughly the same smaller size mass, *up, down*, and *strange*.[379] The diagrams that follow are 4000 years apart, but they both correspond to a

376 Peat, 82.
377 Peat, 89-90.
378 Icke, 208.
379 Icke, 216.

three-fold pattern of symmetry to create a tenfold pattern of resonances. Like Mendeleev's periodic table, these patterns of resonance within the modern Quadrivium predicted missing elements.[380] In Figures 92a & b, and 93a & b, we can compare the ancient and modern patterns of resonances. Interactions between leptons (such as the electron), and between quarks and leptons, occur as the weak SU(2) and electroweak SU(2) * U(1) forces. The gauge field between leptons is the electromagnetic force U(1) carried by neutral, massless photons. The weak force that characterizes radioactive decay, SU(2), is carried by two gauge field vector bosons W+ and W-, as well as the neutral vector boson Z°.[381]

In Figure 95, the exposed hadrons formed nuclei, and ~300,000 years after the Big Bang (13.7 billion years ago), they interacted with leptons to form atoms, then molecules, and gradually, matter as we know it. Galaxies and solar systems were born about 700 million years after the Big Bang. The most primitive forms of life began 3.8 billion years ago, and fossilized worms date to 1.1 billion years ago.

Figure 92a & b – The Resonances of the Quadrivium[382]

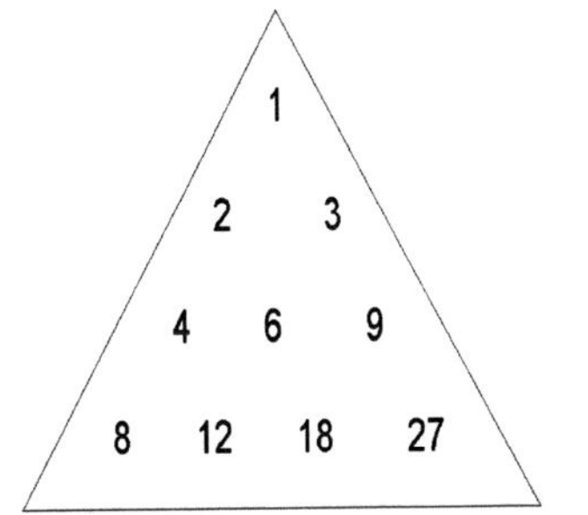

The Ancient Quadrivium - Ten member pattern of elementary resonances derived from three integers within a classical string

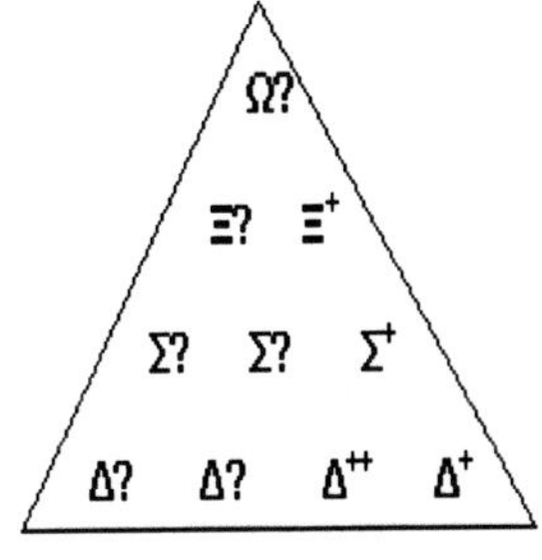

The Modern Quadrivium - Ten member pattern of elementary resonances derived from a three-fold pattern of up, down, and strange quarks within the hadron portion of a superstring.

Figure 93a - The "Wheels of Ezekiel"

Figure 93b - Sub-Atomic Wave-Particles

380 Peat, 78.
381 Peat, 89.
382 Peat, 79.

Superstring Theory & M-Theory

Despite 30 years of effort, Einstein could not come up with a viable unified field theory. Yoichiro Nambu's important pioneering work in the 1970s helped set the stage for success,[383] so that by 1984, Michael Green and John Schwarz could directly apply the theory of relativity and quantum mechanics to the classically vibrating string, and superstring theory was born.

The extra compactified dimensions within abstract mathematical space continues to be explored. Superstring theory has often been called the best hope for a "theory of everything" because it reconciles two of the greatest physics revolutions of the twentieth-century, quantum mechanics and general relativity: "That has been the problem of problems in physics... For some years, it's been clear that string theory does, in fact, give a logically consistent framework, encompassing both gravity and quantum mechanics."[384]

To incorporate both quantum mechanics and relativity, the classic Newtonian string must become a superstring by becoming both "relativistic" and "quantized." In order to get some insight into what is involved, we will start with Newton's classic formula for a vibrating string:

$$f = \frac{1}{2L}\sqrt{\frac{T}{m}}$$

Figure 94- Classic Newtonian String [385]

This formula relates the fundamental frequency *f*, the length of a string *L*, its mass *m*, and its tension *T*. In classical mechanics, we would write down the calculus describing the physical quantities of the oscillating string. These equations map each of the overtone waveforms in terms of their periodic trigonometric functions (sines and cosines) into the geometric coordinates of space-time. Solutions to these equations for any given instant would enable us to determine the velocity and location of any point on the string.

To get a very high level view of the mathematical rigor required to create a superstring, we would first need to transform our Newtonian string into a "relativistic string" with its highest energy wave functions moving at

---

383 Peat, 51.

384 P.C.W. Davies and J. Brown, eds., *Superstrings: A Theory of Everything* (Cambridge: Cambridge University Press, 1988), interview with John Ellis, 165; 97.

385 Peat, 53.

the speed of light. From the formula above we can determine that increasing the frequency of a vibrating string to the speed of light would have an inverse effect on wavelength, reducing it to approximately "Planck's length" of 10^{-32} cm. In order to travel at the speed of light as relativity requires, it must also be massless, while the tension on the string would be enormous: 10^{39} N. Even though the highest energy wave functions of a relativistic string would be massless, lower harmonics would decrease in tension and begin to pick up mass, until we reach the fundamental of the superstring, which would have the lowest frequency, largest wavelength, and would be the most massive wave-particle within any given element.

The next major step in creating a superstring would be to "quantize" this "relativistic string." Heisenberg's uncertainty principle requires that the terms representing the various wave functions be converted to quantum mechanical operators. These quantum operators become statistical and probabilistic determinants of what was previously a definitive process. The final step in creating a superstring requires us to ensure that the string's vibrations are supersymmetric and adhere to the correct particle symmetry groups, as previously discussed, to enable the mathematics to work out appropriately.[386]

After pointing out the similarities between the classical and quantum equations, Einstein and Infeld comment:

> Analogously, in the case of an electron, a certain function is determined for any point in space, and for any moment. We shall call this function the *probability wave*... It does not tell us the position and velocity of the electron at any moment because such a question has no sense in quantum physics. But it will tell us the probability of meeting the electron at a particular spot, or where we have the greatest chance of meeting an electron. The result does not refer to one, but many repeated measurements.[387]

The discrete "packets" of energy, or "quantum numbers" that define each of these different quantum states, give us the various wave resonances. The different masses that we created from the wave functions of a relativistic string now take on the different characteristic energies, quantum numbers, and symmetries associated with each of the subatomic wave-particles.

Princeton professor Ed Witten, touted as the new Einstein in a 1987 *New York times Magazine* article, believes that science will find a way to prove string theory correct within the next 100 years.[388] His description underscores

386 Peat, 109-110.
387 Einstein and Infield, 288-289.
388 K.C. Cole, "A Theory of Everything," *New York times Magazine*, October 18, 1987.

the importance of the harmonic series to the generation of matter within superstring theory. Witten's brief description of superstring theory echoes Einstein's previously quoted description of quantum waves as acoustical standing waves:

> In the case of a violin string, the different harmonics correspond to different sounds. In the case of a superstring, the different harmonics correspond to different elementary particles. The electron, graviton, the photon, the neutrino and all the others, are different harmonics of a fundamental string just as the different overtones of a violin string are different harmonics of one string.[389]

Referring to string theory's "long forgotten" roots, Witten states:

> String theory is a long forgotten theory that turns our current picture of the physical universe on its head... the most revolutionary idea in physics in more than half a century - as revolutionary as relativity; as revolutionary as quantum theory.[390]

"That silly little formula describing vibrating strings,"[391] as Witten put it, "organizes all matter and forces in the universe." Abraham used that "silly little formula" to define God. It also replaces the standard model of particle physics which accounts for only three out of four forces of nature – the strong force, the weak force, and the electromagnetic force — but did not include gravity until the abstract dimensions necessary for supergravity were borrowed from superstring theory. Superstring theory accounts for all four forces of nature.

Alternative Superstring Theories have presented themselves in recent years, and Superstring Theory has evolved into M-Brane Theory, suggesting that we may not really live in a universe, but rather, in a multi-verse in which each universe can been compared to a single slice of bread within a loaf. These "slices of bread," however, are really vibrating multidimensional membranes (3-Brane, 4-Brane,... thus M-Brane Theory). However, it includes the notion that an additional 11th dimension may unite them in an over-arching rainbow structure according to harmonic "first principles."

The *Sefer Yetzirah* encrypts the harmonic series in the holiest name of God, the Holy Tetragrammaton, which can now be understood as the organizing principle of Superstring and M-Brane Theory. Today's empirically minded naysayers are scientists who can't accept the inherent difficulties in devising appropriate experiments to prove them true, since they are unable to touch or see the proverbial stone cast into the lake. Perhaps we need to accept the fact that this stone sits at the bottom of this metaphorical lake and all we may ever able to see and study are

389 Davies and Brown, 93.
390 Cole.
391 Cole.

the "ripples" that travel away from its point of entry. The psychological blow of not being able to locate and touch an object was introduced by Heisenberg. After winning the Nobel prize for establishing uncertainty as a scientific principle, one would hope that the precedent has been set for mankind to reconsider the existence of God in terms of Superstring and M-Brane Theory's over-arching harmonic structure, and that God will one day be recognized in the common terms of the science of religion by both physicists and clergy. That will be a momentous day.

Science may never be able to view the tiny vibrating string at the core of every atom, because it exists at the unviewable size and impenetrable energies of Planck's length and mass (10^{-32}cm and 10^{27} GeV). Since the harmonic series is the heart of superstring mathematics, if scientists can understand the ripples at the surface of a lake, then there may be no need to look for the tossed stone lying at the bottom. Mathematics insists that it is there, but, until it is empirically proven, it remains a theory. Darwin's theory of evolution is still a theory, but the concensus among scientists suggests it is true. Superstring theory and M-theory is the cutting edge of theoretical physics, so it would not be accurate to dismiss it as philosophy. Nevertheless, the harmonic series is empirical fact, and Abraham's definition of God as a harmonic series puts monotheism on unshakeable scientific ground. The Sumerian Clock of Heaven originally defined polytheism in harmonic terms, but the sexual cult of Inanna that integrated divine energies and astrologically emanated those harmonic energies from Heaven to the Sumerian Kings was never transformed into a theory of everything until Abraham defined the *Living God.*

Figure 95 - Creation in Scientific Terms

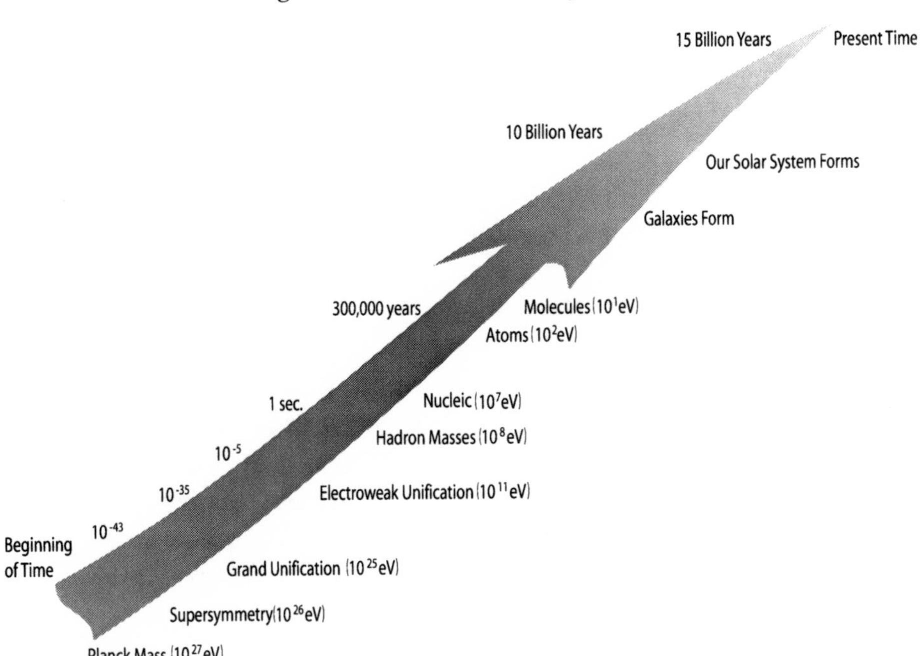

Chapter 20: Searching for a Common Truth

Creationism Versus Evolution

The science of religion can only be discovered through a classical Liberal Arts education. Liberal Arts includes the Quadrivium's four mathematical disciplines and the Trivium's three language disciplines. The Quadrivium dates back at least as far as Sumer (circa 3200 BCE). Sadly, a modern Liberal Arts curriculum is no longer rigorous enough to integrate our knowledge of these separate disciplines. An increased empiricism developed during the Age of Enlightenment, gave rise to a more specialized approach to knowledge.

A recent bumper crop of atheists with a narrow type of empirical mindset have written about religion as superstitious nonsense that has done more harm than good throughout history. Unfortunately, the behavior of religious zealots often lives up to these accusations. But, one man who is in a position to know better is biologist Richard Dawkins (author of *The God Delusion*). He has held the title of "Professor for the Public Understanding of Science" at Oxford. Dawkins is often considered the *de facto* leader of a group called the New Atheists. Ironically, they are also called the *Four Horsemen,* which includes: Dawkins, Sam Harris (*The End of Faith*), Daniel Dennet (*Darwin's Dangerous Idea*), and Christopher Hitchens (*God Is Not Great*). The focus of this New Atheism has been the century old debate between Creationists and Evolutionists that pits science against theology and rationalism against revelation. It is as if mankind were somehow forced to choose between science and religion. The choice is false. This old and heated debate is on-going only because, like most of the world, the New Atheists have no idea that a science of religion exists, and thus, they have passed judgement on religion as if they were experts.

From a Creationist's perspective, the beauty and functionality of a human organism is a masterwork of Intelligent Design that only God could have executed. Dawkins compares Creationism to a steep cliff, and compares natural selection to the other side of the mountain – an easily scalable, gradual slope of Evolution.[392] So, what constitutes the best example of Intelligent Design, scientific theories of Darwinian Evolution or religious theories about Creation. The debate is on-going because it summarizes the classic epistemological argument defining knowledge as the intersection of truth and belief. It remains an open debate because the two greatest forces shaping civilization — religion and science — have never had access to the knowledge that defines the common ground between them.

392 Richard Dawkins, *The God Delusion* (New York: Houghton Mifflin, 2006), 121-123.

Figure 96 - The kernel of truth that lay at the heart of all the various historical religions

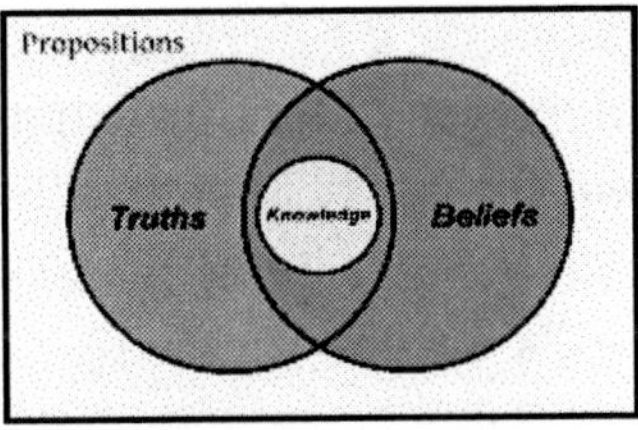

In *The God Delusion*, Dawkins paraphrases Darwin's own admission that "The creationists are right that, if a genuinely irreducible complexity could be properly demonstrated, it would wreck his [Darwin's] theory."[393] In other words, the scientific community maintains that everything is reducible to a gradual, step-by-step process — everything! Today, Darwin's influence has spread well beyond biology. A plausible, step-by-step evolutionary model has even been applied to the creation of matter. Figure 95 suggests a timeline for the evolution of quarks, leptons, hadrons, atoms, and molecules, fractions of a second after the Big Bang. It also includes a chronology for the evolution of planets, solar systems and galaxies. But, neither Creationists nor scientists have ever been able to come up with the "irreducible complexity" that Darwin could call God. This entire text has attempted to make the case that God is the harmonic series. Even before the primordial superstring gave birth to time, space, and matter, the harmonic series structured the complex singularity that gave rise to the Big Bang. Harmonic background radiation is an empirical fact that enables us to pinpoint Creation as a historical event. Once time and space were born, it is fair to impose the laws of Evolution. But, as long as the singularity containing the primordial superstring's harmonic series precedes the Creation of time and space, logically, it would also precede Evolution. Despite the fact that the harmonic series defines Darwin's dreaded irreducible complexity, his fears about the end of his theory are misplaced. The theory of Evolution remains securely intact.

Redefining Intelligent Design

Intelligent Design begins with first principles, namely: the harmonic series as the basis of superstring theory. Abraham's mathematics of the rainbow defined God as Darwin's irreducible complexity. The complex white light that comprises the Monad reveals its constituent colors when refracted through a prism, and reveals its constituent sounds when refracted through a harmonic analyzer. For example, there are degrees of loudness (amplitude) within the mathematical structure of sound that determines how a violin differs in sound quality (timbre) from a clarinet. Similarly, every atom on the periodic table can be understood as a holistic blending of rainbow-like wave-particles that reveals its harmonic structure when "refracted" through a supercollider. Each atom has its own spectral signature that uniquely

393 Dawkins, 125.

identifies it on the Periodic Table of Elements. Differences within wave-particles that are mathematically analogous to the amplitude of different harmonics define how the spectral signature of oxygen differs, for example, from that of helium.

What is most important for our redefinition, is an understanding of how the mathematics of the harmonic series translates across all mediums within the continuum of energy and matter, including: gravity, electromagnetic waves, and the strong and weak forces of the atom. This "common thread" runs through all of Creation to define the God of Abraham. Thus, the great patriarch of monotheism originally defined God in the mathematically valid terms of Intelligent Design.

Stephen Hawking's new book about M-Theory suggests that science's "theory of everything" does not require God. Since scientists and atheists can't really prove that God doesn't exist, Hawkings' new book opts for demonstrating that God is simply unnecessary to complete nature's equations. However, by understanding the science of religion we are in a position to say that M-Theory, and its predecessor: Superstring Theory, and <u>its</u> predecessor: the God of Abraham, all require a harmonic series to define what Euclid called "first principles," a basic foundational proposition or assumption that cannot be deduced from any other proposition or assumption. So, Hawkings is quite correct that God is not necessary to define superstring theory, however, he could not know that the God of Abraham was simply the earliest name for a theory of everything based on the harmonic series.

During the last 28 years, the harmonic series has taken center stage, defining the first principles of both Superstring Theory and M-Theory. Our survey of history explains how the harmonic series describes the shared common ground between polytheism and monotheism. Man had been liberating his Soul since the Ice Age, and he began searching for that Soul in the Heavens immediately after the Ice Age. These explorations evolved into the exact sciences of antiquity, so it is ironic that God has become the target of scientists who argue for the end of religion.

We must consider the possibility that the Bible was created in order to bring Abraham's scientific treatise to the masses. Unfortunately, its parables and allegories have been interpreted literally throughout history. I am convinced that they were intended as an accessible way to grasp the profundity of Abraham's scientific and theological conception. It is not enough to use Scripture in support of a subjective position. Abraham attempted to explain God as an objective reality that transcends individual points of view. The Torah was written in order to describe "the objective truth about God" — what Princeton professor Ed Witten calls that "silly little formula" describing the harmonic series. The harmonic series defines more than just common ground between science and religion, it defines empirical common ground. It is a firm foundation on which to build world peace. The harmonic series is revolutionizing modern physics, and my profound hope for mankind is that it will revolutionize religion before religious martyrdom initiates a self-fulfilling prophecy of destruction.

Conclusion

This text has explored a history of the science of religion from its prehistoric origins to the present day. The scientific evidence suggests that Early Modern Humans migrated out of Africa due to cataclysmic climate changes kicked off by the last Ice Age. EMH then sought refuge in Middle Eastern caves. The underlying speculation here suggests that to cope with the brutality of everyday survival and the harsh constraints of cave life during the perpetual winter of glacial periods, EMH found solace in meditation. By exploring the inner recesses of their own mind, mankind evolved dramatically for anywhere from 20,000 to 50,000 years, transforming themselves from primitive caveman to the sophisticated civilizations of Sumer, Egypt and Harappa.

After the last glaciers melted, EMH left their caves and their gaze gradually turned outward toward the heavens. The first science appears to have been astronomy, followed by arithmetic, geometry, and music (i.e., the integer ratios that define the structure of sound). The invention of a sexagesimal clock was followed by the discovery that the clock's 12 integer ratios could also be found in a distant but parallel realm which they imagined to be the abode of their liberated soul. The priestly astronomers had discovered Heaven, and this marked the birth of religion. The first gods to reach Heaven were thought to have perfected their meditation in caves. The oldest extant Indo-Aryan text, the *Rig Veda*, suggests that Yama was the first man to "cross-over" to life as an immortal god.

Understanding polytheistic gods and monotheism's God requires more than just knowledge of the separate mathematical disciplines in the Quadrivium. Understanding divinity begins with knowledge of how the harmonic series integrates the Quadrivium's disciplines into the Blueprint of Creation. But, even great knowledge does not equate to wisdom. If modern civilization hopes to recapture the knowledge and wisdom of ancient religious texts then we must follow in the footsteps of the Aryan founders of civilization and learn how to optimally utilize our brain. In short, we must strengthen our limbic system through meditation. This practice will give us direct access to the source of all Biblical metaphor: the "wellspring of prophecy," the "elixir of life," the "fountain of youth," "the anointing of kings," a "baptism of the spirit," the "eternal priesthood," etc..

We must learn how to "pray like the prophets," with the same meditation techniques used by the High Priests of Solomon's Temple and the Aryan "shepherd-gods on the mountain." Meditation is religion's great legacy. It has been the point of the entire religious exercise since the dawn of civilization. It provides us a way to integrate our knowledge into wisdom. It empowers us to heal ourselves and others, offers us the vision of a prophet, it raises our IQ, and accesses what Carl Jung called the collective unconscious, which brings creative solutions to whatever problems we are facing. These are just a few of meditation's "divine gifts." The Quadrivium's mathematical disciplines integrated into a science of religion that provided the cosmological context for the meditations of the ancient astronomer priests.

A recent New York Times article[394] describes the three Abrahamic faiths: "While the three share many traits — these are not primarily meditative or contemplative religions, after all, and they are indeed historical faiths, concerned with action, even with mission — their commonalities also lead to profound contrasts." I must take issue with this statement. The original authors of the Torah encrypted the sacred meditation practice far too well. If the three monotheistic faiths could recapture the lost legacy of the science of religion and the practice of meditation, it would be a much better world. So, we must ask ourselves if there is still time to spread the Word? Meditating religiously will cause our worldly wanderings to gradually slow and eventually cease, until we come to a place of contentment within ourselves. As we persist, this contentment gradually transforms into joy and compassion for those who aren't experiencing it with us. This is the point we must all reach, one person at a time, but time is growing short. The goal is to transcend the constraints of time and space, and to transcend the chaos of everyday life.

The science of religion functions as the common denominator for all the religions of the world. It epitomizes what Karen Armstrong referred to as "the kernel of truth that lay at the heart of the world's historical religions." Re-synthesizing knowledge of the science of religion has been my lifelong effort. My mission has been to gather the pieces of the great jigsaw puzzle called comparative religion — its pieces scattered across the ages and around the globe. Ever since the early 1970's, when I majored in music composition and theory in college, and attended classes at an Orthodox rabbinical seminary, the harmonic series has been my obsession. It has enabled me to organize this jigsaw puzzle and to integrate the seeming disparities of science and religion. When everything finally fell into place I realized how the entire process resembled the old parlor game of telephone, where meaning gets distorted as the initial "kernel of truth" is passed from generation to generation. However, it is presumptuous to suggest that each "teller" communicating their version of the "Word of God" might be more or less valid than the next version. But, since the science of reli-

394 *"Abraham's Progeny, And Their Texts,"* New York Times, October 23, 2010

gion was lost very early in history, we also lost the ability to reign in dogma that was no longer consistent with the exact sciences of antiquity. It was then that the various world religions began to splinter and go off in their own direction.

It will be difficult for established religion to integrate with its scientific foundation, but in an age of instant global communication, appealing to hearts and minds can turn the tide. The Church's apology for its treatment of Galileo was an important milestone, and the Church should get credit for taking that first difficult step toward the recognition of scientific reality. It must continue along that path if it hopes to preserve itself as a meaningful part of 21st century life. With this new interpretation of Abraham's writings, rabbis who care enough about peace can find adequate justification to acknowledge Christ and Mohammed as authentic prophets in the Biblical tradition. This leap of faith by Jewish clergy would go a long way toward establishing a peaceful and harmonious world. Similarly, imams must realize that surrendering one's soul to Allah is only possible through the greater *jihad* as defined by Abraham's sacred practice. Mohammed's prophetic insight was born in the cave where he meditated. Mohammed sought and found the true religion of Abraham in that cave. Once Mohammed secured the Kabah for Islam, he advised his followers to end the lesser militaristic *jihad* and return to the greater spiritual *jihad* of "7 circuits around the sacred cube."

Muslim perception of Western materialism is an accurate perception of the West's on-going "inner struggle" between spirituality and materialism. But, it is a Western struggle, and each man or woman, East or West, whether Hindu, Taoist, Buddhist, Jew, Christian, or Muslim, must be free to wage their own *jihad* against materialism and ego. Even the pious of every faith face the same inner struggle to master time and the elements. Hatred and murder had no place in the Torah when Ishmael and Isaac buried their father together, and it has no place in the relationship among their descendants today. From Abraham's perspective, there is no difference between the 7 circuits of the *Kabah*; the 7 circuits of the *Tefillin*; and the 7 tonecircles of angels heralding the descent of the New Jerusalem from Heaven. The prophecy of the New Jerusalem declares that all three Abrahamic faiths will embrace the common spiritual highground of the *Living God*.

The march of science and technology does not imply the end of religion as some hope and others fear. Much to the contrary, our 21st century empirical definition of Divinity ties the Clock of Heaven and Earth to the Ten Commandments, and anchors them both to the harmonics organizing modern theoretical physics. The harmonic series governs man's inner world through electrophysiology. A new field of research called contemplative neuroscience — the brain science of meditation — is moving forward with the help of the Dalai Lama's Mind and Life Institute. Because of the brain's ever-changing potentials called neuroplasticity, recent MRI research has discovered that meditation creates new neural circuits, and that neural systems can be developed in the same way that regular exercise strengthens certain muscle groups. Even novice meditators appear to be able to stimulate their limbic system, the brain's emotional network. One finding verifies that experts in Tibetan Buddhist-style meditation have permanently changed the way their brains operate even when they are not meditating.[395] Other than the obvious long-term spiritual goals, this is also good news for stroke victims, addictive behavior, etc., but the link between self-hypnosis and meditation requires further study. As additional findings unfold, this new research should empirically establish what thousands of years of religious experience established long ago.

Civilization must follow in the footsteps of the Aryan fathers at the dawn of civilization, by striving to reclaim their rich legacy of knowledge and wisdom. Only the dynamic between science and religion can "tear down the walls of Jericho," eliminating the exclusivity of dogma, bigotry, and ignorance separating cultures and religions from one another. We must start a new civilization — a New Jerusalem — founded on the harmonic series as our empirical God, where meditation will ensure that our species survives to meet the dramatic challenges of the new millennium. "Praying like the prophets" means purifying the body and liberating the soul.

> *"Come, let us go up to the Mount of the LORD, to the House of the God of Jacob; That He may instruct us in His ways, And that we may walk in His paths." For instruction shall come forth from Zion, the word of the LORD from Jerusalem. Thus He will judge among the nations and arbitrate for the many peoples, And they shall beat their swords into plowshares and their spears into pruning hooks: Nation shall not take up sword against nation; They shall never again know war.*[396]

My hope is that reconciling science and religion will put monotheists, polytheists, empirical science, and atheists, on common ground for the first time. Reason alone cannot heal our civilization, because it does not speak to man's inner and true self. Only meditation, practiced within the context of the science of religion, can rescue each of us from the cultural differences and ambiguities of language and dogma that have led the world into chaos. A miraculous opening for peace exists because — finally — there is a common ground for all hearts and minds to reconcile within the objective truth of modern science. I believe that the original authors of the Torah not only understood Abraham's writings, but in their prophetic vision, could foresee the peace of a New Jerusalem.

395 Dan Gilgoff, Op.Cit..
396 Isaiah 2:3.

The New Jerusalem by Charles Bentz

Autumn Rhapsody

by Jonathan S. Clark

If there is but a note in one vibrating
String within Your celestial heart, O Lord,
That could soothe the harrowed soul
Of one who has long sought You in vain,
Pluck it now, in the turning of the year,
As the days grow short, and darkness encroaches.
There are melodies which are transporting,
Which have, as their source, Your Eternal power
To save, and redeem, the most tattered of souls.
The misanthropic strain, potent and virulent,
Is rendered harmless in the revelation
Of Your harmonious, supernal Light.
Who could sleep through the torturous night,
Were it not for Your transforming Love?
I hear it in the ancient melody of the Kol Nidre chant,
And in the last portion of Brahms's *Alto Rhapsody,*
When the bitter, wintry chromatics of the earlier music
Give way to alto and male chorus singing a different song,
One of transporting beauty and solace,
Where Brahms found inspiration in Goethe's poem
To go beyond his tendency to misanthropy,
To convey a tender compassion for a suffering soul.
So, dear Lord, put forth shoots of song in the heart,
To flower in the darkening of the year, and give us
Warmth as the winter moves in upon us after our fall,
And knowledge of Your transforming Love.

Appendix: The Ancient Quadrivium

The liberal arts taught in today's colleges can be traced back to the Middle Ages. It was comprised of the mathematical disciplines of the *Quadrivium* (Latin: four roads): arithmetic, music, geometry, and astronomy; plus the language disciplines of the *Trivium*: grammar, logic, and rhetoric.[397] But, the mathematics of the Quadrivium has much more ancient roots that can be traced back to Sumer, Harappa, Egypt, Babylon, Israel, and Greece.

It might be easiest to understand the Aryan mind at the dawn of civilization if we approach them via ancient Greek thought; a culture that is reasonably familiar to us. The Greek Pythagorean tradition is usually identified as the first integrated cosmology based on the mathematics of the Quadrivium.[398] By the time of Pythagoras, Plato, and Aristotle, there were two generally accepted modes of thought: science and theology. In ancient Greece, science and theology were tightly coupled, but a modern mathematician or physicist may well consider the Pythagorean tradition to be pseudo-science since it imbues number with a great deal of extended meaning. If we are to properly understand the mathematical disciplines of the Quadrivium then we must understand them within the context of the ancient Pythagorean tradition. The great minds of science and theology found their voice through number. We cannot fully understand Greek mathematics without appreciating its theological overtones any more than we can claim to understand theology without a firm grasp of its foundation in mathematics and science.

The exact sciences of antiquity included: arithmetic, music (string theory as a predecessor to acoustics), geometry, trigonometry, and astronomy. Although observation and mathematical calculation characterized this early science, a rigorous scientific method would not exist for thousands of years. Astrology and astronomy had not yet been differentiated from one another; and, arithmetic was just beginning to differentiate from "arithmology." Two important treatises on these topics were authored by Nicomachus of Gerasa, an important Neo-Pythagorean of the day.

In his I*ntroduction to Arithmetic,* Nicomachus deals with what he calls "scientific" number, as opposed to what has become known as "arithmology," or the theology of numbers, as described in his other well known work, *Theologumena Arithmeticae*. Here is an excerpt from commentary on his *Introduction to Arithmetic.*

397 An important connection to our knowledge of the 7 Liberal Arts was Boethius (ca. 480-524), a scholar of the early Middles Ages, who is said to be the first to use the term Quadrivium.
398 Joscelyn Godwin, *The Harmony of the Spheres* (Rochester, VT: Inner Traditions International, 1993).

> Nicomachus assumes continuity and discreteness to be qualities always associated with magnitude and multitude... We can know about, and 'scientifically' deal with multitude, if it can be numbered and with magnitude, if it can be measured.[399]

Nicomachus was a dualist, citing Plato's distinction between "that which ever exists, having no becoming," and, "that which is ever becoming, never existent." His *Theologumena* describes the *Monad* as the mind of God, and the *Dyad*, as the first extension leading out of the *Monad's* Oneness into the *Dyad's* Twoness. Because 2:1 is the first ratio, 2 'dares' to separate itself from the original unity. The infinite and eternal, the forever changeless and spiritual ...is associated with "sameness." "For 'same' is predicated of those things whose essential essence is One; and so it is evident that 'sameness' is a kind of 'Oneness' of being." From this perspective we note that the number 1 is the only common factor of all numbers. The Dyad describes "otherness" which is material in nature, and subject to becoming, decay, growth, etc.[400] This dualism became a universal mathematical model for sets of opposites: day and night, man and woman, good and evil, etc. Opposites can be harmonized by a third term, giving meaning to the Triad, which functions as a mathematical "mean." This "mean" harmonizes the spiritual and material opposites within each being. After the number 3, further extensions into matter defines a diversity that is contained within the unity of the Monad. Thus, unity and diversity are flip sides of the same coin. The Quadrivium provides us with a mathematical window into earlier religions describing a "Blueprint of Creation" and a "God principle" in terms of a single beam of sunlight that contains the diversity of the rainbow, or a single complex natural sound that contains the diversity of a harmonic series.

The secret society of Freemasons understands that God's "Blueprint of Creation" was based on the Quadrivium. They believe its mathematical detail was once known, but subsequently lost to civilization. They also believe that rediscovering this Blueprint would reveal religion's great mysteries. Throughout this text, I have attempted to reveal those mysteries based on my knowledge of the Quadrivium. Freemasons often play important roles in government (about half of the US Presidents were Masons), perhaps because their belief that a Divine Blueprint common to all religions implies the need for an even-handed, ecumenical approach to governance. The great spiritual quest of Freemasonry has always been to recover the lost mathematical and scientific details of the Blueprint of Creation, not just for the purpose of understanding how to construct sacred edifices like Solomon's Temple and Saint Peter's Cathedral, but for civilization to embrace God's "Intelligent Design" as the basis of a new world order — a New Jerusalem.

---

399 Nicomachus of Gerasa, Introduction to Arithmetic, trans. by Martin Luther D'Ooge (New York-London: Macmillan & Company, 1926), 92.
400 Ibid., 92-94.

A Primer on Arithmetic

In keeping with the Greek Pythagorean tradition that included Plato and Aristotle, the *Monad* was understood as a world-Creating God that encompasses all things in nature. The Monad embodies all number and numerical forms as the eternal essence of everything...Especially as it relates to the harmonics of the decad (Base-10). "In this the mathematical properties of the first ten numbers were already likened to and identified with physical properties and sometimes with the gods."[401] "Philolaus identified seven with 'the leader of the universe.'[402]

As the Dyad begins its motion out of the Monad, Nicomachus did not consider 1 and 2 to be actual numbers, but rather, as elements of number. He considered them a true "combination of Monads," with the first actual number being the number 3, the Triad, because it has a beginning, middle, and end. Thus, it has a mean. Continuing on from 3, the tetrad is a square, produced from 2+2 and 2x2, and had long been revered as potentially the decad, because 1+2+3+4=10, indicative of the tetraktys by which the Pythagoreans swore. Odd numbers were considered male and even numbers female. It is in this numerical sense that the World Soul of Plato's Timaeus (identical to Abraham's construction in Figure 42b) was considered hermaphrodite.

With the number 3 giving rise to the concept of a mathematical mean, the Greeks focused on three different types: the arithmetic mean, geometric mean and harmonic mean. The simplest of the three is the arithmetic mean. It is what most of us think of as the "average" value of two numbers. The arithmetic mean of two numbers, a and b, is $(a + b)/2$. The arithmetic mean preserves the distances between numbers. The arithmetic mean of 10 and 20 is 15, and the distance between 10 and 15 on a number line is the same as the distance between 15 and 20. An arithmetic progression of more than two numbers will always have equal increments, e.g., 2, 4, 6, 8, 10 ...

A second type of mean is called the geometric mean. Rather than preserving distances, it preserves ratios. The geometric mean of two numbers, a and b, is the square root of their product. The geometric mean of 5 and 20, for example, is the square root of $5*20 = \sqrt{100} = 10$. Look at the sequence of numbers 5, 10, 20. Notice that the ratios, 5/10 and 10/20, are equal. This will always be the case with the geometric mean. A geometric progression of more than two numbers will always have equal ratios, e.g., 1, 2, 4, 8, 16 ...

401 Ibid., 90; *Aristotle, Metaphysics*, I. 5, and XIII. 4, 1078 b 21.
402 Nicomachus, Op.Cit., 90; Philo, *De Mundi Opificio*, 33.

The harmonic mean is probably the least familiar of the three. The harmonic mean of two numbers, a and b, is twice the product divided by the sum, or $2ab/(a + b)$. This is equivalent to taking the product of the two numbers and dividing by their arithmetic mean. For example, the harmonic mean of 6 and 12 is (2*6*12)/(6 + 12) = 144/18 = 8. We'd get the same result by taking the product, 6*12 = 72, and dividing by the arithmetic mean of 6 and 12, which is 9.

We've said that the arithmetic mean preserves distances and the geometric means preserves ratios. The harmonic mean combines the two and preserves the ratios of distances. For example, the harmonic mean of 6 and 12 is 8. If we take the sequence of numbers 6, 8, and 12, and look at the two ratios, (8 - 6)/6 and (12 - 8)/12, we'll get the same number, 1/3, in both cases. This will always be the case for harmonic means. The ratios of distances from the mean to the endpoints are always equal.

The reciprocity of frequency and wavelength is reflected in the reciprocity of arithmetic and harmonic proportions. For example, a harmonic proportion with relative frequency ratios of 6, 8, and 12 when inverted gives its wavelength in an arithmetic progression: 1/6 = 4/24, 1/8 = 3/24, 1/12 = 2/24. This implies that the formulas for arithmetic and harmonic means are in a reciprocal relationship. We can show this to be true if we substitute the reciprocals of a, b and x into the formula for the arithmetic mean $(a + b)/2 = x$, to get $1/x = 1/2(1/a + 1/b)$. When we solve for x, we find that x is equal to the harmonic mean, $2ab/(a + b)$. The three types of mathematical mean could be applied to "moving number" that was understood to be the essence of Creation.

These three types of mathematical mean described relationships defined by the three types of numerical series: harmonic, arithmetic, and geometric which come together in the *lambdoma* table of Abraham and Plato. The mathematical/musical constructions that Abraham and Plato used as the basis of their writings were subsets of this table. Note the lambda lines drawn through Figure 36 and compare these lambdas to Abraham's construction for the soul in Figure 42b. It is so named because it also resembles the Greek letter lambda. Thus, it became historically associated with the Pythagorean tradition; although, both the *Sefer Yetzirah* and the Hebrew Scriptures (the Tree of Knowledge, the Tree of Life, etc.) antedates Plato's use of it. Plato's "Dyad of the Great and Small" are the "superparticular ratios" of music theory, as exemplified by "two trees in the Garden of Eden (Figures 40a & b)"; the Four Wheels of Ezekiel; and the Four Rivers of Eden. Our thesis suggests that the mirror reflection of materiality and spirituality is based on the reciprocity of the harmonic and arithmetic series that was well known to the ancients during the time of Abraham (the Old Babylonian period), but we have traced its origins back to ancient Sumer, and perhaps as far back as the Ice Age caves of the Aryan fathers.

A Primer on Music

In 1984, two professors, Michael Green and John Schwarz collaborated on Superstring Theory, a comprehensive mathematical framework describing a "theory of everything" for all matter and energy in the universe. At the heart of Superstring Theory is the formula for a classic vibrating string that oscillates to generate a harmonic series. Superstring Theory is a direct descendant of Sumerian/Babylonian string theory that described the first "theory of everything" based on the harmonic series — musical ratios formed from integers 1 to 12 within the "Clock of Heaven" — which generate astrological forces that emanate from the polytheistic "Gods in the Clock" (Figures 26b & 27). The second historical "theory of everything" based on the harmonic series was the 10 Commandments giving rise to monotheism.

The harmonic series that reveals the structure of sound can be described in formal scientific terms as "integer multiples of a fundamental sound." Or, to put it more simply — counting. Ancient scientists counted units of string length and compared those lengths in terms of musical ratios. Today, we have the technology to count sine waves: 1 sine wave, 2 sine waves, 3 sine waves, etc., *ad infinitum* (Figure 97a & b). The human ear is limited to about 16 harmonics, but the clock's polytheism only needed 12, and the Ten Commandment's monotheism only needed 10. Without a modern oscilloscope, and armed with only a ruler to measure string length, Sumerian and Babylonians had discovered that superparticular ratios were at the heart of their music theory. Nicomachus describes them in his Introduction to Arithmetic. Algebraically, they follow the following formula:

$$\frac{n+1}{n} = 1 + \frac{1}{n}$$

Substituting for "n" as we count from 1, the ancients generated two sounds as the endpoints of musical intervals determined by the following integer ratios: 2:1 - an octave; 3:2 -a perfect fifth; 4:3 -a perfect fourth; 5:4 - a minor third; 6:5 - a minor third; and 9:8- a minor second. A superparticular number can also be defined as any integer which factors completely into prime numbers. Modern terminology states that a positive integer would be considered *B*-smooth if *B* is the upper limit. For example: 5-smooth implies that a number like 360 can be completely factored by 2, 3 and 5 as $2^3 * 3^3 * 5$; while the number 2560 would be considered 7-smooth as $2^3 * 3^3 * 5 * 7$. Note that the intervals listed here are "5-smooth" which implies that the prime number 7 was not used as a tone generator. This became encrypted within Biblical allegory as God resting on the 7th Day.

Figure 97a - A Harmonic Series Defining the Inner Structure of a Natural Sound

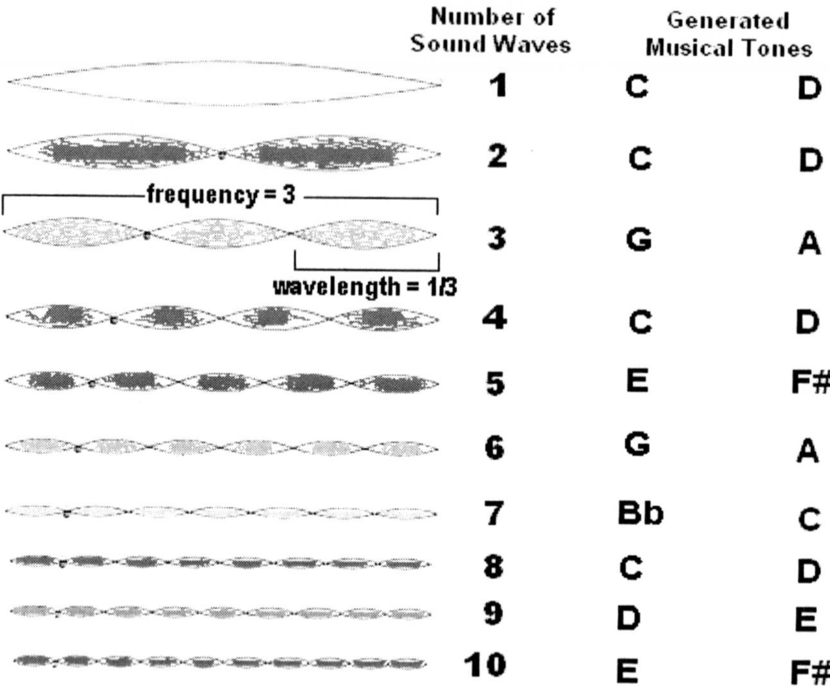

Figure 97b - Locating Integer Ratios as Musical Tones on a Piano Keyboard

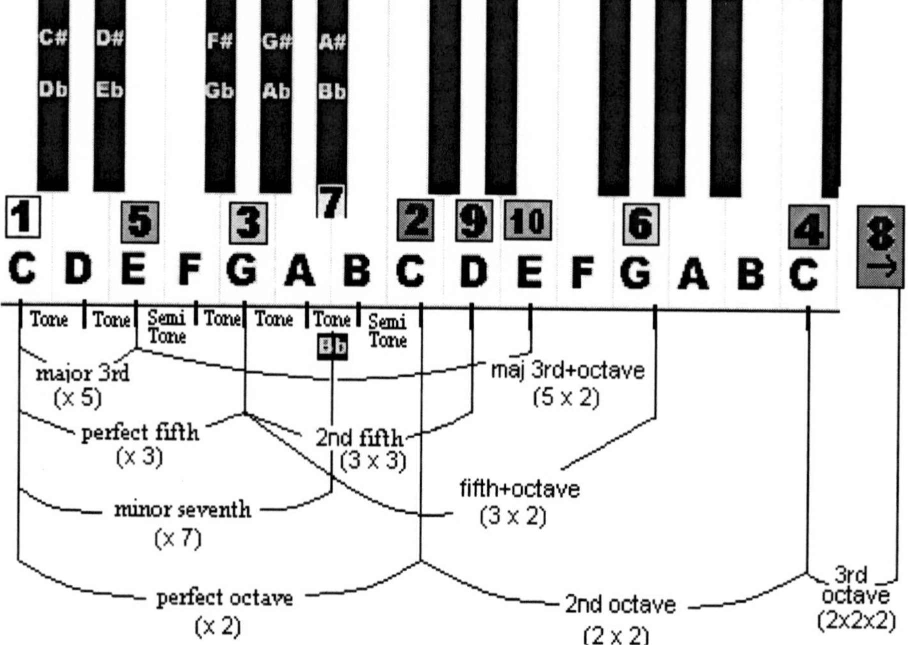

If a violinist plays one of his strings, and with his left hand divides that string exactly in half, a second note would sound exactly one octave above the first note played (Figures 97a & b). A musical interval defines the span between two musical tones. The ratio of 2:1 generates the most basic musical interval possible: an octave (the second note is eight notes higher than the first note). Similarly, 2:4, 4:8, 8:16, and 440:880, all describe musical octaves because the second quantity is always twice the first quantity. In Figures 97a & b, we can see all the superparticular ratios that result from the acoustics of a vibrating string, as well as where it would be played on a piano keyboard.

In Figures 98a, the frequency ratios defined by God's harmonic series of Ten Utterances descends into matter through the "22 Foundation Letters" of the Hebrew alphabet, reflecting God's 10 root frequencies into a reciprocal arithmetic series of wavelengths. Omitting the twenty-second letter, the letter *Tav* (ת), from the 21 x 11 = 231 Gates matrix preempts it from creating a new musical tone. This is in keeping with its function as the essence of the Sabbath, when God rests and refrains from creating. The *Tav*'s (ת) correspondence to the Sabbath is verified in the *Sefer Yetzirah.* This transition from number to sound is Abraham's "hidden" layer of meaning. It is the great "Secret of the Torah" (Hebrew: *Razah D'Oraytah).*[403]

Figure 98a- The 231 Gates Multiplication Table

1	2	3	4	5	6	7	8	9	10	20
2	4	6	8	10	12	14	16	18	20	40
3	6	9	12	15	18	21	24	27	30	60
4	8	12	16	20	24	28	32	36	40	80
5	10	15	20	25	30	35	40	45	50	100
6	12	18	24	30	36	42	48	54	60	120
7	14	21	28	35	42	49	56	63	70	140
8	16	24	32	40	48	56	64	72	80	160
9	18	27	36	45	54	63	72	81	90	180
10	20	30	40	50	60	70	80	90	100	200
20	40	60	80	100	120	140	160	180	200	400
30	60	90	120	150	180	210	240	270	300	600
40	80	120	160	200	240	280	320	360	400	800
50	100	150	200	250	300	350	400	450	500	1000
60	120	180	240	300	360	420	480	540	600	1200
70	140	210	280	350	420	490	560	630	700	1400
80	160	240	320	400	480	560	640	720	800	1600
90	180	270	360	450	540	630	720	810	900	1800
100	200	300	400	500	600	700	800	900	1000	2000
200	400	600	800	1000	1200	1400	1600	1800	2000	2200
300	600	900	1200	1500	1800	2100	2400	2700	3000	6000

403 Tanya, Sharr Hayichud 2: "231 Gates, either in direct or reverse order, as is explained in the *Sefer Yetzirah*...which descend, degree by degree, from the Ten Utterances recorded in the Torah..." *Tanya*, Sharr Hayichud 5" "In it [*Razah D'Oraytah*] is the secret of the twenty-two letters of the Torah..."

Figure 98b - "Opening" 231 Gates to Reveal 231 Musical Paths

1:1=d	1:2=d	1:3=a	1:4=d	1:5=f#	1:6=a	1:7=c	1:8=d	1:9=e	1:10=f#	1:20=f#
2:1=d	2:2=d	2:3=a	2:4=d	2:5=f#	2:6=a	2:7=c	2:8=d	2:9=e	2:10=f#	2:20=f#
3:1=g	3:2=g	3:3=d	3:4=g	3:5=b	3:6=d	3:7=f	3:8=g	3:9=a	3:10=b	3:20=b
4:1=d	4:2=d	4:3=a	4:4=d	4:5=f#	4:6=a	4:7=c	4:8=d	4:9=e	4:10=f#	4:20=f#
5:1=bb	5:2=bb	5:3=f	5:4=bb	5:5=d	5:6=f	5:7=ab	5:8=bb	5:9=a	5:10=d	5:20=d
6:1=g	6:2=g	6:3=d	6:4=g	6:5=b	6:6=d	6:7=f	6:8=g	6:9=a	6:10=b	6:20=b
7:1=e	7:2=e	7:3=b	7:4=e	7:5=g#	7:6=b	7:7=d	7:8=e	7:9=f#	7:10=g#	7:20=g#
8:1=d	8:2=d	8:3=a	8:4=d	8:5=f#	8:6=a	8:7=c	8:8=d	8:9=e	8:10=f#	8:20=f#
9:1=c	9:2=c	9:3=g	9:4=c	9:5=e	9:6=g	9:7=bb	9:8=c	9:9=d	9:10=e	9:20=e
10:1=bb	10:2=bb	10:3=f	10:4=bb	10:5=d	10:6=f	10:7=ab	10:8=bb	10:9=c	10:10=d	10:20=d
20:1=bb	20:2=bb	20:3=f	20:4=bb	20:5=d	20:6=f	20:7=ab	20:8=bb	20:9=c	20:10=d	20:20=d
30:1=eb	30:2=eb	30:3=bb	30:4=eb	30:5=g	30:6=bb	30:7=db	30:8=eb	30:9=f	30:10=g	30:20=g
40:1=bb	40:2=bb	40:3=f	40:4=bb	40:5=d	40:6=f	40:7=ab	40:8=bb	40:9=c	40:10=d	40:20=d
50:1=gb	50:2=gb	50:3=db	50:4=gb	50:5=bb	50:6=db	50:7=fb	50:8=gb	50:9=ab	50:10=bb	50:20=bb
60:1=eb	60:2=eb	60:3=bb	60:4=eb	60:5=g	60:6=bb	60:7=db	60:8=eb	60:9=f	60:10=g	60:20=g
70:1=c	70:2=c	70:3=g	70:4=c	70:5=e	70:6=g	70:7=bb	70:8=c	70:9=d	70:10=e	70:20=e
80:1=bb	80:2=bb	80:3=f	80:4=bb	80:5=d	80:6=f	80:7=ab	80:8=bb	80:9=c	80:10=d	80:20=d
90:1=ab	90:2=ab	90:3=eb	90:4=ab	90:5=c	90:6=eb	90:7=gb	90:8=ab	90:9=bb	90:10=c	90:20=c
100:1=gb	100:2=gb	100:3=db	100:4=gb	100:5=bb	100:6=db	100:7=fb	100:8=gb	100:9=ab	100:10=bb	100:20=bb
200:1=gb	200:2=gb	200:3=db	200:4=gb	200:5=bb	200:6=db	200:7=fb	200:8=gb	200:9=ab	200:10=bb	200:20=bb
300:1=cb	300:2=cb	300:3=gb	300:4=cb	300:5=eb	300:6=gb	300:7=bbb	300:8=cb	300:9=db	300:10=eb	300:20=eb

A Primer on Geometry

In his book *Introductio Arithmetica*, the ancient Greek arithmetician Nicomachus of Gerasa (ca.100 CE) tells us that the first triangle is potentially formed by the number 1 but actually created by the number 3, the next triangle is created by the number 6 … Numbers that can be arranged in triangular arrays are called *triangular numbers*, while those that can be arranged equilaterally in squares became the *squared numbers* (n^2): 1*1 = 1; 2*2 = 4; 3*3 = 9; 4*4 = 16 … As one studies these patterns of equilaterally arrayed pebbles, it shouldn't take long to discern some repeating patterns. For example, every sequential form, whether triangles, squares, pentagons, hexagons,... has sides that increase by 1 pebble with each successive increase in size. We observe that the first triangular number creates a triangle with a side 1 unit in length, the second triangle has a side 2 units in length, the third triangle has a side 3 units in length, and the fourth has a side 4 units in length, etc. The same thing can be said of the length of each side for the other two-dimensional forms – squares, pentagons, hexagons, etc. A second important pattern also becomes evident: if one takes the difference between adjacent sets of triangular numbers 1, 3, 6, 10, 15 ..., we get a difference of 2 between the first two triangular numbers: 1 and 3, and a difference of 3 between the next two triangular numbers, 3 and 6, a difference of 4 between the next two triangular numbers, etc. (Figure 99)

Figure 99 - Calculating Geometric Numbers

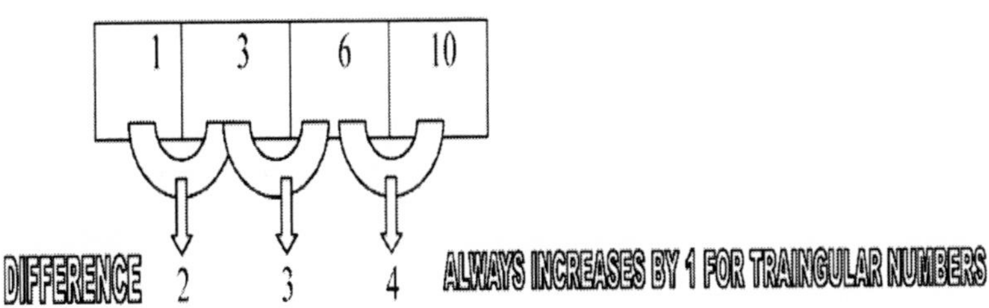

Similarly, when we take the difference for adjacent square numbers 1, 4, 9, 16, 25..., we begin with a difference of 3, and then get a difference of 5, a difference of 7, etc., always increasing the difference by 2. When we consider pentagonal numbers 1, 5, 12, 22, 35,... differences will always increase by 3, while differences between hexagons will always differ by 4.

From this pattern of differences, we can follow Nicomachus' example and create the following table, identifying the various geometric forms by their corresponding number (Figure 100).[404]

Figure 100 - Calculating Geometric Numbers

Triangles	1	3	6	10	15	21	28	36	45	55
Squares	1	4	9	16	25	36	49	64	81	100
Pentagonals	1	5	12	22	35	51	70	92	117	145
Hexagonals	1	6	15	28	45	66	91	120	153	190

Using this method of construction, Table 15 can be extended to as many rows and columns as desired. Nicomachus also points out that every square can be diagonally divided into two triangles, and if we refer to the table we can see that every square number also resolves into two successive triangular numbers: 4 = 1 + 3; 9 = 3 + 6; 16 = 6 + 10, etc. Just as a square is made of two triangles, a pentagon can be made from joining square to a triangle. This also holds true with respect to the numeric table above: 5 = 4 + 1; 12 = 9 + 3; 22 = 16 + 6, etc. Similarly, any hexagon is comprised of the pentagon appearing immediately above it in the table, added to the previous column's triangle, 6 = 5 + 1; 15 = 12 + 3; 28 = 22 + 6,... for every geometric form. We consider the triangle as the most elemental two-dimensional geometric shape because every other shape can be broken down into triangles. On Day 4 God extends the two-dimensional triangular array of "opposites and the mean" into a three-dimensional tetrahedron, by simply juxtaposing a fourth pebble over a 3- pebble equilateral triangular base (Figure 101).

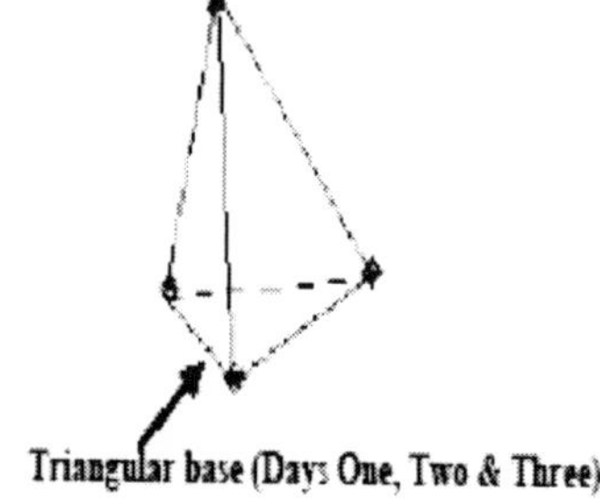

Figure 101 - Day 4's Extension into Matter

404 Nicomachus, Introduction to Arithmetic II, Chapter XII.

If we view the Creation allegory from Abraham's perspective, then a planer triangular base came into existence as a result of Days 1, 2 and 3 of Creation. Day 4 generated the fourth tonal "pebble," extending our structure into three dimensions. This 4-pebble tetrahedral structure can be further "extended into matter" by juxtaposing it over the next successive triangular base of 6, to get a 10-pebble tetrahedron. We can extend it still further into matter by juxtaposing the 10-pebble tetrahedron over the next triangular base of 10 to get a 20-pebble tetrahedron; a 20-pebble tetrahedron over a 15 triangular base is 35, etc. Our three-dimensional tetrahedron series is therefore 4, 10, 20, 35,... which we may notice is a progressive accumulation of the series of triangular numbers: 1, 3, 6, 10, 15, 21… Within the holistic context of the ancient Quadrivium, it is easy to forget that geometry should also be understood from a musical perspective. The God of Abraham extends the geometry of the tetrahedron's triple progression by echoing the geometric proportion of wavelength ratio 3/2 into the lowest realms of matter (Figures 102a & b).

Figure 102a - Extending the Triple Progression

F ← C ← G ← D → A → E → B

$2/3^3$ $2/3^2$ $2/3$ 1 $3/2$ $(3/2)^2$ $(3/2)^3$

Triple progression + Extension into matter

Without a detailed knowledge of the Quadrivium that encompasses the polytheistic and monotheistic musical traditions, most modern music theorists have been taught that Pythagoras invented the diatonic scale (circa 550 BCE) based on the triple progression that forms a succession of musical fifths, called a *circle of fifths* (Figure 102a). A circle of fifths spans several octaves, and transposing them to the same octave requires either multiplication or division by the appropriate power of 2. To create a C diatonic scale from Figure 102a we begin with "C" then take five successive upper fifths and one lower fifth, an "F", and then transpose them all into a single octave to form the scale in Figure 102b.[405]

Figure 102b - The Rising Tetrachord

T T S T T T S

C → D → E → F → G → A → B → C

1 9/8 81/64 4/3 3/2 27/16 243/128 2

405 Willi Apel, *Harvard Dictionary of Music* (Cambridge, MA: Harvard University Press, 1972), 709-710.

The derived notes are sequenced above as a rising diatonic scale, transposed to the key of C, because that key is easily recognizable as the white notes on a piano. Two cumulative intervals of 9/8 (indicated as T for tone), are followed by one semitone interval of 256/243 (indicated as S). This creates the pattern T T S T T T S. The Pythagorean semitone ratio 256/243 was called either a *leimma* ("leftover" interval) or *diesis* (difference) because it was obtained by subtracting two whole tones from the perfect fourth. This pattern of tones and semitones can be maintained when transposing to another diatonic key (bringing black notes of the keyboard into play). With each different key, the scale would still be called diatonic rather than chromatic as long as the pattern of tones and semitones is maintained. It is important to remember that God's extension into matter first took place within musical and geometric terms, until Day 5, when God added motion to geometry and created Astronomy.

A Primer on Astronomy

Astronomy and time are integrally related. We tell time by measuring angles in space. For example, we derive the time of day by measuring the sun's angle in the sky from some location on earth. If it is noon in Greenwich, England, on the first day of Spring, the sun would be at its highest point in the sky for the year. However, if we were observing from the equator, then the sun would be directly overhead, at 90^0 from the horizon, for just a moment, at noon. At that same moment, however, the sun would be rising in Chicago at a 0^0 angle, and Chicago time would be about 6 AM.

Figure 103 - Projecting the Equator into Space and Comparing it with the Sun's Ecliptic

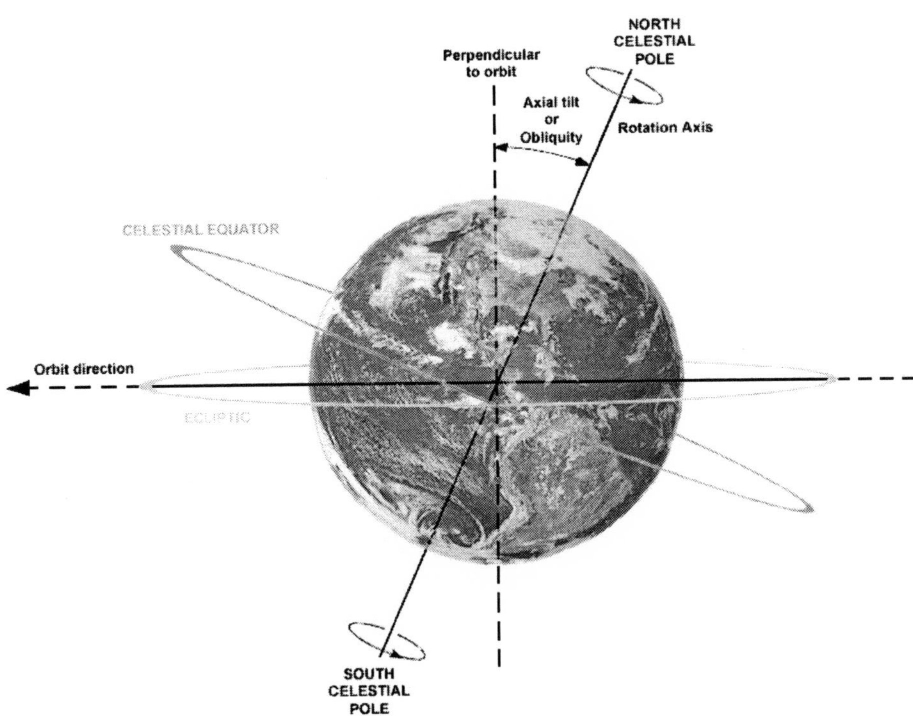

We know that the sun rises in the east and sets in the west, but the path of the sun, its ecliptic, does not line up with the equator, because the axis of the earth is tilted (Figure 103). This causes some confusion when we measure angles to the sun. To help solve that problem, we have established a grid of horizontal and vertical lines extending around the earth, called latitude and longitude. Lines of latitude were created by measuring the angle from the center of the earth to any location on the surface of the earth. Degrees of latitude must therefore be limited to a range of 0^0 to 90^0, with 0^0 latitude corresponding to the equator, and 90^0 latitude corresponding to the North and South Poles. The equator divides the earth into two hemispheres: degrees North latitude, and degrees South latitude (Figure 104a).

Figure 104a - Determining Latitude

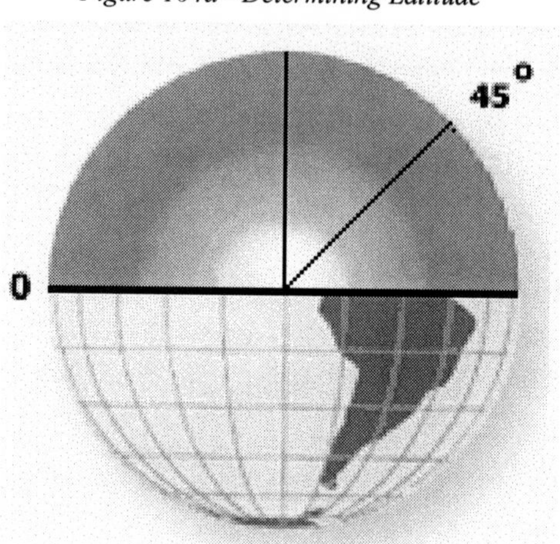

Next, we established lines of longitude, also called meridians, which are determined by measuring angles from the North or South Pole. Once again, the earth is divided into two vertical hemispheres by the Prime Meridian. In this case, we speak of degrees East longitude or degrees West longitude (Figure 104b).

Figure 104b - Determining Longitude

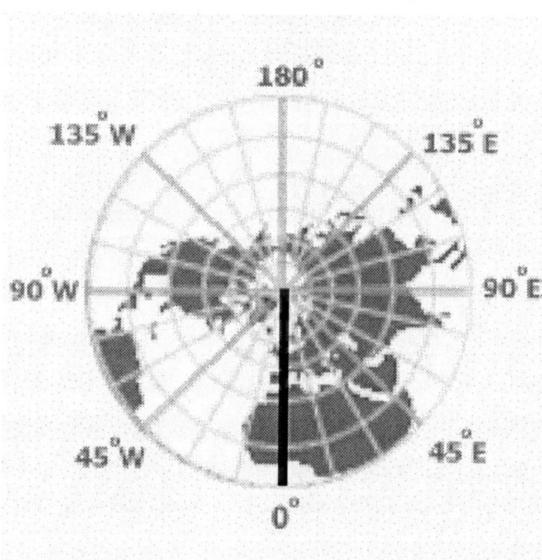

This grid gives us a frame of reference to measure angles to the sun, moon, and stars. It is probably safe to assume that early astronomers didn't realize how the earth spun on its axis, nor how it orbited around the Sun. And, we know that they had no lines of latitude or longitude for reference. They would have had to rely on some version of a "solar ecliptic coordinate system," that maps to a location either north or south of the Sun's ecliptic.

However, when modern astronomers wanted to catalog the locations of stars so that they might aim their telescope in the right direction, they would use an "equatorial coordinate system" (Figure 105a). In this type of coordinate system we can think of the earth as a small sphere that spins and orbits inside of a bigger, celestial sphere of stars. From our grid on earth, we would be looking out at the celestial sphere's grid.

Figure 105a - Equatorial Coordinate System: a Moving Inner and Fixed Outer Sphere

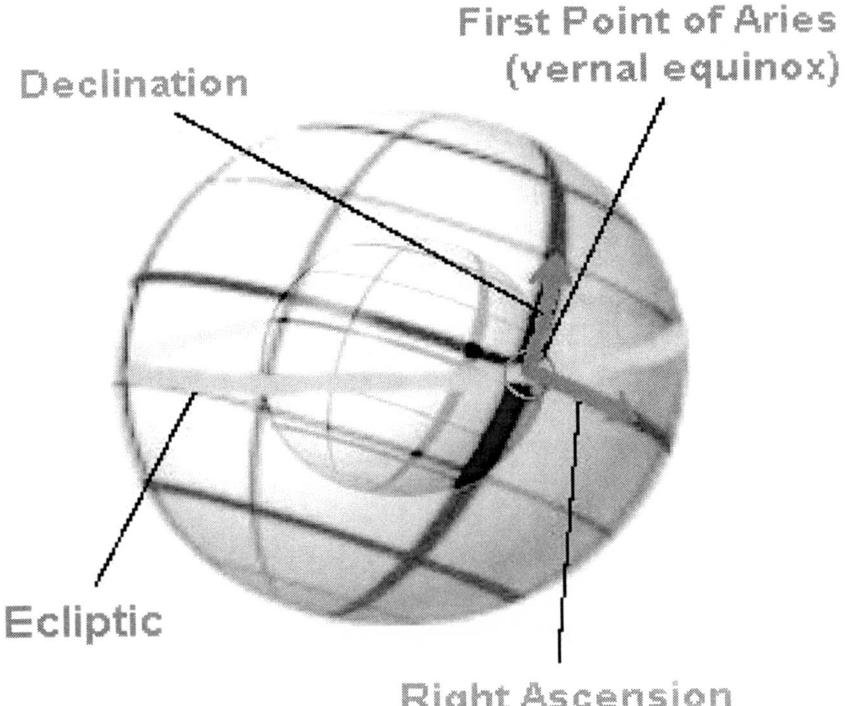

We determine the outer celestial grid by projecting the earth's latitude-longitude grid out into space during the vernal equinox, the first day of Spring. On that day, 0^0 on the earth's "prime meridian" can be projected out to the "first point of Aries" in the celestial grid. Degrees of longitude can then be measured from the prime meridian by angles of "right ascension" which form "hour circles" (see

Figure 105b). In a 24 hour day, each hour of right ascension measures a longitude of 1/24th of 360° or 15°. To pinpoint the position of the sun or a star, we require a second grid coordinate. Degrees of latitude are measured in terms of declination angles ranging from 0^0 to 90^0 for latitudes north of the celestial equator, and 0^0 to -90^0 for southern latitudes. Thus, the pole star Polaris would have a declination of +90, while a southern pole star would have a declination of -90^0.

During the vernal equinox, tracking the Sun's path begins at the first point of Aries, the prime meridian for right ascension. By definition, this starting point is always 0 hours R.A., 0 degrees declination. It is where the Sun's ecliptic crosses the celestial projection of the equator on the first day of Spring.

Figure 105b - Equatorial Coordinate System: Projecting the Earth's Grid onto the Celestial Grid

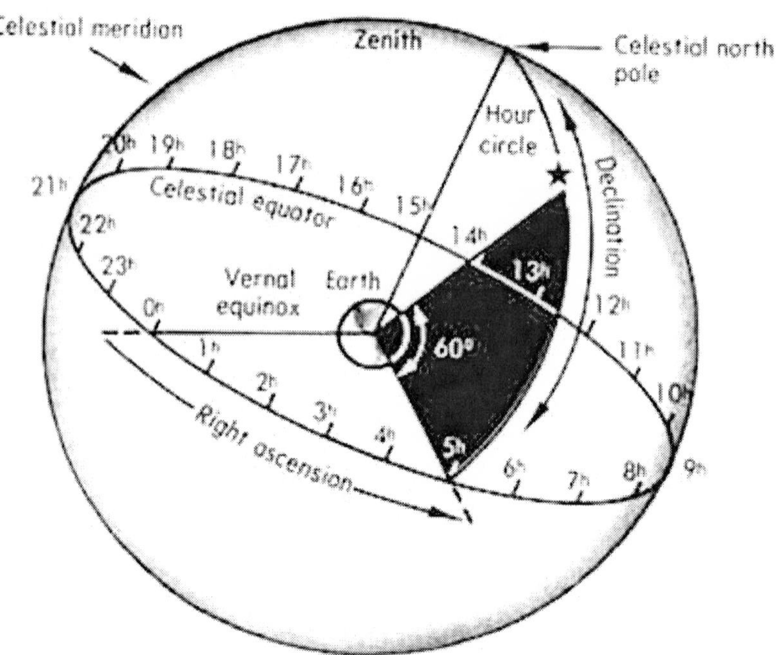

Today, we know that the earth's orbit around the sun creates the solstices and equinoxes that define our four seasons. The positions of the stars with each change of season is no longer considered significant, as it was in ancient astronomy. In modern astronomy, the seasons occur as a function of the Earth's orbit, its tilt, and its relation to the Sun. The Tropical year is defined by a complete cycle of the seasons, and the seasons are largely a result of the Earth's axial tilt, which varies between ~22.1^0 and 24.5^0 in a 41,000 year cycle. Today, this "obliquity of the ecliptic" (as axial tilt is officially called), is about ~23.5^0 and decreasing. The tilt of the Earth's axis is oriented directly towards or away from the Sun; summer occurs in the closest portion, while winter occurs in the farthest (Figure 106a).

Figure 106a - The Earth's Tilt and Orbit Combine to Create the Seasons

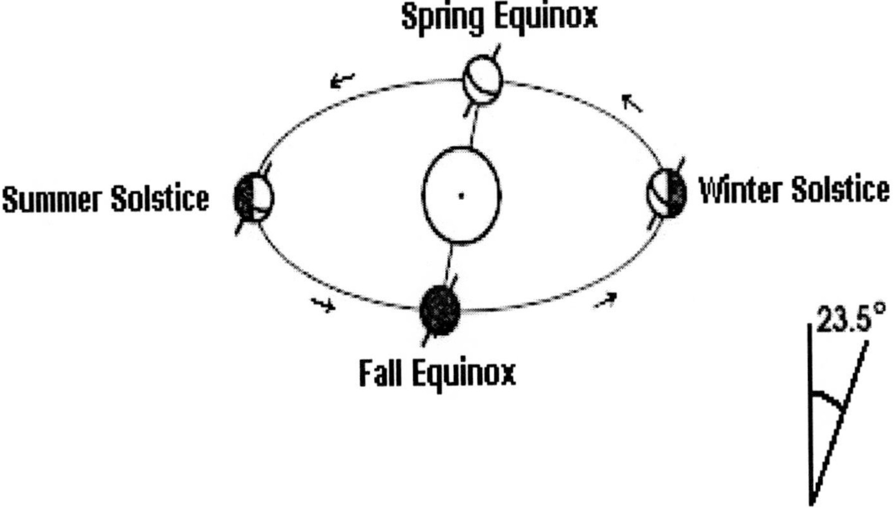

During the summer or winter solstice, the Sun is at either its northernmost or southernmost points in the sky. During the summer solstice, the Sun passes directly over the circle of latitude known as the Tropic of Cancer, which lies at 23° 26′ 22″ north of the Equator. During the December solstice it passes over the Tropic of Capricorn, which lies at the Sun's most southerly latitude of 23° 26′ 22″. If one were standing on one of these lines of latitude during these key times, the Sun would pass directly overhead at noon. The Sun begins to reverse its direction in the sky at the next sunrise while the ecliptic heads toward the equator for another seasonal equinox. The changing of the seasons thus creates a periodic wave (see Figure 106b), back and forth across the Tropics, giving modern astronomy its name: "Tropical Astronomy."

Figure 106b - he Earth's Tilt and Orbit Combine to Create the Seasons

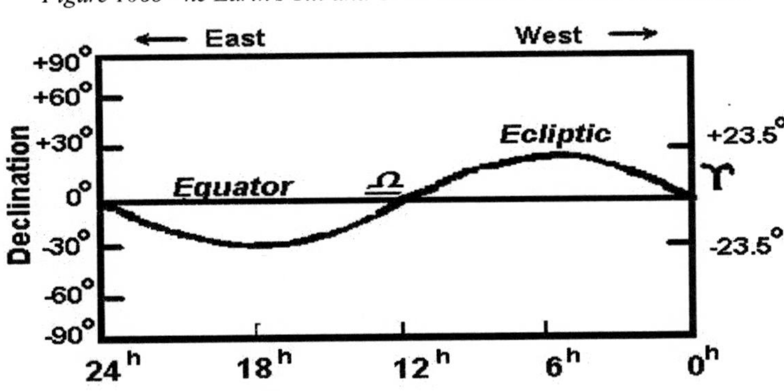

In contrast to modern Tropical Astronomy, ancient Vedic Astronomy, or *Jyotisha*, pays a great deal of attention to the stars. It is based on what the ancient priests could reveal about the Heavens during the first day of spring. *Jyotisha* measures a *sidereal* day, which is a measure of the clock time it takes to observe the position of the Sun against the fixed backdrop of the stars. A sidereal day does not measure 24 hours, because it takes the stars 23 hours 56 minutes and 4.090530833 seconds to actually "travel" the 24 hours and 360° of right ascension. Similarly, a *sidereal* year is the measure of the 365+ days it takes for the Sun to travel 360° in order to return to its original position against the background stars. The Gregorian calendar, which is more accurate, counts 365.26 days for the length of a sidereal year. At noon, on January 1, 2000, it was measured at 365.256363004 days. It is important to realize that sidereal time measures the Sun against the background stars (the hour angle of the vernal equinox), whereas tropical time (solar time or "clock time") is a function of the hour angle of the Sun, and pays no attention to the stars.

Of course, today we know that it is really the motion of the Earth, and not the motion of the stars, that is being measured. The Earth rotates on its axis once per day, and revolves around the Sun once per year. In *Jyotisha*, careful measurement of the Earth against the background stars, reveals a tiny discrepancy of ~50 seconds of arc every year. The sun's ecliptic passes through the twelve constellations of the zodiac at a rate of almost 1° per day, but days and degrees are not quite in a one-to-one relationship. The yearly gap results from the 365+ days that it takes for the Sun to travel a complete circuit of 360°, beginning and ending with the vernal equinox. In scientific terms, we might say that there is a slight mismatch between the sidereal measure of time and the diurnal motion of the stars. This "mismatch" can be observed by astronomers.

Observation of sunrise in the East and setting in the West implies that the Sun takes an elliptical or circular path behind the earth before it reappears. From the star observatory of *Göbekli Tepe,* when the repeating seasons brings the 1st day of Spring exactly one year later, a careful viewing of the Sun's annual reappearance against the celestial dome of background stars has inexplicably shifted by the same tiny amount from the year before. Every year the Sun and background stars would move cumulatively further out of alignment. A superior Aryan race would have been attentive to this detail, especially after constructing a star observatory specifically designed for carefully monitoring the motion of the heavenly bodies from a stone circle's stationary platform. Even to assume that they had no precise metric, they would certainly have been able to determine that the sun's path did not form a perfect circle against the celestial dome as one might naturally expect in an ordered universe. At the moment our Aryan fathers noticed that the sun's path through the heavens formed a spiral and not a perfect circle, they had acquired a working knowledge of precession, and discovered the path of liberation that gave birth to religion.

Bibliography

Ambrose, Stanley, "Late Pleistocene human population bottlenecks, volcanic winter, and differentiation of modern humans," Journal of Human Evolution 34, 1998.

Apel, Willi, Harvard Dictionary of Music, Cambridge, Massachusetts: Harvard University Press, 1972.

Armstrong, Karen, Islam: A Short History, New York: Random House, 2000.

Armstrong, Karen, A History of God, New York: Random House, 1993.

Armstrong, Karen, The Case for God, New York: Random House, 2009.

Austin, James H, Zen and the Brain: Toward an Understanding of Meditation and Consciousness, Boston: MIT Press, 1999).

Austin, William W., Music in the Twentieth Century, New York: W.W. Norton, 1966.

Asimov, Isaac, Asimov's Guide to Science, New York: Basic Books, 1972.

Barbour, J. Murray, Tuning and Temperament: A Historical Survey, East Lansing, Michigan: State College Press, 1953.

Barrett, Helen M., Boethius, New York: Russel & Russel, 1965.

Black, Jeremy and Green, Anthony, Gods, Demons and Symbols of Ancient Meopotamia, Austin, Texas: University of Texas Press: 1992.

Boethius, The Consolation of Philosophy, trans. Richard Green, Indianapolis: Bobbs-Merrill, 1962.

Brinton, Craine and Christopher, John B., and Wolff, Robert Lee, A History of Civilization, Vol. I. Englewood Cliffs, New Jersey: Prentice Hall, 1960.

Burrows, Millar, The Dead Sea Scrolls, New York: Viking Press, 1955.

Campbell, Joseph, The Masks of God, New York: Viking Press, 1964.

Carto, Shannon; Weaver, Andrew; Hetherington, Renée; Lam, Yin; Wiebe, Edward, "Out of Africa and into an ice age," Journal of Human Evolution, Royaume-UNI: Elsevier Journals, 2009 Feb;56(2): 139-51.

Christensen, Duane, Habakkuk, BIBAL.net

Christensen, Duane, Nahum, New Haven, CT: Yale University Press, 2009.

Chumash: Artscroll Series, eds. Nosson Scherman and Meir Zlotowitz, Brooklyn, New York: Mesorah Publications, 1998.

Clawson, Calvin, Mathematical Sorcery, Cambridge: Perseus, 1999.

Cole, K.C., "Theory of Everything," New York times Magazine, October18, 1987, 20-26.

Connolly, Robert, The Search for Ancient Wisdom, Cambrix Publishing, 1995.

Coogan, Michael D., ed., The Oxford History of the Biblical World, New York: Oxford University Press, 1998.

Cozort, Daniel, Highest Yoga Tantra, Ithaca, New York: Snow Lion, 1986.

Dalai Lama, Dzogchen, trans. G.T. Jinpa and R. Barron, Ithaca, New York: Snow Lion, 2000.

Dalai Lama, trans. by Jeffery Hopkins, Tantra in Tibet, Ithaca, New York: Snow Lion Pub., 1977.

Davies, P.C.W. and Brown, J., eds., Superstrings: A Theory of Everything, Cambridge, UK: Cambridge University Press, 1988.

Dawkins, Richard, The God Delusion, New York: Houghton Mifflin, 2006.

DeMar, Gary, "Denying Sola Scriptura: The Attempt to Neutralize the Bible," Biblical Worldview, December 1993.

Durant, Will The Story of Civilization: Caesar and Christ, New York: MJF Books, 1994.

Einstein, Albert and Infield, Leopold, The Evolution of Physics, New York: Simon & Schuster, 1938.

Eisenman, Robert, and Wise, Michael, The Dead Sea Scrolls Uncovered, New York: Barnes & Noble Books, 2004.

Eliade, Mercea, Yoga: Immortality and Freedom, trans. by Willard Trask, Princeton, New Jersey: Princeton University Press, 1969.

English Standard Version Study Bible, Wheaton, Illinois: Crossway Bibles, 2008.

Fairbanks, Arthus, The First Philosphers of Greece, London: Kegan Paul, Trench, and Trauber, 1898.

Farmer, Henry George, "The Music of Ancient Egypt," The New Oxford History of Music, London: Oxford University Press, 1957, Vol.1, 275.

Feurerstein, Georg, Tantra: The Path of Ecstasy, Boston: Shambhala Pub., 1998.

Finegan, Jack, The Archaeological History of the Ancient Middle East, Boulder, Colorado: Westview Press: 1979, 7-9.

Foley, Robert, "The Context of Human Genetic Evolution," Genome Research, vol.8, Cold Spring Harbor, New York: Cold Spring Harbor Lab Press, 1998.

Frankfort, Henri, Ancient Egyptian Religion, New York: Columbia U Press, 1948.

Gaon, Saadia, The Book of Beliefs and Opinions, trans. Samuel Rosenblatt, New Haven, Connecticut: Yale University Press, 1948.

Godwin, Joscelyn, Harmonies of Heaven and Earth, Rochester, Vermont: Inner Traditions International,1987, 1995.

Godwin, Joscelyn, The Harmony of the Spheres, Rochester, Vermont: Inner Traditions International,1993.

Grout, Donald Jay, A History of Western Music, New York: W.W. Norton, 1973.

Greene, Brian, The Elegant Universe, New York: Random House, 1999.

Halevi, Z'ev ben Shimon, Kabbalah and Exodus, Boulder Colorado: Shambhala, 1980.

Hall, Manly P., The Lost Keys of Freemasonry or The Secret of the Hiram Abiff , Richmond, VA.: Macoy Publishing and Masonic Supply Co., 1976, 1923.

Hancock, Graham and Bauval, Robert, The Message of the Sphinx: A Quest for the Hidden Legacy of Mankind, New York: Three Rivers Press, 1997.

Harkavy, Alexander, ed., The Holy Scriptures, New York: Hebrew Pub., 1936.

Helmholtz, Hermann, On the Sensations of Tone, translated by Alexander Ellis, New York: Dover Publishing, Inc., 1954.

Heninger, S.K. Jr., Touches of Sweet Harmony: Pythagorean Cosmology and Renaissance Poetics, San Marino, California: Huntington Library, 1974.

Hill, Carol A., "The Garden of Eden: a Modern Landscape," Perspectives on Science and Christian Faith, 52 (March 2000): 31-46..

Hindemith, Paul, Craft of Musical Composition, Book I, trans. Arthur Mendell, New York: Associated Music Publishing, 1942.

Holy Bible, King James Version, New York: Delair Pub., 1982.

Icke, Vincent, The Force of Symmetry, Cambridge: Cambridge University Press, 1995.

Idel, Moshe, Studies in Ecstatic Kabbalah, New York, State University of New York Press, 1988.

Jones, Rev. F.A., "The Ancient Year and the Sothic Cycle, " Proceedings of the Society of Biblical Archeology (PSBA), Vol. XXX, London: 1908.

Josephus, Flavius, The Antiquities of the Jews, Vol.I, trans. by William Whiston, McLean, Virginia: IndyPublish.com.

Jwing-Ming, Yang, Muscle/Tendon Changing & Marrow/Brain Washing Chi Kung, Jamaica Plain, Mass.: YMAA Pub., 1989.

Kaplan, Aryeh, Bahir, York Beach, Maine: Samuel Weiser,1979.

Kaplan, Aryeh, Meditation and Kabbalah, York Beach, Maine: Samuel Weiser, 1982.

Kaplan, Aryeh, Meditation and the Bible, York Beach, Maine: Samuel Weiser, 1978.

Kaplan, Aryeh, Sefer Yetzirah, York Beach, Maine: Samuel Weiser, 1990.

Hall, H.R. and Woolley, C.L., "Ur Excavations Al-'Ubaid," Oxford University Press, 1927, vol.I, 216-240.

Koran, trans. by J. Dawood, London: Penguin Books, 1956.

Kramer, Samuel Noah, History Begins at Sumer, Philadelphia: U of Penn Press, 1956.

Laurence, Richard, trans., The Book of Enoch, London: Kegan Paul, Trench, and Trauber, 1883.

LaViolette, Paul A., Earth Under Fire: Humanity's Survival of the Ice Age, Inner Traditions/Bear & Company, 2005.

Lawlor, Robert, Sacred Geometry, London: Thames & Hudson, 1982.

Levarie, Sigmund and Ernst Levy, Tone: A Study in Musical Acoustics, Kent, Ohio: Kent State University Press, 1968.

Levy, Ernst, A Theory of Harmony, unpublished, 1951.

Lewis, Bernard, The Arabs in History, New York: Oxford University Press, 2002.

Lippman, Edward A., Musical Thought in Ancient Greece, New York: Columbia University Press, 1964.

Long, G., "On the Site of Susa," Journal of the Royal Geographical Society of London, Vol. 3, (1833) 257-267.

Macoy, Robert, General History, Cyclopedia and Dictionary of Freemasonry, New York: Masonic Publishing Company, 1869.

Malhotra, Ashok, "*Tracing the Origin of Ancient Sumerians,*" syndicated article appearing in the Armenia Encyclopedia; Chayah Bayith Elowahh; EZine Articles.

Mann, Felix, Acupuncture, New York: Vantage Books, 1962, 1971.

Marshall, John, Mohenjro Dara and the Indus Civilization, Asian Educational Studies, 1931.

Mavromatis, Andreas, Hypnagogia: the Unique State of Consciousness Between Wakefulness and Sleep, London: Routledge, 1991.

McClain, Ernest G., The children of Abraham, unpublished

McClain, Ernest G., The Myth of Invariance: The Origin of the Gods, Mathematics and Music from the RG Veda to Plato, New York: Nicolas-Hays, 1976.

McClain, Ernest G., Meditations Through the Quran, New York: Nicolas-Hays, 1981.

McClain, Ernest G., The Pythagorean Plato, New York: Nicolas-Hays, 1978.

McClain, Ernest G., "A New Look at Plato's Timaeus," Music and Man, 1, no. 4, 1975.

Mellaart, James, Çatal Höyük, New York: McGraw-Hill; Thames & Hudson Ltd, 1967.

Mlodinow, Leonard, Euclid's Window, New York: Simon & Schuster, 2001.

Moore, Andrew; Hillman, Gordon; Legge, Anthony, Village on the Euphrates: From Foraging to Farming at Abu Hureyra, London: Oxford University Press, 2000.

Mullin, Glen, Tsongkhapa's Six Yoga's of Naropa, Ithaca, NY: Snow Lion, 1996.

McClain, Ernest, Narmer, unpublished.

Gevork, Nazaryan, Armenia: the Cradle of Civilization, unpublished.

Neugebauer, Otto E., "The Alleged Babylonian Discovery of the Precession of the Equinoxes," Journal of the American Oriental Society, Vol. 70 No. 1, Jan - Mar., 1950.

New Testament, New York: Catholic Book Publishing, 1952.

Ni, Maoshing, trans., The Yellow Emperor's Classic of Medicine, Boston: Shambhala Publications, 1995.

Nissen, Hans J., The Early History of the Ancient Near East, trans. by Elizabeth Lutzeier and Kenneth Northcott, Chicago: University of Chicago Press, 1988.

Odeberg, Hugo, ed., Hebrew Book of Enoch, New York, KTAV, 1973.

Pagels, Elaine, The Gnostic Gospels, New York: Random House, 1979.

Painter, Nell Irvin, Why White People are Called Caucasian?, New Haven, Connecticut: Yale University Press, 2003.

Pargiter, Frederick E., Ancient Indian Historical Tradition, London: Oxford University Press, 1922.

Patch, Howard Rollin, The Tradition of Boethius, New York: Oxford University Press, 1935.

Peat, F. David, Superstrings and the Search for the Theory of Everything, Chicago: Contemporary Books, 1988.

Petrie, Flinders, Wisdom of the Egyptians, London: British School of Archeology in Egypt and B.Quaritch ltd., 1940.

Plato, The Republic, trans. G.M.A. Grube, Indianapolis: Hackett Publishing Company, 1974.

Plato, "Laws," in The Collected Dialogues of Plato, ed. by Edith Hamilton and Huntington Cairns, trans. A.E. Taylor, Princeton, NJ: Princeton University Press, 1961.

Plato, "Timaeus," in The Collected Dialogues of Plato, ed. by Edith Hamilton and Huntington Cairns, trans. by Benjamin Gowett, Princeton, NJ: Princeton University Press, 1961.

Porter, J.R., The Lost Bible, Chicago: University of Chicago Press, 2001.

Rameau, Jean-Philippe, Treatise on Harmony, trans. Philip Gosset., New York: Dover Publications, 1971.

Rameau, Jean Philippe, Harmonic Generation, trans. Deborah Hays, doctoral dissertation, Stanford University, 1968.

Rand, Edward Kennard, Founders of the Middle Ages, Cambridge, Massachusetts: Harvard University Press, 1928.

Reese, Gustave, Music in the Renaissance, rev.ed., New York: W.W. Norton,1959.

Renard, John, Understanding the Islamic Experience, New York/Mahwah: Paulist Press, 1992.

Riemann, Hugo, History of Music Theory, trans. R.H. Haggh, Lincoln, Nebraska: University of Nebraska,1962.

The Rig Veda, trans. by Wendy Doniger O'Flaherty, New York-London: Penguin Books, 1981.

Rinpoche, Sogyal, The Tibetan Book of Living and Dying, ed. P.G. Gaffney and A. Harvey, San Francisco: Harper Collins, 1994.

Sachs, Curt, Our Musical Heritage, New York: Prentice Hall, Inc., 1948.

Schatz, Howard, ed.by Schneck, Dr. Daniel J. & Judith K., "The Chord of Nature and the Evolution of Music Theory," Music in Human Adaptation, Blacksburg, Virginia: Virginia Tech, 1997.

Schatz, Howard, The Lost Word of God (New York: Tone Circle Pub., 2007).

Scherman, Rabbi Nosson, ed. The Chumash, Brooklyn, New York: Mesorah Publications, 1998.

Schneck, Daniel J., and Dorita S. Berger, The Music Effect: Music Physiology and Clinical Applications, London: Jessica Kingsley Pub., 2006.

Schneider, Marius, "Primitive Music," The New Oxford History of Music, vol. I, London: Oxford University Press, 1957.

Scholem, Gershom, Kabbalah, New York- Jerusalem: Keter Publishing House, 1974.

Scholem, Gershom, Origins of the Kabbalah, ed. R.J. Zwi Werblowsky, trans. Allan Arkush, Princeton, New Jersey: Princeton University Press, 1962, 1987.

Sells, Michael A., trans. and ed., Early Islamic Mysticism, New York-Mahwah: Paulist Press, 1996.

Soltysiak, Arkadiusz, "Physical Anthropology and the Sumerian Problem," Studies in Historical Anthropology, Vol.4: 2004[2006] 145-158.

Sperling, Harry and Simon, Maurice, trans. Zohar, London: Soncino Press, 1984.

Sutton, Daud, Platonic & Archimedean Solids, New York: Walker & Co., 2002.

Tanakh: The Holy Scriptures, Jerusalem: Jewish Publication Society, 1985.

Waite, Arthur Edward, A New Encyclopedia of Freemasonry, New York: Random House, 1970.

Wilhelm, Richard and Baynes, Cary F., trans., The I Ching, Princeton, New Jersey: Princeton University Press, 1950, 1977.

Wilkinson, Tony, Genesis of the Pharaohs, London: Thames & Hudson, 2003.

Yasser, Joseph, A Theory of Evolving Tonality, New York: American Library of Musicology, 1932.

Yasuo, Yuasa, The body, Self-cultivation and Ki-energy, Albany: State University of New York Press, 1993.

Yeshe, Lama Thubten, The Bliss of Inner Fire, Boston: Wisdom Pub., 1998.

Yu, Lu K'uan, Taoist Yoga: Alchemy & Immortality, York Beach, Maine: Weiser, 1973.

Yu, Lu K'uan, The Secrets of Chinese Meditation, York Beach, Maine: Weiser, 1964.

Zalman, Schneer, Likutei-Amarim-Tanya, New York-London:Kehot Publication Society, 1972.

Index

Symbols

A

B

E

K

L

N

O

P

Q

R

S

T

U

V

W

CPSIA information can be obtained at www.ICGtesting.com
Printed in the USA
BVOW080109180912

300626BV00003B/1/P

9 780978 726416